Oppositional Consciousness

Oppositional Consciousness

The Subjective Roots of Social Protest

Edited by

Jane Mansbridge

and

Aldon Morris

The University of Chicago Press • *Chicago & London*

The University of Chicago Press, Chicago 60637
The University of Chicago Press, Ltd., London
© 2001 by The University of Chicago
All rights reserved. Published 2001
Printed in the United States of America
10 09 08 07 06 05 04 03 02 01   1 2 3 4 5

ISBN: 0-226-50361-5 (cloth)
ISBN: 0-226-50362-3(paper)

Library of Congress Cataloging-in-Publication Data

Oppositional consciousness : the subjective roots of social protest / edited by
    Jane Mansbridge and Aldon Morris.
        p.   cm.
    Includes bibliographical references and index.
    ISBN 0-226-50361-5 (cloth : alk. paper)—ISBN 0-226-50362-3 (pbk. : alk.
paper)
    1. Social movements—Psychological aspects.   2. Civil rights
movements—Psychological aspects.   3. Group identity.   4. Oppression
(Psychology).   5. Social movements—United States—Case studies.   6. Civil
rights movements—United States—Case studies.   I. Mansbridge, Jane J.
II. Morris, Aldon D.

HM881 .O66 2001
303.48'4'0973—dc21   2001027560

The Negro must . . . work passionately for group identity. This does not mean group isolation or group exclusivity. It means the kind of group consciousness that Negroes need in order to participate more meaningfully at all levels of the life of our nation.

Martin Luther King Jr., *Where Do We Go from Here: Chaos or Community?*

Contents

Acknowledgments

Northwestern University—particularly its Departments of Sociology, Political Science, and History and its Institute for Policy Studies—served as the crucible in which the various elements in this volume coalesced. The mixture of intellectual challenge and comradeship that we found there typified academic interaction at its best. As is so often the case, it was our graduate students who first pointed out the synergies emerging across our disciplines on the question of oppositional consciousness. To them, as well as to the institutions that nurtured us, we express our considerable gratitude.

Contributors

Naomi Braine works in HIV research and policy in New York City. She received her Ph.D. from Northwestern University in the Department of Sociology. She is currently the project director for a multicity study of HIV prevention services for injection drug users at Beth Israel Hospital, Chemical Dependency Institute. Her work addresses issues of gender, sexuality, identity, and social movements.

Sharon Groch is a consultant in Chicago working with disability rights groups. She received her Ph.D. from Northwestern University in the Department of Sociology. She is the author of several articles on disability rights issues and is working on a book entitled *Pathways to Protest: The Making of Oppositional Consciousness by People with Disabilities.*

Fredrick C. Harris is associate professor of political science and director of the Center for the Study of African-American Politics at the University of Rochester. He received his Ph.D. from Northwestern University in the Department of Political Science. His publications include *Something Within: Religion in African-American Political Activism* and "Will the Circle Be Unbroken? The Erosion and Transformation of African-American Civic Life" in *Civil Society, Democracy, and Civic Renewal,* edited by Robert K. Fullinwider. He has published articles in the *Journal of Politics* and *Policy Studies Review* and was a 1998–99 visiting scholar at the Russell Sage Foundation.

Jane Mansbridge is the Adams Professor of Political Leadership and Democratic Values at the John F. Kennedy School of Government at Harvard University and was a professor of political science at Northwestern University. She is the author of *Beyond Adversary Democracy* and *Why We Lost the ERA,* editor of *Beyond Self-Interest,* and coeditor (with Susan Moller Okin) of *Feminism.* She is currently working on a book on the role of nonactivists in social movements, entitled *Everyday Feminism.*

Anna-Maria Marshall is assistant professor of sociology at the University of Illinois, Urbana-Champaign. She received her Ph.D. from Northwestern University in the Department of Political Science. She is the author of "Closing the Gaps: Plaintiffs in Pivotal Sexual Harassment Cases" in *Law and Social Inquiry* and is working on a book examining the relationship between law and social change in the area of sexual harassment.

Aldon Morris is professor of sociology at Northwestern University. Morris's *The Origins of the Civil Rights Movement* emphasized the structural and cultural aspects of that movement. His current research extends that analysis to subsequent decades in the United States and to movements of liberation in other societies. His current research also includes work on theoretical issues in social movements, first developed in the edited volume *Frontiers in Social Movement Theory* (coedited with Carol Mueller), a study of social protest in Chicago during the 1960s, and a study of the National Baptist Convention. He is also acting as editor of and contributor to an encyclopedia of American social movements.

Marc Simon Rodriguez is assistant professor of history at Princeton University. He received his Ph.D. from Northwestern University in the Department of History and his J.D. from the University of Wisconsin Law School. Before working at Princeton he taught at Northwestern University; the University of Wisconsin, Madison; and the University of Wisconsin, Parkside. He is revising for publication his dissertation, "Obreros Unidos: Migration, Migrant Farm Worker Activism, and the Chicano Movement in Wisconsin and Texas, 1950–1980."

Brett C. Stockdill is assistant professor of sociology at California State Polytechnic University, Pomona. He received his Ph.D. from Northwestern University in the Department of Sociology. He is the author of "Blood at the Roots: Analyzing Racist Violence," "AIDS, Queers, and Criminal (In)justice: Repressing Radical AIDS Activism," "(Mis)treating Prisoners with AIDS: Analyzing Health Care behind Bars," and other articles. He is currently working on a book entitled *AIDS Activism at the Crossroads: Social Movement Rifts and Alliances*.

Lori G. Waite is assistant professor of sociology at Trinity College in Hartford, Connecticut. She received her Ph.D. from Northwestern University in the Department of Sociology. Her Ph.D. dissertation is entitled "Overcoming Challenges and Obstacles to Social Movement Mobilization: The Case of the Chicago Freedom Movement"; she is a contributor to the volume *Civil Rights in the United States* and is currently working on an oral history of the Chicago Freedom Movement.

1   The Making of Oppositional Consciousness

Jane Mansbridge

How can human beings be induced to give their lives—even one minute of their lives—for their group? This is a question every nation, every social movement, indeed every social organization, has had to face. One answer is somehow to arrange incentives so that in doing what is good for themselves, people also do what is good for the group. The market often works this way. So do Nobel prizes. Another answer is to convince people that because of the principles they hold or how they feel about the group, they *should* contribute to the group, even when this is not rewarding in other ways— and sometimes even when it will cost them their lives.

Successful social movements, like other successful social organizations, tap into as many kinds of incentives as possible. This book looks at one constellation of incentives that applies to historically subordinated groups—a constellation composed of the principles, ideas, and feelings that we call "oppositional consciousness." Although we will explore the meanings of the term at length in the last chapter, for now the easiest way to understand oppositional consciousness is to think about what people have meant with the words "class consciousness" and apply the same logic to other groups, such as women or African Americans. We say that members of a group that others have traditionally treated as subordinate or deviant have an oppositional consciousness when they claim their previously subordinate identity as a positive identification, identify injustices done to their group, demand changes in the polity, economy, or society to rectify those injustices, and see other members of their group as sharing an interest in rectifying those injustices. "Oppositional consciousness" is the umbrella term. Class, race, and other forms of group consciousness are specific instances.

Our project is fundamentally inductive. We present six cases from recent United States history, based on participant observation and interviews, that reveal in some historical detail how different groups actually develop and use what we call oppositional consciousness. Each of these cases features groups—African Americans, people with disabilities, sexually harassed women, Chicano workers, and gay men and lesbians— whose outrage at their situation had at one point been kept under

1

control by a dominant set of ideas that portrayed their situations as natural, normal, or in any case not unjust. Each group, and each case, demonstrates some complexity in the practice and theory of oppositional consciousness. In focusing on complexity rather than order, we try to follow the empirically oriented path blazed by E. P. Thompson, who detailed how the nineteenth-century English working class overcame the dominant ideas of its time and began to see itself as a distinct class whose interests conflicted with those of factory owners. We ask how versions of this process have applied to other subordinated groups and those who identify deeply with such groups.

By a subordinated group we mean a group subordinate in a system of social organization in which members of one group create and reinforce inequalities between themselves and members of another group through the exercise of power, that is, the threat of sanction and the imposition of constraint.[1] That exercise of power may be conscious and intentional, as in the institution of slavery. It does not, however, require individual intent, as in many cases of gender inequality. Members of a group with the power to make a decision that affects others may, without conscious intent, simply not take into account the interests or perspectives of members of a group with less power. They may only choose a course of action that is in their interests with little recognition of how that choice affects others. Everyone has had the experience of harming others by "just not thinking." When harm or disadvantage is imposed this way consistently over time, because the members of one group consistently have more power than the members of another, the process creates and reinforces a pattern of domination and subordination.[2]

The essays in this book use the word "oppression" to describe the unjust exercise of power by a dominant group over a subordinate group. The concept of oppression as English speakers use it today derives in the most influential early instance from the experience of the Jews in Egypt. Although all the well-known Mediterranean philosophies and religions evince a strong concern for injustice, the Hebrew Bible carved out a special concern for a form of injustice that in English is traditionally translated as "oppression." The Hebrew, indeed, has at least four separate roots for words that the King James Bible translates as "oppression."[3]

When these words appear (particularly in the books of Exodus and Deuteronomy), the context reveals that "oppression" involves the unjust use of power by the more powerful against those less powerful and more vulnerable by virtue of their social position. Conceptually, oppression usually applies to groups rather than individuals, and it is used when members of more powerful groups use their power to take advantage of members of more structurally vulnerable groups. The Jewish people's slavery in Egypt is archetypal. Jewish tradition makes that experience central, in both the yearly Seder and many other group-defining references. In the Exodus story, God's command forbids oppression: "Thou shalt neither vex [wrong] a stranger, nor oppress him: for ye were strangers in the land of Egypt." That command is strong and personal. It reminds the Jews of their own group's past experiences in Egypt, and so may even ask for, or draw upon, some form of empathy for those vulnerable to oppression.[4] The groups whom "thou shalt not oppress" include not only widows and orphans, for whom the New Testament and the Koran urge compassion and charity (without mentioning oppression), but also, more challengingly, the "stranger within your midst" and your "hireling." Neither Christianity nor Islam suggests a particular care for either strangers or workers. The Hebrew Bible singles them out, along with widows and orphans, presumably because their weaker structural positions vis-à-vis the powerful make them vulnerable to others' power.

This underlying meaning of oppression as the unjust use of greater power by one group against another, maintained without emphasis in the European Middle Ages, was picked up and used extensively both in the American Revolution and in the early antislavery movement.[5] In Europe the concept then became much used in socialist and Marxist writing. In the United States it peppered abolitionist and populist thought. Christian slave spirituals preserved intact the meaning from Exodus: "When Israel was in Egypt's land—Let my people go—Oppressed so hard they could not stand. . . ." Although the New Testament rarely uses words that are translated into English as "oppression," Christianity nevertheless treats the Hebrew Bible as a sacred text. Thus in the Christian as well as the Jewish tradition the embedded heritage of God's implacable opposition to oppression gave subordinate groups a strong claim for rectification of wrongs rooted in the unjust power that one group could wield against another.

A group is oppressed only if its position in a particular hierarchical system derives from unjust inequalities that result from the exercise of power (in the sense of threat of sanction or imposition of constraint). Injustice and power are central. But any conclusion that a particular group has been deeply affected by this form of power is subject to contest.[6] So is any conclusion that a particular hierarchy is unjust. In any given system of inequality, those higher in the hierarchy will have an interest in claiming that existing inequalities derive not from the unequal exercise of power but from other causes; those lower in the hierarchy will have, to some degree, an interest in the opposite claim.

Yet those lower in the hierarchy also have incentives *not* to challenge the naturalness of inequality. Challenging the interpretation of the dominant group can result in punishment so severe or pervasive that subordinates will go a long way toward adopting the dominant interpretation. Inequalities in power have their most insidious effect when the dominant group has so much control over the ideas available to other members of the society that the conceptual categories required to challenge the status quo hardly exist. Ideological hegemony of this sort pervades every human society in ways that are, by definition, hard to bring to conscious awareness.[7]

We have only recently come to understand how hard it is to resist the dominant ideas of one's time. By the mid–nineteenth century, doubts had begun to emerge about the eighteenth-century vision in which the free play of ideas would eventually produce a rational world. Karl Marx and John Stuart Mill, who differed dramatically on many things, agreed that the distribution of power in a society had a profound influence on its receptiveness to particular ideas. Marx wrote, "The ruling ideas of each age have ever been the ideas of the ruling class." Mill's judgment was almost identical: "Wherever there is an ascendant class, a large portion of the morality of the country emanates from its class interests." More than a century later Michel Foucault carried this line of thinking to its logical conclusion. "Power," he wrote, "*is* 'already there' . . . one is never 'outside' it, . . . there are no 'margins' for those who break with the system to gambol in. . . . [P]ower is co-extensive with the social body; there are no spaces of primal liberty between the meshes of its network."[8]

Foucault is also famous for recognizing that "there are no relations of power without resistances . . . formed right at the point where relations of power are exercised." But his own writing stressed the effects of power rather than the creation of resistance. When in one essay he encountered instances of such resistance he called them "curious," "strange," and "amazing."[9] His theory of resistance—which he did not elaborate—seems to have assumed a gut refusal to be subordinated rooted somewhere in every human being. This is where oppositional consciousness comes in. To form an effective basis for collective action, gut refusals need cognitive and emotional organizing. They need an injustice frame. They need ideology.[10] They need an apparatus involving both reason and emotion that can trigger the switch from shame to anger.

Oppositional consciousness as we define it is an empowering mental state that prepares members of an oppressed group to act to undermine, reform, or overthrow a system of human domination. It is usually fueled by righteous anger over injustices done to the group and prompted by personal indignities and harms suffered through one's group membership. At a minimum, oppositional consciousness includes the four elements of identifying with members of a subordinate group, identifying injustices done to that group, opposing those injustices, and seeing the group as having a shared interest in ending or diminishing those injustices. A more full-fledged oppositional consciousness includes identifying a specific dominant group as causing and in some way benefiting from those injustices. It also includes seeing certain actions of the dominant group as forming a "system" of some kind that advances the interests of the dominant group. Finally, it can include a host of other ideas, beliefs, and feelings that provide coherence, explanation, and moral condemnation.[11]

It is not easy to describe a particular "consciousness." As we use it, the term implies some special sensitivity to certain features of the outside world rather than others. A particular consciousness draws one's rational and emotive attention to big and small things—big political events, reported in the media, and small inflections of voice, or the way of "owning the world" in which one person sits and the way of taking orders (or notes) in another's stance. Consciousness also transforms. Oppositional consciousness takes free-floating frustration and directs it into anger. It turns strangers into brothers and sisters, and turns feelings for these strangers from indifference into love. It builds on ideas and facts to generate hope. Cognitive and emotive processes mix together, as an emotion focuses a cognition and a cognition triggers an emotion. (Indeed, in such processes the very words "cognition" and "emotion" may impede our understanding if we take each to imply that it is the antonym of the other.)[12]

Although consciousness is, by definition, internal to an individual's mind, the kind of consciousness that we describe is inextricably derived from the social world. We learn who we "are" from the social world. We appreciate those who like us and "our kind," and we react defensively toward those who seem to attack us and our kind or seem not to have our interests at heart. We learn the meaning of justice from our own and others' interpretations of the social world. We develop particular forms of consciousness in particular historical moments when certain political opportunities, certain mobilizing institutions and certain repertoires of action and self-understanding become available.[13]

Our social settings and our particular needs and proclivities always give us both many forms of identity and many forms of consciousness prompted by our senses of identity and our experiences. We make some identities more salient at some times, and events make some identities more salient at some times. Sometimes our identities articulate relatively harmoniously with one another; sometimes they conflict and we need consciously to insist on their multiplicity or craft social situations that reinforce their multiplicity; sometimes we can compartmentalize and emphasize our different, perhaps conflicting, identities in different places. In all situations, when we give names to who we "are" we analogize ourselves with others and think of ourselves as members of a group. In many situations, however, this identity is not simply self-chosen; it is also partly given by others. When an identity at least partly given by others is a marker for social injustices imposed on members of one's group, one's consciousness will inevitably reflect those injustices, but not in predictable ways. Only in some historical situations will what we call "oppositional consciousness" arise. We cannot disentangle the individual and social elements in such a group-based consciousness, because the group-based element is irreducibly social, even more than other elements of the self.[14]

Just as the meaning of "class consciousness" is highly contested, so too must the meaning of "oppositional consciousness" be contested. Yet most scholars agree that such a consciousness, however hard to define, plays an important causal role in the motivation to work for those social movements that we call "liberation movements."[15] The last chapter of this book will explore further the components we have identified in the meaning of oppositional consciousness, while leaving the field open for further reflection, analysis, and observation. The examples in the substantive chapters will illustrate how a consciousness based in part on defending oneself and one's kind from domination differs in some important ways from other forms of moral commitment. Most importantly, we want to show that oppositional consciousness is not a single thing that one "has" or "doesn't have." We want to show that it is not one point in a binary but a loose continuum, not a unity but a congeries of competing elements, and not static but constantly changing in its content.

As this book describes the making of various forms of oppositional consciousness among several different groups in the United States, it aims to open up subtleties in the concept, helping us understand better the way oppositional consciousness is formed—through struggles among different oppositional traditions, clusters of both cognate and competing elements, divides and continua in cultural strands, syntheses of previously disparate elements, borrowings from likely and unlikely sources, and the transmutation of new inflections into central themes, which then serve as the ideational source for further inflections and transmutations. Oppositional consciousness is not the same for different groups. It is deeply colored by the objective structural position of a group within a system of domination and subordination, the obvious injustice versus the presumed naturalness of its subordination, the degree of the group's physical and cultural segregation from the dominant group, and the degree of voluntariness in its distinctness from the dominant norm.[16]

The pattern we see is not "the stronger the oppression, the stronger the oppositional consciousness." That is true in some cases. But, as we stress constantly, consciousness is historically contingent. Oppositional consciousness requires ideational resources—ideas available in the culture that can be built upon to create legitimacy, a perception of injustice, righteous anger, solidarity, and a belief in the group's power. It requires emotional involvement and commitment. It also requires institutional resources. The cultural materials required come in sedimented layers. Individuals in the subordinate group must be brought together by existing or developing institutions in order to help one another dig into those layers, recognize, borrow, modify, inflect, and selectively inflate and suppress elements from the existing culture to craft what then become new ideas.

Luck plays some role in the evolution of ideas. A catchy name, like a catchy tune, can carry an idea forward independently of its intrinsic merits. The existing schemas of all participants—dominant, subordinate, and mixed—also count heavily. As the chapters in this book will reveal, some religious traditions (such as the Judaic), some past practices (such as physical segregation), some legal and institutional settings (such as a law against discrimination), some geographical patterns (such as migration routes), some patterns of self-interest among the players (such as those of elected politicians), and some conscious strategies (such as those of movement activists) can greatly facilitate or impede the development of both oppositional consciousness and group unity.

As members of subordinate groups try to recognize, name, and challenge the structures of power that often underlie even the seemingly most neutral or benign of surfaces, they can usually draw on one or more of the following resources—as each of our chapters will indicate. An existing *oppositional culture* provides ideas, rituals, and long-standing patterns of interaction that overt political struggle can refine and develop to create a more mature oppositional consciousness. Other key resources include: a history of *segregation* with some autonomy, providing "free spaces" for the elaboration and testing of ideas; *borrowing* from previous successful movements; the *synthesis* of more than one oppositional strand, creating more than the sum of its parts; mutually supportive *interaction*, bridging divides in emotional commitments, political opinions, and material interests; and *conscious creativity* by activists, drawing on the traditions and practices of everyday life. Each chapter in this book investigates at least one of these resources.[17]

Making Sense of the Patterns

The chapters in this book illustrate the complex patterns of negotiation, struggle, coalescence and division, borrowing, and crafting that characterize the formation of oppositional consciousness. Perceiving injustice, recognizing a need for collective action, feeling efficacy, and all the other components of an oppositional consciousness emerge (or do not emerge) from the warp and woof of everyday experience. These patterns are all undergirded by certain material relations, including, at the base, the underlying structures of historical domination with which each group must deal. Each chapter is grounded in a specific historical reality and shows how oppositional consciousness works in the concrete experience of a particular group. Each chapter illustrates a particular theoretical point about the character of oppositional consciousness.

Bringing Domination Back In

In chapter 2, "Social Movements and Oppositional Consciousness," Aldon Morris and Naomi Braine point out that symbolic and ethnomethodological approaches tend to underemphasize issues of domination and oppression. "Liberation movements," or movements based on historical structures of domination, differ in several important ways from movements based on concern about social problems. In movements based on historical structures of domination, like the civil rights movement, a group's segregation often plays a key role in generating oppositional consciousness. When segregation is minimal, as between men and women, subordinate groups need to create autonomous spaces in order to craft an oppositional consciousness. Consciousness-raising in small groups, for example, helped launch the "second wave" of the women's movement. This particular dynamic, of developing oppositional consciousness in "safe spaces" controlled by the oppressed groups themselves, does not apply to movements based on concern for social problems.

"Equality-based special issue movements," such as the pro-choice movement, address social problems that disproportionately affect a particular oppressed group. Some of the participants in these movements do not address the full struggle to reform or overthrow large-scale systems of human domination. They focus on the special issue in and of itself, while nevertheless appropriating the symbols and operating styles of liberation movements. Other participants have developed a commitment to the issue only because they see it as an integral part of the larger struggle. Such participants are members both of the larger liberation movement and the special issue movement. Equality-based special issue movements differ both among themselves and over time in how much their members are committed to the larger liberation movement and how much to the special issue.

"Social responsibility movements," such as the antinuclear movement, address social problems that affect humanity in general. Participants usually do not have a personal history, directly related to the movement, of being oppressed through the most obvious systems of human domination. They thus find it harder to draw from a long-standing oppositional culture as they try to create their collective identities and injustice frames.

This distinction between liberation movements and other forms of social movement draws attention to the particular challenges faced by groups that are subordinate in an existing system of human domination. It is they who develop oppositional consciousness and use it in their struggle to end that domination. As other groups face power structures that oppose their ends, their activists too must craft new identities as part of their commitments to their cause. Members of liberation groups, however, have both an easier and a harder task. They do not need to create almost from scratch an identity primed for collective action. They already have a deeply meaningful identity embodying the pride, strength, and hope collectively nurtured by their group since that group gained any consciousness of itself. But that identity is also already externally—and oppressively—described. The task of calling on past cultural resources in the struggle to redefine that identity often releases immense creativity, giving rise to symbols, rituals, strategies, and other cultural inventions that have lasting meaning and that, on occasion, other groups can fruitfully adapt.

All of the chapters in this book analyze facets of oppositional consciousness within liberation movements. The great diversity in the situations of the groups they describe is anchored by a strong common structural similarity: each of these groups is, or claims to be, subordinate in an ongoing system of domination. This structural position has major effects on the identities of the individuals in these groups as well as on the symbolic and cultural repertoires available to them for collective action.

Borrowings, Inflections, Continua, Synthesis: Oppositional Civic Culture in the Black Church

In chapter 3, "Religious Resources in an Oppositional Civic Culture," Fredrick C. Harris visits a prayer breakfast on the campaign trail of former senator Carol Moseley-Braun. In this breakfast, Moseley-Braun and her supporters draw upon an existing oppositional culture in the African American community to create a moment of political solidarity and inspiration. In the tradition of the civil rights movement, they freely borrow from both the Old and New Testaments. Familiar stories come out of this process inflected in new ways. David, of the David and Goliath story, becomes female. Moseley-Braun herself, working for the Black community in the halls of White power, becomes a "modern-day Esther," who saved the Israelites by standing up for her people. Passages from the New Testament urging on the faithful take on political overtones: " . . . for in due season we shall reap, if we faint not." Gospel hymns stress the power of the weak ("Little becomes much when you place it in the Master's hand"), as do New Testament prophesies that "the last shall be first, and the first shall be last." Each story from the Bible, now many times recounted over the centuries of African American slavery, the Jim Crow era, and the civil rights movement, undergoes one more iteration, one more inflection, one more subtle interpretation. The process brings into a moment of late twentieth-century politics strands of ideas forged by the civil rights movement, strands forged earlier in slavery, and some strands forged generations ago by the oppositional movements of Judaism in Egypt and Christianity in Israel.

Moseley-Braun's breakfast meeting and Harris's other observations from the politics of the Black church reveal the uses of biblical imagery to craft what Harris calls an "oppositional civic culture." That culture performs at one time the two seemingly contradictory functions of opposing the prevailing racial hierarchy and rooting its participants more deeply in the civic structures of the United States.

The chapter introduces the concept of oppositional civic culture and at the same time illustrates some of the differences between oppositional "culture" and oppositional "consciousness." Oppositional consciousness focuses on injustice. Leaders in the Moseley-Braun breakfast, working within both traditional electoral politics and social movement politics, brought together participants with varying degrees of oppositional consciousness. In the ceremony itself they did not draw heavily on the theme of injustice that is central to oppositional consciousness. Rather, reaching into the available oppositional civic culture, they drew on strands—such as the power of the weak against the strong—more appropriate to a mainstream electoral event.

Negotiations, Struggles, Clusters, Divides, Borrowing, Inflection:
A Story of Physical Segregation and "Free Spaces"

In chapter 4, "Free Spaces: Creating Oppositional Consciousness in the Disability Rights Movement," Sharon Groch documents how activists in the disability rights movement consciously created images, slogans, literature, humor, rituals, and other cultural expressions by drawing from the deaf and blind cultures formed in segregated residential schools and from the legacy of the civil rights movement.

The oppositional consciousness of deaf people in the United States has traditionally been much stronger than that of blind people. Groch's nuanced history shows why. Segregation itself, she reveals, helps create collective identity, but only the control by members of some autonomous ("free") spaces, as in the history of deaf people in the United States, allows the development of the full counternarrative and conviction of injustice necessary for oppositional consciousness. Blind people did not have as much autonomous control of their own spaces, and so developed a less thoroughgoing oppositional consciousness.

In contrast to segregation, integration permits developing the weak ties that promote elite connections. Mobility-impaired people, who were far more integrated into nondisabled society than deaf or blind people, had these advantages of integration. Yet they had had no history of autonomous spaces in which to develop their consciousness. Accordingly, they attained oppositional consciousness only through interaction with the civil rights movement. Keeping the disability movement creative and nonhierarchical often requires careful negotiation between members of groups whose past and present segregation has brought them the advantages of forming an oppositional consciousness and members of groups whose past and present integration has brought them the advantages of elite contact.

The comparison among disability groups in this chapter gives powerful evidence for the effects of physical segregation and autonomy on oppositional consciousness.

Borrowing, Inflection, Continua, Synthesis: Movement Permeability,
with Actors along a Spectrum of Oppositional Consciousness

For chapter 5, "A Spectrum in Oppositional Consciousness: Sexual Harassment Plaintiffs and Their Lawyers," Anna-Maria Marshall interviewed nineteen attorneys and four plaintiffs in landmark sexual harassment cases. Based in the lives and choices of these different individuals, her analysis reveals how disparate are the incentives for participating in social change through legal action. Some of her attorneys and plaintiffs were steeped in the oppositional consciousness of the feminist movement and supported by movement institutions. Others were only distantly or not at all connected. One plaintiff, reporting an act of harassment, checked "sex discrimination" on the complaint form at her workplace only because she could not find a more appropriate box to check. That act helped her lawyer to think of the harassment as a form of discrimination and present it that way in court. One lawyer took what would become a precedent-setting case only because he needed work and some friends of his had given his business card to the waitress at a restaurant where they were having lunch. Yet each of these different actors borrowed the institutional machinery and interpretive frame of the civil rights movement, which had produced the concept and practice of antidiscrimination legislation. All also borrowed, in greater or lesser degrees, an interpretive frame introduced by the feminist movement.

This massive borrowing from a set of congruent conceptual frames and institutional guarantees made it possible for some individuals who had little or no oppositional consciousness to take steps that matched the steps of others who lived and breathed the work of the movement. Together, their individualistic and collective moves combined with the existing institutional machinery of the legal system to generate the interpretive and institutional outcome that we now know as sexual harassment law. This chapter introduces the idea of permeability in a social movement's boundaries. Most importantly, it illustrates how individuals can contribute to a social movement from different places on a spectrum of oppositional consciousness (including not having even a minimal oppositional consciousness). It reveals how social movements are brought forward by a mix of activists, steeped in oppositional consciousness, and nonactivists, influenced only indirectly in their ideas and actions by the movement.

Borrowing, Inflection, and Negotiation: A Story of Synthesis and Historical Contingency

In chapter 6, "Cristaleño Consciousness: Mexican-American Activism between Crystal City, Texas, and Wisconsin, 1963–80," Marc Simon Rodríguez locates the origin of the La Raza movement in the historically specific confluence of two originally separate strands of oppositional culture and consciousness. Mexican-American workers in Crystal City, Texas, had traditionally practiced many forms of resistance to the Anglo landowners and power holders of the area. They had also developed a rich linguistic and cultural apparatus for interpreting the injustice of their situation. This tradition encountered a second strand when the Political Association of Spanish-Speaking Organizations and the Teamsters began to integrate the town of Crystal City into the larger world of organized politics and labor. In 1963 these two organizations helped five Chicanos run for city council and win. But the crucial moment came when the traditional migration patterns of picking beets, corn, and tomatoes took the now politically primed Cristaleño workers to the states of Wisconsin and Minnesota and brought them together with the strong progressive "Farmer-Labor" culture and institutions in these states. Because many younger workers now had the high-school degrees required for employment in many industries, they could finally get union jobs and "settle out" in these new states, creating a political and union base on which the migrants could rely. The two traditions, from Crystal City and the progressive Midwest, created a heady synthesis made even more explosive by institutional and cultural interaction with the civil rights movement in Milwaukee. That synthesis resulted in several successes and the eventual creation of the La Raza Unida Party. This chapter illustrates vividly both the processes of synthesis and the historical contingency in the formation of oppositional consciousness.

Negotiation, Struggle, and Divides: Internal Differentiation within Oppositional Consciousness

In chapter 7, "Divided Consciousness: The Impact of Black Elite Consciousness on the 1966 Chicago Freedom Movement," Lori G. Waite details the problems the Reverend Martin Luther King Jr. encountered when he brought the Freedom Movement to Chicago in 1966. All of the African Americans who actively struggled both for King's intervention in Chicago and against him were imbued with some form of oppositional consciousness, deriving from African American oppositional culture and from their identification with (although not always participation in) the recent civil rights movement in the South. Yet that oppositional consciousness did not bring them unity. The disunity that doomed King's intervention was rooted both in class divisions and in elite power divisions. King's forces were unable in the new circumstances of Chicago to find an issue that united African Americans across class. Most importantly, both the Black politicians of the Daley machine and many local Black ministers had material and ideological interests that differed from King's. They were not excluded from the polity, as in the South, but were in many ways participants in the polity. Thus although all elite participants in this struggle partook in some ways in an oppositional consciousness, their differing structural positions, material interests, and strategic or ideological perspectives prevented political unity. Waite's interviews suggest that these structural positions and material interests rarely affected political stances directly, but instead worked through interpretive schemas that generated variations in oppositional consciousness that participants on both sides of the issue could use to defend their political stances to themselves.

This chapter introduces the concept of internally differentiated oppositional consciousness. It reveals how structural variations within a system of oppression—in this case different degrees of inclusion within the polity—produce dramatically different and conflicting visions of oppositional consciousness, resulting in this case in disunity that was for that moment politically disabling.

Borrowing, Inflection, Negotiation, Synthesis, and Conscious Cultural Creation: Fighting Oppression by the Oppressed

In chapter 8, "Forging a Multidimensional Oppositional Consciousness: Lessons from Community-Based AIDS Activism," Brett C. Stockdill chronicles the efforts of the AIDS movement in three U.S. cities to create a consciousness that opposes all oppression. As AIDS activists struggled within their own groups against dominance by sex, race, and class, they also found it crucial to build coalitions, devise strategies, and recruit activists in ways that drew upon the existing culture and institutions in Black, Latino, and Asian communities. Cultural forays on many fronts had the goal of creating both new attitudes toward sexuality and new, empowered identities for gays and lesbians of color. In the process, the activists found themselves fighting not only the power of the dominant groups but also the dynamics of the oppressed as oppressor.

This chapter introduces the concept of multidimensional consciousness. It also reveals both how the experience of one sort of oppression does not easily generalize to understanding another's oppression and how conscious cultural creativity can foster that process of generalization.

Definitions, Power, Problems

Our understanding of oppositional consciousness casts this mental state as the analogue of "class consciousness" extended to all groups subordinate in an ongoing system of human domination. Future scholars may, however, find it useful if we try to tease apart the different components of oppositional consciousness as we see it. Chapter 9, "Complicating Oppositional Consciousness," analytically distinguishes stages of realization that one's own group is different from another group, that the groups are unequal, that the inequalities are unjust and systemic, that only group action can eliminate the inequalities, and that group action can succeed. It distinguishes these stages from the other states of identification, warmth, opposition, and anger, which can enter at almost any time. It argues that the four components of a "minimal" oppositional consciousness—identifying with the group, recognizing injustice, demanding rectification, and seeing shared interest—all must center on the recognition of injustice. A more "full-fledged" or "mature" oppositional consciousness includes other elements, such as identifying some of the ways a dominant group systematically uses power to initiate and maintain its position, a moral condemnation of the forms of domination, and usually some set of strategies—historical, culturally derived, or borrowed—for ending the system of domination.

Our case studies and theoretical formulations, however, repeatedly make the point that oppositional consciousness is not one thing but many. It comes in a continuum, not a dichotomy—and a messy continuum at that. There are many points of entry and many cognitive and emotional features that differ from individual to individual. Oppositional consciousness is negotiated in particular cultural contexts, blending many historical and cultural streams.

Throughout we argue that a group's structural position in a complex of power relations affects both its likelihood of developing an oppositional consciousness and how its movement will develop. The deaf had a different relation to the system of power in which they were embedded than did the mobility impaired. Martin Luther King's followers had a different relation to the system of power in Chicago in 1968 than in Birmingham in 1966. The Cristaleños developed a different relationship to Anglo landholder power when the Teamsters entered Crystal City, and a different relation still as their migrations introduced them to the ideas and institutions of the Farmer-Labor states of Wisconsin and Minnesota. Political opportunities affect the process, as do cultural opportunities.

A central theme in this volume is that cultural forms and institutions created for one purpose can be appropriated for another and differently inflected. So African American politicians appropriated and transformed ideas and symbols from the Old and New Testaments. So sexually harassed women appropriated and transformed ideas and legal forms that had developed from the civil rights movement, from an existing U.S. culture that gave rights a central place, and from legal institutions that had themselves developed from both the civil rights movement and that larger culture.

Activist intentions play a major role in the process of creating oppositional consciousness, as activists consciously decide to synthesize ideas,
symbols, collective identities, injustice frames, and cultures of solidarity.
The mobility impaired in the disabled movement, for example, engaged
in conscious culture work. ACT UP and other organizations in the AIDS
movement deliberately engaged the culture of the communities in which
they were active.

In the emergence of an oppositional culture, by contrast, activist
intentions play a far smaller role. Here the usual process is that incrementally throughout history members of a group, often unconsciously,
select and play up some themes in the larger culture while they ignore
and downplay others. Both in the creation of oppositional culture and in
the maintenance of social movements, nonactivists play critical roles as
they selectively adapt and use either existing cultural themes or themes
that activists have promoted.

Oppositional consciousness is not always good for the subordinate
group. The cases here primarily chronicle successes, but in chapter 9
we look briefly at certain drawbacks. The problems inherent in oppositional consciousness include exaggerating both one's difference from the
dominant group and the identity of interests within one's own group, a
learned inability to process information that does not fit one's ideological
context, and the dangers of essentialism.

In the analysis presented here, oppositional consciousness functions
as an intermediate factor, or variable, that is caused by and also causes
some of the important dynamics of social movements. When the members of some groups systematically exercise coercive power over the
members of others, the resulting pattern of domination is the first, primal
cause of the oppressed group's eventual liberation movement. To the
degree that the coercive power is overt, it will be noticed. The coerced
will form first an oppositional culture that simply resists, and eventually
an oppositional consciousness that spells out the workings of injustice,
the need to act collectively, and the possibilities of success in collective
action. When political opportunities open and sufficient resources, including social networks, are in place, oppositional consciousness then
acts as a cause, helping to bring an effective social movement into being.

Notes

Many thanks, with absolution from responsibility, to the reviewers, Sidney Tarrow, Aldon
Morris, Christopher Jencks, Anita McGahan, and for NSF Grant #SBR-9601236, Center for
Advanced Study in the Behavioral Sciences.
   1. These terms need some explanation. A good broad definition of "power" is "the
actual or potential causal relation between the interests of an actor or a set of actors and

the outcome itself" (adapted from Nagel 1975, 29). By focusing on cause, Nagel's definition avoids imputations of intent and allows anticipations of future events to cause present behavior. As a broad conceptual umbrella, this definition also covers what Mary Parker Follett, William Connolly, and many feminist theorists have called "power to" or "power with" as well as "power over." (For "power to," "power with," "power as energy," and "power-from-within," in contrast to "power over," see Follett [1935] 1942; Arendt [1963] 1965; Connolly 1974; Hartsock 1974; Starhawk 1987. For the positive uses of "power over," see Wartenberg 1990, Mansbridge 1996.) We adopt here a narrower meaning, covering only those kinds of power that derive from the threat of sanction and the imposition of constraint. These are kinds of "power over," or "coercion." (Note that this definition of power does not encompass positive inducement—an important form of power that, if asymmetries are great enough, may amount to coercion; see Barry [1975] 1991).

By "threat of sanction" we mean an inducement produced by the perception of future harm conditional on nonperformance of a desired action or inaction. By the "imposition of constraint" (sometimes called "force," e.g., in Bachrach and Baratz 1963, Lukes 1974, Mansbridge 1996), we mean a method of causing B to act in A's interests that does not involve B's choice. If I carry you out of the room in such a way that your will on the matter is irrelevant, my action involves constraint (or "force"). By contrast, if I threaten a sanction, by telling you I will shoot you unless you leave, my getting what I desire (your leaving) involves, to a small degree, your will. You can always refuse to leave, and although I shoot you, I will not have gained your leaving. The imposition of constraint, which does not involve the will of the constrained, is implicated in many systemic attributes such as language. It includes building a set of structures in which some choices are not possible. It includes making decisions that preclude different later decisions. It differs from the threat of sanction in one important way: Although power as the threat of sanction always involves resistance or the possibility of resistance, power as the imposition of constraint is sometimes impossible to resist. Although Michel Foucault seems not to have recognized this distinction (see below, text and notes 9 and 11), it comports best with experience to interpret his statement that "there are no relations of power without resistances" as applying only to power as the threat of sanction.

2. See Young 1990, 45, on intent.

3. Young 1936, 721–22. I thank Noam Zohar for consultation on this point.

4. Exodus 22:21. Although Cohen (1972) and others have argued that "empathy" is a modern phenomenon, these passages may suggest otherwise.

5. E.g., the Declaration of Independence (1776) refers to the English crown's unjust exercise of powers as "Oppressions"; in Federalist 10 (1788) James Madison warns against the majority's "oppression."

6. Young 1990, for example, identifies five "faces" of "oppression." Her analysis usefully helps identify the many ways in which dominant groups can exert their power. As a definitive set of criteria by which one can identify "oppression" it too has been contested (see Kymlicka 1995, 145).

7. This process appears, for example, in language that encodes subtle patterns of subordination but that all members of the society "naturally" speak, as when women express their solidaristic yearnings with the word "fraternity" and English-speaking people of African descent describe an evil heart as "black."

8. Marx and Engels [1848] 1954, 52; Mill [1859] 1947, 6; Foucault [1977] 1980b, 142.

9. Foucault [1977] 1980b, 141; [1976] 1980a, 80. Foucault also stressed what others might call "power to," both by pointing out the creativity and ubiquity of power and by making the many forms of power analytically inseparable from one another (see Fraser 1989 and McCarthy 1990 on the strengths and weaknesses in Foucault's analysis of power).

10. Early in the recent study of social movements, Snow et al. (1986) and Snow and Benford (1992) built on Goffman's (1974) concept of framing and Gamson, Fireman, and Rytina's (1982) concept of an "injustice frame" to show that one central function of social movements is to frame or reframe "objects, situations, events, experiences, and sequences

of actions" to either "underscore and embellish the seriousness and injustice of a social condition or redefine as unjust and immoral what was previously seen as unfortunate but perhaps tolerable" (Snow and Benford 1992, 137; see also Snow et al. 1986 on frame bridging, frame amplification, frame extension, and frame transformation). As Goodwin and Jasper (1999) point out, and as the Harris, Marshall, and Stockdill chapters in this volume indicate, both activists and nonactivists, leaders and the rank and file participate incrementally in these framing processes. The processes are emotional as well as cognitive (Taylor 1995, Tarrow 1998, Goodwin and Jasper 1999, McAdam 1999). For more on injustice frames, see Gamson 1992, esp. 68 ff., and Mansbridge chap. 9, this volume, esp. nn. 1, 5, and 6. The concept of ideology has been much disputed. We mean by it only a system of beliefs that frames and guides one's general understanding of, and interaction in, the world (Cohen 1999, 41).

11. Adapted from Morris 1990, 1992; see also Morris and Braine, chap. 2, this volume. See Mansbridge, chap. 9, this volume, for a more detailed analysis. Note that this definition is intended to apply primarily to members of the oppressed group, as the challenges of recasting consciousness apply primarily to those who have experienced the relevant processes of subordination, both blatant and subtle, triggered by membership in the group. (See also Conover 1988 and Conover and Sapiro 1993 for the effects of group membership.) Our experience prompts us, however, to include individuals who are not members of the group but who have come sufficiently to identify with the situation of members of the group to be thought of as having an oppositional consciousness themselves (see Kalmuss, Gurin, and Townsend 1981 on "sympathetic consciousness"). When we enter the realm of a "multidimensional consciousness" (Stockdill, chap. 8, this volume), the identification across group boundaries becomes explicit.

12. See Rorty 1985; Nussbaum 1995; Jasper 1997.

13. For political opportunities, see Tarrow 1998; for mobilizing institutions, see McAdam 1982 and Morris 1984; for repertoires see Tilly 1995, esp. 392–95; for the continual interaction of "culture" and "structure," see Polletta 1999 and Tarrow 1999.

14. For more on the relation between individual and social in the concept of consciousness, see Gamson 1992, 55, 65 ff.; Taylor and Whittier 1992, 114 ff.; see also Morris and Braine, chap. 2, this volume; and Mansbridge, chap. 9, this volume. It is helpful to see identity as a process of negotiation (Minow 1997; see Cerulo 1997 for a review). See Mansbridge, chap. 9, this volume, for the temptation to essentialism when identity is mistakenly seen as fixed.

15. For parallels, see, e.g., Shingles 1981 (on "black consciousness"); Sigel and Welchel 1986 (on "minority consciousness"); Gurin 1985, Miller, Hildreth, and Simmons 1998, Sapiro 1990, and Rinehart 1992 (on "gender consciousness"); Kalmuss, Gurin, and Townsend 1991, Klein 1984, Cook 1989, Conover and Sapiro 1993, and Reingold and Foust 1998 (on "feminist consciousness"); Kaplan 1982 (on "female consciousness"), King 1988 and Higginbotham 1993 (on the "multiple consciousness" of race, class, and gender); and Sandoval 1991, 1993, 2000 (on the "equal rights," "revolutionary," "supremacist," "separationist," and "differential" forms of "oppositional consciousness").

16. Groups characterized by oppositional consciousness thus differ in their relations to existing systems of domination and subordination from those "new social movements" that are characterized as resulting from a "quest" for identity (see Johnston, Laraña, and Gusfield 1994, 22, 23, 29; and Johnston 1994, 267). The women's and gay rights movements are often listed as among the new social movements because they are thought to involve the "emergence" of dimensions of identity that, although not new, are at least "formerly weak" (Johnston, Laraña, and Gusfield 1994, 7). McAdam puts the point better, however, by saying that "what is 'new' about the new social movements—including the women's movement—is the central importance they attach to the creation of new collective identities as a fundamental goal of the movement" (1994, 50). Members of groups embedded in a longstanding pattern of domination and subordination do not need

to engage in a "quest" for identity. A central feature of their socially given identities is already the recognized cause of their subordinate status. Yet, like workers in the era that E. P. Thompson ([1963] 1966) chronicles (an "old" social movement), African Americans, colonized peoples, women, people with disabilities, and gays and lesbians all have to forge new understandings of their identities as a means to their liberation. For members of all these groups, new understandings of their identities also become to some degree a goal of the movement rather than simply a means. Groups that are subject to oppression may differ from one another in the degree to which crafting new understandings of their identities plays a central role in their struggle for equality. Yet all differ from, for example, New Age movements in having as the central goal not an identity quest, but rather ending their already recognized subordinate status in an existing historical pattern of domination and subordination (see Morris and Braine, chap. 2, this volume).

17. Our analyses draw from many strands in the current debates among analysts of social movements. We stress both structure and culture, and assume that each of these factors determines and gives meaning to the other. We draw to some small degree from "rational choice" analysis. We think that we have embedded the "collaborative meaning-making" that we describe here in the mix of relevant historical contexts that McAdam (1999, xii) prescribes, although we in no way claim to have produced a full analysis of the causal forces operating in any of the settings. We want to stress what Tilly calls "continuously negotiated interchanges among specific interlocutors" with "constraint and mediation by historically-accumulated understandings concerning identities and relations of the parties" and "incessant modification of those identities and relations" (1998, 494). To the degree that we emphasize cultural forces, this emphasis seems appropriate in a study of consciousness. We do not want to underplay the importance of structural forces. In the most overarching sense, our analyses are deeply structural, because they take the larger structures of domination and subordination that cause a group's oppression as the primary cause of the need to develop an oppositional consciousness. In the more proximate sense, we try to identify spatial, geographical, political, and organizational structures that have important effects on developing oppositional consciousness. "Free spaces" (Groch, chap. 4, this volume), legal structures (Marshall, chap. 5, this volume), migrant patterns (Rodríguez, chap. 6, this volume), and the positions of polity member versus challenger (Waite, chap. 7, this volume) all play key causal roles in our analyses. We could not investigate all the relevant structural forces in these short chapters, and we may have neglected some extremely important ones. But this neglect will not have been due to a decision that such forces are not important.

We have two primary goals within the field of social movements. The first is to make more salient in future analyses the distinction between "liberation groups," whose members are working to end their own subordination, and other groups, so that this does not get lost. Our second goal is to extend and underscore analyses that make consciousness (and its moral, psychological, cultural, and structural causes) a critical factor in the chain of causation that produces social movements. Charles Tilly's important early model of the causation of collective action differed from his model of Marx's theory of causation in several respects, one of which was the omission of "Common Consciousness" (Tilly 1978, 43, 56). McAdam's later model (1982, 51) put "Cognitive liberation" back in, as a third and last step (mutually interacting with "Indigenous organizational strength") in a path whose final outcome was "Social movement." His more recent model (McAdam 1999, xvi) put "Interpretive processes" first after the primordial cause of "Broad change processes," followed by four other processes before the outcome of "Sustained contention." In our analysis, consciousness and interpretation interact with other factors all along the causal chain. Notes in the specific chapters will indicate where we agree and differ with other interpretations by social movement analysts on more specific points.

2   Social Movements and Oppositional Consciousness

Aldon Morris and Naomi Braine

Culture has made a triumphant return to sociology generally, and to social movement analysis specifically. While the resource mobilization and political process perspectives provided a much-needed challenge to collective behavior and related theories of social movements, their emphasis on rational movement actors and the material capacity for action by challenging groups obscured the importance of cultural factors in political activism. It is altogether proper that culture has returned to social movement analysis, for social movements are intensely cultural as well as structural phenomena. However, in turning attention to the cultural aspects of movement activity, it would be analytically costly to lose sight of the interconnected nature of culture and social structure in determining the terrain on which any particular social movement operates. Theoretical work on social movements has too often assumed that all movements confront basically similar tasks and operate out of the same internal logic. This assumption is problematic when applied to the organizational and material factors structuring movement activity; it completely breaks down when applied to cultural dynamics. Thus, in order to pursue a more comprehensive explanation, we examine one important way in which movements differ systematically and how such variation affects the tasks confronting movement leaders and organizers.

The new work (e.g., Jasper 1997; Goodwin and Jasper 1999; Johnston and Klandermans 1995; Morris and Mueller 1992; Snow et al. 1986; Snow and Benford 1992) that seeks to construct appropriate cultural and social psychological analyses of social movements addresses many issues crucial to understanding culture and social movements. For example, Gamson (1992) identifies four central problematics in the social psychology of movements—collective identity, solidarity, consciousness, and micromobilization. All these problematics address how actors are embedded in social networks and how they interpret events and construct meaning systems conducive to movement participation. The social constructionist paradigm provides relevant analytical tools to address these issues.

This new cultural and social psychology work is a vast improvement over the collective behavior tradition as well as the cultural blind spots of resource mobilization and political process models, but it still has significant gaps. Although most contemporary work no longer views individuals in social movements as isolated or pathological, it still does not adequately situate individuals and social networks within systems of human domination. Taylor and Whittier (1992) are an exception to this generalization with their study of how lesbian-feminist communities provide collective support for individuals fighting such a system. Gamson's (1992) review of the recent social psychology literature on social movements suggests that questions of identity, solidarity, and consciousness are framed in a way that presumes the absence of the kind of oppositional communities revealed in Taylor and Whittier's work.

This lack of attention to the role of oppositional communities in struggles against larger systems of domination may result directly from the character of the movements that appear to be the empirical base for much of the new theoretical work. Environmentalists and antinuclear activists have to build identity, solidarity, and consciousness "from the ground up" because generally they are not mobilizing in the context of either personal identities that have an existing subordinate meaning in the social system or entrenched oppositional communities. An identity as an "environmentalist" is fully chosen rather than externally imposed by a dominant group (unlike the situation for, e.g., racial groups), and creating this identity often requires considerable education and persuasion. Even when sociological work concentrates on oppositional communities, however, we also have to be attentive to how the "frame" provided by an existing theoretical perspective may shape the "answer" found in the data. For example, Josh Gamson's (1989) study of ACT UP emphasizes the use of boundaries and the emergence of "new" categories/identities, and overlooks the roots of AIDS activism (especially in ACT UP) in earlier gay liberation and feminist movements. The extent to which movement activists have to create a collective identity and ideological basis for action—quintessentially cultural tasks—is heavily determined by the position of the group being mobilized in existing structures of domination and subordination.

As analyses in the new social movement tradition (Cohen 1985; Melucci 1989) have pointed out, one of the central goals of many movements is to bring about cultural change within their own constituencies and within target groups. The essence of such cultural change is to convince people to see things differently, to interpret social reality differently. The civil rights movement, for example, attempted to convince both Blacks and Whites that race relations in this country could be structured and practiced differently. Yet that movement did not have to carve out a Black collective identity and an injustice frame because Blacks internalize and learn them as routinely as they learn to talk, to walk, and to socialize with peers, parents, and Whites. Nor was the development of a master frame a crucial task because historically Black people have consistently espoused a "freedom and justice" and an "equal rights" position in their quest for racial equality (Morris 1993b).

The existence of collective identities and injustice frames within oppressed populations does not mean that such groups can be easily mobilized to engage in risky and protracted collective action. Indeed, within oppressed populations certain cultures of subordination inhibit collective action. These cultures of subordination arise because oppressed populations devise survival strategies that enable them to cope with adverse social conditions they encounter on a regular basis. These strategies generate a language of submission that permeates a subordinate group's religion, music, literature, folklore, and educational experiences. Scholars of the Black experience, for example, have long documented the otherworldly aspects of Black religion that encourage passivity rather than militant action. This submission language appears in the blues, as in one popular tune during the era of Jim Crow: "I've been down so long that being down don't seem to bother me." Dominant groups actively encourage and enforce such cultures of subordination.

Such cultures of subordination play an important role in decreasing the possibility of large-scale mobilization and sustained collective action. They also encourage the view among scholars of social movements that collective action is possible only if such populations develop new collective identities and injustice frames. However, these accounts often overlook the coexistence of oppositional cultures with cultures of subordination. Opposition is often present in the same cultural materials that promote submission. Rather than running along parallel tracks, cultures of subordination and cultures of opposition travel crisscrossing routes with frequent collisions and cross-fertilization. Thus, much of Black religion speaks simultaneously of overthrowing oppression and rewarding meek souls in a blissful afterlife.

These cultures embody, therefore, an internal contest between opposition and subordination. This contest has received little scholarly attention and is obscured by frameworks that privilege emergent cultural properties. Indeed, members of oppressed groups tend to vacillate between their oppositional and subordinate cultures. In this delicate dance, movement leaders and organizers try to crystallize and elevate the oppositional side of the equation, making it an effective tool of combat. The analytical challenge is to illuminate the conditions that determine whether and when an oppositional culture will develop in ways that a social movement can utilize for its purposes. The presence or absence of an existing oppositional culture creates radically different challenges for movement leaders and organizers.

The crucial task of the civil rights movement was to undermine the existing culture of subordination while elevating the existing oppositional culture in such a way as to convince Black people that their engaging in a set of nonroutine, risky actions could change the very nature of race relations, to the end that Blacks could become equal with Whites. Preexisting oppositional ideas embedded in music, prayer, ritual, the presentation of speeches, oratory, the written word—in short, culture—were pivotal in convincing large numbers of African Americans to embrace nonroutine collective actions. These cultural items had to be refined and refocused through consciousness-raising activities to be made combat-ready for the civil rights movement.

The growth of gay and lesbian activism since World War II illustrates the importance of oppositional culture in another way. In spite of the increased repression of the McCarthy era, the 1940s and 1950s were a period of rapid community development among lesbians and gay men in major urban areas. Bars and coffeehouses were established; gay neighborhoods became increasingly identifiable in major cities despite chronic police harassment; publications and organizations were established and maintained; more autonomous and increasingly oppositional gay and lesbian cultures came into existence (D'Emilio 1983; Faderman 1991). The Stonewall rebellion and the sudden appearance of gay liberation organizations throughout the country were rooted in a process of community development and politicization that had been gathering force for many years (D'Emilio 1983; Adam 1987). The ideology of gay liberation that heterosexuals heard for the first time in 1969 had been debated, refined, and circulated through different gay and lesbian organizations and publications for decades before emerging into public view. The examples of the civil rights and gay liberation movements suggest that the complex and often obscure relationship between culture and power needs to take a central place in social movement analyses.

Much of the recent cultural analysis of social movements contains the conceptual biases embedded in symbolic interactionism, classical collective behavior theory, dramaturgical analysis, and ethnomethodological approaches. In those frameworks, concepts such as emergence, social construction, negotiating, framing, and identity work are the key analytical concepts through which social processes are examined and interpreted. These frameworks tend to conceptualize the social world as a drama in which actors are always constructing meanings, identities, rights, and privileges, and even social reality itself through complex social processes and interactions. The bias here is toward process rather than enduring social relations backed by both naked and symbolic power.

These kinds of cultural analyses are useful in understanding collective action. Social construction, the formation of collective identities, consciousness-raising, framing, media packaging, defining grievances, and developing ideologies are key internal dynamics of social movements. Such approaches to movement analysis have a great deal to contribute to the understanding of how fluid processes and subjective interpretations affect collective action. The new cultural approaches rooted in a constructionist framework have begun to illuminate these processes.

Nevertheless, we argue that these theoretical traditions have underemphasized issues pertaining to domination and oppression. The emphasis of these perspectives on fluid processes and the social construction of reality makes them sometimes slow to acknowledge the relatively stable aspects of most systems of domination. These perspectives often avoid explicitly dissecting systems of human domination, such as racial, class, and gender domination. Marx's analysis ([1866–67] 1970) of class domination and Weber's analysis ([1922] 1947) of various systems of domination demonstrate how central power, social inequality, and culture are to such social arrangements.

On the other hand, some analysts utilizing the perspectives that take power dynamics into account have become overly structural. Too often such analysts assume a mechanistic relationship in which structural inequality or some other social condition leads directly to collective action. The best classical analysts, such as Weber ([1922] 1947), Gramsci ([1929–35] 1971), and Thompson ([1963] 1966), focused on how objective structures of domination interact with subjectively experienced domination to produce collective action. In these approaches, culture functions either to inhibit or to facilitate collective action, depending on the mix of hegemonic or insurgent characteristics in that culture. By returning to this classic agenda in our studies of culture and social movements, we will give considerable weight both to systems of human domination and to cultural processes. We can then explore the intersection between structural and cultural factors.

This combination of structural and cultural analyses appears frequently in feminist and gay-lesbian theory, particularly gay-lesbian social history. D'Emilio (1983), Faderman (1991), Rubin (1975, 1984), Vance (1984, 1989), Collins (1990), and others have explored the role of the social construction of masculinity/femininity and heterosexuality in establishing and maintaining deeply entrenched systems of political, economic, and cultural power. These social constructions themselves are products of power relations and historical forces, not neutral negotiations among individual or collective actors of equal social resources and standing. The social construction of gender in capitalist and colonial societies, for example, cannot be understood in isolation from the expansion of capital and capitalism, the social organization of sexuality, systems of racial and ethnic domination, and shifts in family structure. Symbolic interactionists and ethnomethodologists have tended to back away from a serious engagement with the links between these structures of social and economic domination on the one hand and identities and other constructions on the other hand. Feminist and gay/lesbian scholars, to the contrary, insist that human domination is fundamentally cultural and structural, and that the social construction of identities, ideologies, and symbolic systems is intimately embedded in the major systems of domination structuring a society.

A system of human domination can be defined as that constellation of institutions, values, ideas, and practices which successfully enables one group to achieve and maintain power and privilege through the control and exploitation of another group (Morris 1992). In any given society several major systems of human domination usually coexist and interact in complex ways. American examples include the systems of class, race, and gender. As Marx ([1846] 1965) and Gramsci ([1929–35] 1971) understood, dominant groups that benefit from the most powerful systems of human domination usually develop and disseminate a hegemonic culture that symbolically legitimizes their rulership. Such symbolic legitimation is never perfectly achieved. Such a culture must be reproduced, reshaped, and disseminated on an ongoing basis to counter the cultural and social forces at work attempting to undermine it (see Fantasia 1988; Scott 1985).

One of the most important cultural forces working against a hegemonic culture is the oppositional consciousness of oppressed groups. An oppositional consciousness is an empowering mental state that prepares members of an oppressed group to act to undermine, reform, or overthrow a system of human domination. Minimally, that mental state includes identifying with a subordinate group, concluding that the mechanisms that have produced at least some of the group inequalities are unjust, opposing the injustice, and seeing a common interest within the subordinate group in eliminating the injustice. The magnitude of oppositional consciousness ranges from this minimal level to a fully mature state. A more full-fledged oppositional consciousness includes seeing some actions of the dominant group as forming in some way a "system"—that is, as linked and roughly functional for advancing the interests of the dominant group. It also includes a variety of other insurgent ideas and beliefs that provide coherence, explanation, and moral condemnation. Oppositional consciousness in the restricted sense we give it characterizes members of groups that have long been subordinate within a system of domination and subordination, along with those who identify deeply with them.

The existence of oppositional group consciousness presupposes the prior existence of an oppositional culture (see Mansbridge, chap. 9, this volume). An oppositional culture contains the frameworks of oppositional ideas and worldviews that permeate the larger culture of certain subordinate communities. These frameworks also contain partially developed critiques of the status quo as well as knowledge of isolated rebellious acts and prior episodes of organized collective action. These frameworks provide the raw materials that help shape and crystallize the collective identities that are in large part externally imposed on oppressed communities by dominant groups. In short, these frameworks facilitate the process by which collective identities become internalized and experienced subjectively by members of oppressed groups.

Yet oppositional cultures usually fail to provide shared definitions of experience that make clear the need for collective action. An oppositional culture, for example, may generate the familiar complaint within the Black community that Whites mistreat Blacks. This assessment falls short of directing members of that community toward lines of action that would collectively change their situation. Oppositional cultures often do not provide potential collective actors with the directions and strategies required to overcome repression. As a result, when cultures of opposition and subordination weave back and forth in their crossing, the culture of subordination often wins out because it focuses on the abundant knowledge of the negative consequences associated with rebellion.

A mature oppositional consciousness, in contrast to oppositional culture, challenges dominant beliefs and ideologies by distilling and synthesizing the ideas already present in that culture, giving them a coherence that forges them into symbolic blueprints for collective action and social change. As Taylor and Whittier have pointed out, one major purpose of oppositional consciousness is to supply subordinate groups with concrete accounts that challenge dominant understandings; indeed, oppositional consciousness is "an ongoing process in which groups reevaluate themselves, their subjective experiences, their opportunities, and their shared interests" (Taylor and Whittier 1992, 14).

In contrast to most oppositional cultures, oppositional consciousness directs individuals away from explanations of their fate based on neutral impersonal forces or personal shortcomings and identifies dominant groups and their structures of domination as the source of oppression. Oppositional consciousness thus critiques and undermines the submissive messages that sprout from the cultures of subordination. The mobilizing work of organizers and leaders has a major effect in crystallizing and disseminating oppositional consciousness.

Thus, although there is no hard and fixed line between what we mean by "oppositional culture" and a minimal oppositional consciousness, except that consciousness lodges more within the individual, oppositional culture alone can live more easily intertwined with a culture of subordination. The more an oppositional culture stresses not just group identification and opposition but the injustice of a group's subordination, the more it will breed individuals who will automatically have a minimal oppositional consciousness and actively resist the culture of subordination. In the evolution to oppositional consciousness that we describe, mere sense of difference, self-preservation, opposition, anger, and resentment develops into an understanding of unequal power, injustice, and finally the systemic quality of the oppression. We agree with Gamson that consciousness "involves a mesh between individual and cultural levels" and that oppositional consciousness pertains to the process by which "the meaning that individuals give to a social situation becomes a shared definition implying collective action" (Gamson 1992, 55).

Carriers of an oppositional consciousness perform several tasks. They identify the enemy as an oppressor, thus politicizing preexisting "we" vs. "they" dichotomies. They describe the nature of the oppression and the ways in which it is maintained. They highlight and reinterpret countercultural expressions previously somewhat camouflaged in rituals, religious ceremonies, music, poetry, dance, and jokes. They create free spaces where resistance can be contemplated, acted out, and condoned. They attach moral wrongness to their oppression while imbuing thoughts and acts of resistance with the mantle of rightness. Like hegemonic culture, oppositional consciousness must constantly be reproduced and refined to address the conditions of oppression as they appear in real time and space. Oppositional consciousness flows from historical and social processes, not from biology.

Systems of human domination thus give rise to the conditions that generate oppositional cultures as well as oppositional consciousness. Oppositional communities are the dialectical opposites of the dominant communities that espouse and disseminate hegemonic consciousness.

Victims of a system of domination usually possess at least some rudimentary forms of an oppositional consciousness, although the specific analyses and critiques of the dominant group will evolve as the precise dynamics of oppression change in minor or major ways (Scott 1985). There is considerable variation in the extent and level of maturity of such an oppositional consciousness and how entrenched it is in any given oppressed community. This variation is affected by levels of repression, the cohesiveness of the oppressed group, the institutional autonomy of the oppressed group, and the group's communication networks, including its media.

Collective identities are never created from a vacuum. Movement participants never develop full-fledged injustice frames on the spot. Only sometimes do those participants have to be schooled about who the enemy is; only sometimes do they have to be taught to interpret their situation as a social problem. The theoretical language of "emergence" and "becoming" distracts analytical attention from preexisting communities of oppositional culture and fledgling oppositional consciousness, which in some instances have been in place for decades, centuries, or even millennia.

When applied to historic oppressed groups, the conceptual language of emergence privileges the moment at which an oppressed group mobilizes and commits itself to public conflict with the dominant group. In actuality, open challenge usually follows the internal development of a community of resistance that includes a maturing oppositional consciousness, collective identity, and organizational infrastructure. African Americans have had long-standing communities of resistance in the United States (Harding 1983; Morris 1993b) with a well-developed sense of identity and at least some oppositional consciousness. In contrast, lesbians and gay men had to create communities of resistance before a social movement could arise to challenge the dominant heterosexual population. All too often the theoretical language of emergence privileges the perspective of the dominant group by defining a movement as emerging only at the moment that it gains sufficient internal resources to sustain an open challenge. For oppressed groups, the creation of important forms of identity, solidarity, and oppositional consciousness must precede public challenge in order for the challenge to be sustained and the movement leaders to survive.

Analysts who emphasize emergence and becoming as key movement characteristics often portray the tasks of movement leaders and organizers as far more difficult than they may be. Building on and refining preexisting collective identities and injustice frames is easier than creating them anew. Indeed, in communities where oppositional cultures already exist, movement leaders often face the challenge of how to address existing inequities of power and how to use preexisting forms of oppositional culture and consciousness to convince oppressed people that at that moment it is advantageous for them to engage in risky collective action. Such populations have to be moved beyond the inertia created and maintained by cultures of subordination.

Theoretical approaches that underemphasize preexisting communities of at least fledgling oppositional consciousness also fail to understand the symbolic readiness of many groups to engage in collective action. They thereby reify the power and control of dominant groups. Gamson addresses this point head-on: "Are social scientists, in emphasizing how this culture of quiescence is produced and maintained, themselves promulgating yet another set of reasons for inaction, another discouragement to agency? Where are the cracks where some ideas of collective agency stay alive, ready to grow and prosper under the proper conditions, as they did so dramatically and to everyone's surprise in Eastern Europe, for example?" (1995, 97). In these cracks live preexisting cultures of opposition from which oppositional consciousness can be consciously developed by the activists in social movements.

Physical Segregation and Oppositional Consciousness

Ironically, most systems of human domination themselves produce many of the conditions that develop oppositional consciousness. Many such systems physically segregate those whom they oppress—for example, on the basis of race, ethnicity, or relation to the means of production. In racial systems of domination, the oppressed are normally segregated and treated differently on the basis of skin color. Distinct working-class communities dot the social landscape because workers are indirectly segregated on the basis of how much they are paid for the role they play in the economy.

The degree of segregation and community development varies across oppressed groups. Groups oppressed on the basis of race, ethnicity, or class are likely to live in geographically segregated communities where oppositional culture becomes a part of the bonds of family and neighborhoods. In contrast, most women in the United States have had close relationships with and live in close proximity to the dominant male population (Gurin 1985; Conover 1988; Sapiro 1990). These women were to some degree separated from one another through relative isolation in private households. Professional political women who came together in the nation's capital and activist women who came together in the civil

rights and antiwar movements soon found that their previous relative isolation required the conscious creation of organizations and institutions
where the elements of a developed oppositional consciousness could be
hammered out. The early consciousness-raising groups in the women's
movement and the later pressure for women's centers at universities
exemplified the movement's need for segregated safe spaces in which
women could socialize, forge bonds of solidarity, and puzzle out together
their own analysis of their oppression.

In yet a third pattern, in Europe and the United States throughout
the twentieth century, the development of independent gay-lesbian social worlds preceded the development of lesbian and gay oppositional
consciousness. In the first half of the twentieth century, gay-lesbian
bars and other social spaces developed originally in Europe, as did the
earliest articulations of a nascent gay-rights discourse. Before World
War II, gay-lesbian social and political activity centered in Germany.
The rise of the Nazis both destroyed the European gay communities
and set back the oppositional discourse that was developing at these
sites. In the United States, homophile organizations and national publications arose after World War II. The combination of social disruption
and economic opportunity caused by mobilization during the war and
boom in the postwar period produced a massive expansion of gay-lesbian
social networks, commercial establishments, and proximate settlement
in urban enclaves. When a period of renewed repression began in the
1950s, political organizations were founded in 1951 (Mattachine) and
1955 (Daughters of Bilitis) with the goal of organizing gays and lesbians
and improving social conditions, although from an assimilationist stand-
point. Throughout the 1950s and 1960s, gay-lesbian organizations and
publications (particularly *One* and *The Ladder*) provided a collective
forum for the gradual development of political analysis and action. The
first visible protests occurred several years before the Stonewall Riots
and the Gay Liberation Front (Adam 1987; D'Emilio 1983).

Sharon Groch (chap. 4, this volume) also provides considerable
evidence that the primary factor influencing the strong oppositional
consciousness of deaf people, as compared to the blind and the mobility
impaired, was the physical segregation of deaf people plus at least partial
control of their own spaces.

These different patterns of physical segregation and the capacity to
talk together in unmonitored spaces powerfully affect consciousness and
mobilization. In general, we theorize, the higher the degree of physical
segregation, the greater the likelihood of a widespread mature oppositional consciousness.

The relationship between physical segregation and the development of oppositional cultures and oppositional consciousness is not, of course, inevitable. Subordinate groups can be highly segregated without substantial control of "their" space. The more closely segregated spaces are monitored, the harder it becomes for autonomous cultures to take root. The key is the degree of independent internal organization subordinate groups can forge within segregated spaces. Churches, schools, unions, and voluntary associations, coupled with explicit cultural products including newspapers, music, literature, and humor, are especially relevant in producing oppositional cultures in segregated spaces.

Despite even close monitoring by repressive regimes, subordinate communities residing in the most highly segregated spaces are often the most likely to find the privacy and cultural resources to develop oppositional cultures and oppositional consciousness. In many cases segregated institutions present a facade of normalcy that reassures dominant groups while fomenting oppositional cultures and oppositional consciousness behind the scenes. This facade/backstage division sheltered the growth of oppositional consciousness in Black churches and colleges in the south, in Iranian mosques during the shah's regime, and in working-class churches and universities in Chile during Pinochet's rule. In these spaces cultures of subordination struggled with cultures of opposition, but when political opportunities arose or repression for one reason or another was relaxed, the culture of opposition could blossom into oppositional consciousness and intense movement activity.

Although in general historically oppressed groups who are highly segregated are more likely than other marginalized groups to develop an oppositional culture and oppositional consciousness capable of facilitating and sustaining full-fledged liberation movements, this association is not perfect. Before the "second wave" of the women's movement in the United States around 1968, middle-class White women did not experience the spatial segregation from men conducive to the development of an oppositional culture or an oppositional consciousness. With their lives effectively entrenched in private households, they were to some degree segregated from one another. Betty Friedan captured their situation by pointing out that with the kitchen at the center of their lives "many women no longer left their homes, except to shop, chauffeur their children, or attend a social engagement with their husbands" (1983, 17).

Indeed, these women came to believe that their "problem" was a personal problem. So relatively absent was an oppositional culture that, in Friedan's words, "nobody argued whether women were inferior or superior to men; they were simply different. Words like 'emancipation' and 'career' sounded strange and embarrassing." A woman was "so ashamed to admit her dissatisfaction that she never knew how many other women shared it" (Friedan 1983, 19). Without much of an oppositional culture, women became victims of a "problem that had no name."

In contemporary America, middle-class women confront a different reality. As women organized, they borrowed oppositional ideas, symbols, and practices from the Black movement. The phrase "women's liberation" took the concept of liberation directly from the civil rights movement, and the word "sexism" was coined as a direct parallel to racism. At the same time women began entering the work force in increasing numbers and interacting more often in both segregated and integrated work spaces. The activists consciously created segregated spaces such as women's bookstores and music festivals, at which at least some women could feel safe and develop their thinking. (Differences in class, race, sexual orientation, and activism did not make any one place feel safe for all women.) As a result of building a movement and interacting in the public sphere, women began to develop a fuller oppositional culture and an oppositional consciousness, transforming themselves into a group from whose more developed cultural apparatus the social movement could draw.

In short, physical segregation (by which we do not mean purely residential segregation) and the distinct oppressive treatment of dominated groups often converge to produce an ongoing culture of opposition. Although physical segregation is not necessary, it greatly facilitates the growth of such a culture. The culture then helps provide members of the group with a collective identity, an injustice frame, and some experience with resistance, whether at the level of contemplation or actuality. This oppositional culture and the oppositional consciousness that can be derived from it make collective action possible when other economic and social conditions are met. This culture and consciousness also enable collective action to spread rapidly once it is sparked. Thus, the majority of African Americans understood what one Black man meant when he exclaimed to the crowd in Los Angeles following the Rodney King verdict, "Justice is for the White man not the brother man!" The Los Angeles rebellion could never have become such an explosive force in a matter of hours had it not been rooted in a historical injustice frame on which the average African American, and even the average Latina/Latino, in Los Angeles could easily draw.

Oppositional Consciousness and Movement Type

For some movements the conceptual language of "emergence," "becoming," and "social construction" is more applicable than in others. Movements such as Mothers Against Drunk Driving, environmentalism, and the peace movement do not grow directly out of preexisting systems of human domination. While they may be linked to broad structures of domination like capitalism or military power, these movements are not tied to specific populations, such as social groups or social classes, that have a preexisting identity and culture. These movements attack what they perceive as undesirable conditions or future human catastrophes affecting humanity in general. Through one's own effort and self-education one chooses to become an environmentalist, an antinuker, or an active opponent of drunk driving. Each individual, in a facilitating or impeding context, voluntarily develops such an identity and takes on such a role for social and political purposes. In contrast, members of oppressed groups acquire their status involuntarily, often through classification at birth. The social consequences of their identity are externally imposed and enforced. An environmental activist may suffer some penalties for social movement activity, but a woman is penalized socially and economically whether or not she engages in feminist political activity.

Throughout this chapter we have emphasized the need to refocus theoretical attention on the interconnection of structure and culture and the resulting differences in the cultural tasks faced by different movements. Sociological analysts sometimes make a loose distinction between "new" social movements and another, even vaguer, category—presumably "old" social movements. If this distinction is temporal, it is not clear which time period constitutes the dividing line. If the distinction is based on targets for action and change, the criteria for categorizing the targets are not clear. Is second-wave feminism a "new" movement and women's suffrage an "old" movement? Both waves of feminist activity addressed similar issues of women's political and economic roles, treatment by men within and outside of the family, and the importance of women controlling their own sexuality and reproduction. Rather than focusing on the temporal dimension of old and new, we find it more useful to focus on preexisting structures of domination and subordination and the kinds of preexisting oppositional cultures in which movement leaders have to work.

In a recent work James Jasper has pointed out how important it is to distinguish between types of movements when examining the interaction between social structure and cultural processes. He argues that a distinction should be drawn between what he calls "citizenship" and "post-citizenship" movements. Citizenship movements consist of "efforts . . . organized by and on behalf of categories of people excluded in some way from full human rights, political participation, or basic economic protections." These types of movements direct their demands to the state. On the other hand, post-citizenship movements are "composed of people already integrated into their society's political, economic, and educational systems. . . . These protestors are especially interested in changing their society's cultural sensibilities" (1997, 7). This useful distinction roughly maps onto ours but is too restrictive for our purposes. In our view, the movements that Jasper calls citizenship movements usually direct their demands at a variety of targets depending on the nature of their domination. They often demand deep social changes that the state is only partially able to facilitate. From our perspective, it is the relationship between social movements and systems of domination that provides the key distinction between them. Our typology thus rests on both movement goals and systems of domination.

Relating the goal of the movement to its preexisting group base produces a typology consisting of three types of movements: "liberation movements," "equality-based special issue movements," and "social responsibility movements." Each of these movements stands in a different relationship to enduring systems of human domination.

Liberation Movements

These are movements whose carriers have a historically subordinate position within an ongoing system of social stratification. This type of movement is aimed at overthrowing the relevant system of domination and is conducted almost entirely by the individuals whose daily existence is negatively impacted by those systems. The carriers of liberation movements are almost entirely members of oppressed groups for whom group membership is externally imposed, often from birth. Members of such groups are often differentiated from dominant groups on the basis of some social identifier such as race, gender, ethnicity, or social class position. Most are also physically segregated. Because of this long-standing state of oppression and segregation, such groups usually have developed both a culture of subordination and an oppositional culture. The two cultures of subordination and opposition coexist in tension, engaged in an ongoing contest for supremacy. As Scott (1985) has shown with respect to peasants, such groups often develop a rich culture of resistance as they and their interests routinely collide with concrete systems of domination.

It is from these infrastructures of oppositional culture that liberation movements rapidly take hold when other necessary conditions are met. The cultural challenge for movement leaders and organizers in this context is to refine, focus, and shape a preexisting consciousness rather than create it anew. Thus, the theoretical language of "emergence," "becoming," and "identity creation" is least relevant to an understanding of the cultural dynamics of liberation movements.

Equality-Based Special Issue Movements

These movements address specific issues that exclusively or disproportionately affect a particular oppressed group. In contrast to liberation movements, these special issue movements mobilize preexisting liberation ideologies and oppressed groups to fight a limited battle against a specific threat or mechanism of group oppression. These movements often appropriate the oppositional consciousness and culture of resistance generated by populations who are the carriers of liberation movements. The carriers of these special issue movements usually have a smaller goal than the full struggle to reform or overthrow large-scale systems of human domination. However, it is not rare for some participants in equality-based special issue movements to have been participants in the relevant liberation movement and to view their activism in this more limited movement as a part of the larger struggle waged by the liberation movement.

Examples of equality-based special issue movements include the pro-choice movement, the environmental racism movement, and the grass-roots AIDS movement. The pro-choice movement seeks to keep abortion legal by relying on activism fueled by the ideologies and oppositional consciousness of the larger women's movement, which is, in our analysis, a liberation movement. Similarly, the environmental racism movement appropriates the ideology and oppositional consciousness of the Black liberation movement in its quest to improve the environment in poor minority communities.

The cultural tasks for movement leaders and organizers of equality-based special issue movements differ in some respects from those of liberation movements. In these special issue movements the task is to align the grievances and cultural interpretations of the movements with those of liberation movements in such a manner that these special movements can both adopt the legitimacy and the cultural capital of liberation movements and, in the best instances, contribute to that legitimacy and capital. The activism generated by involvement in the special issue movements can either strengthen or dilute the larger liberation movement, in which the activists and leaders of the special movements are often participants. Their background in the larger movement provides the special issue movement with cultural resources and helps give it credibility and legitimacy. At the same time, these leaders and activists may see their work in the special issue movement as critical to the goals of the larger liberation struggle. The frame alignment analyses of Snow et al. (1986) are especially applicable to the cultural work carried out by these special issue movements. Yet the consciousness and ideologies of these movements are often the results primarily of cultural borrowing rather than emergence.

Social Responsibility Movements

These are movements that challenge certain external social conditions affecting the general population, conditions that a challenging group views as undesirable. Such movements seek to make individuals, corporations, and governments act in ways that are socially responsible in order to benefit humanity. Such movements include the antinuclear movement, the peace movement, and Mothers Against Drunk Driving.

The cultural realities confronting social responsibility movements differ sharply in one critical respect from the other two types of movements. The fundamental difference is that a member of such a movement chooses to assume and internalize the appropriate movement identity. Such identity transformations usually require considerable effort and self-education. In most cases, activists in these movements suffer penalties only for their social movement activity; in liberation movements, members of the oppressed groups are penalized socially and economically whether or not they engage in activist liberation politics.

Thus, participants in social responsibility movements are not directly connected to the most obvious oppressive systems of human domination. Movements of this type are not constructed by populations who have been exposed to extreme physical segregation or been the targets of oppressive regimes designed to keep them subordinate. They cannot, therefore, tap into their own segregated culture to access pre-existing frameworks or ideological weapons. When they do not emerge from a religious or political background oriented toward such issues, participants in these movements must develop almost from scratch their collective identities, appropriate injustice frames, and an oppositional consciousness. In short, they must become activists by learning how to understand, for example, what a nuclear holocaust would be like or what would happen to earth and its inhabitants in the event of total environmental breakdown. Their activism depends in part on their ability to construct collective action identities and injustice frames. Yet even in this process of construction, such movements often borrow from some aspects of liberation and special issue movements.

Conclusion

This paper has emphasized the need to refocus theoretical attention on the interconnection of structure and culture and the resulting differences among the cultural tasks faced by different movements. Movements vary systematically in the issues they address and the constituents they mobilize. An appropriate cultural analysis must distinguish among types of social movements and the variety of cultural challenges that different types of movements face.

The three types of movements identified here are ideal types. They and the nature of their oppositional consciousness overlap in concrete societies. Yet we believe they correspond, albeit imperfectly, to social reality and should be distinguished for analytic purposes. Our analytic typology distinguishes three kinds of groups: liberation movements, which are based in historically subordinate groups and aim at overthrowing the system of domination that subordinates those groups; equality-based special issue movements, which are based in historically subordinate groups and aim at removing a specific mechanism of group oppression; and social responsibility movements, which are based in groups that have no particular history of subordination and aim at removing a specific threat to humanity or the planet as a whole or some non–historically subordinate subset of humanity on the planet.

In creating oppositional consciousness, liberation movements can draw on cultural strands nourished through a long history of subordination. Social responsibility movements draw eclectically from a diverse set of cultural strands, of which only the religious components normally have the psychological depths of the oppositional cultures nourished by subordinate groups. Equality-based special issue movements fall in between, drawing from the preexisting oppositional consciousness fostered by liberation movements and also from diverse other social responsibility strands. One cultural model does not fit all. Social movement theory at this point in its history needs analyses characterized by a specificity that attends to the effects of systematic human domination.

Religious Resources in an Oppositional
         Civic Culture

Fredrick C. Harris

Breakfast with the Candidate

Each of the church leaders gathered at the Carter Temple CME Church
that August morning had, two weeks earlier, received a letter written on
the campaign stationery of Carol Moseley-Braun.[1] Addressing them as
"Dear Leader of Faith," it invited them to "a good morning of fellowship
with Illinois Democratic nominee for Senate Carol Moseley Braun." On
one side of the invitation was a head shot of the smiling candidate, on
the other a list of forty ministers who made up the event's steering and
organizing committees. It was clear that the Moseley-Braun campaign
was strategically targeting religious leaders to mobilize Blacks for the
upcoming election.

This letter was signed by Moseley-Braun's own minister, the Reverend Addie Wyatt of the Vernon Park Church of God. Wyatt was chair
of a group of ministers who would campaign on Moseley-Braun's behalf;
this committee was part of Moseley-Braun's official campaign organization. Wyatt's interdenominational work, activism in electoral and protest
activities, and longtime involvement in Chicago's labor union movement
had made her a familiar colleague to these clerics. In addition to her
involvement in the meatpackers' union, Wyatt had helped to organize
Black women for Harold Washington's mayoral campaign. Under her
leadership, she estimated, these women had raised more than one hundred thousand dollars for the candidate. In fact, Wyatt claimed to have
delivered a prophesy from God to Harold Washington telling him, two
weeks before he announced his candidacy, "God has sent me to tell you
that you suppose to be mayor of Chicago." She assured the future mayor:
"[God] will deliver the city into our hands."[2]

In her letter, Wyatt pointed out the historic nature of Moseley-
Braun's potential election: "Never before has an African-American
woman been elected to the U.S. Senate." To the uncommitted she suggested, "If you have not endorsed any candidate, we ask that you attend
this breakfast and hear what Carol Moseley Braun has to say." She
urged supporters of Moseley-Braun to "include her in your prayers and
meditations, and join us."

The steering and organizing committees for the event included not only Moseley-Braun's renowned minister but also locally based national leaders of various Christian denominations, including the bishops of the predominantly Black African Methodist Episcopal Church (AME) and the Church of God In Christ (COGIC), as well as Roman Catholic priests and ministers of the National Baptist Convention and the Pentecostal Assemblies (also a predominantly Black denomination), the United Methodist Church, and several nondenominational congregations.

Copies of the printed program for the breakfast were handed to participants as they entered the room. The cover read, "Religious Leadership Breakfast for Carol Moseley Braun"; the names of committee members appeared inside. Some parts of the program duplicated the structure of a religious service, with a congregational hymn, a scripture reading, an opening prayer, sacred music selections, and a benediction. In other ways, it read like a political event. Crammed inside the program was a "Blitz for Braun" flyer requesting volunteers to distribute campaign literature.

After the audience sang a couple of verses of the hymn "Leaning on the Everlasting Arm," Bishop Brazier, the master of ceremonies for the event, observed that it was a great honor to be "a part of the election campaign of a great woman." Brazier then quoted scripture from Psalm 127. "Except the Lord build a house," he uttered, as a chorus of voices from the audience chimed in to help him finish, "they labor in vain that build it." He went on: "We know that the Lord is with us today. We know that we are on our way." He urged the assembled to labor for Moseley-Braun's candidacy by registering eligible voters in their churches.

Carter Temple's minister, the Reverend Henry Williamson, who had recently been elected president of Operation PUSH—a nationally known civil rights group based in Chicago and founded by Jesse Jackson during the early seventies—was unable to attend the breakfast, so a representative gave the welcoming remarks in his place. Voter registration material was handed out to the audience by members of Project Vote, an organization registering Black voters in Chicago for the November general election. Williamson's representative urged the audience to "participate and support our very own, God's child, Carol Moseley Braun," and asked interested ministers to see Project Vote's clerical coordinator.

The registration handout noted that "the unregistered in our communities potentially represent the critical swing vote in both the presidential and senatorial election." It outlined how churches could participate, instructing religious leaders to appoint a voter registration coordinator, devote a Sunday to registration at their church, put registration material in church bulletins, set up booths at church events and programs, encourage ten lay members to become volunteer deputy registrars, and publicize registration activities through their religious radio and television broadcasts. The leaflet appeared to be specifically designed for clerics, noting on the form that "churches have historically been the key base for successful voter registration activities in the African American community," and adding, "[W]ith their large memberships and commitment to social justice, they provide both volunteer deputy registers and a forum to reach the unregistered."

The leadership breakfast continued with a reading from John 27:20–26. Father Martini Shaw of the Saint Thomas Episcopal Church read these passages, containing Jesus' prayer for unity among His disciples—and all believers—before His imminent crucifixion. This reading appeared to symbolize the importance of oneness among politically fractured elements in the audience:[3]

> I do not pray for these only, but also for those who believe in me through their word. That they may all be one, even as Thou Father art in me and I am in Thee, that they also may be in us. So that the world may believe that Thou hast sent me, the glory which Thou hast given me, I have given to them, that they may be one even as we are one.

Father Michael Pfleger, a White Roman Catholic priest whose voice resonated like that of a Baptist preacher, led a prayer that called for divine recognition and guidance for the candidate and her campaign. The Reverend Willie Barrow, a former president of Operation PUSH, once described Pfleger's preaching this way: "The first time I heard him, I had to look twice to make sure what was happening. Most white preachers, you know, don't have a lot of spirit and emotionalism. But this [white] boy, he can whoop!"[4] Father Pfleger serves as priest at the nearly all-Black Saint Sabina's on Chicago's South Side and often dresses in kente cloth; he combines Catholic liturgy with West African music and rituals during Mass. His renown comes in part from his past work with Father George Clements, mobilizing protests against stores and companies that sell and manufacture drug paraphernalia in Chicago's minority communities. Their activities led to the passage of a state law that made the sale of such merchandise illegal.

Pfleger began his prayer that morning by acknowledging God's presence:

> Father God, we thank You and we pray to You first for the gift of this day. We thank You Lord, for each and every person here that You will

allow to gather in Your name. And we thank You for the purpose for which we gather. We have to thank You, Lord, that You would continue to reveal Yourself to us in Your all-divine way and fashion.

Pfleger also thanked God for sending a candidate of faith.

We thank You for our sister Carol. We thank You first of all that she knows You, that she loves You, and is faithful to You and Your word. We thank You Lord that through Carol, You have given us the privilege and the opportunity to continue to renew the face of the earth, to open up the rivers of righteousness and the streams of justice.

Quoting fragments of a scripture, the prayer portrayed Moseley-Braun's candidacy as a divinely decreed challenge to societal inequalities. The Old Testament scripture that Father Pfleger invoked (Amos 5:24) commands God's people to challenge social oppression ("But let judgement run down as waters, and righteousness as a mighty stream"). Pfleger's prayer then turned to the gathering's participants, asking for divinely inspired commitment to political action and prophetically envisioning Moseley-Braun's imminent victory:

All we ask, Lord, is that You continue to use us, from morning until sunset. We ask You, Lord, that You will stir up Your word within us, that we might work with an urgency and not grow faint and in remembering that even as we stand the victory is already ours.

Pfleger then asked God to provide sacred protection and feelings of strength and empowerment for the candidate:

Oh Lord, we thank You and we pray to You and we ask that You would protect our sister. Dispatch now Your angels from Heaven to watch over her in her comings and in her goings. Strengthen her on the journey, and make her ever and always dependent upon You.

The prayer ended "[f]or we are no longer ourselves, but now it is Christ who lives in us."

Next stood the newly appointed bishop of the United Methodist Church, Charles Jordan. A former regional administrator of the church, Jordan had been instrumental in organizing Black Methodist clerics for Harold Washington's 1983 mayoral race.[5] Indeed, Jordan's involvement in secular politics extended back over two decades. Brazier noted, when introducing Jordan, that he had known him for over twenty-five years "and worked with him . . . when we were in the throes of organizing The Woodlawn Organization [TWO]."

Taking on some part of the role of prophet, Jordan proclaimed that one purpose of this gathering was to "celebrate that God is about to do something new in our midst" and that the candidate was a religious sacrifice "offering herself as a part of a fulfillment of God's new day." Another reason for the event, the bishop stated, was to organize support for Moseley-Braun by "commit[ing] ourselves to the task" of mobilizing "our prayers, our time, our money, our energy, our votes—and we have to get the votes."

After Jordan's talk, some audience members lined up for a breakfast of eggs, sausage, bacon, biscuits, orange juice, sweet rolls, and coffee, while others mingled. Then the featured speaker entered the room from a side door and was introduced by the master of ceremonies as "the next senator of Illinois!" Welcomed with thunderous and sustained applause from the audience, most of whom were still standing, the candidate sat down next to the speaker's podium, and participants began to settle back into their seats. As the applause slowly dwindled, Brazier introduced elected officials and candidates who were, as he put it, making "contributions to [the] city." These included several members of the Board of Education, the local head of the NAACP, a few candidates running for public office, and the newly crowned Miss Black Illinois. Alderman Bobby Rush, an Illinois Democratic congressional nominee who had been shaking hands and conversing with ministers throughout the event, stood and waved to the audience. As the seats began to fill again and the breakfast line shortened, the musical selections began.

Sung a cappella, with collective hand clapping and foot tapping keeping the tempo upbeat, the first song, a slave spiritual, subtly repudiated otherworldliness and encouraged the political involvement of the faithful:

Well, I keep so busy working for the Master
I ain't got time to die.
Oh, I keep so busy singing for Jesus
Ain't got time to die.
Well, I keep so busy working for the kingdom
Ain't got time to die.

Phrases like "singing for Jesus," and "working for the kingdom" could perhaps be taken to refer to pie-in-the-sky desires, diversions from worldly concerns like electoral politics, distractions that might even amount to "working for the master," or serving "White" interests. But it is unlikely that anyone present experienced this song that way in this context—a political gathering to elect an African American to the U.S. Senate. The soloist sang the bridge to the tune:

Get out of the way, let me praise my Jesus.
Get out of the way, let me praise the Lord.
If I don't praise him the rocks are gonna cry out
Glory and honor, glory and honor
I ain't got time to die.

Many in the audience responded with a wave of a hand, a nod, or a shout of "Yes, that's right." Any outsider bothered by the hint of submission imagery in "Ain't Got Time to Die" would have been immediately reassured by the next number, "Ordinary People." In this performance the soloist, with piano accompaniment, sang several of the first verses in a melancholy yet earnest mood. They seemed to articulate the merits of collective action through divine guidance, especially for those who might lack material resources:

Just ordinary people, God uses ordinary people.
He chooses people, just like me and you
Who are willing to do everything that He commands.
God chooses people that will give Him their all
No matter how small it all seems to you
Because little means much when you place it in the Master's hand.

"Yes, it does," "That's all right," "Amen," the audience fervently agreed. The next verses seemed to symbolize the link between collective action and divine guidance. Referencing biblical miracles that illustrate personal sacrifice and divine intervention, the soloist continued:

Just like the little lad, who gave Jesus all he had
Oh multitudes were fed with a fish and loaf of bread
What you have may not seem much
But when you yield it to the task
The Master's loving hand appears
Then you understand how your life could never be the same.

Repeating the first stanza, the tune slowed and modulated to a higher octave. The soloist improvised verses by stretching syllables and emphasizing phrases, bringing most of the audience to its feet. Listeners swayed back and forth, shouting "Glory" and "That's right" in chorus. The boundary between performer and audience blurred, showing even more clearly the mission of the political gathering.

Rocking side-to-side with a microphone in one hand and gesturing with the other hand to emphasize particular phrases of the song, the singer trumpeted:

Just ordinary people, my God uses
Plain old ordinary people.
He uses the rich and the poor,
The Black and the White, the strong and the wounded.
I just stopped by to tell you that.
My God uses people who will give Him their all
No matter, no matter how small it may seem to you
Because little becomes much
When you place it in the Master's hand.

As the performance ended, the master of ceremonies returned to the podium, and members of the audience began to settle back into in their seats. With approving murmurs still stirring the gathering, Brazier began to chant, as if he were about to deliver a sermon, "If this were Sunday morning . . . I would be ready." Repeating a line from the previous selection—"A little becomes a lot"—Brazier continued the program with an introduction that likened Moseley-Braun's primary victory over incumbent Allen Dixon to David's victory over Goliath. As he spoke, some listeners joined him in a call and response.

Brazier: As I sat there I began to think of how so often we fail to see the hands of God.
Response: Think about it.
B: Because sometimes He moves in mysterious ways.
R: Oh, yes, yes!
B: When this candidate started out . . .
R: Yes, think about it!
B: I would expect that ninety percent of the people in this room thought it was a useless task.
R: Well.
B: She was coming up against a giant . . .
R: Yes, oh yes, a giant.
B: . . . one who had never lost an election . . .
R: Come on, Bishop.
B: . . . who was already ensconced on the throne . . .
R: Yes. Come on, Bishop!
B: . . . who was an incumbent, an incumbent rarely loses.
R: That's right.

Attempting to renegotiate the gender distinction between Moseley-Braun and David, the bishop proclaimed:

Here comes a little, almost unknown person, who, I hate to call on Jesus, but is it possible to say Davidess? If it wasn't so unbiblical I would talk about a little David who comes along and strikes a mighty giant. I can see the hand of God. . . . That was the hand of God, leading us out of the wilderness.

Then, referring to Moseley-Braun as "our keynote speaker," Brazier introduced the candidate as "our next United States senator from the state of Illinois!" The event immediately began to feel like a political rally as participants shouted and clapped in unison—"Carol! Carol! Carol!" Her wide-striped blue and white dress strikingly coordinated with the red, white, and blue lettering on the poster above the podium, Moseley-Braun took the floor.

She thanked the organizing committee for putting the event together. Recognizing—and perhaps exaggerating—the political resources of the ministers, Braun claimed that "this room right now easily represents . . . five million people." On a rush of applause from the audience, she added that reaching out to churches had helped her win the Democratic primary; she thanked Brazier and other ministers for letting her "come to their pulpit" to "talk to [their] congregations about my platform and my programs for Illinois and why I was running . . . for the United States Senate." Moseley-Braun quickly reminded the ministers that her campaign still needed their support, asking them to contact for her everyone else "that I was not able to contact [or] did not contact [or] did not have a chance to interface with in the primary." She told them, "I am so grateful to you because really the race is not over 'til it's over. It's not over until November and I am going to need all your help."

Moseley-Braun then began what appeared to be a modified campaign speech. "You know, Rev. Brazier," she exclaimed, "when [you] talked about David, really the fact of the matter is, [you] really struck a responsive chord in me." Weaving the biblical story of David and Goliath into a narrative that justified her race for the Senate, she declared: "We really did just start out with an idea and concept of doing that which was right. Doing the right thing, that's all that we were trying to do." She contended that her campaign was for "stand[ing] up for the principles about the appropriate role of government, and how government should serve all people, and what should be done."

Commenting on the program's musical selections, Braun began to testify about how her religious beliefs had sustained her physically and emotionally during the campaign. Noting that "this campaign trail has been a rough one," and that with the long hours campaigning "every now and then I get weak in the knees," Moseley-Braun began to describe how her religious beliefs had supported her through the hard work of the primary:

> We walked into a church in Urbana-Champaign last week and as I walked in the church, the scripture on the church program—now I don't have it with me and I don't know my Bible well enough to know where this book comes from, but it had to do with—we shall win the race if we don't faint.

The scripture that Moseley-Braun wanted to recall, from Galatians 6:9, speaks of the perseverance of those who seek to do good. It reads: "And let us not be weary in well doing; for in due season we shall reap, if we faint not." As the audience exploded with laughter and shouts of amen, Moseley-Braun continued her testimony:

> Now I don't know where that comes from, . . . but I'm sure that some-body will let us know, because I would like to find that again. But it had lifted me up. For that whole day of activities in Urbana-Champaign, and that quote, walking into that church that morning, lifted me up and held me up for the rest of the service. And I have to tell you, all during the dark days of that primary it was that faith that lifted me up and carried me through even when my own strength was failing me. When my own strength was failing me, I was able to keep going.

Attributing her physical health to this faith, Moseley-Braun continued to recognize divine intervention in her primary victory:

> I didn't even get a cold once this year and I've had chronic bronchitis ever since I was sixteen. I did not get a cold once. Because it was my faith that carried me through it. Yes, that carried me through it.

Moseley-Braun went on to talk about the goals of her candidacy. Throughout her thirty-minute speech, she kept returning to the theme of ordinary people, from the musical selections played earlier: "I can't get over the notion that an ordinary person went out there to do the right thing." Moseley-Braun described the Senate as a closed institution "without the voices of working people, ordinary people," saying she entered the senatorial contest to get democracy to "serve ordinary people." She charged that the Bush administration didn't understand the economy because "they don't hear ordinary people" who "built this country to begin with," and governed only for "the one percent at the top that got richer in the last ten years."

Toward the end of her talk, Moseley-Braun began to focus on the organizational resources of churches. She first asked ministers in the audience to help "get the word out" about her campaign. Then, recognizing the participants' networking capacity, their ability to bring campaign and voter information to potential voters, Moseley-Braun made this request:

> I need your help; there are 102 counties in this state. I have to try to be in as many of them as I can. I will not always be able therefore to be here in Chicago physically or even in Cook County and so I thought . . . about how to do this. The church is the single most important institution we have and so if you are willing to help me spread the word in your respective denominations, to spread the word through your own congregations, to help spread out and spread the word and make introductions for me even in southern and central Illinois [and] throughout the state, that will give me the ability to have the kind of statewide network, so that Illinois will be able to send a signal . . . that will be unmistakable.

With that, Moseley-Braun returned to her seat while the audience applauded enthusiastically. Brazier then introduced ministers who would talk about how everyone present could get involved in Moseley-Braun's campaign.

Reverend Elmer Fowler of the Third Baptist Church, who had recently served as president of the Chicago chapter of the NAACP, spoke first about the electoral challenge that lay ahead. Referring to the rift among both religious and secular Black leadership over who would become Harold Washington's successor as mayor of the city, Fowler remarked that "we have a second chance in Chicago," adding, with an edge of ridicule to the mostly male audience: "If the Lord don't use men, He will use women!" Many in the audience laughed and amened; others nodded in agreement. Fowler recalled famous African American women leaders of the past: Harriet Tubman, Sojourner Truth ("who never apologized for being a woman"), Mary Macleod Bethune, Madame C. J. Walker, and "that school teacher from Memphis, Tennessee, who wrote, 'There is something within me that holdeth the reins, there is something within me that I cannot explain.' These are the women who have come [before us]."

Urging members of the audience to "talk to every Black person you see and get them registered to vote," Fowler also asked them to make a financial contribution to Moseley-Braun's campaign, declaring that "you got to have money to get into the game," so "give some money for the cause." He then went on to caution them not to give out of self-interest, asserting that "you ain't supposed to get nothing for yourself." Instead, "you're supposed to get something for the folks and in turn they will give something to you."

After he announced an upcoming political rally at his church, Fowler's voice turned angry as he contested the religious claims of political conservatives:

> . . . these Republicans. They think that being a conservative is a blessing, a gift from God to this earth. But ain't nothing to no Republican conservative; to conserve, you got to have something to conserve. I'm so sick and tired of Bush. . . . Yes, I am a liberal and I hate Republican conservative voters as well, as much as they hate them liberal Democrats. . . .

Fowler's spirited talk ended with these partisan remarks, which provoked an eruption of laughter and applause from his listeners. Brazier then introduced the next speaker, the Reverend Shelvin Hall, who had served as president of a West Side ministerial group and during the midsixties had been active in Martin Luther King's Chicago Freedom Movement. Before Hall reached the podium, Brazier informed the audience that he had to leave for a previous engagement, but was contributing a thousand dollars to Moseley-Braun's campaign.

Asking all the ministers from his own Baptist organization, the Illinois Baptist Association—some thirty—to stand before the audience, Hall noted that his denominational group had Moseley-Braun as a guest speaker at one of its statewide meetings in East Saint Louis. He informed the audience that his was the "largest [organization of] structured Baptist churches in the state," suggesting that he represented a significant communication network. He noted that Moseley-Braun's appearance at his group's statewide convention would help her win in November, because ministers from key cities would be in attendance. He ended his remarks by announcing that he too would pledge a thousand dollars to Moseley-Braun's campaign.

At that point Reverend Leon Finney, a political operative for the Moseley-Braun campaign, took over as master of ceremonies and introduced the next and last speaker, Reverend Willie Barrow. A minister of the Church of God and a former president of Operation PUSH, Barrow, known as the "little warrior" for her short stature and tenacity on civil rights issues, had been involved for decades in both electoral and protest politics in Chicago. She approached the podium, which nearly hid her from view, to start raising funds for Moseley-Braun's campaign.

Quoting a phrase from the gospel of Matthew that seemed to legitimize Moseley-Braun's underdog victory in the primary, "the last shall be first, and the first shall be last," Barrow explained that the candidate was last in political organization, campaign advertising, endorsements, and funds but was the first woman during the election year to break "the glass ceiling," allowing other women to win nominations to the Senate.

Proclaiming that twenty-five thousand dollars would be raised from breakfast participants, she then asked the audience to bow their heads in prayer for the candidate. Acknowledging the racial and gender importance of Moseley-Braun's candidacy, Barrow began to pray for perseverance:

> *Eternal God our Father, we pause because we know that the strength of God endures forever. This is a woman of God. You have placed her in this position not for herself, but for all of Your people, Black, White, Brown, rich, poor. Here's a woman that's not taking it. She lives on our side, don't live in the suburbs. She lives right here on the South Side with a Black child. . . . Preserve her strength.*

With these blessings, Barrow began to target those present for thousand-dollar contributions. Disclosing the names of the ministers who had already given that amount, Barrow thundered: "I know that we've got about ten people here who could give a thousand dollars," asking the hushed audience, "How many of you will join the thousand-dollar crowd?" Barrow then asked those willing to raise their hands. In Barrow's first ten minutes of soliciting, a dozen or so individuals gave or pledged a thousand dollars each.

Adopting a fund-raising technique used at many Black churches, Barrow began to lower dollar amounts in increments to encourage more people to give. Many of the several hundred participants of the breakfast came forward to put their contribution into a round wicker basket, as if it were collection time at a regular Sunday morning worship service. This ritual went on for about twenty minutes, as the candidate left for another campaign stop and the participants slowly drifted from Carter Temple's basement.

This ministerial breakfast easily revealed how a church could furnish political actors with organizational and institutional resources: the indigenous leadership, the communication networks, the easy availability of mass membership, and the social interaction of political actors at the breakfast. Anyone looking through the door could see key campaign actors socializing with ministers of various denominations, broadening the capacity of networks, disseminating information about their campaigns to various churches and denominational groups, and facilitating the involvement of ministers and congregants in the political process. As a political entrepreneur in search of electoral support, Moseley-Braun got "hard" resources—from a place to hold the ministerial breakfast to financial support.

The leadership breakfast also confirmed what past scholars of social movements have demonstrated: that preexisting networks are a key part of the mobilization process. Not only in civil rights protest in many southern communities (Morris 1984), but also in the post–civil rights era, clerical networks continue to function as a source of Black mobilization. At the breakfast, these formal clerical networks assisted Moseley-Braun's efforts on at least two levels. At the religious level, participants were linked through groups like the West Side Ministers Alliance and denominational organizations like the statewide Illinois Baptist Association, the African-American Religious Connection, the United Methodist Church, and the governing districts of the African Methodist Episcopal Church (AME). On the political level, networks also brought together ministers who had been previously involved in Chicago politics. Many had been involved in labor and civil rights mobilization efforts for decades— ranging from The Woodlawn Organization (a Saul Alinsky group) and Martin Luther King's crusade against slum housing during the sixties, to electoral campaigns in the eighties, such as Harold Washington's bids for mayor, to demonstrations against stores and companies that sold and manufactured drug paraphernalia in minority communities in the nineties. Still other ministers at the breakfast were active in civil rights organizations like the NAACP and PUSH.

The social ties of ministers at the breakfast reflected the socioeconomic diversity within Chicago's African American communities, a critical feature for successful collective action in any Black community. Clerics at the breakfast represented religious institutions that included large working- and middle-class congregations like Brazier's Apostolic Church of God, as well as small storefront churches with less affluent congregants like Lucius Hall's First Church of Love and Faith, a spiritualist sect.

As micromobilization scholars argue, social networks facilitate collective action not only through institutional alliances like these but also by engaging individual participants who are socially embedded within their groups and communities. In addition to the leadership, the church networks at the breakfast may have, in Moseley-Braun's words, "easily" represented "five million people." Asking the audience to "spread the word in your respective denominations . . . in your own congregations . . . and make introductions for me . . . throughout the state," Braun understood that the churches would give her "the ability to have the kind of statewide [communication] network [needed to win]" the election. As part of her outreach to individuals, Operation Vote asked ministers at the breakfast to designate a Sunday for voter registration at their church, put voter registration material in Sunday bulletins, set up voter registration booths during morning worship services, and recruit church members as volunteer registrars.

The event also allowed the church participants as well as leaders to become part of the political process. It gave some the opportunity to make political speeches, contribute money to a candidate, and work for a political campaign. Equally important, but less obvious, were the simple acts of collecting money, preparing food, setting up chairs and tables, performing a song, or leading a prayer. These activities are normally not thought of as political actions but rather routine activities of church life. Nevertheless, they contributed not only to the overall success of Braun's campaign but also to the political engagement, education, and empowerment of the participants.

As several analysts of Black religious institutions have pointed out, these smaller tasks, which help sustain religious institutions throughout Black communities, are overwhelmingly performed by women, although men hold the bulk of powerful leadership positions within these institutions. This gender inequality persists despite the fact that women outnumber men considerably in regular church attendance and membership. The same religious institutions that give Black women the opportunity to develop civic and organizing skills also reinforce the ideals and practices of male authority.

Religious Symbolism and Black Consciousness

Most of the material institutional and individual capacities that the church could mobilize were revealed in their general outlines at that church breakfast for Carol Moseley-Braun in August 1992. These material resources are critical for helping the Black population redress the power imbalances caused by the legacy of racism and their generally lower-than-average social and economic status.[6] In addition, Moseley-Braun's candidacy tapped the spiritual and cultural resources of the Black church that have sustained Black resistance and organization since the time of slavery.

During the leadership breakfast, one central theme, drawn from a history of Black religious culture, was the divinely endowed strength that allowed an ordinary person to overcome obstacles to making a difference in the political world. Prayers asked for personal fortitude for the candidate herself ("strengthen her on the journey"; "we know that the strength of God endures forever"). And Moseley-Braun herself bore witness to how her religious beliefs sustained her commitment to the campaign during moments of uncertainty ("during the dark days of that primary it was that faith that lifted me up and carried me through even when my own strength was failing me").

A second prominent theme drew from Jesus' exaltation of the weak over the strong, supplemented by key Old Testament stories, such as that of David and Goliath. At the breakfast, musical lyrics stressed this power of the weak when strengthened by God ("God uses plain old ordinary people"), the importance of coalitions to electoral success ("God uses the rich, poor, Black, White, the strong and the wounded"), and the virtue of cooperative efforts given limited material resources ("a little becomes much when you place it in the Master's hand").

The Moseley-Braun candidacy created an opportunity for the theme of weak/strong reversal to be applied to gender. Later that year, on the Sunday before the election, at Carol Moseley-Braun's own church, the Vernon Park Church of God, a female clerical assistant spoke on the subject.[7] After the choir had sung "We Are All More than Conquerors through Jesus Christ," she thanked the Lord for allowing the congregation

> to see the scriptures unfold before our eyes. When we read in Jeremiah the 31st chapter [31:22] that this new thing was going to be created in the earth. A woman—glory to God—would compass a man, not surpass, but go around and about in Your kingdom-building work and be effective.

The minister continued to pray on Moseley-Braun's behalf, characterizing her as the biblical heroine Esther:

> *We thank you for the wonderful opportunity that we have of presenting Carol to you, Jesus. We thank You, Lord God, we lift her up, she our modern-day Esther, standing in the gap for us. We bless her right now in the name of Jesus. We connect with every other prayer of faith that has already been prayed in her behalf and we believe that You are going to deliver us on Tuesday. We claim the victory.*

In the Old Testament book of Esther, Esther had used her influence on the royal court to save her people from extermination (Esther 7:1–10).

Black politics and political movements have often drawn on this Judaic and Christian theme of weak/strong reversal. Marcus Garvey's post–World War I Black nationalist movement, for example, considered Blacks scattered throughout the African diaspora to be the Lord's chosen people (Burkett 1978). Indeed, the Garvey movement reconstructed Scripture into a catechism for members (Burkett 1978, 34):

Q. What prediction made in the 68th Psalm and the 31st verse is now being filled?

A. Princes shall come out of Egypt, Ethiopia shall soon stretch forth her hands unto God.

Q. What does this verse prove?

A. That Negroes will set up their own government in Africa, with rulers of their own race.

Today, the theme of weak-made-strong is easily appropriated by Black politicians. In 1992, while preparing to run for governor, Illinois attorney general Roland Burris attributed his election to public office to God's support:

> I'm in there every day working with the people because that's what the Lord has directed me. Can you all imagine a young, Black kid in Centralia, Illinois, at the age of sixteen saying he wanted to do two things? One, to be a lawyer and the other, to be a statewide elected official. Reflect on this, my Christian friends. There weren't that many Black lawyers in 1953, let alone any Black politicians in 1953. That wasn't me, that was the Lord! As the thirty-ninth attorney general of the sixth-largest state in America, that's the Lord's work.[8]

Drawing on both the New Testament and the Old Testament, these evocations stress the need, from positions of both individual and collective material weakness, to rely on God's help in the ongoing imbalance of power. They also stress the need for collective action and community vision as against individualist apathy and the other individual incentives that might lead voters to stay home and indulge themselves rather than contributing money to a candidate and getting out to vote on election day.

Take the 1991 primary rally for mayoral candidate Danny Davis.[9] At a church on Chicago's South Side, with the church pulpit and choir stand packed with political activists and elected officials, the Reverend Cornelius Haynes, the pastor of the church, began by proclaiming that "if we put our hearts and our resources together, success will be ours." Another minister offered a prayer, saying, "As our Bible [Proverbs 29:18] says, 'Where there is no vision, the people perish.' . . . But Lord, we thank You for Your amazing grace, and for Your power."

Invoking biblical figures known for their personal strength and divinely granted wisdom, the minister then asked the Lord for strength and wisdom on behalf of the candidate as well as those attending the rally:

> Father God, we ask that Thou will anoint for us
> The head of our brother Danny K. Davis,
> That Thou will give him the wisdom

Of a Solomon and the strength of Samson, Lord.
And Father God, bless all of Your people
Who are here, for we must choose
Between chaos or community.
Our Lord, our Savior, our Redeemer
Bless us, keep us, strengthen us,
Guide us. Amen.

The unifying songs, "Everybody Say Amen" (transformed into "Everybody Say Danny"), "Lift Every Voice and Sing," and the slave spiritual "Oh Mary Don't You Weep," symbolized the strength of the weak by combining the Old Testament account of the Exodus and the New Testament account of God's comforting Mary and her sister Martha after the Crucifixion:

Oh Mary don't you weep, tell Martha not to moan.
Oh Mary don't you weep, tell Martha not to moan.
Pharaoh's army drowned in the Red Sea;
Oh Mary don't you weep, tell Martha not to moan.
If I could, I surely would
Stand on the rock where Moses stood.
Pharaoh's army drowned in the Red Sea;
Oh Mary don't you weep, tell Martha not to moan.

Although the comparison was not explicitly articulated, the challenger Danny Davis could easily be personified as Moses, incumbent Richard Daley and supporters as Pharaoh and his army. Mary and Martha, like southern Blacks in slavery and, arguably, Black voters as a 12 percent minority in an 80 percent White-Anglo world, were in a position of relative powerlessness, as were the Jews in their exodus out of Egypt.

Similarly, when Chicago alderwoman Dorothy Tilman introduced Davis at a church visit months later, she drew on this imagery:

There is a quiet storm going on in our community. There's a storm that folks who don't understand God don't understand. . . . *We don't have no money, but neither did Jesus, he was born in a manger.* We don't have money for colorful television commercials or colorful radio commercials, but we have God and we have Jesus [emphasis mine].[10]

In all these cases, this spiritual and the larger ritual reminded participants that God's help allowed the objectively weaker to prevail.

A final example derives from an entirely sacred setting, in which Bishop Paul Morton, a politically active minister in New Orleans who pastors a charismatic congregation called the Greater Saint Stephen Full Gospel Baptist Church, mobilized opposition to the candidacy for governor of Louisiana of David Duke, a White supremacist.[11] Using phrases from Matthew 20:16 that, according to Morton, have a special reference for African Americans,[12] the bishop declared:

> I'm here to tell you that God has not sent David Duke to put African Americans in their place. The reason why I know this is not true [is] because God has already put us in our place. Now some of you don't know what God has told me in the last days. And He told me what would happen, and He told me what my place would be in the last day. What is my place? What is your place? Listen to what the Bible says: "The last shall be first and the first shall be last." Now I didn't make that up. That's what God said in the last days. And He's trying to tell White brothers and White sisters, Wake up! You've been first a long time. We've been in slavery, we didn't have education, we were saying "yes ma'am" and "no sir," but God is saying it's time to take our place.

As the Hebrew seder reminds the Jews of past oppression, so too Morton adapted to this important election God's promise of power reversal. The Lord having brought Black Americans from slavery, it is now up to them to support God and not to go back. Nearing the end of his sermon, Morton justified Blacks' active opposition to Duke's candidacy by quoting Joshua 17:17–18, an Old Testament scripture that details the post-Exodus promises of the territory awaiting the Israelites when they reach the promised land:

> *And Joshua spake unto the house of Joseph, even to Ephraim and to Manasseh, saying, Thou art a great people, and hast great power: thou shalt not have one lot only. But the mountain shall be thine; for it is a wood, and thou shalt cut it down: and the outgoings of it shall be thine: for thou shalt drive out the Canaanites, though they have iron chariots, and though they be strong.*

Proclaiming, "This is what God is saying to African Americans," Morton reinterpreted the verse "Thou art a great people, and hast great power" as a call to direct action. His reinterpretation simultaneously promoted group efficacy and racial consciousness, both psychological resources for Black mobilization. Morton added:

> Black man, Black woman, Black child, you are great in God's sight. Thou art a great people and hast great power. We got to learn more and more to begin to help one another because our world is waxing colder and colder and colder.

Again:

> Look what it says: 'Though they have armed chariots and though they
> be strong.' I'm not going to tell you that when you look at the polls and it
> says it's mighty close, so it means that they're strong and all the [Black]
> registered voters in the state of Louisiana is 28 percent. I mean they
> look strong, but I got some news for you. You see, everybody out there
> don't hate, thank God. There are some White brothers and sisters who
> love God's plan, who are listening to God's voice today and what God
> will do is He'll take our 28 percent and He's got some White brothers
> and sisters who are saying, "No Duke, because you are not going to
> destroy what God has sent to Louisiana." And God will touch White
> brothers and White sisters in the body of Christ, and there's enough
> White Christians out there, help me Holy Ghost, because if you say you
> love Jesus you better hear what God is saying to you today.

God's spirit, working in the souls of others, will redress what looks on
the surface like an unequal balance.

People are inherently "symbolizing, conceptualizing, meaning-
seeking animal[s]" (Geertz 1973a, 140). Their rituals, their symbols, and
their deepest religious beliefs can all act as culturally based resources
for mobilization. People construct frames of action through, among other
things, the religious meanings of their lives. The sacred symbols do not
work in isolation from secular ones; often they complement one another,
working together to strengthen frames of action.

The use of religious rituals and symbols for Black political mobilization had its most powerful recent evocation in the modern civil
rights movement, as several scholars have explored in detail (Morris
1984; Branch 1988; Raines 1977). Former civil rights activist Andrew
Young aptly summarizes the process in his comments on organizing in
the Mississippi Delta (Hamilton 1972, 132–33):

> Nobody could have ever argued segregation and integration and gotten
> people convinced to do anything about that. But when Martin [Luther
> King] would talk about leaving the slavery of Egypt and wandering
> into a promised land, somehow that made sense to folks. And they
> may not have understood it; it was nobody else's political theory, but
> it was their grass roots ideology. It was their faith; it was the thing
> they had been nurtured on. And when they heard that language, they
> responded. You could go into Mississippi and tell people they needed
> to get themselves together and get organized. And that didn't make
> much sense. But if you started preaching to them about dry bones
> rising again, everybody had sung about dry bones. Everybody knew
> the language.

Young reported that the organizers in the South had the job of helping people see "in their faith also a liberation struggle that they could identify with." From an organizer's perspective,

> They all wanted to be religious. And when you finally helped them to see that religion meant involvement in action, you kinda had 'em hooked then. You had a ready framework around which you could organize people. You had people in churches. And usually in the smallest country town, you had people in those churches. And that was what, I guess, gave us kind of [a] key to the first organizing phases.

The mixture of religion and the existing oppositional culture in the South produced the heady mixture that made the civil rights movement possible. Inspired by the civil rights movement, later movements have adopted important elements, such as the anthem "We Shall Overcome," with little recognition of the vitality of its religious meaning in the originating movement.

The influence of religious culture on Black mobilization had a significant history before the modern civil rights movement. Eric Foner's analysis of Black mobilization during Reconstruction notes that throughout this period "religious convictions profoundly affected the way blacks understood the momentous events around them," as they expressed in religious language their "aspirations for justice and autonomy" (1988, 93). Then as now, Black political entrepreneurs were keenly aware of the political importance of religious culture; they drew, often from sacred texts, on shared symbols and rituals that made meaning out of actors' immediate situations. For these political actors, "the Bible—the one book with which they could assume familiarity among their largely illiterate constituents—served as a point of reference for understanding public events" (Foner 1988, 94). Blacks during Reconstruction constructed a worldview that resisted White supremacy, drawing on Christianity as a major source of political meaning and thus creating an oppositional space that challenged their domination within the framework of a religion that ostensibly legitimized Black servitude and subordination.

As we have seen, Marcus Garvey also built grassroots support for his movement by basing the beliefs and rituals of the UNIA "on the solid foundation of the religious faith of black folk," which reflected their "shared experience of oppression" (Burkett 1978, 8).

The use of religious culture for Black activism also played a significant part in Black radical organizing during the Depression era. Robin Kelley's history of Alabama Communists details how Christianity supported a "rich source of oppositional culture" for Black party organizers by providing them with a ready framework for conveying meaning. Although Black church leaders mostly opposed both unionization and Communist Party activity, the Black organizers of the Alabama Communist Party came to rely on the "prophetic tradition of Christianity" to give meaning to class struggle. Against the early expectations of some of the organizers, participants in this struggle appeared to learn more about class exploitation and domination from Christianity than from Marxist ideology. Christianity, Kelley concluded, was a "major factor in drawing blacks into the Communist Party and its mass organizations." For these activists, "grassroots understanding of exploitation was based on scripture" (Kelley 1990, 107). Sacred songs were transformed into political anthems as they were during the Garvey movement and the modern civil rights movement; both opposition and allies were symbolized by biblical figures. Thus was forged a Christian-influenced oppositional culture for radical mobilization during the 1930s.

During the Great Migration of southern Blacks in the interwar period, and also after World War II, religious culture supported Black electoral mobilization. Incorporated into the urban machines of northern cities, this mobilization relied on the institutional resources of the Black church and on its cherished ritual and symbols. Harold Gosnell's analysis of Black politics in Chicago in the 1930s details how religious culture served to motivate voters. He reported that "[b]iblical and religious references are common even in the mouths of speakers who are known to be non–church members," and ministers were "frequently part of the program of meetings" and were "expected to introduce some of the atmosphere of a revival" ([1935] 1967, 184).

Theologian James Cone, writing about the meanings of spirituals to African slaves reminds us that "[r]eligion is not a set of beliefs that people memorize and neither is it an ethical code of do's and don'ts that they learn from others. Rather religion is wrought out of the experience of people who encounter the divine in the midst of historical realities" (1972, 29). Cone's interpretation of African American Christianity provides a framework in which to explore how and why sacred symbols and rituals are (or can become) politicized, action-oriented vehicles of meaning that help actors interpret their political goals and construct strategies for action.

African American religious worldviews—perspectives carved from Blacks' acceptance of Christianity and their historical experience with racial and economic domination—have provided, and continue to provide, actors in Black communities with an oppositional culture through which to articulate grievances, opportunities, and collective identities during episodes of protest and electoral activism.

Religion, Domination, and Black Oppositional Culture

Scholars have long viewed the cultures of dominated groups as forces undermining their political engagement. The often fervently emotional religious practices of African Americans have historically been disparaged by many intellectuals, who have seen them as a way for Blacks to vent their earthly frustrations yet still submit to a divine authority.

This perspective underestimates the ways that the cultural practices of subordinated groups promote resistance to domination—often subtly, and at times overtly. Cultural practices that have traditionally been viewed as instruments of acquiescence may actually serve as disguised forms of resistance (Scott 1990). Stressing the role of religious culture in understanding African American political thought and action, Cornel West points out that "any political consciousness of an oppressed group is shaped and molded by the group's cultural resources and resiliency as perceived by individuals in it." He notes further that "the extent to which resources and resiliency are romanticized, rejected, or accepted will deeply influence the kind of political consciousness that individuals possess" (West 1982, 71). Sidney Peck also reminds us that the culture of oppressed groups should not be understood simply as the result of racial or class domination and urges cultural analysts to "look beyond obvious appearances to more subtle, liberating tendencies residing beneath the surface" (Peck 1982, 161).

The construction of meaning for political goals occurs in the context of specific collective action frames, or "purposely constructed guides to action" (Tarrow 1992, 177). Collective action frames "organize experience and guide action" and are a "necessary condition for movement participation, whatever its nature or intensity" (Snow et al. 1986, 469). As Sidney Tarrow points out, action frames operate within the culture of politicized groups, providing "leaders with a reservoir of symbols with which to construct a cognitive frame for collective action" (1992, 177).

Responding to value-centered approaches that link culture to action, sociologist Ann Swidler implicitly argues that the construction of action frames through culture is critical to mobilization. More than a mechanism that inculcates participatory values to actors, culture acts instead as a "tool kit" for constructing "strategies of action" that are indigenous to a group's culture. As Swidler explains, "people do not build lines of action from scratch." Instead they "construct chains of action beginning with at least some pre-fabricated links," where "culture influences action through the shape and the organization of those links, not by determining the ends to which they are put" (1986, 277).

By such linking or framing of action through culture, goals are readily communicated to targeted groups, according legitimacy and certainty to action, and in turn, mobilizing. Conferring legitimacy to political action is crucial because, as Murray Edelman argues, actors are able through symbols to construct diverse meanings for political events that "shape support for causes and legitimize value allocations" to actors (1985, 195). Movements that lack an existing, easily grasped, and mutually important cultural framework through which to communicate meaning will find group-based mobilization a far greater challenge.

Sacred symbols, like secular ones, may be used to clarify and legitimize political goals. Culture traffics in symbols that give meaning to reality and experience. Culture is performed through ritual, a means of inventing and sustaining symbols. For those with whom sacred symbols resonate, such symbols may be more persuasive vehicles for political meaning than their secular equivalents. Sacred symbols have, as Clifford Geertz points out, a "peculiar power" that comes from "their presumed ability to identity fact with value at the most fundamental level, to give what is otherwise merely actual, a comprehensive normative import" (1973a, 127).

Culture further enhances the political resources of dominated groups by shaping political reality and being shaped by it (Geertz 1973b, 93). Thus, when opportunities for activism arise, people can, by actively resisting domination and adapting the symbols available to them, draw on cultural perspectives and practices that are lodged in the oppositional tendencies of their own cultural group.

Many of the cultural resources through which Blacks shape oppositional worldviews evolve from their religions (Thurman 1981; Genovese 1974; Raboteau 1978; Cone 1969, 1972, [1970] 1986; Levine 1977). The use of religious language and icons in the political discourse of the Reverend Jesse Jackson, the former Democratic presidential candidate, served as a valuable cultural resource for the mobilization of Black voters during his 1984 and 1988 candidacies (Henry 1990; Barker 1988; Washington 1986; Wills 1990). Similarly, as we have seen, Martin Luther King Jr. and other civil rights movement activists used religious language and art to articulate views and motivate participants (Branch 1988; Raines 1977; Walker 1979; Washington 1986).

As Cheryl Townsend Gilkes observes, indigenously expressed forms of African American Christianity like sermons and testimony "speak directly to the structures of oppression which cause black suffering" (1980, 36). This collective perspective on racial domination appears in other cultural forms of the African American religious experience as well, particularly in music. Wyatt T. Walker theorizes that African American religious music operates in at least two ways. It creates an oppositional space for political reflection by "locat[ing] the people's strength of heritage, their roots, where they are and where they want to go." It also "mobilizes and strengthens the resolve for struggle," functioning as an agent of oppositional consciousness by serving as a "primary reservoir of . . . Black people's historical context," and performing as an "important factor in the process of social change" (1979, 181).

Scholarship on Black electoral mobilization has, however, largely neglected the effects of culture on mobilization. With a few notable exceptions regarding political behavior in general (Edelman 1985; Kertzer 1988; Laitin 1988) and African American political behavior in particular (Henry 1990), most scholarly work on culture and political action supports the "civic culture" perspective, viewing culture as a mediating factor indirectly promoting participation by facilitating democratic values that support the existing social order (Almond and Verba 1963).

The Black political experience in the United States, however, reveals that opposition and democratic values can go hand in hand, creating an oppositional civic culture.[13] The same symbols and rituals that strengthen oppositional mobilization can also strengthen the capacity for participation in mainstream politics. Carol Moseley-Braun's campaign breakfast in 1992 is only one instance of the way religious symbols, imagery, and meaning, which in the past have sustained oppositional movements from Nat Turner's rebellion through the civil rights movement, can also work to sustain the practice of more everyday democratic politics for those whose objective material situation makes them individually less powerful than the average citizen and collectively a distinct minority. The phrase "oppositional civic culture" is not a paradox, but expresses the dual role of religion for African Americans, in both undergirding opposition to oppression and at the same time rooting its practitioners more deeply in the civic practices of democracy.

The way religious symbols and ritual undergird an oppositional civic culture for large numbers of African Americans also helps illustrate the difference between an oppositional culture and an oppositional consciousness. An oppositional culture is the attribute of a group. It is usually broad and has many sometimes incompatible strands. An oppositional consciousness is the attribute of both individuals and groups. It focuses on injustice and domination. Presumably not all of the African American citizens gathered at the Moseley-Braun breakfast had a full-fledged oppositional consciousness as we describe it in this volume. Many had undoubtedly taken the minimal steps of identifying with other African Americans, recognizing the injustice in White rule, opposing White supremacy, and seeing a common interest with other African Americans in ending that injustice. Some of the supporters at the breakfast—for example, the Reverends Shelvin Hall, Addie Wyatt, and Albert Sampson—had been activists in the movement for a long time. Indeed these three had been allies of Dr. Martin Luther King in the 1966 Chicago Freedom Movement (see Waite, chap. 7, this volume). Each had developed a strong and mature oppositional consciousness. Yet on that particular morning those leaders did not draw from the Bible to stress the themes of injustice, oppression, or systemic exploitation. The religious themes stressed at the breakfast—the strength sent from God that allows ordinary people to make a difference in the world, and the exaltation of the weak over the strong—undoubtedly built upon the perception of injustice, but did not highlight it. The oppositional culture was there, providing the soil and fertilizer for oppositional consciousness. The explicit call to collective action was there. An enhanced sense of efficacy was central to the event. But the specific theme of injustice—and particularly the form of systemic, group-based injustice that we call oppression and whose recognition is a key component of an oppositional consciousness—was implicit rather than central. The event was designed primarily to draw upon an oppositional civic culture for a collective good. That collective good was related to injustice, because the election of Moseley-Braun to the Senate had the potential to help remedy injustices to the African American community. The event was not, however, designed specifically to forge among the participants a more mature oppositional consciousness. That task would have encouraged drawing out additional themes from the oppositional culture.

This mainstream political moment opens up, under scrutiny, to reveal political and religious actors creatively inflecting for a different time and place oppositional themes from Hebrew stories and early Christian experiences. The religious themes that had given strength to the sharecroppers organizing in the 1930s now gave inspiration again to those who without the oppositional civic consciousness so created might not have given their money or worked to register their neighbors to vote. Their work then helped bring to office the first Black woman elected to the U.S. Senate.

Notes

The observations in this chapter are from my own ethnographic accounts and tape record-ing of a ministerial breakfast for Carol Moseley-Braun on August 1, 1992. The campaign breakfast was also attended by other elected and appointed officials as well as by reporters from local newspapers. I would like to thank Father Martini Shaw for inviting me to the event. Portions of this chapter appeared in *Something Within: Religion in African-American Political Activism* (New York: Oxford University Press, 1999), copyright © 1999 by Oxford University Press, Inc. Used by permission of Oxford University Press, Inc.

1. When Carol Moseley Braun was a candidate in 1992 her surname was "Braun," but shortly after she was elected her name became "Moseley-Braun."

2. See Addie Wyatt, "The Role of Women in the Harold Washington Story" in Young 1988, 95–103.

3. This may have been the first time since the death of Chicago's first Black mayor that diverse factions of clerics had supported the same candidate. During the primary, thirty-six ministers had endorsed one of Braun's opponents, Al Hofeld. When asked by reporters why the group was not supporting Moseley-Braun, the only Black candidate, Reverend O'Dell White of the Spirit of Love Missionary Baptist Church responded that "it is a simple percentage ratio . . . she cannot win." Lynn Sweet and Mark Brown, "Black Clerics Back Hofeld; Steinem Stumps for Braun," *Chicago Sun-Times,* March 11, 1992, 4.

White had also favored a White candidate over popular Black candidate Harold Wash-ington during the 1983 Chicago mayoral election. When explaining why he preferred Richard Daley over Washington at an endorsement session for Daley attended by over 150 Black ministers, White responded that the election of Black mayors in other cities caused economic devastation to those cities, maintaining that "[w]e know what happened in Cleveland, Gary and Detroit. When Mayor Richard Hatcher was elected, the White officials took all the money to Merrillville, Indiana. Gary is now a ghost town." He insisted that Daley would "pull together businesses to generate jobs."

One of White's colleagues at the ministerial endorsement session, Reverend E. J. Jones, echoed these sentiments, saying that the election of a Black mayor in Chicago would be futile. Speaking on behalf of the group, Jones claimed: "It is our spiritual insight and my better judgement—and I am not an Uncle Tom, but I believe the homework should be done [on Washington's potential election as mayor]. I guess we got too excited with the extra few thousand voter registration." See Mitchell Locin and Jane Fritsch, "Black Clergy for Washington Hit Pro-Daley Colleagues," *Chicago Tribune,* January 13, 1983, 4.

A paid political advertisement in the *Chicago Sun-Times* made public the political divisions among Black clerics over whether to endorse Richard Daley or incumbent Jane Byrne. Referring to other politically active ministers as the "splinter group which backs the 'Daley regime' who opposed Dr. [Martin Luther] King" and the "other splinter group which rolls over and plays dead in the face of insult after insult to the Black community from the 'Byrne regime,' " Harold Washington's clerical supporters proclaimed that—unlike the other two groups of ministers—they were "not looking for 'political favors' or plums from the patronage orchard." See "The Black Church Supports Harold Washington for Mayor!!!," *Chicago Sun-Times,* February 12, 1983, 10.

For insights into the political behavior of Black ministers in the post-Washington era of Chicago politics, see Barnaby Dinges, "Mayor Daley Courting Black Ministers," *Chicago Reporter,* December 1989, 1, 6–7, 11; Ray Hanania, "12 Ministers to Boycott King Affair," *Chicago Sun-Times,* January 10, 1990, 4; Chinta Strausberg, "Ministers Split on Mayoral Support," *Chicago Defender,* January 30, 1991, 3.

4. See McClory 1989, 1.

5. Jordan stated that his role in the campaign was merely that of facilitator, insisting that Black ministers of the United Methodist Church in Chicago "were sensing the need for my support," noting that "my pastors were on the front line. They were the ones that were knocking on the doors and doing the precinct work, going to the meetings and so forth," acknowledging that his role was "not that of a campaign worker." See Charles Wesley Jordan, "The Role of the District Superintendent in the Harold Washington Story," in Young 1988, 30–34.

6. Verba, Schlozman, and Brady 1993.

7. Cassette tape, Vernon Park Church of God, Chicago, Illinois, November 1, 1992.

8. Observation, Interfaith Religious Commemoration of Dr. Martin Luther King, Chicago NAACP, First Church of Deliverance-Spiritual, Chicago, Illinois, January 20, 1992.

9. Observation, rally for Danny K. Davis, Bethel African Methodist Episcopal Church, Chicago, Illinois, November 24, 1990.

10. Observation, Omega Baptist Church, Chicago, Illinois, February 24, 1991.

11. Cassette tape, "Take Heed," Elder Paul S. Morton Sr., Greater Saint Stephen Ministries, tape number 253, New Orleans, Louisiana, November 3, 1991.

12. See the Reverend Willie Barrow at the Carol Moseley-Braun breakfast, p. 48 above.

13. See Harris 1999a, 1999b, for further discussion of the concept of "oppositional civic culture."

4   Free Spaces: Creating Oppositional Consciousness in the Disability Rights Movement

Sharon Groch

To develop oppositional consciousness, oppressed groups usually need physical space in which to communicate and share perceptions of their experiences with relatively little interference from or control by the dominant group. These arenas, or "free spaces" (Allen 1970; Evans and Boyte 1986),[1] often provide the networks, funds, and repertories of strategies and tactics that make social movements possible (see resource mobilization theory, e.g., McCarthy and Zald 1973, 1977; Oberschall 1973; Tilly 1978). In this chapter, however, I emphasize the effects of free spaces on the formation of oppositional culture and oppositional consciousness. Specifically, I examine how three different groups within the disability community—the deaf, blind people, and people with mobility impairments—took different routes in the creation of oppositional consciousness. Their differences, I argue, derive largely from their differing abilities to create autonomous free spaces.

Before members of oppressed groups can act collectively, they usually must develop an oppositional consciousness. That is, they must come to see themselves as members of a group, regard their life situations as unjust, find a common interest with other members of the group in opposing that injustice, consider the injustice due to structural inequalities, and believe the injustice can be diminished or ended through their collective actions. To come to this interpretation of their life situation, oppressed groups must create shared meaning. All three disability groups created shared meaning on each of the interdependent levels that Klandermans (1992) suggests: (1) through interactions within social networks; (2) through the conscious attempts of social actors to create shared meaning; and (3) through participating in collective actions or observing the collective actions of others. The first level, consensus formation, involves the unplanned convergence of meaning. The second level, consensus mobilization, involves the deliberate attempts of activists to influence others' beliefs. The third level, action mobilization, involves the creation of shared meaning, planned or unplanned, through discussions that occur among participants and observers of collective action.

Consensus formation, the first level, occurred easily among both deaf and blind people who had been placed in residential schools at a young age. Interactions within these early schools created an early culture of opposition and eventually a sense of collective identity that included an understanding of identity of interests, an injustice frame that included opposition to those injustices, and a belief in the power of collective action. Once an oppositional consciousness with these components emerged, members of these groups perpetuated that consciousness deliberately (consensus mobilization) and developed that consciousness further through participation (action mobilization). By contrast, children with mobility impairments (i.e., who use wheelchairs, walkers, canes, and crutches) traditionally have not been segregated in residential schools. They have sometimes attended separate classes or even separate schools within local public school systems, and have sometimes attended classes with the non–mobility impaired. Consequently, although a strong sense of collective identity has eventually emerged among many members of this group, it has required conscious consensus mobilization and action mobilization through observing other groups. Unlike deaf people and blind people, people with mobility impairments have attempted to mobilize people with all types of disabilities, with the goal of creating an inclusive disability consciousness.

Images, slogans, literature, humor, rituals, and other cultural expressions facilitate the shared interpretations that animate oppositional culture. Some groups, such as African Americans, have developed strong oppositional cultures from which oppositional consciousness can arise (Morris 1984). Other oppressed groups, such as women, who also historically have formed injustice frames (Lerner 1993), have been less successful in creating all that is needed for a supportive oppositional culture.

The experiences of these three different segments of the disability rights movement supports Aldon Morris and Naomi Braine's contention that the degree of physical segregation that an oppressed group experiences influences the emergence of an oppositional consciousness (chap. 2, this volume). Segregation does indeed make it easier for an oppressed group to create free spaces. However, the experience of the different disability groups suggests that both the *degree* and the *nature* of the segregation influence the formation of oppositional consciousness. Segregated groups that are controlled by nonmembers and allowed little unsupervised time have little opportunity to create free spaces. In such conditions, segregation facilitates a collective identity but inhibits the growth of either an oppositional culture or oppositional consciousness.

Two paths thus appear to developing an oppositional consciousness. First, a group can experience the kind of segregation that allows considerable group autonomy. Alternatively, a group that has experienced segregation without autonomy can build from its existing collective identity by applying the model of another group to its own conditions. In both paths "free spaces" play a critical role.

People with Disabilities

Data from the 1990 and 1991 panels of the Survey of Income and Program Participation (SIPP) reveal that 34.2 million noninstitutionalized Americans of fifteen years and over report a disability.[2] A "disability" is defined as having difficulty with or being unable to perform one or more activities, including seeing, hearing, speaking, lifting and carrying, climbing stairs, and walking. Of these 34.2 million individuals, 15.2 million are severely disabled, that is, unable to perform one or more of these activities (McNeil 1993).

People with disabilities resemble members of other oppressed groups in two important ways. First, individuals with disabilities acquire their identity involuntarily; they do not choose to become disabled. Second, as a group, people with disabilities historically have been marginalized and even oppressed on the basis of this identity.[3] However, unlike members of most oppressed groups who enter their group at birth,[4] individuals become members of the disability community at various times in their lives: some at birth, some during childhood, some during adolescence, and some during adulthood. These varying entrance times bring together individuals with an array of life experiences and attitudes toward disability, making the formation of any type of oppositional consciousness particularly hard (Groch 1994). Also unlike most other oppressed groups, the identifying characteristic that places an individual in this group varies greatly across the community in form and degree. A disability may be physical, sensory, cognitive, and/or emotional in nature, and its extent slight to severe. Traditionally, education and health care systems have segregated people with disabilities according to their type of impairment. These structural practices, which diminish the similarities and emphasize the differences between individuals with disabilities, have fostered the formation of distinct versions of oppositional consciousness among subgroups of the disability community. The same structural conditions have hampered the development of a broad-based oppositional consciousness among these groups. People with disabilities did not create a "disability consciousness"[5] until the early 1970s.

Today the disability population includes several specific forms of oppositional consciousness in addition to a general disability consciousness, making this group particularly useful in exploring the conditions that generate various forms of oppositional consciousness. I collected data on these forms of oppositional consciousness in six ways. I (1) interviewed thirty activists with various disabilities; (2) observed and participated in protest actions organized by disability rights activists; (3) attended meetings and conferences of specific disability groups; (4) examined the pamphlets, annual reports, newsletters, position papers, and other documents of nineteen organizations that support the cultures of oppositional consciousness analyzed in this chapter; (5) reviewed published primary material written by individuals with various disabilities; and (6) obtained feedback on an early draft of this chapter from four interviewees.[6]

I have supplemented these observations with secondary sources on the history and cultures of specific disability groups written by nondisabled and disabled scholars (on the deaf: Barnartt 1994; Gannon 1981, 1989; Higgins 1980; Lane 1984, 1992; Padden and Humphries 1988; Sacks 1990; Van Cleve and Crouch 1989; on the blind: Cheadle 1993; Jernigan 1992–94; Koestler 1976; Lowenfeld 1975; Matson 1990; on the mobility-impaired: Frampton and Rowell 1938; Garwood 1983; Lynch and Lewis 1988; Maddox 1993; on cross-disability groups: Berkowitz 1980; DeJong 1979; Johnson 1983; Levy 1988; Shapiro 1993; Scotch 1984, 1988; Treanor 1993).

I recruited the thirty disability rights activists interviewed through snowballing procedures. Interviews lasted from forty minutes to two hours, and were taped unless taping seemed to make the respondent uncomfortable or the interviews occurred in informal settings. The activists range in age from approximately thirty to sixty years old. Nine respondents are visually impaired, three hearing impaired, fourteen mobility impaired for various reasons (polio, spinal cord injury, cerebral palsy, muscular dystrophy, and head trauma), two of short stature, one visually and hearing impaired, and one upper-extremity impaired. Thirteen of the respondents are men and seventeen are women. Twenty-one of the activists are White, three Hispanic Americans, and six African Americans. The activists are located primarily in the eastern and Midwestern regions of the country: Washington, Baltimore, New York City, Rochester, Knoxville, Chicago, and Phoenix.

Because I have collected data from disability rights activists and organizations, the conclusions drawn here are generalizable only to this subset of the broader disability population. Many individuals with disabilities do not identify with the disability rights movement.

Deaf Consciousness

Recent measures of disability by the Census Bureau (McNeil 1993) find that among Americans fifteen years old and over, 10.9 million individuals have a hearing impairment; that is, they have difficulty hearing what is said in a normal conversation. Of this 10.9 million, 900,000 individuals are completely unable to hear what is said in such a conversation. Although these numbers do not tell us the degree of hearing difficulty most of these individuals experience, these numbers reveal that at least 900,000 Americans are profoundly deaf. Individuals within this subgroup of the hearing-impaired population, made up primarily of persons who were born deaf or became deaf at an early age, have forged an oppositional consciousness that they themselves call "deaf consciousness" (McWhinney 1991).

Individuals who possess a deaf consciousness express beliefs similar to those held by other oppressed groups who have developed an oppositional consciousness. These individuals (1) have a collective identity; (2) believe that, as a group, they are subject to unjust treatment and so reject the legitimacy of their subordinate position; (3) recognize a common interest in ending the unjust treatment, (4) blame that treatment on a system of domination created by hearing people; and (5) believe that collective action is their best form of redress. Persons who are blind or have mobility impairments have developed similar oppositional interpretations of their life situation. Unlike these groups, however, people with a deaf consciousness do not consider their impairment a disability.

Instead of identifying themselves as disabled, people who possess a deaf consciousness see themselves as members of a linguistic and cultural minority (Dolnick 1993; Lane 1992). They "share a language . . . and a culture . . . , have inherited their sign language, use it as a primary means of communication among themselves, and hold a set of beliefs about themselves and their connection to the larger society" (Padden and Humphries 1988, 2). To emphasize this point, deaf activists and scholars use the uppercase "Deaf" when referring to people who share the Deaf language and culture.

As with many linguistic minorities, the primary identifying characteristic of the Deaf community is its language. A visual language, American Sign Language (ASL) has a particular spatial grammar and unique syntax (Sacks 1990, 85–92). Deaf individuals consider ASL the natural, inherited language of their people and ridicule other means of communication such as lip reading or Signed English. Since ASL does not have a written form, Deaf individuals have created other expressions to preserve and pass on their language and culture. Signed poetry (Jepson 1993), plays such as those performed by the National Theatre of the Deaf, folktales (Padden and Humphries 1988, 32–33), and jokes (Gannon 1981, chap. 8) are shared through live performances and videotapes. These cultural forms often express the oppositional nature of deaf consciousness. In the poetry, plays, folktales, and jokes, people who hear are called "the others" and their mannerisms and habits ridiculed. Stories are told and retold of hearing educators insisting that Deaf children use oral communication techniques and discouraging students from marrying one another. Many cultural forms celebrate the Deaf community's ability to persevere, maintaining their language, culture, and social ties despite the oppression they have experienced.

Believing that the Deaf community constitutes a linguistic minority group, Deaf individuals value their deafness. When asked if they would rather hear, many Deaf people respond that they do not want to hear (Dolnick 1993). Deaf parents often refuse to let their Deaf children have cochlear implants, a procedure that provides some hearing (Barringer 1993; Dolnick 1993; Lane 1992). These parents argue that supporting cochlear implants is like supporting skin-lightening procedures for people of color. Both procedures attempt to change an integral characteristic of a person, a characteristic which should be a source of pride, not of shame.

Their experiences of oppression have caused many Deaf people to develop separatist views. Approximately nine out of ten Deaf individuals marry other Deaf people (Lane 1992, 17). Most Deaf parents send their Deaf children to residential schools for the deaf. Both intermarriage and separate schooling help ensure the continuation of a deaf consciousness. Deaf individuals also choose to socialize primarily with other Deaf people. As a result, Deaf individuals have established their own fraternal insurance society, travel agencies, social clubs, athletic associations, theater groups, and places of worship. These institutions function as free spaces in which Deaf people can interact with one another uninhibited by the presence of hearing people.

Political organizations form part of the network of organizations created and controlled by Deaf people. The oldest and largest of these organizations is the National Association of the Deaf (NAD). In 1880, Deaf individuals founded the NAD on the belief that Deaf people made up "a class by themselves" and "need[ed] to control their own destinies"

(Van Cleve and Crouch 1989, 94). The members of the NAD held this belief so strongly that they denied hearing people membership for eighty-four years. NAD aims to secure the civil rights of Deaf people, to preserve and expand the language, culture, and heritage of the Deaf, and to develop future Deaf leaders. Members of NAD lobby state and national legislatures, provide legal defense funds in discrimination cases, organize workshops on ASL, sponsor summer youth camps, and award college scholarships to Deaf children. Implicit in these tactics is the goal of perpetuating deaf consciousness.

Gallaudet University plays an institutionally crucial role in the transmission of deaf consciousness. Founded in 1864 (Gannon 1981, 38), Gallaudet is the world's only liberal arts college for Deaf students. Many deaf individuals first encounter deaf consciousness at Gallaudet. Most deaf children born to Deaf parents form a deaf consciousness the way children of other ethnic and racial groups do, through their interactions with their parents and their communities. But only ten percent of all deaf children are born to Deaf parents (Lane 1992, 138). Moreover, most of the old segregated schools have been closed. By 1992, nearly three-quarters of the children who were deaf were attending integrated schools with hearing children (Lane 1992, 135). Integrated schools stress learning English in the form of speech, lip reading, written English, finger spelling, Signed English, or speech accompanied by ASL. In this system, deaf children of hearing parents typically graduate from high school knowing little about the culture of deaf consciousness. Some of these learn about deaf consciousness as adults when they seek out or stumble upon one of the organizations of the Deaf.

Many of the college oriented are introduced to deaf consciousness at Gallaudet, in what are not always easy lessons. A Deaf interviewee educated in integrated schools describes his initial experiences at Gallaudet as "a cultural shock. . . . I actually had to interact with Deaf persons twenty-four hours a day!" Gallaudet gave this person his first lesson in ASL, his first Deaf adult role models in his teachers, his first group of Deaf friends, and his first awareness of deaf consciousness.

In 1988, Gallaudet University students forced the newly appointed hearing president to resign and replaced her with a Deaf president, the first in the university's history. The protest, called Deaf President Now (DPN), showed Deaf people beyond the university the power of collective action (see Christiansen and Barnartt 1995 for a comprehensive review of the protest). Although the mass media and many disability rights activists have claimed the DPN protest as "a touchstone event, a Selma or a Stonewall" for people with *disabilities* (Shapiro 1993, 74), for the

Gallaudet students this was a specifically *Deaf* protest. The Gallaudet takeover was not the Selma of the disability rights movement; it was the Selma of the Deaf (Gannon 1989, 136; also see Barnartt 1994). While the DPN protest undoubtedly increased public awareness of the rights of disabled people, this broader aim was not the intent of the Gallaudet students.

The DPN protest sparked similar actions by the Deaf at residential schools across the nation. It has also drawn the attention of many journalists (Dolnick 1993; Solomon 1994) and social scientists (Barnartt 1994; Lane 1992; Sacks 1990) to deaf culture and consciousness. Many of these authors suggest that deaf consciousness is a relatively new phenomenon. However, a closer look at the history of Deaf people (Gannon 1981; Van Cleve and Crouch 1989) reveals a long-standing tradition among the Deaf of collectively acting on their own behalf.

Consensus Formation in Deaf Consciousness

The beginnings of a deaf consciousness can be traced to the establishment of the first residential school for deaf children in 1817. Founded by three men, one of whom was a Deaf teacher in France who communicated using French Sign Language and writing, this school brought a substantial number of deaf children together for the first time. Having acquired or developed various forms of sign language before entering this school, these children, with the help of their Deaf teacher, began developing their own common language (which became ASL), along with their own beliefs, expressions, and practices. Upon graduating from school, many Deaf students passed on their culture by encouraging other states to open residential schools for the deaf and teaching in these institutions.

Although state funded, these early residential schools for the deaf were essentially indigenous institutions. Deaf administrators, staff, and teachers usually controlled the early schools. Within their schools, individuals communicated using ASL. Students lived segregated from the hearing world. They shared similar life experiences and had adult role models. The schools thus functioned as free spaces, within which deaf children developed the collective identity and "cultural attributes that marked deaf Americans as a distinct subculture within America" (Van Cleve and Crouch 1989, 30).

Upon graduating from these residential schools, Deaf friends maintained their ties by establishing alumni associations. Out of the alumni associations came many of the other organizations of the Deaf: their social clubs, political organizations, and independent newspapers. These organizations too functioned as free spaces, which helped create and transmit deaf consciousness as, after 1880, the schools for the deaf became increasingly controlled by hearing people. In this historical move, prominent educators led by Alexander Graham Bell convinced the world that Deaf children should no longer be taught ASL but should learn to communicate orally, by speaking and lip reading. With this change, what I will call "the culture of deaf consciousness" lost its influential position in the schools. Hearing teachers replaced Deaf teachers, eliminating important adult role models. Children were rewarded for their ability to speak and punished for using ASL. Yet by this time deaf consciousness had solid roots and continued to be passed on outside of the formal classroom settings, in the dormitories of the residential schools and in the many organizations founded by the Deaf.

Deaf people have believed in the power of collective action for over a century. In 1889, members of the NAD fought for equal employment in federal agencies by lobbying and writing letters. In 1913, a Nebraska Deaf group lobbied against teaching oralism in their schools. In the 1920s, Deaf groups across the nation fought successfully for the right to drive. The collective actions of Deaf people turned more disruptive in the early 1970s, as Deaf activists followed the lead of the Black civil rights movement and began to demonstrate publicly and to picket. Deaf students in residential schools organized demonstrations in Louisiana, New Jersey, and Pennsylvania over the lack of Deaf administrators and ASL instruction. Deaf actors picketed television stations to protest their use of hearing people to play Deaf individuals. The student protest at Gallaudet University in 1988 had many precursors.

Although the culture of deaf consciousness appears both stable and mature, individuals who are hearing impaired vary in many ways (Higgins 1980, 48–69). Any person who has a hearing impairment can become a member of the Deaf community by becoming proficient in ASL and accepting the values, norms, and behaviors of Deaf culture. However, variations in demographic characteristics such as race, socioeconomic level, and gender make some groups less likely to form a deaf consciousness than other groups.

People of color, for example, are less likely to become members of the Deaf community than are Whites. Although today most Deaf organizations actively recruit people of color, the Deaf community, created primarily by White deaf men, has traditionally either excluded or marginalized women and people of color.[7] As a White Deaf interviewee regretfully states, "Blacks and Latinos are not totally in the White man's Deaf world." The Deaf community's marginalization of people of color stems partly from past racist practices that segregated African American children in their own residential schools for the deaf. As a result of this early segregation, Deaf African Americans developed a distinct form of ASL. Although Black ASL and White ASL have many similarities, the differences between them are enough to produce occasional misunderstandings and to inhibit interactions between the groups (Higgins 1980, 52). Having created their own distinct oppositional culture and organizations to support this culture, African Americans have been reluctant to join the larger, mostly White, Deaf community.

Variations in time of onset and degree of deafness also influence the likelihood of a person joining the Deaf community. Individuals who become deaf as adults, either completely or partially, are far less likely to become members of the Deaf community than those who are born with profound deafness. People who have once heard usually find it hard to learn both ASL and a new culture that values deafness. Having grown up nondisabled, these individuals are likely to view their deafness as a disability and prefer to remain in the hearing world with their hearing families, friends, and associates. Because of these views and preferences, individuals who have lost their hearing as adults have founded their own organizations to express their unique identities and to address their specific issues.[8]

Hearing-impaired individuals outside of the Deaf community have nevertheless developed some degree of oppositional consciousness. The Deaf community and other organizations of the deaf have worked together on that basis to secure legislative protection for communication accessibility. However, the specific culture of deaf consciousness inhibits many members of these groups from developing a broad oppositional consciousness based on disability. This is particularly true for the Deaf who maintain that their group is not disabled but a linguistic minority.

Blind Consciousness

Census Bureau data (McNeil 1993) indicate that there are 9.7 million Americans fifteen years of age or older who have difficulty seeing words and letters in ordinary newsprint even when wearing corrective lenses. Of the 9.7 million people with visual impairments, 1.6 million individuals are completely unable to see words and letters in ordinary newsprint. Thus, nearly twice as many Americans are blind as are profoundly deaf.

Like the Deaf, a subgroup within the blind population has constructed a form of oppositional consciousness that I call "blind consciousness." Individuals who possess blind consciousness experience a collective identity with other blind people and believe that, as a group, they historically have been dominated and oppressed by the sighted. For these individuals being blind is much like being a member of any other minority group, not in a cultural sense as the Deaf assert, but in the sense that blind people are "subject to much the same differential treatment and suspicious regard as other minorities" (Matson 1990, 372). Blind activists argue that, in parallel with African Americans, blind people historically have been enslaved in asylums, exploited in workshops, and marginalized in education and employment opportunities.

With these beliefs comes the view, as a blind female interviewee asserts, that "blindness is a civil rights issue." Just as for the Deaf the problem is not being deaf, "the principle problem of blindness is not the blindness itself but the mistaken notions and ideas about blindness which are held by the general public" (Jernigan 1976, 20). Individuals with blind consciousness believe that the best way to change these ideas is to act collectively.

While many of the elements of blind consciousness are similar to those of deaf consciousness, blind consciousness differs from deaf consciousness in several important ways. Unlike persons with a deaf consciousness, those with a blind consciousness are more likely to believe that their impairment is a disability. Moreover, many blind individuals emphasize that blindness is a *sensory* disability, not a *physical* disability like paraplegia. In making this distinction, they imply that being blind differs from other physical disabilities.

People who have a blind consciousness do not value their blindness the way Deaf individuals value their deafness. Most say that, given the choice, they would prefer to see. However, these individuals do not view blindness as a tragedy, as many sighted people do. Instead, blind activists contend that blindness is a "serious inconvenience," a "constant annoyance," and a "nuisance."

Unlike the Deaf, individuals with a blind consciousness do not adopt a separatist stance. Rather, they insist on the complete integration of all blind people into the larger society. The value that blind activists place on integration appears in their rhetoric and daily actions. We have no statistical data on the degree to which blind individuals intermarry. Organizations of the blind report that data on intermarriages are not kept because their constituents have little interest in such data. Unlike the Deaf, who value intermarriages, blind interviewees explain that in their community intermarriage is neither encouraged nor discouraged; it is "simply not an issue."

Integration is also the goal for blind activists in educating their children. Like deafness, blindness can be hereditary. However, unlike the

Deaf, blind parents whose children are blind seldom demand that their children attend residential schools for the blind. People who possess a blind consciousness neither value nor devalue educating their children with other blind children. These parents value schools that employ teachers who have high expectations for their children and can teach them important alternative skills, such as cane travel and braille.

People who are blind have created a network of institutions to meet their needs. Professional organizations, recreational clubs, alumni associations of blind residential schools, and theater groups offer the newly blinded as well as those who lost their sight at an early age the opportunity to meet other blind people, often for the first time. Like the organizations of the Deaf, the organizations of the blind foster the development of a collective identity among blind people. However, while a strong oppositional culture prevails in most Deaf organizations, this is not true of many blind organizations. The degree to which each group transmits a blind consciousness varies.

Individuals with a blind consciousness can be found primarily in two organizations: The National Federation of the Blind (NFB) and the American Council of the Blind (ACB). Founded as one organization by alumni associates of blind residential schools in 1940, these organizations split in 1961. Although these organizations have similar goals, much animosity remains between them. Seldom is a blind person a member of both the NFB and the ACB.

The purpose of the ACB is "to promote the independence, dignity, and well-being of blind and visually impaired people" by enhancing their civil rights, job opportunities, access to public services and facilities, and Social Security benefits. To achieve its purpose, the ACB monitors governmental policies, promotes public awareness, provides legal advice and assistance, and offers college scholarships. The ACB also advocates the public use of adaptive devices such as textured surfaces on curb cuts and alarm-sounding cross lights. Since the early 1970s, the ACB has worked in coalition with other disability organizations to secure the rights of all disabled people.

The NFB also promotes the independence, dignity, and well-being of blind people. However, the NFB adds a militant tone by demanding "the complete integration of the blind into society on a basis of equality." For NFB members, the "independence, dignity, and well-being" of the ACB are not enough. They demand as well security, opportunity, and equality. Many NFB tactics mirror the tactics used by the ACB. The NFB monitors governmental activities, lobbies for the passage of legislation, educates the public, and offers scholarships to blind students. However, unlike the ACB, the NFB does not support using adaptive devices for the blind. NFB members see these adaptations as perpetuating their second-class position. They declare, "We don't need the world re-engineered for us. We use it as it is. What we need is good training and good attitudes about ourselves" (National Federation of the Blind 1992).

The NFB also views working within disability coalitions differently from the ACB. An NFB member explains:

> There are very distinct and often rather devastating disadvantages to aligning ourselves with the large disability groups, and being involved, caught up in, the "pan-disability movement." We oppose it. We think it is definitely a bad idea. . . . We feel that we are such a tiny minority, if we involve ourselves in a coalition, that the issues of the coalition will supersede and subvert our issues . . . that our issues would not ordinarily get the kind of emphasis, the kind of commitment from a coalition that we feel is needed to get things done to benefit blind people.

In 1974, NFB members passed a resolution that prohibits them from joining in permanent coalitions with other disabled groups.

Although the NFB will not form coalitions, it remains one of the most aggressive disability organizations in America. When traditional methods of effecting social change fail, the NFB turns to more disruptive tactics. NFB members have held annual marches on Washington for increased representation in accreditation procedures and have picketed television stations for their negative portrayals of blind people. They also have organized strikes among sheltered-care workshop employees for better wages and for the right to form unions.

Like other groups that have developed a culture of oppositional consciousness, NFB members demand the right of self-definition. NFB members call themselves Federationists to distinguish themselves from ACB members, other blind people, and sighted people. They describe themselves as being "blind," not "visually impaired." To Federationists, refusing to use the word "blind" implies that being blind is shameful, and for them "it is respectable to be blind." Defining blindness broadly as the inability to drive a car, read ordinary print, or recognize faces at a distance, they believe that people who call themselves visually impaired are attempting to distance themselves from the blind community and denying their collective identity. Although NFB members do not use the uppercase "Blind" to refer to themselves, NFB members use the words "Federationist" and "blind" to express and build their oppositional consciousness.

NFB members also have created cultural symbols to express and transmit their oppositional consciousness. The NFB logo, with the initials "NFB" triangulated by the words "Security," "Opportunity," and "Equality," is printed on various everyday items such as coffee mugs and T-shirts. Members proudly wear NFB rings and lapel pins and use NFB white canes. Federationists have made the white cane itself an important cultural symbol. Unlike many individuals who see the white cane as stigmatizing, Federationists believe the white cane symbolizes freedom and independence. Members express their oppositional consciousness by walking briskly with their long NFB canes.

Braille is another symbol of blind consciousness. NFB members shun the use of talking books and computers, insisting that braille is the most effective means of writing and reading for blind people. At meetings, Federationists can be seen using braille slates and styluses and braille typewriters to take notes. For NFB members, using braille reaffirms that being blind is respectable; its use becomes an important symbol in building a culture of blind consciousness.

In addition to these other cultural symbols, NFB members have written songs to "promote the attitudes of the Federation." Using familiar melodies so that the songs can be learned and remembered easily, these "songs of freedom" tell of society's exploitation and marginalization of blind people (National Federation of the Blind 1991). Sung primarily during national conventions, the songs remind NFB members of past and ongoing struggles and victories, perpetuating a sense of blind consciousness.

Unlike deaf consciousness, the well-developed blind consciousness that Federationists have created is seldom seen outside this group. Members of the ACB also have a blind consciousness. Yet because of their animosity toward the NFB, they do not share the NFB's cultural expressions. Apart from the ACB and the NFB, most other organizations of the blind have a collective identity, but not an injustice frame.

Much of the difference in the degree to which deaf consciousness and blind consciousness have been developed and accepted by their respective populations derives from the fact that the Deaf share a language. ASL inherently sets the Deaf apart from those who speak. Blind people do not share such a language. Yet, like the Deaf, blind people historically have been segregated in residential schools. Today some segregation continues in work and recreational settings. Blind people also share a unique method of reading and writing, setting them further apart from those who see. These methods had particular salience before tape recorders, talking books, and computers were developed.

Consensus Formation in Blind Consciousness

The history of blind education in America (Koestler 1976; Lowenfeld 1975) indicates why blind people have never developed the same degree of oppositional consciousness as the Deaf. In 1832, fifteen years after deaf children had begun to be educated in residential schools, blind children began receiving their education in similar schools. Some of the blind schools opened as separate departments within schools for the deaf. Other blind schools were freestanding and, like most schools for the deaf, state administered and publicly funded. The major difference between these two school systems was that Deaf individuals helped create the residential schools for the deaf while sighted individuals founded the schools for the blind. Although many schools had some blind teachers, the schools for the blind were primarily controlled and run by sighted people. Moreover, influenced by the eugenics movement of the 1800s, sighted administrators and educators allowed little contact between the blind boys and girls. Although administrators of schools for the deaf had similar fears about perpetuating deafness, the educators of blind children went to a far greater extent to keep the sexes segregated. Separate classrooms for boys and girls were common. Casual conversations between the sexes outside of class often meant expulsion. Many schools prohibited class reunions. Some schools went so far as to open and close their schools at different times of day for the girls and for the boys so that the children would have no chance to meet on the trains.

Once blind children began to attend integrated day schools in the 1900s, the practice of placing boys and girls in separate classrooms ceased. However, even in these situations instructors and parents repeatedly stressed the dangers of two blind people dating and marrying. A blind respondent who went to a public grade school in the mid-1950s remembers that his teachers "made it seem nasty to socialize with other blind kids. It made you want to get away [from blind people] as far as you could!" Another recalls being in college in the 1960s and "purposely avoiding other blind students."

These educational practices reinforced the stigma that society places on individuals who are blind, inhibiting the growth of a positive, collective identity and an oppositional culture. Internalizing the views of their educators, early blind leaders, many of whom were educators themselves, actively discouraged the creation of organizations of the blind. In 1901, blind leader Robert Irwin declared that "every educator of the blind knows the deleterious effect of collecting the blind together in isolated groups" (Koestler 1976, 33). In 1937, another blind leader, Henry Latimer wrote, "At best, blindness is a negative bond of common action . . . There is, nevertheless, no advantage accruing from membership in an all-blind organization which might not be acquired in greater measure through membership in a society of sighted persons" (Maurer 1993). These two men played key roles in the development of the American Foundation for the Blind, a nonmembership organization historically headed by sighted individuals. They did little to encourage and much to discourage the growth of an oppositional culture among the blind.

More recently, negative experiences in residential schools for the blind inspired some blind men to establish integrated schooling for blind children. The results were dramatic. Whereas in 1910, 96 percent of all blind children attended residential schools for the blind, by 1960 only 53 percent of the blind children attended residential schools. By 1970, this number had fallen to 32 percent (Koestler 1976) and by 1993 to only 9 percent (American Printing House for the Blind 1992–93, 26). This history contrasted with that of the deaf, who were mostly segregated in residential schools up until 1975.

Integrated in schools with the sighted and discouraged from socializing with one another, blind children had few opportunities to establish free spaces where an oppositional culture and consciousness could develop. The students of residential schools eventually created some crucial autonomous spaces by establishing alumni associations. Indeed, the NFB grew from interactions within and between these alumni associations. Yet blind students did not establish their first alumni association until 1871, thirty-nine years after the first schools for the blind opened. Members of the alumni associations did not create a national organization of the blind until 1940, sixty-nine years later. By contrast, although it took them nearly as long (thirty-seven years) to establish their first alumni association, Deaf individuals created their first national organization within twenty-six years.

Because of the concern for integration among most of today's blind people, most residential schools for the blind have closed, with those remaining serving primarily children with multiple disabilities. The history of segregation without autonomy produced a greater acceptance of stigma, which in turn generated a resistance to self-segregation. Combined, these structural and cultural conditions have inhibited the growth of a mature, widespread blind consciousness.

As in the deaf population, time of onset affects one's likelihood of forming a blind consciousness. Those most likely to form such a consciousness were born totally blind or became totally blind at an early age. However, today the majority of people who are blind have lost their sight later in their lives, after their sixty-fifth year. The needs and responses of these individuals differ from those who became blind early in life. Having lived most of their lives as sighted people, many in this group do not want to learn braille or how to use a white cane. Like the newly deaf, who prefer the hearing world, they prefer the sighted world. Those who have only a partial visual loss, regardless of time of onset, also often prefer to associate with sighted people. With little sense of collective identity, individuals who become blind late in life and/or are partially blind have found it hard to embrace the oppositional culture of blind consciousness.

Again, as among deaf people, race affects one's likelihood of developing a blind consciousness. The two organizations of the blind that perpetuate a blind consciousness have been founded and are still controlled primarily by White individuals. Many African Americans and Hispanic Americans who are blind find that these organizations fail to address their specific problems of living in a society with multiple systems of domination. Although some people of color are members of the NFB and the ACB, their numbers are few.

As the ACB has begun working in coalition with other disability groups, some blind individuals have transformed their blind consciousness into a broader disability consciousness. Nevertheless, although they see the advantage to such coalitions, most blind persons proceed cautiously for fear that the issues of the blind will be superseded by the issues of people whose disabilities are more visible and occur in greater numbers. As mentioned earlier, the most aggressive and culturally developed organization of the blind, the NFB, refuses to form permanent coalitions with other disability groups. Combined, these factors greatly hamper the growth of a broad disability consciousness among blind people.

Mobility-Impaired Consciousness

Functional measures of disability find that 17.3 million Americans fifteen years old and over have difficulty walking three blocks. Of the 17.3 million individuals with mobility impairment, 5.5 million use assistive devices to walk: 1.5 million persons use wheelchairs and 4 million use canes, crutches, or walkers (McNeil 1993). Thus, people with severe mobility impairments outnumber the profoundly deaf six to one and the totally blind a little more than three to one.

Historically, people with mobility impairments have been subject to some of the same discrimination as people who are deaf or blind. They have been denied access to public and private services and buildings and to equal opportunities in education and employment. Various forms and degrees of oppositional consciousness are evident among mobility-impaired people who share a specific physical condition. Since 1946, veterans who have been paralyzed because of spinal cord injuries, multiple sclerosis, or other neurological disorders have fought for legislative protection against discrimination by establishing the Paralyzed Veterans of America (PVA). The civilian arm of the PVA, the National Spinal Cord Injury Association (NSCIA), has fought similar battles. Polio survivors have created the National Polio Society to secure their civil rights and equal opportunities, and individuals born with spina bifida have established the Spina Bifida Association of America (SBAA) to protect their rights. Members of all of these groups, feeling a sense of collective identity and believing to various degrees that they are discriminated against, have created organizations to express, support, and spread their specific forms of oppositional consciousness.

At times, members of these disease-specific groups have come together to secure a mutual goal. In the 1930s, three hundred New York pensioners who were mobility impaired by cerebral palsy and polio formed the League of Physically Handicapped and occupied the Works Progress Administration (WPA) offices in Washington, D.C., to protest the WPA denying them jobs (Shapiro 1993, 63–64). More recently, mobility-impaired individuals have annually picketed television stations across the nation for broadcasting Jerry Lewis's muscular dystrophy telethon, which they see as perpetuating the view that disabled people are like helpless children, deserving pity rather than equal opportunities. Despite these actions, members of these groups have found it hard to develop an oppositional consciousness based broadly on mobility impairment. Instead, groups who share a physical condition have founded organizations to protect their particular rights and propagate an oppositional agenda based on that specific condition. With the exception of the PVA, most of these groups focus their attention on increasing medical services, funding research, and providing peer counseling to their constituents. NSCIA's motto of "care, cure, and coping" (Maddox 1993, 510) sums up the major goals of many such organizations of mobility-impaired individuals. Being more therapeutic than political in nature (Zola 1983), these organizations have been able to create strong collective identities among their members, but as yet have not developed either specific oppositional cultures or a general mobility-impaired consciousness.

Consensus Formation in Mobility-Impaired Consciousness

As with the deaf and the blind, the extent of oppositional consciousness among mobility-impaired people derives from the way mobility-impaired children have traditionally been educated (Frampton and Rowell 1938; Garwood 1983; Lynch and Lewis 1988). Children with mobility impairments have never been educated in residential schools. Since 1899, these children have been educated in day schools, that is, ordinary public schools. Yet although they usually attended local schools, these children were often segregated from their nondisabled peers by being placed in separate classrooms or wings of buildings. Some attended separate schools for the disabled. In 1975 federal law ordered an end to this "separate but equal" schooling for children with disabilities, but the practice remains in several cities today.

Separation within day schools allows mobility-impaired students to share their feelings, ideas, and personal experiences during school hours—in their classrooms, at lunch, during recess, and on the bus. Through these interactions students sometimes develop friendships and a sense of collective identity. However, these interactions seldom continue outside of school. Most public school systems bus the mobility-impaired students from various neighborhoods to one central location. Before accessible public transportation, many students could not meet with their friends after school unless driven by their nondisabled parents or older siblings. Living within nondisabled families, these students met few adults with mobility impairments. Given little opportunity to create "free space" to reinterpret their life situations and few adult role models to help shape their beliefs, most of these students had little chance to question the legitimacy of their subordinate positions.

The educational experiences of mobility-impaired people contrast sharply with those of deaf people. Unlike the indigenously founded residential schools for deaf children, the few schools for the mobility impaired have been established and controlled by nondisabled individuals. In this sense, the experiences of mobility-impaired students resemble those of blind students. However, unlike the schools for the mobility impaired, the first schools for the blind were residential; students lived together nine months out of the year. Although educators attempted to keep the students apart, the residential schools did bring blind individuals together and so facilitated the formation of a culture of blind consciousness. Mobility-impaired individuals have never experienced this degree of educational segregation. It seems reasonable to assume that these structural and cultural conditions have inhibited people with mobility impairments from creating a strong oppositional culture.

Disability Consciousness

Although no oppositional consciousness that includes all people with mobility impairments has been constructed, some activists have developed the broader oppositional consciousness I call "disability consciousness." Unlike deaf consciousness, blind consciousness, or mobility-impaired consciousness, disability consciousness includes all forms of disability—deafness, blindness, mobility impairment, psychiatric impairment, and intellectual impairment.

Crucial to disability consciousness is the belief that all people with disabilities are oppressed in the sense of having been unjustly deprived of power, status, and opportunities. Citing the findings of the ICD survey of Americans with disabilities, a mobility-impaired interviewee reports that:

> the disabled, as a whole, are the least well educated subgroup of this society. We are its poorest subgroup. . . . We have a lesser—both in terms of frequency and in terms of quality—social life than our nondisabled peers. We are less involved in community life than our nondisabled peers. Two-thirds of us are not working and . . . most of those people want to be working. Those people who are working are making significantly less money to the dollar compared to their nondisabled counterparts.

Like members of other oppressed groups who have developed an oppositional consciousness, people with a disability consciousness contend that their subordinate position is not due to personal failure. Rather, their negative status results from a system of domination that historically has segregated them in schools, nursing homes, and other institutions, subjected them to prejudicial treatment, and discriminated against them in employment opportunities, housing, and public services. Identifying with other minorities, another mobility-impaired interviewee explains that "the problem is not skin color, language, sex, or disability . . . the problem is the environment, in society's attitudes." Individuals with a disability consciousness believe that changes must be made within the system of domination, not within themselves.

As with other forms of oppositional consciousness, disability consciousness is expressed through cultural artifacts and practices. Yet unlike the members of many other racial and ethnic groups, disability rights activists have had purposely to create their culture. A mobility-impaired Latino interviewee remarks, "most groups start out forming cultural relationships and then get into political social movements. We [the disabled] are doing it in the reverse."

Most of the cultural expressions of a broader disability consciousness—such as novels (Finger 1994; Stewart 1989), short stories (Bellarosa 1989), autobiographies (Hannaford 1985; Panzarino 1994; Zola 1982a, 1982b), "survival" manuals (Milam 1993), humor (Callahan 1989, 1991, 1993), music (Crescendo 1993), poetry (Wade 1989), monthly publications (*Mouth: Voice of the Disability Nation*, published by Free Hand Press in Topeka, Kansas), and plays (Nussbaum and Ervin 1990)— have been created by mobility-impaired people, although they tell stories of disabled people in general or of individual and collective struggles against oppression.

Disability rights activists have also created cultural symbols to express and transmit their oppositional consciousness, often borrowing the successful symbols of the Black civil rights movement, the Black power movement, and the anti–Vietnam War movement. Activists have altered the universal symbol of disability (i.e., an outline of a figure sitting in a wheelchair) by drawing the Black power symbol of a clenched fist in the center of the wheel. Although continuing to perpetuate the myth that "disability" equals wheelchair use, this new symbol transforms the benign yet highly impersonal symbol of disability into an image of group strength and pride. In a similar borrowing from the struggles of earlier groups, during a Washington, DC march protesting the institutionalization of disabled people, activists waved banners reading "Separate is never equal" and "Hell no, we won't go."

Disability activists have also created symbols unique to their own movement. Some symbols adapt sacred American icons, such as an image of the Statue of Liberty seated in a wheelchair. Others invent completely new images, such as "Phyllis," the adult-size, wooden and acrylic female bird dressed in brightly colored clothing and high, black boots, who sits defiantly with her legs and arms crossed in a wheelchair. On postcards, Phyllis is pictured with the words "Disability Cool." This phase is meant to convey the belief that disability "will someday become not only tolerated, but—well, trendy. Like [eye]glasses. . . . [It's] countercultural chic—taken to its outer limits" (*Best of the Rag* 1985, 13).

Like other oppressed groups that have formed a culture of oppositional consciousness, disability rights activists insist on their right of self-definition. They reject the language of rehabilitation medicine and special education. Activists replace "architectural barriers" with "segregation," "mainstreaming" with "integration," and "attitudinal barriers" with "prejudice." They convey the negative connotations of various disability labels by comparing them with the labels given African Americans:

> "Disabled" is like "Black" or "Afro-american"
> "Handicapped" is like "Colored"
> "Crip" is like "Homeboy"
> "Physically challenged" is like "non-white"
> "Handicapper" is like "Negro"
> "People with differing abilities" is like "those people"
> "Cripple" is like "nigger." (Mauro 1991, 36)

Other cultural practices also express and transmit disability consciousness. People with a disability consciousness usually try to live as independently as possible; that is, to live outside of institutions and away from their families' homes, have paid personal assistance if needed, use public transportation (not the special transit services for disabled people), and work for pay. They insist on being integrated in all areas of life, from eating in a neighborhood restaurant to attending a prestigious university. They will file complaints and sue if integration is denied. Disability rights activists want to "normalize disability," that is, "to live normal lives . . . be seen as ordinary people." The cultural practices of disability consciousness resemble in this way those of blind consciousness.

To support the culture of disability consciousness, people with mobility impairments have established Centers for Independent Living (CILs) across the nation. Controlled and run by people with various disabilities, CILS are private, nonprofit, nonresidential centers that serve as social-change agents, working for the integration of all people with disabilities. To achieve this goal, CILS offer independent living services, promote an awareness of disability rights issues, and advocate on the behalf of individuals with disabilities. Although similar to the organizations of the Deaf and of people with a blind consciousness, CILS differ from these groups in addressing issues relevant to all types of disabilities— hearing, visual, mobility, cognitive, or emotional impairments. Their staff members have various disabilities. They offer both general services, such as ADA workshops, and specific services, such as distributing teletype communication devices (TTY) to the deaf. The CILS' public-education programs include information about people who are deaf, blind, and mobility impaired. To be accessible to all people with disabilities, CILS list both TTY and voice phone numbers. These tactics often pull together for the first time individuals with various disabilities, encouraging the growth of a unifying disability consciousness.

To ensure that CILS continue perpetuating disability consciousness, members of CILS have formed the National Council on Independent Living (NCIL). NCIL links many of the over four hundred CILS in this country by disseminating pertinent information through newsletters, meetings, and conventions, and by protecting the centers' funds through legislative monitoring and lobbying. In return, CILS must meet strict NCIL membership criteria. The membership requirements demonstrate CILS members' commitment to disability consciousness by demanding that the majority of the governing board members be individuals with disabilities and that the services they provide meet the needs of people with a variety of disabilities.

In addition to CILS, individuals with mobility impairments have formed a direct action group. Once called American Disabled for Accessible Public Transit and now American Disabled for Attendant Programs Today (ADAPT), ADAPT has played a critical role in fostering the growth of disability consciousness. ADAPT is the militant branch of the disability rights movement. Its major activities are organizing and participating in local protest actions and semiannual national demonstrations. Strategically, ADAPT members address only one issue at a time and make their demands known through civil disobedience. ADAPT's two national offices and various local chapters have no paid staff or permanent meeting spaces. Rather the organization exists through member contributions, fund-raising events, and in-kind donations such as office space, photocopying privileges, and telephone use from disability rights organizations, usually CILS. Traditionally, members of ADAPT have been mobility impaired. Today, individuals with all types of disabilities can be found among its ranks.

The tactics used by ADAPT members resemble those used originally by Black civil rights activists. They are part of a repertory that has now become standard (Tilly 1986, 1995). The tactics are now "modular" (Tarrow 1998) in the sense that they can be duplicated and inserted in several forms of organizing. The tactics include organizing sit-ins at federal buildings, staging "crawl-ins" at the Capitol building, and chaining themselves to the doors of state and federal buildings. ADAPT leaders meticulously organize each event, identifying before any action the participants who are able and willing to be arrested, contacting lawyers, securing bail money, and notifying the media.

Consensus Formation in Disability Consciousness

While the deaf and the blind have constructed specific forms of oppositional consciousness, people with mobility impairments have been primarily responsible for the emergence of a more general disability consciousness. Individuals with mobility impairments are statistically more likely than those who are hearing or visually impaired to identify themselves as disabled.[9] Identifying oneself as disabled is the first step in forming a collective identity with other disabled people. Moreover, unlike those who are deaf or blind, people with mobility impairments never developed an oppositional culture based on the experience of being mobility impaired. When individuals with mobility impairments began to develop an injustice frame and a belief in the power of collective action, they saw people with all types of disabilities as being treated unjustly.

Berkowitz (1980) documents one of the first attempts to create a disability consciousness among people with various disabilities. Berkowitz reports that Paul Strachan, an experienced labor organizer and legislative lobbyist who became mobility impaired and deaf as a result of an accident, founded the American Federation of Handicapped Persons in 1942. This group was the first to demand the passage of a federal civil rights bill protecting people with disabilities against discrimination. Although the bill passed in the Senate, it died in a House committee and never again received serious attention. The American Federation did successfully pressure the government to establish the President's Committee on the National Employment of the Handicapped, a federal agency that continues today. Yet by the early 1950s, Strachan had become discouraged with his group's inability to influence Congress further. The American Federation of Handicapped Persons ceased to exist.

By the 1940s, therefore, some people with various disabilities had formed a unifying oppositional consciousness. However, unlike the NFB, this cross-disability group failed to grow. In this period it seems to have been possible to mobilize a relatively small number of people who shared a specific type of disability and attended the same schools, but not to organize a large, diverse, and scattered population such as the "handicapped." What happened in the early 1970s? Among the conditions that made the broader movement possible was the emergence of what Snow and Benford (1992) call an "innovative master frame." In this case, the oppositional consciousness created by African Americans and brought to the public's attention during the Black civil rights movement of the 1950s and 1960s served as an innovative master frame for people with disabilities. It (1) reinforced their belief in the injustice of their position; (2) taught them effective strategies and tactics; and (3) demonstrated the power of collective action. A brief analysis of the lives of the founders of the Centers for Independent Living demonstrates this process.

Social scientists (Scotch 1984), journalists (Shapiro 1993), and disability rights activists (Levy 1988) credit Edward Roberts and Judy Heumann with developing CILS. The eldest of four sons of a White, working-class family living outside San Francisco, Ed Roberts contracted polio in 1953 at the age of fourteen. Needing an iron lung eighteen hours a day, Roberts spent the first twenty months of his illness in a county hospital. Returning home, he attended school via telephone from his iron lung. With his health improving, Roberts attended classes in a wheelchair during his senior year of high school, only to be told by the principal that he could not graduate because he failed to meet the driver's education and gym requirements. Roberts's mother fought that decision and Roberts received his diploma. After high school, Roberts attended a two-year community college, having friends and attendants lift him out of his wheelchair and carrying him to inaccessible classrooms. As a result of the urging of his academic advisor, Roberts applied to the University of California at Berkeley. Initially, California's Department of Rehabilitation refused to pay for his education and Berkeley was reluctant to admit him because of the accessibility problems posed by his iron lung and wheelchair. Failing to convince the Department of Rehabilitation to finance Roberts's university education, the community college's top school officials took Roberts's case to the local newspapers and forced the department to relent. Berkeley admitted Roberts when he agreed to live in the university's student infirmary.

These early experiences taught Roberts two important lessons. First, he concluded that society judges and treats individuals with disabilities unjustly by denying them equal opportunities. Second, he realized that to eliminate this injustice, individuals need to fight. Roberts learned that injustice could be fought successfully by taking a case to higher-ranking officials and by informing the media. These lessons began to develop in him an oppositional consciousness, even as his fight remained individual rather than collective. Not until he observed the 1960s protest actions of the anti–Vietnam War movement and the Free Speech Movement at Berkeley did Roberts learn the power and specific tactics of collective action. Armed with these lessons and those he learned as he worked on his master's degree and doctorate in political science, Roberts began to organize other students with disabilities. Together, these students established the first program for students with disabilities run by people with disabilities. In 1972, after expanding this program to nonstudents, Roberts and the others founded the first Center for Independent Living.

The collective actions of Roberts and the other Berkeley students with disabilities centered around demands for independence—that is, freedom to control their own lives, to live how and go where they wanted. For Roberts, the concerns of people with disabilities did not become an issue of civil rights until 1974, when he taught community organizing in an African American community outside the university. After this brief experience of direct exposure to the oppositional consciousness of African Americans, Roberts began consciously to use parallels from the African American struggle to explain the plight of people with disabilities in American society (Shapiro 1993, 54).

On the east coast, Judy Heumann was having a similar experience. Born in 1947, Judy Heumann contracted polio when she was eighteen months old. Her German-Jewish mother fought New York City's public school system for four years in order to shift Heumann's schooling from home instruction to a segregated public school for disabled children. Finishing elementary school, Heumann was told she would have to resume home instruction because wheelchairs were not allowed in the public high schools. Once again, her mother, along with other parents, fought back and in 1961 forced the school officials to accept high school students in wheelchairs.

Heumann's early experiences taught her, as they did Roberts, that people with disabilities were unjustly being subjected to discrimination and prejudicial treatment based solely on a physical trait. Like Roberts, Heumann also learned by watching her mother's actions that individuals needed to fight for their rights. Undoubtedly, Heumann's mother and the parents who joined her had been influenced by the actions of Black civil rights activists at that time. Yet Heumann herself did not become an activist until she attended Long Island University. Observing and participating in anti–Vietnam War protest activities on campus, she learned organizational skills and effective collective tactics, which she then used to mobilize students with disabilities to fight for increased wheelchair accessibility on campus. The second stage in the formation of her oppositional consciousness came when she began tutoring a group of African American children as part of her schooling. At this point she "made a connection between the injustices suffered by that minority group and those endured by the disabled. More and more she saw evidence that the disabled, like the Blacks, should not be passively accepting the whims perpetuated by society's institutions" (Bliss 1972, 6–7). In an almost exact parallel to Roberts's case, it was Heumann's interaction with African Americans that helped crystallize her oppositional consciousness. By 1970 she had started a cross-disability rights group, Disabled in Action (DIA), which two years later became one of the first disability rights groups to demonstrate in Washington, D.C. In 1973, Heumann moved to Berkeley to help Roberts build the disability movement.

African American oppositional consciousness provided the innovative master frame upon which disability consciousness grew. Having been exposed to the culture of the Black civil rights movements, Roberts and Heumann internalized and then extended this culture to reinterpret their lives as people with disabilities. This convergence of meaning was unplanned. Black civil rights activists did not deliberately attempt to change the beliefs of these individuals. Rather, experience with the Black civil rights movement encouraged the development of a disability consciousness among individuals with mobility impairments. Roberts, Heumann, and other early disability rights leaders then deliberately attempted to promote such a consciousness among other disabled people, often explicitly using lessons and symbols they had learned from the civil rights movement.

Consensus Mobilization and Action Mobilization in Disability Consciousness

Disability rights activists attempt to alter the beliefs of individuals with various disabilities primarily by frame extension (Snow et al. 1986), that is, by extending the oppositional consciousness of African Americans to cover the situation of people with disabilities. In this process, disability becomes framed as a civil rights issue. The life situation of people with disabilities, previously taken for granted, becomes intolerable and immoral, and their desires are transformed into legitimate demands. Disability rights activists explicitly invoke the memory of the Black civil rights struggle through their rhetoric, their choice of cultural expressions, and their forms of collective action. In so doing, the activists hope to inspire their constituents to act collectively and to justify their actions to society as a whole.

Frame extension is particularly effective in fostering disability consciousness among disabled individuals who already have formed another form of oppositional consciousness, such as a Hispanic, feminist, or race consciousness. White interviewees who describe themselves as having been "political . . . active in the antiwar movement and the feminist movement" report that their disability consciousness emerged relatively effortlessly once activists framed disability as a civil rights issue. Interviewees from other racial and ethnic groups recall having similar experiences. Upon being introduced to a civil rights frame for disability, these interviewees quickly saw the similarities between their experiences as disabled people and their experiences as members of other oppressed groups.

Frame extension is less effective in promoting a disability conscious-ness among two groups: (1) people who already have formed a specific disability consciousness, such as deaf consciousness or blind conscious-ness; and (2) disabled people who have never developed any form of oppositional consciousness. Individuals in the first group are unable to extend their specific injustice frame to the larger disability population because their collective identity centers on their experiences with a specific disability. Many such people do not see themselves as disabled, or disabled in the same way as people with other types of disabilities. They find it difficult to extend their more specific oppositional consciousness to a broader group. People who have never formed any kind of injustice frame to explain their situation have the opposite problem. They must reinterpret their experiences as unjust and subject to change through collective action. Both groups must experience some form of frame transformation (Snow et al. 1986).

Interacting at the Centers for Independent Living helps members of each of these groups experience frame transformation. Although they were attracted to CILS originally only because of the services offered, interviewees from Deaf and blind cultures recall meeting and talking to people with other disabilities for the first time at these centers. They began to see that people with various kinds of disabilities nevertheless shared similar experiences, feelings, and ideas. They began to create a collective identity. Discussions with disability rights activists at the CILS clarified and crystallized this new identity. Over time, these interviewees redefined themselves as members of the larger disability community and extended their disability-specific oppositional consciousness to a more inclusive general disability consciousness.

The process of frame transformation is even harder for individuals who have never formed any kind of oppositional consciousness. These interviewees describe themselves as initially having strong reservations about the ideology and actions of disability rights activists. They recall feeling that the activists were "strange and actually militant . . . too force-ful . . . [and] went for the throat." Although many of my respondents identified with other individuals with disabilities and acknowledged that this group had in general been treated unfairly, they did not define their own life situation as unjust due to external forces. Rather, they had been socialized to believe that their disability alone, rather than the lack of acceptance of that disability in the larger world, was responsible for their unfortunate life situation. With this background, they only gradually accepted what they originally saw as a radical ideology.

Disability rights activists often mobilize people who have never had an oppositional consciousness by offering at CILS various essential services (e.g., housing and attendant care referrals). Such services attract large numbers of people with disabilities and bring people with all types of disabilities together. Once at the CILS, individuals interact with disability activists in one-to-one conversations and group discussions, which over time encourage them to reinterpret their life situations. Daily experiences that they had always viewed as simply unfortunate they now see as unjust violations of their civil rights. And they begin to think of specific ways to confront these violations. In short, activists at the CILS use the "politicization of everyday life" (Taylor and Whittier 1992, 119) to transform the frames of individuals with disabilities.

Disability rights activists also promote frame transformation by organizing and encouraging participation in protest actions. As Klandermans (1992) points out, action mobilization not only brings a group's demands to the public's attention but also fosters oppositional consciousness in both protest participants and spectators. Participating in protest is a powerful tactic for raising the consciousness of all individuals, but seems to be particularly useful for people with no previous oppositional consciousness. Commenting on her experience in a recent demonstration, an interviewee who before her involvement in the disability rights movement had never participated in a political movement declared, "There is no better way to be connected . . . than to participate in a rally." Others like her agreed, asserting that they "got an incredible sense of grassroots empowerment" while protesting. Although these interviewees had formed a collective identity as "disabled" before participating in protest actions, it was during these actions that they first felt the power of "we."

Weaknesses of Mobilization Tactics

The first public expression of disability consciousness occurred in 1977, when individuals with various disabilities staged sit-ins in federal buildings across the nation. They were protesting the government's failure to implement a bill protecting people with disabilities against discrimination in federally funded programs and facilities (Johnson 1983; Scotch 1984). More recently, disability rights activists organized one of the largest gatherings of disabled people in history, the Wheels of Justice campaign. During the week of March 12, 1990, disabled people from all over the country came to Washington, D.C., to stage demonstrations and lobby for the passage of the Americans with Disability Act (ADA). Nearly a thousand individuals with various disabilities and their nondisabled supporters marched down Pennsylvania Avenue. On reaching the Capitol Building, disability rights activists and legislators gave speeches linking the passage of the ADA to the passage of the 1964 Civil Rights Act (Treanor 1993). Staged during a time when other interest groups were lobbying to weaken specific ADA regulations, these actions gave a major impetus to the bill's passage.

Although the Wheels of Justice protest demonstrates some of the possibilities for success in mobilizing for disability rights, it also demonstrates some of the tensions within the movement. Precisely because of their lack of segregation, the mobility impaired sometimes have the connections and "weak ties" (Granovetter 1973) that facilitate organizing in a social movement. Partly for these reasons, the Deaf and members of the National Federation of the Blind remain reluctant to join the disability rights movement. These groups sometimes see the disability rights movement as exclusive, marginalizing many members of the disability community, rather than being inclusive, as the original activists intended.

Just as Patricia Hill Collins (1991) and other African American feminists have felt marginalized in the women's movement, people of color in the disability community have had similar experiences. Few directors of CILS or other leaders of the disability rights movement are people of color. Issues pertinent to disabled individuals of color are seldom a priority. As a White interviewee reports, "The same racial biases that exist outside the movement exist inside the movement." These biases mean that although the disability rights frame resonates with their own belief systems, many disabled people of color are unwilling to become active members of the disability rights movement.

Finally, individuals forced to live in nursing homes also feel that the disability rights movement has marginalized them. They assert that most of the activists' goals, such as accessible transportation and equal employment opportunities, benefit them little. The first demand of individuals in nursing homes is to be able to live outside institutions. They believe that securing federal funding for home care assistance should be a major priority of the disability rights movement. Although the culture of disability consciousness may resonate with the values and beliefs of these individuals, much of its language and many of its goals do not. Like disabled people of color, these individuals are reluctant to develop a disability consciousness.

Recently, disability rights activists have begun reaching out to these specific groups. CILS are actively recruiting disabled people of color for staff positions. Other disability rights organizations are holding workshops on the diversity of people with disabilities, and ADAPT is demonstrating across the nation to secure federally funded home care programs. Despite these attempts, however, many disabled people still believe that the disability rights movement is fighting primarily for the rights of individuals with mobility impairments. Disability rights activists help perpetuate this conclusion through the cultural forms they choose to express and transmit disability consciousness. Most of these cultural expressions rely on wheelchair images, words, and themes: the Statue of Liberty seated in a wheelchair, the stars on the American flag rearranged in the shape of a wheelchair, a raised fist replacing the spokes of a wheelchair, and a protest action called Wheels of Justice. Such cultural expressions act to distance disabled people who do not use wheelchairs. A blind interviewee, for example, explains that these symbols create, "a problem for the blind. . . . We want to make sure that disability is not just seen as a wheelchair."

Conclusion

This chapter has explored the formation of cultures of oppositional consciousness among people with disabilities. Lacking the necessary structural and cultural conditions, individuals with disabilities did not form a broad-based oppositional consciousness until the early 1970s. Up until this time, subgroups in the disability population constructed their own distinct versions of oppositional consciousness. Of the three forms of oppositional consciousness analyzed here, deaf consciousness was the most widely accepted and developed and mobility-impaired consciousness the least accepted and developed.

The variance in the extent and maturity of the forms of oppositional consciousness that people with disabilities have formed derives primarily from their differential ability to create free spaces, or spaces of autonomous action. That ability in turn derives in great part from the degree of a group's physical segregation. The more physically segregated a group has been, the more likely it is to have created free spaces in which its members could develop an oppositional consciousness.

Traditionally segregated in residential schools, the Deaf have been most able to create spaces in which, interacting, they could create a deaf culture and consciousness. From these roots, deaf consciousness has endured and grown despite hearing people gaining control of their schools. In greatest contrast, individuals with mobility impairments have never been segregated in residential schools. Typically segregated for six hours a day in separate classes within public school systems, mobility-impaired children have returned each night to predominantly nondisabled families. They develop many ties that they can later use for organizing, but have little chance to interact autonomously in spaces where they could form an oppositional culture. Although individuals with mobility impairments have often constructed strong collective identities, their injustice frames have been weak.

Blind consciousness falls in the middle of the continuum. Like deaf consciousness, blind consciousness has a distinct collective identity, a mature injustice frame, and a full repertoire of collective actions. Yet blind individuals have formed an oppositional consciousness much less often than the Deaf. The early residential schools for the blind allowed their members to develop some degree of oppositional culture, but the relatively quick integration of the blind students into public day schools inhibited the growth and spread of this culture in the blind community.

Although the degree of physical segregation plays a crucial role in the creation of free spaces, equally important is the *nature* of the segregating institutions. Segregating institutions that are controlled by nonmembers and allow little unsupervised time or space facilitate the formation of a collective identity while dampening the development of an oppositional consciousness.

Many of the early residential schools for the deaf were founded and run by Deaf individuals. Although the Deaf ultimately lost control of these institutions, these schools laid the foundation on which the Deaf have since built a complex system of institutions supporting and transmitting their oppositional consciousness. In contrast, the sighted established and ran the early residential schools for the blind, and the mobility abled established and ran the day schools for the mobility impaired. Under these conditions, many blind and mobility-impaired children internalized the subordinate positions of their groups, avoiding and refusing to associate with other disabled people. Although the resulting disability groups have established various institutions, only a handful of these institutions support and transmit an oppositional consciousness.

When the degree and nature of group segregation allows for little development of free spaces, another path to the creation of oppositional consciousness results from adopting an external master frame. This was the path followed by people with mobility impairments. Once exposed to the oppositional frame created by African Americans, mobility-impaired individuals extended it to their own struggle. In the process, they created a new oppositional consciousness based on the life experiences of people with all types of disabilities. Activists with this consciousness then deliberately spread it to others by creating new free spaces (the CILS) where frame extension and frame transformation could occur.

Today, as a result of the work of disability rights activist, the number of free spaces available to people with all types of disabilities has grown. New cross-disability organizations such as the American Association of People with Disabilities (AAPD), Justice for All (JFA), and the Consortium for Citizens with Disabilities (CCD) have been established to defend and advance broad disability rights. These organizations help organize massive protest activities, sponsor national meetings for disability rights leaders, and support e-mail networks, all of which promote disability consciousness among people with various disabilities. Free spaces that had earlier been established to protect the rights of people with only one type of disability are beginning to include people with other disabilities. For example, organizers of the 1995 Alternatives Conference, traditionally a conference where only people with psychiatric disabilities would gather, scheduled several cross-disability sessions and invited a prominent disability rights activist who uses a wheelchair to speak at their luncheon. By opening previously exclusive spaces and by creating new spaces that include all people with disabilities, disability rights activists are succeeding in transmitting and maintaining an oppositional culture based on the larger experience of being disabled in America.

Notes

I would like to thank Jane Mansbridge and Aldon Morris for their insightful comments and suggestions on earlier drafts of this chapter. I am especially indebted to the individuals with disabilities who allowed me to interview them and to join in their protest activities.

1. Other analysts have called these arenas "segregated spaces" (Morris and Braine, chap. 2, this volume), "sequestered social sites" (Scott 1990), "a world apart" (Taylor and Whittier 1992), "subaltern counterpublics" (Fraser 1992), or "enclaves" (Mansbridge 1994).

2. This figure is based on limitations of functional activities. When other measures of disability are included—such as limitations in activities of daily living (e.g., dressing, eating, toileting), limitations in instrumental activities of daily living (e.g., keeping track of money, getting around outside the house, preparing meals), the presence of impairments (e.g., learning disabilities, mental retardation, mental/emotional conditions), and the use of wheelchairs and other aids—the figure rises to 48.9 million (McNeil 1993).

In this chapter I focus on groups with physical disabilities. However, people with psychiatric and intellectual disabilities also have created oppositional cultures. See Chamberlin 1990 and Dain 1989 for historical overviews and Emerick 1995, 1989, for a descriptive analysis of the psychiatric survivors liberation movement. For overviews of the self-advocacy movement created by people with intellectual disabilities, see Williams and Shoultz 1982, Edwards 1982, and Dybwad and Bersani 1996.

3. Young (1990, 47–63) suggests that whether or not a group is oppressed "depends on whether it is subject to one or more of the [following] five conditions": exploitation, marginalization, powerlessness, cultural imperialism, and violence. In Groch 1998 I argue

that disabled people as a group are particularly vulnerable to each of these conditions. When members of these groups consider themselves oppressed, they point specifically to the elements of injustice in their treatment.

4. Activists and scholars alike debate whether gays and lesbians are "born" with their sexual orientation or "learn" this orientation. See Taylor and Whittier 1992, 114–17, for a clear summary of this debate. In either case, gay and lesbian individuals seldom have been raised by a homosexual parent. In this sense, gays and lesbians are more likely to resemble most disabled people, who are the only person with a disability (either acquired or congenital) in their family, than to resemble members of most other oppressed groups.

5. Scotch (1988, 162) seems to have been the first to use the term "disability consciousness." Although Scotch does not specifically identify disability consciousness as a form of oppositional consciousness, he does use the term to represent the willingness of individuals with disabilities to identify themselves as disabled and to act collectively on their own behalf.

6. I purposely selected the four interviewees to represent the populations I studied— a Hispanic man who uses a wheelchair, an African American woman with a hearing impairment, a White man who is Deaf, and a White woman who is blind (the manuscript was printed in braille for her review).

7. While women have been members of NAD since its beginning in 1880, African Americans were not allowed to become members until 1949 (Buchanan 1993, 197). Another of the earliest Deaf organizations, the National Fraternal Society of the Deaf (founded in 1901) excluded women until 1951 and African Americans until 1967 (National Fraternal Society of the Deaf n.d.).

8. The two largest groups are the Association of Late-Deafened Adults (ALDA) and Self Help for Hard of Hearing People (SHHH). The president of a local ALDA chapter recently called for members to identify themselves as "a group separate from the Deaf culture" (Hering 1996, 1).

9. My reanalysis of the International Center on Disabilities (ICD) Survey of Americans with Disabilities (1986) reveals that when respondents were asked if they identified themselves as disabled or not, 54 percent of the 349 mobility-impaired respondents said yes, compared to 34 percent of the 61 blind/visually impaired respondents and 23 percent of the 60 deaf/hearing-impaired respondents ($p < .001$). The disability variables derived from answers to the survey question, "What is the medical diagnosis or description for your disability or health condition?" In the data set provided, these were grouped into eighteen values, including "Deafness/Hearing," which I report as "deaf/hearing-impaired," "Blind/Visual," which I report as "blind/visually-impaired," and "Nonparalytic Ortho" and "Neuromotor/Neuromuscular," which I collapsed and report as "mobility-impaired." The self-identification question reads: "Do you consider yourself a disabled or handicapped person, or not?"

5　A Spectrum in Oppositional Consciousness: Sexual Harassment Plaintiffs and Their Lawyers

Anna-Maria Marshall

Claiming Their Rights

The development of the legal claim for sexual harassment poses a puzzle for social movement theory. Sexual harassment has been a central issue in the United States women's movement for more than two decades. Women's organizations have conducted public education campaigns to raise consciousness about the prevalence of unwanted sexual attention in the workplace and have lobbied employers to adopt policies designed to prevent sexual harassment. Part of this public education campaign has involved informing women of their legal right to be free of harassment. Yet this legal right—the cornerstone of official policy against sexual harassment—is not primarily the product of concerted social movement activity. Instead, the right was established through hundreds of lawsuits brought by individual women against their employers.

The first sexual harassment plaintiffs were not activists in the women's movement, nor were they even self-identified feminists. Instead, they were working women, struggling for economic independence, whose efforts were thwarted by the supervisors and coworkers who placed sexual demands on them as a condition of keeping their jobs. Without calling themselves members of the women's movement, they were on-the-ground feminists: having suffered extreme injustice because they were women, they blamed their harassers and not themselves, and they challenged their harassers in a public forum. In their lawsuits, they were primarily trying to vindicate their own interests. Sometimes, however, those cases set judicial precedents that helped other women.

A few of these early plaintiffs were represented in court by feminist litigators who won crucial victories in appellate courts. The precedents from these victories created future legal liabilities for employers who knew about sexual harassment in their workplaces and did not take steps to prevent it. The fear of legal liability, in turn, induced many employers to adopt sexual harassment policies. Feminist legal organizations also submitted briefs in support of plaintiffs in many landmark cases. But these organizations did not "sponsor" sexual harassment litigation in the way that the NAACP coordinated the effort to dismantle segregation in education or restrictive covenants (Vose 1955; Kluger 1975). Lawyers with varying levels of commitment to the principles of women's rights and feminism also contributed to the effort. Some of these lawyers were simply trying to win the case for the client and had little interest in the broader implications of the legal theory, much less in dismantling the system of domination that made women subject to sexual exploitation in the workplace.

This chapter will use the early history of sexual harassment law, with its array of actors and motivations, to investigate the way a spectrum in oppositional consciousness can influence a social movement. It will describe two ways in which oppositional consciousness may be "borrowed" by others.

First, this analysis will show how the women's movement "borrowed" the legal tools of antidiscrimination laws developed in response to the civil rights movement to challenge the subordination of women at work. Legal categories are one way that a movement's oppositional frames can eventually translate into public policies. The early decisions on sexual harassment reflect a larger societal debate over the interpretation of sex at work: in the course of these decisions, the dominant view that sexual harassment was a personal problem eventually gave way to the oppositional interpretation that the practice of sexual harassment was a systematic source of discrimination against women. The analysis of sexual harassment as discrimination was thus inspired by the civil rights movement and the conceptual apparatus and concrete legislative enactments developed to challenge race discrimination.

Second, the variety of actors who participated in this legal development reveals the permeability of the boundaries of a social movement. The oppositional consciousness generated by a social movement can never be the exclusive property of that movement. Members of other movements and even sympathetic bystanders may "borrow" the ideas of the movement that circulate widely. A movement's frames may reach individuals and even change their life choices, even if those individuals are not willing to identify with the movement or participate in collective action. A movement may be successful in major ways if its oppositional frames help ordinary individuals to reinterpret their experience and to act on those reinterpretations.

Analyzing some of the earliest sexual harassment cases in the United States, this chapter asks what motivated the plaintiffs and the lawyers who brought the cases. Among the lawyers, it portrays a spectrum in oppositional consciousness, running from the committed movement activist to the lawyer primarily trying to make a living. Among the plaintiffs, it depicts a similar spectrum, moving from women with heightened race and gender consciousness but little interest in collective action to women who are actually antifeminist. This chapter shows that while the activist attorneys were moved by a mature feminist oppositional consciousness, even the most skeptical attorneys and plaintiffs were influenced to some degree by oppositional frames of justice and equality for women. The analysis explores what I call the "borrowed oppositional consciousness" of the less committed. It will show that the ideas of the feminist movement stretched into the lives of nonactivists in part through the law and legal institutions available to them, which they in turn shaped through their own actions.

Methodology

This chapter is based on interviews with attorneys and plaintiffs in key cases that led to the development of sexual harassment law. These cases fall into two general categories—quid pro quo harassment and hostile working environment. I consulted Lindemann and Kadue's hornbook on sexual harassment, *Sexual Harassment in Employment Law* (1992), which includes a comprehensive discussion of the early development of the sexual harassment claim. I also consulted the Federal Digest and the digest to the Federal Employment Practices reporter. This research generated a list of fourteen quid pro quo cases[1] from twelve different states and the District of Columbia and twelve precedent-setting cases in the area of hostile working environment. These cases established critical rulings relied on extensively by other courts, particularly on the issues of the "reasonable woman" standard and the necessity of establishing psychological harm. Finally, one case filed in the late 1970s, *Henson v. Dundee Police Department* (1982), contained allegations of both forms of sexual harassment. In addition to the cases described above, I also included three significant cases that did not fit neatly into the quid pro quo or hostile working environment categories of employment discrimination, for a total of thirty cases.[2] The entire list of crucial cases in the area of sexual harassment is provided in the appendix to this chapter.

After compiling this list, I attempted to contact the attorneys of record in each of the cases. I used Martindale-Hubbell's directory of attorneys, as well as phone directories on CD-ROM and microfiche. I was able to locate twenty-two of the fifty-two attorneys of record. I was able to arrange interviews with nineteen attorneys in seventeen different cases. Because the attorneys came from a number of different states, I conducted the interviews over the telephone. The interviews lasted from forty-five minutes to one and one-half hours. With one exception, I tape recorded and transcribed the interviews.[3] The names of the cases whose attorneys I interviewed are marked with an asterisk at their first mention in the account that follows and in the appendix.

I also attempted to contact the plaintiffs in the cases by asking the attorneys I interviewed whether they were still in contact with the plaintiffs. Unfortunately, most of the attorneys had lost track of their clients. I then tried to find all the plaintiffs using other sources, including telephone books and telephone listings available on CD-ROM and the Internet, but because many of the plaintiffs had changed their names or moved, I was unable to contact them. I did locate and interview four plaintiffs. Diane Williams, Sandra Bundy, and Deborah Katz were all victorious plaintiffs whose cases established crucial precedents in the areas of quid pro quo harassment and hostile working environment. I also interviewed Roxanne Smith, whose sexual harassment claims were dismissed in 1978 for failing to state a claim. These interviews were also conducted over the phone and lasted from one and one-half hours to three hours. These interviews were also taped and transcribed.

I used semistructured interview schedules for the attorneys and plaintiffs, following up with additional questions where necessary. I also encouraged the subjects to discuss any issues they thought were important. I asked the attorneys about the conduct of the litigation, their views on the practice of law, their political views, their educational and class background, as well as about their clients in the sexual harassment cases. Thus, the attorneys were able to act as informants about the plaintiffs' educational and class background, about the plaintiffs' reactions to the litigation, and about the plaintiffs' views about politics and the legal system in general. When I could find them, I asked the plaintiffs about the events giving rise to the litigation, about their social networks, their political views, and their educational and class backgrounds.

There are several limitations associated with these data. First, my reliance on published opinions creates a bias because the many cases that terminated without a published opinion are not represented (Siegelman and Donohue 1990). I miss the many cases that ended without a published opinion, or, more likely, never got to the courthouse at all. In addition, the focus on precedent-setting cases generates a very small sample. Yet these published opinions set the precedents used by attorneys in future cases, and their small number allows me to study their cases in detail. Nor do I make causal inferences in this account. The point of this chapter is instead to illustrate the permeability of a movement's boundaries, as it gives rise to a spectrum in oppositional consciousness among two critical sets of actors: the plaintiffs whose sense of injustice leads them to want to bring a suit, and the lawyers who craft the language that will eventually influence policy.

Oppositional Consciousness into Legal Claims

The United States women's movement of the 1960s and 1970s had deep roots in the civil rights movement. Through their involvement in the civil rights movement, female activists acquired "a language to name and describe oppression; a deep belief in freedom, equality, and community— soon to be translated into 'sisterhood'; a willingness to question and challenge any social institution that failed to meet human needs; and the ability to organize" (Evans 1980, 100). Using these tools, feminists began to analyze the sources of women's social, political, and economic inequality. As part of this endeavor, feminists studied many institutions, including family, religion, education, law, and the workplace, identifying both blatant and subtle practices that produced inequality.

Some of the major policy achievements of the civil rights movement, like antidiscrimination laws, also benefited large numbers of women. At the last minute, sex was added to Title VII of the Civil Rights Act of 1964, causing much joking in Congress and the near-failure of the act. Although some feminists, notably the National Women's Party, had been lobbying since suffrage for greater equality for women, "the civil rights movement, and the various civil rights bills, opened up a window of opportunity of which the activists took advantage" (Freeman 1991, 184). Aimed at the social experience of African Americans, the antidiscrimination laws resulting from the Civil Rights Act were flexible enough to cover the experience of other marginalized groups (MacKinnon 1979, 127–29).[4]

For example, the employment discrimination laws derived from Title VII responded to the feminist critique of sex in the workplace. In the feminist formulation, men occupy most of the high positions in corporate hierarchies, giving them economic power in the workplace.[5] This power enables them to set rules and standards for appropriate behavior at work. For women, these standards are often sexualized, requiring women to adopt "an ingratiating, flattering, and deferential manner which projects potential sexual compliance" (MacKinnon 1979, 22). These sexualized standards of behavior are working conditions imposed on women and not on men. This conceptualization emphasizing inequality in social conditions brings the problem within the ambit of the antidiscrimination laws.

Once sex at work was identified as a source of discrimination rather than a personal problem, the women's movement challenged it with a variety of strategies, including public education and lobbying employers to adopt policies against sexual harassment (Weeks et al. 1986). This chapter documents, however, that the main source of official policy was the legal system, deriving ultimately from individual complaints of sexual harassment. Only later did legislatures and regulatory agencies pick up the issue and use the language previously crafted in the courts to produce legislation specifically targeting sexual harassment. Contrary to some claims of judicial inability to lead in creating policies reflecting social change (Rosenberg 1991), this was one case in which the legal system moved first. It could not have so moved without the initiative of the individual women whose legal claims were based on laws shaped by the civil rights movement and adapted by the women's movement. These women, in turn, shaped those laws and influenced the agenda of the women's movement.

The Early Cases: Quid Pro Quo Sexual Harassment

In 1972, Paulette Barnes began working as an administrative assistant in the equal opportunity division of the Environmental Protection Agency (EPA). Soon after she took the job, the supervisor who hired her made sexual overtures and promised her job benefits if she complied with his request. After she repeatedly refused his advances and offers, he belittled her, took away job responsibilities, and finally abolished her job. When she went to file a complaint against this supervisor, EPA officials told her to file a race discrimination complaint, even though both she and her supervisor were Black. After a lengthy hearing process, an administrative law judge rejected her race discrimination claim.[6] When she sought a new trial from the district court on the new grounds of sex discrimination, the court in *Barnes v. Train** rejected her appeal, stating:

> The substance of plaintiff's complaint is that she was discriminated against, not because she was a woman, but because she refused to engage in a sexual affair with her supervisor. This is a controversy underpinned by the subtleties of an inharmonious personal relationship. Regardless of how inexcusable the conduct of plaintiff's supervisor might have been, it does not evidence an arbitrary barrier to continued employment based on plaintiff's sex. (*Barnes v. Train* 1974)

Barnes's case was the first, but certainly not the last, time that a federal district court would reject a woman's claim of sexual harassment against her supervisor. In *Corne v. Bausch & Lomb** (1975) brought one year later, Jane Corne and Geneva DeVane reported that their supervisor had given preferential treatment to women who gave in to his physical and verbal advances. His behavior became so intolerable that they were forced to quit. The trial court also rejected their claim for sex discrimination, observing that their supervisor's behavior was no more than a "personal proclivity" and did not advance a company policy. Employers could be liable only for their discriminatory *official* policies. The court also fretted about the potential flood of litigation that might be caused by allowing this type of claim:

> An outgrowth of holding such activity to be actionable under Title VII would be a potential federal lawsuit every time any employee made amorous or sexually oriented advances toward another. The only sure way an employer could avoid such charges would be to have employees who were asexual. (*Corne v. Bausch & Lomb* 1975)

Two other trial courts soon dismissed women's claims for sexual harassment in decisions that would later be appealed. In *Miller v. Bank of America** (1976), Margaret Miller's supervisor wondered what it would be like to have sex with a "Black chick" and fired her when she refused his advances. The court emphasized the company's policy of discouraging sexual relations between employees, but also relied on biological explanations for the behavior at stake: "The attraction of males to females and females to males is a natural sex phenomenon, and it is probable that this attraction plays at least a subtle part in most personnel decisions." The court concluded that it would be best to protect this "subtle" process from judicial consideration.

Finally, in *Tomkins v. PSE&G** (1976), Adrienne Tomkins was a secretary for PSE&G when her boss took her out to lunch. During the meal, he told her that if she wanted to keep her job, she would have to have sex with him. When she tried to leave, he physically restrained her and threatened to fire her. When she complained about the incident, she was transferred to a series of worse positions and was finally fired. The court rejected the plaintiff's claim for sexual harassment, again citing the inevitability of sexual attraction among men and women at work:

> If the plaintiff's view were to prevail, no superior could, prudently, attempt to open a social dialogue with any subordinate of either sex. An invitation to dinner could become an invitation to a federal lawsuit if a once harmonious relationship turned sour at some later time. And if an inebriated approach by a supervisor to a subordinate at the office Christmas party could form the basis of a federal lawsuit for sex discrimination if a promotion or a raise is later denied to the subordinate, we would need 4,000 federal trial judges instead of some 400.[7]

These first judicial opinions framed sexual harassment as a personal problem between men and women, emerging from biological urges, rather than as a social problem between employers and employees based on unequal economic power. The judges regarded the supervisors' conduct as reflecting personal idiosyncrasies, certainly crude but not discriminatory because no official policies were at stake. The judges also attributed sex at work to the "natural" attraction of the opposite sexes. Finally, the judges were unwilling to commit judicial resources to resolving "personal" problems between supervisors and employees (MacKinnon 1979, 83–99).

Judicial hostility to sexual harassment claims finally ended in 1976 in the case of *Williams v. Saxbe*.* As in the other cases, Williams's supervisor at the Department of Justice (DOJ) had repeatedly asked her out and had left her notes and cards professing his attraction to her. When she declined his advances, he began giving her negative evaluations and finally fired her in 1972. As a federal employee, she filed an internal complaint in the DOJ. After the case had spent years in the administrative process, the administrative law judge decided against her. In overruling that decision, the district court held that "the conduct of the plaintiff's supervisor created an artificial barrier to employment, which was placed before one gender and not the other" (*Williams v. Saxbe* 1976, 657). Instead of assuming that the supervisor's conduct was "an isolated personal incident," the district court gave Williams and her lawyer the opportunity to prove that the conduct was an impermissible condition of employment (*Williams v. Saxbe* 1976, 660–61).

But district court cases do not bind other courts. For a case to set a binding precedent, it must be issued by an appellate court. In 1977, three appellate courts, the Third, Fourth, and D.C. Circuits, recognized a cause of action for sexual harassment as sex discrimination. In all these cases, *Garber v. Saxon Business Products* (1977), *Barnes v. Train* (1977), and *Tomkins v. PSE&G* (1977), federal circuit courts of appeal reversed the district courts and held that employees who had been fired for refusing their supervisors' advances could sue their employers for employment discrimination under Title VII. The judges in these cases reasoned that such sexual demands were a condition of employment imposed on women but not on men and therefore constituted sex discrimination. The appellate courts were careful, however, to limit their holdings to situations where the supervisor explicitly made a promotion, salary, or the job itself contingent on sexual favors. They reserved judgment on whether employers had to provide a working environment free of sexual conduct or conversation when such conduct was not tied to compliance with sexual demands (*Tomkins v. PSE&G* 1977, 1046).[8]

Appellate decisions are binding only in their own circuits, although their holdings may influence courts in other jurisdictions. When the Third, Fourth, and D.C. Circuits recognized the cause of action for sexual harassment in 1977, courts in other parts of the country took notice. For example, in the next case to be decided, *Munford v. James T. Barnes & Co.** (1977), the trial court relied on the D.C. Circuit's reasoning in *Barnes* to recognize Munford's claim of employment discrimination, even though the court sat in Detroit and was not bound by the *Barnes* decision. Similarly, the trial court in *Heelan v. Johns-Manville** (1978) surveyed the growing body of sexual harassment law before recognizing Heelan's claim for employment discrimination.[9] Both Munford and Heelan had lost their jobs, hired their attorneys, and filed their lawsuits before these favorable precedents appeared.

The Hostile Working Environment

By 1978, the cause of action for quid pro quo harassment seemed well established in most of the federal trial and appellate courts. However, by now women were filing lawsuits with more expansive claims. They complained of being exposed to sexual jokes, as well as to sexual threats and demands that did not have negative job consequences when they refused compliance. Nevertheless, they argued, the working environment imposed a substantial burden on their ability to perform their jobs. For example, in 1977, Roxanne Smith filed a complaint for sex discrimination against her employer. In one of the counts of the complaint, she told the court that she had been "subjected to sexual advances and remarks" but conceded that her rejection of these demands did not affect her job (*Smith v. Rust Engineering** 1978). The court dismissed this count of the complaint.[10]

Although courts were reluctant to recognize this form of sexual harassment, the federal Equal Employment Opportunity Commission, an office of the executive branch, had been following the legal issue closely and had adopted regulations matching the growing body of case law. In November 1980, it issued regulations including conduct such as jokes, threats, and demands in its definition of sexual harassment. According to the EEOC, sexual harassment would include "such conduct [that] has the purpose or effect of unreasonably interfering with an individual's work performance or creating an intimidating, hostile or offensive work environment" (29 C.F.R. 1604.11). Although courts give great deference to the regulations issued by administrative agencies, regulations are merely advisory and do not have the force of law until adopted by a court (*Meritor Savings Bank v. Vinson** 1986). Not until 1981 would a case based on such facts win judicial recognition. In *Bundy v. Jackson** (1981), Sandra Bundy described sexual advances made daily by her supervisors and coworkers. For over three years, they constantly asked her out to lunch, invited her to go on vacations, made sexual jokes, and even physically molested her by pinching or caressing her. Once, when she complained about all this to a supervisor, he told her he would investigate but then justified his coworkers' actions by observing: "Any man in his right mind would want to rape you." Although the D.C. Circuit found that Bundy did not suffer any adverse job consequences as a result of her refusal of these offers, the court still held that the hostile working environment itself was sex discrimination. It thus became the first court to recognize a hostile working environment claim for sexual harassment. Shortly thereafter, the Fourth Circuit acknowledged a claim with similar facts but no physical acts of harassment, thus acknowledging that a hostile working environment could consist of verbal harassment alone (*Katz v. Dole** 1983).

It was not until 1986, when sexual harassment cases had been in the federal courts for almost fifteen years, that the Supreme Court issued a decision that put to rest any question that sexual harassment—in quid pro quo or hostile working environment situations—constituted sex discrimination in employment. In *Meritor Savings Bank v. Vinson* (1986), the Court recognized a claim for hostile working environment, but placed restrictions on that claim. The plaintiff, it declared, must show that the conduct was unwelcome, which allows the trial to address issues such as the plaintiff's dress and manners. This inquiry can deflect attention away from the harasser's behavior (MacKinnon 1987; Pollack 1990). However, in 1993, the Supreme Court held that a plaintiff does not have to demonstrate that she experienced psychological distress to state a claim for sexual harassment (*Harris v. Forklift Systems** 1993).

During its 1997–98 term, the Supreme Court answered several outstanding questions about what kinds of conduct constitute sexual harassment and about when employers can be held liable for such behavior. Early in the legal history of sexual harassment, perplexed courts pondered how the legal framework would deal with the case of a bisexual supervisor who harasses an employee of the same gender. For example, the trial court in *Corne* observed: "It would be ludicrous to hold that the sort of activity involved here was contemplated by the Act because to do so would mean that if the conduct complained of was directed equally to males there would be no basis for suit" (*Corne v. Bausch & Lomb* 1975, 163). The Supreme Court resolved this question by holding that same-sex sexual harassment violated Title VII as long as the plaintiff could prove the statutory requirements: that the harassment was severe and pervasive and that it was discriminatory (*Oncale v. Sundowner Offshore Services* 1998). The Court observed:

> In same-sex (as in all) harassment cases, the inquiry requires careful consideration of the social context in which particular behavior occurs and is experienced by its target. . . . Common sense, and appropriate sensitivity to social context, will enable courts and juries to distinguish between simple teasing or roughhousing among members of the same sex, and conduct which a reasonable person in the plaintiff's position would find severely hostile or abusive. (*Oncale v. Sundowner Offshore Services* 1998, 82)

The Court also clarified the rules on an employer's liability for the sexually harassing behavior of its supervisors and employees. Although the Court stated in *Meritor* that "agency principles" should govern this determination, lower courts struggled with applying these principles, particularly in the context of hostile working environments. When a supervisor engages in sexual taunting or threats but never takes any action against the target, the employer itself derives no benefit from this conduct, making courts unwilling to hold the employer liable for the supervisor's actions. Similarly, courts were unwilling to impose liability on employers that were not aware of sexual harassment by their supervisors and employees.

The Supreme Court used two 1998 cases to clarify these questions. The Court held that an employer is liable for a hostile working environment created by its supervisors, whether or not the plaintiff has suffered a direct, negative job consequence. When the plaintiff does not suffer direct consequences—that is, when the employee is not fired or denied a promotion or raise as a result of her refusal to engage in sexual activities—the employer may avoid liability by showing first that it "exercised reasonable care to prevent and correct promptly any sexually harassing behavior" (*Burlington Industries v. Ellerth* 1998) and second that "the plaintiff employee unreasonably failed to take advantage of any preventive or corrective opportunities provided by the employer or to avoid harm otherwise" (*Faragher v. City of Boca Raton* 1998).

In *Burlington Industries v. Ellerth* (1998), a supervisor propositioned Kimberly Ellerth and implied that he would fire her if she was not sexually cooperative, but he never fulfilled his threats before she quit the job. Under previous law, these facts would not have constituted quid pro quo harassment and thus the employer would not have been held liable. The Court remanded the case for further proceedings to determine whether Burlington had a reasonable complaint mechanism in place and whether Ellerth made reasonable efforts to resolve her problem on her own. In *Faragher v. City of Boca Raton* (1998), Faragher was a lifeguard working at a beach that was physically remote from the city's offices. Although the city had a sexual harassment policy, neither the lifeguards nor their supervisors were aware of it. The Court held that the city was liable because it failed to take reasonable measures to prevent sexual harassment among the lifeguards:

> Unlike an employer of a small work force, who might expect that sufficient care to prevent tortious behavior could be exercised informally, those responsible for city operations could not reasonably have thought that precautions against hostile environments in any one of many departments in far-flung locations could be effective without communicating some formal policy against harassment, with a sensible complaint procedure. (*Faragher v. City of Boca Raton* 1998, 808–9)

In spite of the Supreme Court's recent activity, it left some unanswered questions in the application of sexual harassment law. For example, one unresolved issue is the standard for evaluating whether or not a working environment "unreasonably interferes" with a woman's job performance. Should the courts view the environment through the eyes of a reasonable person, a reasonable woman, a reasonable victim, or someone else (Bernstein 1997)?[11] Most circuits follow the traditional "reasonable person" standard. The most famous—and most criticized—articulation of this standard came in *Rabidue v. Osceola Refining** (1986). Vivienne Rabidue was the only female manager in the company, and one of her coworkers routinely treated her with contempt, using vulgar language to address her. In addition, men posted in their offices pictures and calendars of naked women in demeaning positions. The trial and appellate courts denied that this conduct constituted sexual harassment. Citing the prevalence of near-naked women in magazines and television, the court observed that Rabidue could not have been offended by her coworkers' behavior. The court stated: "The sexually oriented poster displays had a de minimis effect on the plaintiff's work environment when considered in the context of a society that condones and publicly features and commercially exploits open displays of written and pictorial erotica at the newsstands, on prime-time television, at the cinema, and in other public places" (*Rabidue* 1986, 622).

However, several courts since *Rabidue* have adopted the differing "reasonable woman" standard. In the leading case in this area, *Ellison v. Brady* (1991), a woman received notes from a coworker, asking her out on dates and expressing his hope for a physical relationship with her. Ellison was "shocked" and "frightened" by his notes. In considering whether her harasser's conduct was sufficiently severe, the Ninth Circuit adopted what is called a "reasonable woman" standard, which attempted to account for the different reactions of men and women to sexual attention.[12] In another case, a female welder working in a shipyard was confronted with pornographic pictures, sexual jokes, and threats every day. The trial court's opinion, documenting every picture, poster, and comment, went on for pages. Admitting that men might not be offended by this environment, the court found that "a reasonable woman would find that the working environment was abusive" (*Robinson v. Jacksonville Shipyards* 1991).

Other Possible Legal Remedies

Sex discrimination was not the inevitable avenue for sexual harassment claims. Several cases brought during the same time reveal other possible grounds of legal relief that were possible. In 1972, Cleo Kyriazi filed a class action sex discrimination case against her employer, Western Electric Company. Although that claim was based on the way that the employer treated all women, she included specific facts about the way she was treated. In addition to her problems with lower salaries and worse job assignments, she endured physical and verbal harassment from her coworkers. Her lawyer included a tort claim for "tortious interference with work," which the court recognized in the case *Kyriazi v. Western Electric Co.* (1978). Similarly, Norma Rogers's attorney could not get the EEOC to proceed through its administrative process, which foreclosed a sex discrimination complaint. Instead, he drafted a complaint based on the tort of intentional infliction of emotional distress (*Rogers v. Loews L'Enfant Plaza** 1981).

Tort claims are designed to remedy private harms. In contrast, based on Title VII, the law of sexual harassment acknowledges that unwanted sexual attention at work is a social problem, affecting thousands of women (MacKinnon 1979). The women's movement generated this broader oppositional analysis, giving women new ways to frame their experiences with sex at work. The analysis drew on previously articulated concepts of rights and equality, potent ideological weapons in many social movement struggles, particularly the civil rights movement. These concepts, and their instantiation in antidiscrimination laws, resonate with many different people, from movement activists to sympathetic bystanders.

The Fluid Boundaries of a Social Movement

The active members of all social movements try in various ways to establish a sense of group identification among the movement's members. Taylor and Whittier argue that one strategy for creating the needed sense of "we" is to erect boundaries, to "promote a heightened awareness of a group's commonalities and frame interaction between members of the in-group and out-group" (Taylor and Whittier 1992, 111). Within these boundaries, movements struggle to transform group identification into group consciousness. "Consciousness" here is the set of interpretive frameworks that allow members to reinterpret everyday experience as being unjust and to attribute the blame for that injustice to external causes rather than personal failing (Taylor and Whittier 1992, 114). Movement actors also try to mobilize others to devote time and energy to work within the movement's boundaries, advancing its goals. To carry out such work, they develop institutions and networks that offer movement members resources, strategies, and moral support (Taylor and Whittier 1992).

Even though a movement's activists create and circulate oppositional consciousness primarily among other activists, the boundaries of a social movement are also permeable, subject to influences both inside and outside the movement (Whittier 1995). For example, movements take anticipated opposition into consideration in formulating their demands, or they may borrow oppositional frames that have been successful in other movements. Thus, actors and institutions outside the boundaries of the movement influence its work. Defining who is "inside" or "outside" derives from an actor's interactions with the movement. If the actors' work is politically motivated, and if they draw on movement networks and institutions for financial or strategic support, they are for present analytic purposes "inside" the movement. But individual actors that by this definition fall "outside" the movement may also have adopted, sometimes quite deeply, the movement's interpretive frameworks.

Oppositional consciousness is thus not a dichotomous variable, a thing people either have or do not have. Rather, oppositional consciousness with several different dimensions is usually arrayed across a spectrum. In the most simplified version of this spectrum, at one end, people completely outside a movement do not identify with members of the group. Even if they share salient traits of group membership, such as gender or skin color, the extreme outsiders perceive few similarities between themselves and movement members; they share no sense of a common fate; and group membership is not important in their self-definition (Gurin and Townsend 1986; Miller et al. 1980). Further along the spectrum, when a person comes to identify with a group, she may begin to attribute the problems associated with group membership to external forces rather than to personal failings, and she may develop discontent about the position of the group in society. Still, such a person may not seek widespread change to alter these conditions. Further along the spectrum are those who believe collective action is the best means of overcoming inequality. On the far end of the spectrum are activists whose high levels of oppositional consciousness have led them to commit themselves and many of their resources to the political work associated with dismantling the systems of subordination the movement has identified as inhibiting its members' fulfillment.

The political work mounted by movement activists may include legal strategies and litigation. Without extensive resources or political power, most subordinate groups have little access to legislative or executive offices, the most conventional sites of policy making. In these circumstances, the judicial branch sometimes appears to be an attractive alternative (Vose 1959). Social movement organizations, particularly those emerging from the civil rights and women's movements, coordinate litigation to challenge legal barriers to equality. Famous examples include the NAACP's efforts to dismantle school segregation (Kluger 1975; Tushnet 1987) and racial restrictive covenants (Vose 1959). But critics have noted that litigation is a flawed means of achieving policy change (Scheingold 1974; Rosenberg 1991). Even large-scale litigation reduces complicated social problems to discrete disputes among only a few parties, thus isolating a case from its broader context. Because they aim only to remedy the dispute among the parties, judicial remedies are poorly suited to bring about widespread social change (Handler 1978; Horowitz 1977). Critics also suggest that legal strategies may contribute to the "myth of rights," luring subordinated groups into believing that accumulating formal rights is sufficient to achieve justice (Scheingold 1974).

Although legal remedies are indeed imperfect for achieving large-scale social change, social movements may use litigation as one piece of an overall strategy of organizing and consciousness raising. Activists use litigation campaigns to educate the public and to attract new members to the movement (McCann 1994; Olson 1984; Milner 1986). McCann's study of the comparable worth movement, for example, illustrated the way that union activists used novel legal claims in organizing efforts among public employers.

Large-scale public interest litigation is a direct means for movements to translate demands for reform into official policy. But a movement's struggle over social values may also reach the courts through individuals who use the law to resolve conflict in their everyday lives. Group members who adopt a movement's oppositional frames may develop new expectations about their treatment at work, at home, or in their neighborhoods. Based on these altered expectations, individuals may place demands on others. Because they threaten existing social relations, those demands are likely to be met with resistance and to give rise to conflict. As in many conflicts in the United States, individuals may turn to the courts to resolve them. Although individuals bring "private" claims, those claims may have political significance. Litigants structure the agenda of the judicial system, and when cases result in written opinions, they establish precedents binding on future litigants. Moreover, by invoking the law, individuals enforce public norms that might otherwise lie dormant: "What the populace actually receives from government is to a large extent dependent on their willingness and ability to assert and use the law on their own behalf" (Zemans 1983, 694). Mobilizing the law is thus a form of democratic political participation (Zemans 1983; Lawrence 1991a, 1991b). In that process, individuals can borrow elements of oppositional consciousness from social movements to formulate demands and press them on the government.

Studying the development of sexual harassment law helps us understand the circulation of oppositional consciousness beyond the boundaries of the activist women's movement. The oppositional frames reinterpreting sex at work as a form of employment discrimination and a violation of rights were developed among feminist actors and institutions. But others "outside" the movement borrowed these frames, often to vindicate their own personal interests. The permeability of the movement's boundaries and the circulation of oppositional consciousness contributes to movement success when people "outside" the movement use its frames to reinterpret their experience and to challenge the status quo.

In the analysis that follows, I categorize the actors in the early sexual harassment litigation according to their level of identification with the women's movement and their participation in the networks and institutions associated with that movement. The actors "inside" the movement were self-identified feminists working for explicitly feminist goals in the litigation. They were immersed in feminist legal networks. The actors "on the borders" were sympathetic to feminist principles but were primarily interested in the rights of African-Americans and other racial and ethnic minorities, and their networks reflected those interests. Their familiarity with the rights claims of these other groups helped them translate their clients' experiences into successful legal arguments. Finally, the actors "outside" the movement were sympathetic bystanders. They were reluctant to think of themselves as feminists, and they did not identify themselves particularly with the civil rights movement. They simply did not think of their legal work as making a political statement. They did not participate in feminist networks or in any other movement circles. Yet, in spite of their relative isolation from movement ideology, they used feminist frames to understand the experiences of their clients and to challenge sexual harassment in the courts.

Central Actors: The Lawyers

Lawyers are critical to the translation of individual experience into legal claims. Their familiarity with legal rules and procedures makes them the gatekeepers between individuals and legal institutions (Jacob 1994). In the course of their work in translation, lawyers often reshape individuals' experience to fit into legal categories. These strategies often narrow the dispute to exclude aspects extraneous to the legal decision-making process. Occasionally, however, lawyers may also expand individual disputes "by linking subjects or issues that are typically separated, thus 'stretching' or changing accepted frameworks for organizing reality" (Mather and Yngvesson 1980–81, 779). Expanding the conflict challenges accepted categories and sets the stage for legal change. In the history of the sexual harassment claim, attorneys challenged the acceptable legal categories of sex discrimination by stretching it to include sexual harassment. In the process, they drew on a variety of ideological and material resources, depending on their relation to the movement.

In the Movement

Of the nineteen lawyers I interviewed, six were feminist activists strongly influenced by the oppositional consciousness of the women's movement. All six closely identified with women, opposed the inequalities facing women as a group, and deeply believed that the economic and social injustices facing women could be challenged using legal strategies. Their legal work reflected these beliefs: three worked in feminist social movement organizations seeking social change through the courts, while the other three, as private practitioners, took on political cases as they tried to earn a living. Regardless of their practice settings, all six participated in networks of feminist litigators and activists that provided support for their efforts. Members of these networks, lawyers and nonlawyers, helped litigators assume the expenses associated with the litigation process. They also wrote amicus curiae briefs, explaining to courts the harms of sexual harassment and the need for a remedy. Finally, these networks provided feminist litigators with much-needed moral support and creativity in the long and sometimes frustrating course of a sexual harassment case. The lawyers' participation in the women's movement equipped them with a relatively mature oppositional consciousness, making it possible to translate women's experience into a claim for employment discrimination.

Nadine Taub was one of the first attorneys to handle a sexual harassment case, *Tomkins v. PSE&G* (1977), and was a crucial figure in organized feminism's efforts to fight sexual harassment in the courts. In 1972, she became the director of the Women's Rights Litigation Clinic at Rutgers University School of Law. Before this appointment, she had spent several years working in various legal services positions, representing the urban poor and racial minorities. At the clinic, Taub's work on sex discrimination and abortion rights expressed her political commitment to improving women's lives through law. Describing the development of the legal claim for sexual harassment, she remembered: "I have to say that this is the example of how wonderful it was to work together with [other women]. . . . We were women sitting around trying to figure out how to explain to somebody that this was wrong, and how to fit it into the legal requirements."

In developing Adrienne Tomkins's legal claim, Taub turned for help to other feminist activists. Some of the law students who helped draft pleadings and motions were activists in the parts of the women's movement "more to the left than NOW [the National Organization for Women]." Taub also worked with an organization, Working Women's Institute (WWI), that had done some early research and public education on sexual harassment. WWI's representatives helped Taub "articulate what the harm is, and really why it was discrimination and not just some bad thing that happens to you."

Taub was at the center of a wide network of feminist lawyers who were working on similar cases at the time. Taub had met Catharine MacKinnon and Ann Simon at a Women in Law Conference in 1974. She and MacKinnon were in contact while the Tomkins case was proceeding. At the time, MacKinnon was writing the paper that would later become the book *Sexual Harassment of Working Women* (1979). Taub received a copy of the paper from MacKinnon and cited it in her appellate briefs. "We were crazy for something to cite," Taub remembered. Through these connections, Taub also received help from and provided assistance to other attorneys working on sexual harassment cases.

Mary Dunlap, who worked on *Miller v. Bank of America* (1979), was one of the attorneys Taub consulted. Dunlap was a founding member of Equal Rights Advocates (ERA), a public interest law firm working on women's rights litigation. She and three feminist colleagues from law school had received grants to open a women's rights firm: "We were all sort of gambling it would happen, and it happened, and so then we all got to do our hearts' desire, our passion, which was women's rights cases." They handled cases involving girls' access to Little League sports, pregnancy leave, and lesbian rights. When the trial judge dismissed Margaret Miller's claim for sex discrimination, her original attorney, Stuart Wein, called Dunlap. Wein had met Dunlap while studying for the California bar exam and knew that Dunlap handled women's rights cases. Upon hearing the facts, Dunlap immediately agreed to handle Miller's appeal. Although she thought the facts presented an "analytically easy" case of sex discrimination, Dunlap recognized that the decision presented political problems. But she credited women's organizations, like WWI and Women Organized for Employment in San Francisco, for expanding the political opportunities for the litigation:

These groups, I think, had probably the most catalytic role in making certain that the question of harassment got litigated, pursued, and made itself known to management and got its way into the employment picture. . . . They were out raising consciousness. They were in the newspaper, talking about the phenomenon; they were doing local actions. . . . I would say they were the political element at the time that had people paying attention.

While working on the appellate brief, Dunlap also strategized with Taub about defining issues, and they even traded briefs.

Taub and Dunlap both worked in settings where legal work on behalf of women's rights was subsidized by outside funding. Law school clinics and public interest law firms were more able than private practitioners to absorb the financial risks associated with taking controversial cases where small amounts of money are at stake and where attorneys' fees might not be available.[13] Then as now, private practitioners did not find such cases attractive, especially when the client could not afford to pay for the legal services. For some private practitioners, however, the political goals involved in such a case outweigh these material considerations.

Ann Simon, the lead lawyer on *Alexander v. Yale University** (1997) was one of three lawyers in the New Haven Law Collective, which had a general practice handling cases involving family law, bankruptcy, landlord-tenant disputes, and employment discrimination. Although they sought to make money from their law practice, the attorneys in the collective also took cases that presented novel political or legal cases: "It created issues about how much time can we afford to spend on this thing that we're not getting paid for. I don't think they were any different from any other kinds of pro bono hassles in private practices. There were a lot less than in many because we all agreed it was politically important to do."

The collective handled the *Alexander* case with extensive help from the Yale Undergraduate Women's Caucus. The young feminist activists in the caucus conducted an informal investigation to uncover incidents of sexual harassment on the Yale campus; they raised money to cover some of the New Haven Law Collective's expenses in the litigation; they volunteered to do the clerical work associated with litigation in federal court; and they filled the courtroom to watch the proceedings. The caucus also conducted its own organizing efforts on this litigation: it used the case to lobby for a grievance procedure at Yale and to educate the campus community about sexual harassment.

Also working for the collective at this time was Catharine Mac-Kinnon, still a law student at Yale and writing *Sexual Harassment*. According to Simon, "There was virtually nothing going on about sexual harassment that MacKinnon didn't already know, hadn't already talked to people about." Both Simon and MacKinnon were tightly enmeshed in the network of feminist lawyers, which led them to seek assistance from Susan Meredith, of the Connecticut Women's Education and Legal Fund, another public interest law firm. When the plaintiffs in *Alexander* lost at trial, Simon turned to these contacts to help with the appeal. The contacts included Nadine Taub, who wrote part of the appellate brief and performed the oral argument in *Alexander*. Simon also arranged for amicus curiae briefs from the Women's Legal Defense Fund (WLDF).

This network of feminist activists was held together, in part, by institutions like the Women in Law Conferences held in the 1970s. Lacking formal organizational sponsorship, feminist lawyers, academics, and law students coordinated the conferences each year. The conferences offered seminars and workshops for lawyers working on women's rights issues, whether in public interest or private practice. In these settings, legal professionals and feminist activists shared ideas, strategized, and made important contacts. Taub, Dunlap, and Simon all attended these conferences and cemented the relationships there.

Other feminist private practitioners also attended the Women in Law Conferences. For example, Linda Singer, the appellate attorney for Paulette Barnes in *Barnes v. Costle** (1977), was a private practitioner but also a cooperating attorney with the Lawyers' Committee for Civil Rights under Law (LCCRUL). As a cooperating attorney, she occasionally handled employment discrimination or civil rights cases on a pro bono basis. In working on the appeal, Singer sought assistance from the LCCRUL and WLDF. The WLDF helped by filing an amicus curiae brief and giving her a copy of MacKinnon's paper on sexual harassment. Although Singer never spoke to MacKinnon, she cited the paper in her brief and also distributed the paper to other lawyers who called asking to see her briefs. Singer attended and gave presentations at the Women in Law Conferences.

Heather Sigworth, attorney for Jane Corne and Geneva DeVane in *Corne v. Bausch & Lomb* (1974), also attended the conferences. Sigworth became a feminist after a radicalizing life experience, when she was denied a teaching position because of a university's antinepotism rules. At the time, antinepotism rules were used almost exclusively to deny women employment. When she sued the university for sex discrimination, she became a high-profile symbol of the women's movement in Tucson, Arizona. After going to law school, she built a practice around that reputation. As an attorney, she represented women who complained about sex discrimination in their unions. Her reputation among working-class women brought Jane Corne and Geneva DeVane to her office when their supervisor began making sexual demands. In conducting the litigation, Sigworth sought advice and moral support from another women's litigation organization, the Women's Law Fund (WLF) in Cleveland, Ohio. She was on the litigation committee that monitored cases for WLF. Although WLF did not finance the *Corne* case, Sigworth nevertheless discussed legal strategy with friends there. Because of her base in Arizona, Sigworth was not as tightly connected with the east coast feminist networks as Taub and Simon. She did not have access to their briefs or to MacKinnon's paper when she was preparing her case.

These six lawyers were motivated by a mature oppositional consciousness. Their articulation of the claim for sexual harassment flowed from a well-worked-out theory of male domination in the workplace. They saw, even when their clients did not, that the injustices stemming from this domination included sexual exploitation on the job. Trained as lawyers, they saw litigation as the most effective way to use their talents to end or diminish this system of domination. They passed along effective strategies and interpretive frames among themselves and others like them. The oppositional frames that they helped to develop then became freely available to other lawyers litigating similar claims and to ordinary women confronting sexual harassment in their own lives.

On the Borders

Among the lawyers who litigated the first sexual harassment cases were seven men and women whose oppositional consciousness was rooted in the civil rights movement rather than in the women's movement. When these attorneys attended law school, the Civil Rights Act of 1964 had recently been passed, and the civil rights movement had established a tradition of using the courts to dismantle the legal underpinnings of segregation. In this political atmosphere, law schools trained students to see law as a potent weapon against inequality (Scheingold 1974). Although these civil rights attorneys were sympathetic to the women's movement, they did not necessarily identify as feminists. They believed that discrimination rather than personal flaws caused women's inequality, and that sex discrimination, like race discrimination, was unjust. Yet they did not necessarily identify with women as a group, nor desire to commit themselves exclusively to collective action on behalf of women. Like the feminist litigators, they considered their work political, but they were dedicated to working for all subordinated groups, including racial and ethnic minorities. When seeking advice and support in preparing their sexual harassment cases, they naturally turned to networks of civil rights lawyers who handled many different kinds of discrimination cases. Thus, these attorneys had a relatively multidimensional oppositional consciousness (see Stockdill, chap. 8, this volume). They found it conceptually easy to borrow oppositional frames from the civil rights struggle in the courts and to use those elements to support their legal strategies against sexual harassment.

The very first judicial decision recognizing a cause of action for sexual harassment, *Williams v. Saxbe* (1976), was litigated by Michael Hausfeld, now a noted civil rights attorney in Washington, D.C. Although Hausfeld is willing to consider himself a feminist, he emphasized in our interview that he has always been more concerned with "minority rights." He traces this interest to his youth: "I didn't like McCarthyism. I was young, but I really grew up hating it. I personally witnessed young people getting beaten by police during the riots of 1968 and 1969 for no reason other than that they were young. I didn't think that was right." After graduating from Georgetown Law School, Hausfeld began practicing at a large law firm in Washington, D.C. but soon left to pursue what he considered more interesting civil rights cases. Accordingly, his name appeared on an LCCRUL list of civil rights attorneys. After Diane Williams was fired and filed an administrative complaint in 1972, she used that list to find an attorney to handle the case. Several other lawyers on the list had turned her down before she finally met Hausfeld. Although in 1972 no one had yet suggested that sexual harassment could be understood as a form of sex discrimination, Williams herself, Hausfeld remembers, had checked the sex discrimination box on the DOJ's internal complaint form because it was the only box that seemed relevant. But Hausfeld's own previous work on race discrimination cases made the legal analysis of sexual harassment seem simple:

> It was basically, at least in my mind, and that of my two partners who discussed this with me, it was a natural and logical outgrowth of the intention of Title VII to create a workplace that provided for equal employment opportunities for persons of whatever race, sex, or color. And you were not being given an equal employment opportunity if, because of your sex, you were being denied promotions and/or tenure because you refused to provide sexual favors or accede to sexual stereotypes.

In handling the Williams case, he had only sporadic contact with other civil rights attorneys and no contact with feminist activists. When he called the LCCRUL for advice in 1972, they were not very helpful. "They felt it was wrong," he reported, "but nobody really knew how to proceed."

Although Hausfeld has always been in private practice, he believes that litigation can be significant political work: "A lawsuit can focus possibly as good as, if not better than, a congressional hearing on a particular social issue, and determine where in society the arguments are for and against. Many of them first bring to public attention an issue that should be brought up but may not be brought up in the political arena." During his career, he has worked on many highly visible cases of racial and ethnic discrimination, including the race discrimination case against Texaco that was settled in 1997. Although Hausfeld believes his work is political, he works largely outside of political organizations and networks.

Thomas Oehmke, the attorney in *Munford v. James T. Barnes Co.* (1977) would have called himself a feminist when Maxine Munford hired him in 1976, but that label was connected to his wider ideological commitments to equality for subordinated groups. He had taken a class on sex discrimination while in law school. His paper for that class was a comprehensive account of the law in this area, which he later published as a book. This expertise made it easier for Oehmke to frame Munford's experiences as sex discrimination:

> There were no reported cases at the time. . . . There was no literature on the subject, there were no discussions in the journals, and those of us who were doing discrimination work, you know, hadn't really talked about it. But after having written the book on sex discrimination in employment, I just figured that this was misbehavior, and this was— I mean, I just looked at it from a raw sex standpoint. . . . [I]f Maxine Munford were not a woman but were a man, [her supervisor] wouldn't have put the moves on her.

Oehmke had begun his career in New Detroit, a public interest organization committed to community development, but he also maintained a small private practice on the side. Most of his work was in race and sex discrimination, with some family law matters as well. He met Munford through his contacts at New Detroit. Oehmke also had some contacts with the public interest lawyers who helped him with the case. He was a member of the National Lawyers Guild (NLG), an organization of politically progressive lawyers interested in civil rights and other public interest work. Through the NLG, Oehmke met an attorney at the EEOC who helped him develop a strategy for the case. That attorney also prepared an amicus curiae brief when Oehmke filed an appeal in *Munford*.[14]

Oehmke is less willing to label himself a feminist today: "I don't like calling myself anything. I like to confront issues one at a time." Preferring to call himself an "egalitarian," Oehmke observed that he lived his life in a feminist way:

> I guess I wouldn't call myself that today but I behave that way. I mean, for example, we had some guy come over here trying to sell us a fence this morning. And, he said, "I thought I would just call and give one of the girls in the office the message." You know, and my immediate response is: "Girls in the office?" I said, "Are you hiring children under twelve? You should be ashamed of yourself; would you call the man a boy and give him a message?" So, I'll immediately confront these situations and I don't care who it is, whether it's a paying client or not, or whether it's an opposing party, I think we ought to confront, you know, discrimination whenever it occurs and rears its ugly head, whether we do it one on one—and you make converts only one at a time.

In private practice, Oehmke also views his work as political: "We are spending our time and money on those kinds of cases that are our way of politically addressing problems that we think ought to be changed." Oehmke's broad-based commitment to social change includes improving the lives of women, but only in the broader context of improving the lives of members of many different subordinated groups.

In the late 1970s, as the claim for sexual harassment became more established in legal circles, lawyers specializing in employment discrimination began to take notice and pursue the cases that would eventually establish the claim for hostile working environments. After graduating from Harvard Law School in 1976, Barry Gottfried, one of the attorneys in *Bundy v. Jackson* (1981), wanted to do what he described as "good-guy work." He began his career at the Civil Rights Division of the Department of Education where he worked on desegregating the University of Georgia. He left this work after two years to practice law in a small law firm in Washington, D.C., where "we were all kind of liberal people. The politics of the place were Democratic and liberal," but "we were trying to make money." In 1975 (before Gottfried arrived), Sandra Bundy was referred to this firm by a friend who occasionally consulted lawyers about race discrimination questions. Like many other young attorneys in Washington, Gottfried was a cooperating attorney with the LCCRUL. He and other attorneys working on the case periodically consulted with lawyers who had experience with sexual harassment cases, such as Linda Singer, who had handled the appeal in *Barnes*. Although not in contact with feminist activists, Gottfried nevertheless had access to feminist interpretive frames. In Bundy's appeal he cited MacKinnon's book, which had only recently been published.

Some of these civil rights lawyers had feminist networks come to them, particularly when sexual harassment law began developing in many different directions. Then as now, women's rights litigation groups monitored appellate court dockets, looking for cases that presented important legal issues. These organizations offered their services in significant cases when they thought they could play a role in shaping a precedent affecting many women in the future. They helped with brief writing; they coordinated amicus curiae briefs; and they organized moot courts for attorneys to practice their oral arguments. Once the claim for sexual harassment became established, these organizations encouraged its expansion by watching the docket and offering assistance to willing civil rights attorneys handling the cases.

For example, Patricia Barry was Mechelle Vinson's only attorney before both the trial court and the court of appeals in *Vinson v. Meritor Savings Bank** (1985). Barry had a private practice in which she handled a great deal of discrimination work but also worked on family law and consumer cases. When she met Vinson, she was trying to develop a private practice that reflected feminist ideals of empowering women, but she also handled cases of race discrimination and other more routine work. She did not work closely with feminist litigation networks, but once Vinson's case reached the appellate docket, the WLDF contacted Barry. Eventually the WLDF contributed an amicus curiae brief to the circuit court of appeals. When the case went to the Supreme Court, under the name *Meritor Savings Bank v. Vinson* (1986), Catharine MacKinnon wrote the brief, and the WLDF and the NOW Legal Defense and Education Fund coordinated amicus curiae brief-writing efforts. These organizations also sponsored several moot courts in which Barry practiced her oral argument before she appeared before the Supreme Court.

These organizations also gathered around Irwin Venick, attorney in *Harris v. Forklift Systems* (1993), when Teresa Harris's case reached the Supreme Court. In 1989, when Harris hired him, Venick was a private practitioner in a small law firm. While he did employment discrimination work, it was not his only area of expertise.[15] He did the *Harris* trial and appellate work himself, but when the time came to handle the appeal to the Supreme Court, Venick turned for help with the brief to professors at Vanderbilt Law School. Also assisting were women's litigation organizations. In fact, before the Supreme Court ever contacted him, Venick heard from one of these organizations that the Supreme Court had decided to take the *Harris* case. These organizations wanted Venick's brief to reflect their own positions on important legal issues, especially the "reasonable woman" standard. Venick commented: "Well, they all had their own agendas. I would imagine that nothing sort of aggravates those organizations more than to have these cases pop up that they have not been involved in. Because, I mean, their job is to basically shape the development of legal theories. And then, some cockamamie lawyer out of Nashville, Tennessee, comes up with the next big case." These groups coordinated an amicus brief in support of Harris, consulted with Venick and the law professors on the main brief, and helped Harris handle media requests for interviews.

Finally, one lawyer developed a feminist oppositional consciousness while working on cases involving sexual harassment and sex discrimination. Lynn Feiger handled an early sexual harassment case in *Heelan v. Johns-Manville* (1978). Feiger was raised in a political family in whose structure she did not see much sexual inequality. Her mother was a labor lawyer, and her sisters all pursued careers. She herself organized laborers for the United Farm Workers while she was in college. "When I went to college, my career goal from high school was to be a radical sociologist. Just accomplishing social change was what interested me."

In 1976, Feiger had just opened a private practice with another lawyer, Leslie Lawson. Although Feiger had a political interest in the larger field of employment discrimination, she and her partner attracted mostly sex discrimination cases because they were among the few female attorneys in private practice at the time. She met Lawson while they were organizing Lawyers for Colorado Women, a bar association for women, but she did not think of herself as a feminist or any kind of activist: "It's just the issue that was there to get involved with. I had been involved with other liberal causes and had done a lot of work for the farm workers, and I never even thought of the women's movement back then." Mary Heelan's original lawyer arranged for Feiger to be local counsel, but he soon dropped out of the case, leaving Feiger and Lawson to take it to trial. In preparing the *Heelan* case, Feiger did not contact any women's organizations or civil rights lawyers, although she remembers attending an EEOC seminar on employment discrimination when she first opened her practice. When asked if she ever consulted with other attorneys about strategy, she reported: "No, we were just blundering along. I mean, we had no idea what we were doing at all. . . . Really and truly, we were just sort of following our instincts."

Since working on the *Heelan* case, Feiger has developed a stronger feminist oppositional consciousness. She herself has experienced discrimination as an attorney: "Nobody took women lawyers seriously, anyway, and people would—in the court system and clerks and clients— nobody would take you seriously." Handling sex discrimination cases made her even more sensitive to women's problems: "I did sex discrimination cases for years without considering myself a feminist in any way, shape, or form, and I think just seeing that and experiencing it through the eyes of my clients really radicalized me." Feiger still takes cases that reflect her desire to create social change. Her office is now handling a sex discrimination case against a company where women have been isolated from each other, working in offices far from each other but surrounded by men. Feiger and others have made efforts to organize these women to support each other through the litigation.

The lawyers described in this section as "on the borders" of the women's movement had a range of attitudes toward that movement that ran from complete feminist identification to more general support for the goals of women's equality and equality for all subordinated groups. They were committed to doing civil rights work for members of many such groups, and they were trying to earn a living from it. The law they practiced gave them access to networks of civil rights and employment discrimination attorneys who provided support for their work on sexual harassment cases. And when the cases became sufficiently significant, they also attracted the attention of the feminist legal community. Although the feminist legal community often helped, these attorneys were essentially lone actors "doing good-guy work." That work made a major contribution to the development of oppositional frames for sexual harassment and to legal rights for women.

Outside the Movement

Also involved in these critical cases were five lawyers who were completely outside the women's movement, and probably did not meet the minimal criteria for what we are calling oppositional consciousness. Although they generally supported equal rights for women, they did not identify with women's interests, nor did they particularly care about the larger power disparities between men and women. Some of them, in fact, were skeptical of many elements of feminist oppositional culture. They did not dwell on the systematic injustices confronting women and were more interested in developing a successful legal practice than in making political statements. For these lawyers, material considerations prevailed over social ones. They did not participate in feminist networks, or even in civil rights networks, at the time of the litigation. Yet their contributions to the development of sexual harassment law should not be overlooked. Indeed, it was one of these lawyers, Warwick (Bud) Furr III, the trial attorney in *Barnes v. Train* (1974), who framed Paulette Barnes's complaints about sexual harassment as a sex discrimination action, laying the groundwork for the very first appellate decision recognizing sexual harassment as a violation of Title VII. Similarly, George Chuzi won the first appellate recognition of a claim of hostile working environment based solely on verbal harassment in *Katz v. Dole* (1983). Thomas Mauro was the first attorney to establish that sexual harassment constituted the tort of intentional infliction of emotional distress in *Rogers v. Loews L'Enfant Plaza* (1981). Despite their minimal contacts with feminist oppositional culture, these attorneys crafted strategies for these significant sexual harassment cases using legal tools made available by years of activity in court by the civil rights and feminist movements.

In 1972, Bud Furr, the attorney in *Barnes v. Train,* had recently left a large law firm to open a new law practice in Washington, D.C. He was sharing office space with another young lawyer, who in turn was a cooperating attorney with the LCCRUL. His office mate was too busy to take Paulette Barnes's case and gave it to Furr. Although Furr knew Barnes could not pay him, he hoped to get a contingency fee from a settlement. Furr felt very isolated in preparing Barnes's claim. Although Furr did not himself work extensively with the LCCRUL, he occasionally called the staff to ask for advice. The staff suggested he call NOW for help in preparing the case. Although NOW provided him with anecdotal evidence about the problems of sexual harassment, he could not use that evidence in court. When the judge granted the employer's motion for summary judgment, Furr asked the LCCRUL to find another lawyer to handle the appeal. His aim was, in effect, to spread the financial losses associated with handling a losing employment discrimination case. Furr generally endorsed the idea of women's equality, but he was not surprised or shocked when the trial judge ruled against him on the *Barnes* case. Although he thought the ruling was "intellectually conservative," he did not consider it clearly wrong. In his work on the *Barnes* case, Furr was a zealous advocate for his client, but insisted he was not trying to make any social or political points with his conduct of the case.

When Deborah Katz hired him, George Chuzi, the attorney in *Katz v. Dole* (1983), worked in a law firm that specialized in representing employees of the federal government in the complex administrative procedures accompanying employment disputes. Describing himself, Chuzi said: "I think I'm just one of these idealistic liberals. When I graduated college, I went into the Peace Corps, and when I came back I was a teacher in Bedford Stuyvesent in New York. And, you know, I think I did a lot of these things because I thought, you know, working with people and helping people is one of the nobler things to do." While going to law school, he worked for the federal government, processing discrimination claims. Still, Chuzi did not think of this legal work on employment discrimination as political work; he did not see these complaints as a symptom of systematic injustice. Rather, he was an idealist trying to help individuals with their particularistic problems.

Chuzi was familiar with sexual harassment law largely through his own legal research. While he was preparing the case, Katz described dozens of times she had confronted vulgar language and sexist insults at work. Having read and analyzed appellate opinions in other cases, Chuzi thought her complaints might constitute a hostile working environment, although Katz had not been the object of any physical assaults. Chuzi did not himself have any contacts with feminist or civil rights networks. When he lost in the trial court in 1982, he asked for help preparing the appeal from rights organizations, but he could not arrange any assistance.

Like Furr and Chuzi, Thomas Mauro, the attorney in *Rogers v. Loews L'Enfant Plaza* (1981) was new to the practice of law when Norma Rogers hired him in 1980. Two of his friends were regular customers at the restaurant where she worked on a day when her harasser was particularly annoying. Exasperated, she told them she needed a lawyer, and they gave her Mauro's card. Familiar with sexual harassment law through his own legal research, Mauro pursued her case as a traditional employment discrimination case and filed a charge with the EEOC. For reasons Mauro could not explain, the EEOC did not process the charge, which kept Rogers from filing a complaint in district court. Feeling pressured for time, Mauro filed a complaint based on the tort of intentional infliction of emotional distress. The court rejected the employer's motion to dismiss and acknowledged that the plaintiff could proceed to trial on her tort claim. But because the trial would have been costly and there was no guarantee of winning, Rogers decided to settle the case. Mauro had no contacts with women's organizations or other civil rights networks, but he did have some contact with feminist ideas. Browsing in a bookstore while he was working on the case, he discovered a copy of *Sexual Harassment of Working Women* (1979). He credits MacKinnon's book with clarifying for him the seriousness of sexual harassment: "It was very helpful, I thought, at the time, very helpful. You know, and it educated me to the problem. Which a lot of people, you know, didn't understand at the time. Clearly, it was something that most people didn't think was a problem."

Even among the attorneys who initially resisted many elements of feminist oppositional culture, the act of representing female clients carried the potential for transformation and the development of mature oppositional consciousness. Marion Walker, the attorney in *Smith v. Rust Engineering* (1978), had been left on her own at the death of her law partner in 1978. That was the year Roxanne Smith hired her. Although Walker had participated in some college protests during the Vietnam War, she did not consider herself a particularly political person, let alone a feminist:

> I fought that word [feminism] for a very long time. . . . I was raised in a country club atmosphere in a small town [in Alabama]. And, I came from pretty well-to-do, upper middle-class families, and I never really knew a lot about anything else. But my mother was always wanting to work outside the home, and my father didn't want her to. It was very early on that I realized that women needed to do stuff. And I have the energy to do it, so, from the age of sixteen, I wanted to be a lawyer, and it never occurred to me that there was any reason I couldn't be. Fortunately, I had the support of my parents saying, "You can be whatever you want."

Walker had not developed a political law practice. Many of her clients were police officers fired without notice and trying to get reinstated. Smith found Walker through mutual friends. Walker had no access at that time to any feminist litigators or activists: "It wouldn't have occurred to me that such organizations existed."

Since working on *Smith,* Walker's experiences as a lawyer have radicalized her, making her much more active in politics and the women's movement. She had had a difficult time finding a job in Birmingham, Alabama, after she graduated from law school:

> It was only when I got through law school and after law school and all the men were getting these nice jobs, and you know, people were saying to me, "If you'd have been a guy with that résumé, I would have hired you on the spot." Then it was finally occurring to me, there were some different things going on. . . . I am much more liberal. I am much more political. Since that time [the *Smith* case], I've had my own experiences in the world that point to who has power and who doesn't and who is going to get it and who is not. And it's generally gender based, in my experience.

Through her own experiences, and through her relationships with her clients, Walker has developed a full-fledged oppositional consciousness that attributes discrimination to systematic forces that she opposes in her practice of law. Walker now participates extensively in fund-raising activities on behalf of liberal women candidates for office. She now views her legal work, consisting largely of sex and race discrimination, as political. "I'll never run out of discrimination cases, as long as I live here, I imagine. People are just not willing to curb their appetites for bigotry." Walker no longer rejects the label of feminist: "I got over worrying about the word when I got angry enough at the way things were. When I realized that if my past life was not going to be able to be reconciled with my current life of being a feminist, then so be it."

These lawyers had little or no feminist consciousness at the time they handled the sexual harassment cases, and they were completely unaware of the feminist legal activists who were working on the same issue at roughly the same time. Yet they were able to borrow elements of feminist consciousness from books and legal opinions. Although they had no political goals themselves, their use of feminist legal frames helped develop the claim for sexual harassment. That claim has been widely publicized by the women's movement. As a result, sexual harassment has become a familiar concept, a label that women can now apply to their everyday experiences at work. Yet the legal struggles that underlie the label were waged by lawyers arrayed all along the spectrum of oppositional consciousness.

Central Actors: The Plaintiffs

The legal claim for sexual harassment could never have emerged without the plaintiffs themselves—the working women who came forward to complain about sexual exploitation on the job. Although sexual harassment was not a familiar term to these women at the time, they recognized the injustice of their working conditions. They believed they had a right to a workplace free of harassment and decided to pursue that right by going to court. In particular, their experiences with sexual harassment conflicted with their belief that men and women of equal abilities should be treated equally. Like the lawyers, the plaintiffs I interviewed were arrayed all along a spectrum of feminist oppositional consciousness, but they were less likely than the lawyers to view their cases as political statements. They were chiefly trying to vindicate their own interests and reputations, although they expressed satisfaction knowing that their experiences in court probably improved conditions for other women. Their life experiences, in their families and in their working environments, provided them with potent evidence of women's abilities along with women's vulnerable position in society. This section examines the ways that these plaintiffs borrowed oppositional frames from the civil rights and feminist movements to interpret their experiences and to challenge harassment in court.

The Intersection of Race and Gender

Two of the plaintiffs I interviewed, Diane Williams and Sandra Bundy, were African American. Both of them had strong racial and gender identification; they were both aware that race and sex erected barriers to economic opportunities affecting not only them but other Black women as well. Although they identified with other Blacks and women, they were not activists participating in social movement organizations. They did not file their lawsuits as part of a planned program of litigation. Rather, they challenged sexual harassment as a form of personal resistance, which ultimately had wide-ranging effects on legal rules and on the women's movement itself.

Black women are often omitted from feminist and antiracist theory and policy. Race discrimination is often thought of as discrimination against Black men, and sex discrimination as discrimination against White women; the lives of Black women are ignored, although they experience both forms of discrimination (Crenshaw 1989). This intersectionality provides a unique perspective, uncovering specific sources of subordination. For example, sexual harassment is accompanied by racial slurs and epithets for many Black women. According to Kimberlé Crenshaw: "Perhaps this racialization of sexual harassment explains why Black women are disproportionately represented in sexual harassment cases. Racism may well provide the clarity to see that sexual harassment is neither a flattering gesture nor a misguided social overture but an act of intentional discrimination that is insulting, threatening, and debilitating" (Crenshaw 1992, 412). One of the leading attorneys in the development of sexual harassment law, Nadine Taub, observed: "I don't think it was an accident that many of the early cases were brought by Black women, because I would think that a lot of White women could be tricked into thinking that it could be worked out. Whereas for Black women, they knew. They'd been exploited since day one." In fact, Black women were overrepresented among the plaintiffs in the early cases of sexual harassment. They filed six of the fifteen reported quid pro quo cases in the 1970s, the first opinions that recognized a claim for sexual harassment.[16]

The facts of these early cases demonstrate the way racism and sexism mingled to interfere with women's economic lives (Lerner 1972; Crenshaw 1989; Collins 1990). For example, Margaret Miller's supervisor wondered what it would be like to have sex with a "Black chick" and fired her when she declined his advances (*Miller v. Bank of America* 1979, 212). Similarly, Maxine Munford's supervisor, Glenn Harris, asked her on her first day of work "if she would make love to a White man and if she would slap his face if he made a pass at her."[17] After Munford had been only two weeks on the job, Harris fired her for continually declining his advances. Her attorney, Thomas Oehmke, thought the harassment was racially motivated: "He thought she was an easy touch, because she was a Black woman. And, you know, he treated her as if she were the local hooker that just came into town. And rather than treating her as a professional woman, to do the job he hired her to do."

Diane Williams, who closely identifies with both women and the Black community, was the first woman to win a judicial acknowledgment of her claim for sexual harassment in *Williams v. Saxbe* (1976). Her strong sense of justice was deeply offended by the treatment she received at the Community Relations Service of the DOJ, her first job after graduating from college. Nothing in her brief career had prepared her for the unfair treatment she would receive: "It was a rude awakening for me because I had been brought up to believe that if I obtained a good education and training and worked hard, that my efforts would be rewarded, recognized and rewarded appropriately. So it was something out of the way for me to discover that something more was required simply because I was a woman." Soon after she arrived, her supervisor and another employee began sending her cards and asking her out on dates. When she declined, she started receiving poor evaluations. Williams complained about these evaluations, but complaining only made things worse. Soon, other employees avoided her, except for two other women who had filed sex and race discrimination complaints against other supervisors in the division. After Williams was fired in 1972, she too filed a complaint. Although sexual harassment was not yet recognized as a form of sex discrimination, she chose to pursue sex discrimination because "I don't think he would have treated a man that way."

The case was important to Williams for personal reasons and to prove a larger point: "I wanted to vindicate my position that women should not have to be the paramour of the supervisor or anybody else to succeed in the workplace. And I was trying to show that my job performance was not the reason for my being subjected to that kind of treatment or being fired." After eight years of litigation, Williams obtained only a small back pay award in 1980 because she had found a new job almost immediately after being fired.[18] She also won attorneys' fees. Although she is disappointed by the large numbers of women who do not seem aware of laws against sexual harassment, she feels her case has been helpful to other women: "They don't have the same battle, they don't have to prove that sexual harassment is awful, so that part of the battle is now closed."

Williams identifies with other Black women, and is chiefly concerned with racism and sexism as barriers to economic equality. When she identifies herself as a feminist, she is careful to specify that her chief concern is securing "equal opportunities for women whether it's in the field of education or employment, or elsewhere." Williams is less sympathetic to other causes that some feminists support: "I guess there are just different factions of the women's movement that are not really responsive to my needs or interests. Or perhaps their means of seeking some objective, whatever that might be, would not be things with which I would feel comfortable. . . . Employment and education and housing and health care are much more serious problems for women, especially Black women, than gangster rap."

Williams is keenly aware of the effects of racism on economic opportunities for Blacks. Considering the Texaco case, where White executives were taped making racist slurs, Williams thought there were more important economic issues at stake: "They're focusing on the alleged racial slurs rather than on the thing that I think is perhaps even more important, and that is the dignity of people in the workplace, and being treated fairly, and being compensated on the basis of their own merit and abilities. And so those folks have been fighting, not only to be treated with fairness, dignity, and respect in the workplace, but also to be compensated accordingly."

While she is greatly concerned about structural barriers to economic opportunity, Williams's experience with her sexual harassment case has made her skeptical of organizations that seek to dismantle those barriers. During the litigation, Williams sought but could not obtain assistance from women's organizations.

> I'm disgusted with a lot of women's organizations, unfortunately. . . . They have a mediocre track record, as far as I'm concerned. You write to these groups, and you call them, and you can't get any help. And then, after you start winning, then everybody wants to jump on the bandwagon. The Women's Legal Defense Fund—I had contacted it and could not get any help. . . . And after you start winning and getting decisions in your favor, then other people start taking on these cases, and they want to claim credit for the victories.

In spite of her doubts about women's organizations, Williams is motivated by a relatively strong oppositional consciousness. She identifies with women and Blacks, sees and opposes the group injustices they experience, and looks for occasions to challenge these injustices. She continues to engage in activities, sometimes in organizational settings, that enhance women's economic opportunities. Since winning her case in 1980, in *Williams v. Bell*,* Williams has prepared newsletters and press releases for Federally Employed Women, a group that provides training and networking opportunities for working women and runs a clothing bank for poor women trying to enter the working world. She has testified before Congress about the harms of sexual harassment. And while she was working at a government agency years after the case, she mounted her own career development program for female employees, particularly clerical workers. She invited speakers and organized workshops on job training, investment advice, and even "dressing for success." In spite of her contacts with groups like Federal Employed Women, she prepared the sessions herself to avoid the red tape that she associated with organizations and bureaucracies: "Because when you do things on your own, you don't have to ask for approval." Williams also entered law school while the litigation was proceeding. She is currently in private practice and works as an investigator for the Equal Employment Opportunity Commission. She advises her own clients to pursue discrimination complaints, but encourages them to find supportive networks to help them through the emotional ordeal. She also encourages them to find other people in the workplace who are having similar experiences.

Sandra Bundy's sense of oppositional consciousness emerged from her participation in personal and political struggles against racism. In her youth, Bundy had attended civil rights demonstrations, including the March on Washington. As a factory worker, she had also organized

Black employees for a union whose demands included an end to race discrimination in job assignments. Bundy had also engaged in personal acts of resistance: she was thrown off a bus in Wilmington, North Carolina when she refused to sit in the back. This early development of oppositional consciousness prepared her for her experiences with sexual harassment.

At the District of Columbia Department of Corrections, Bundy's male supervisors and coworkers approached her often with sexual jokes about her anatomy and her weekend plans. They invited her to parties and out for dinner. They routinely used vulgar language around the office. She was used to such language from the inmates, but "when it came from coworkers, with their lack of respect for women, it became intolerable." Bundy was not the only woman affected by this environment. Although many women went along with the joking and teasing, most confided to her that they too were uncomfortable. The discomfort of others helped Bundy see the systematic nature of sexual harassment. "If men were perpetrating these things on women in a sexual way, yes, that's discrimination." Bundy complained about her treatment, but found that her complaints were met with demotions and transfers to worse assignments. She also suspected that her supervisors sent bad references to prospective employers when she tried to change jobs. She felt that she had no alternative but to hire an attorney. "That was the real reason I did it, because I wanted to leave. I did not want to pursue this case. I just wanted to pack up and leave and go somewhere else. But my back was against the wall." She chose to sue to restore her professional reputation and to protect her livelihood.

When asked if she was a feminist, Bundy replied "Of course." She felt that her case helped all women: "I felt that I was making a statement for not only myself but for many, many women, for all women, whether the women who felt that they had nothing else to offer but themselves or felt that . . . this was their obligation. . . . This is what you have to do in order to get along in this man's world." Bundy also believes that women ought to work together, across racial divisions, to bring about social change: "The only time that women will get credit for anything they do, they have to do it collectively. It cannot be done on an individual basis; the women have to stick together and they have to really fight together to get anything they want. . . . Regardless of color. Color should never matter to women."

In spite of her belief in the importance of collective action for women, Bundy herself does not participate in any political organizations. In the aftermath of her case, she made television appearances to publicize the problem of sexual harassment. One of those appearances was arranged by NOW. Bundy was very grateful for that opportunity, but her participation ended after she made the appearances. She describes herself as "a member of [her] community," as when she recently pursued a complaint with local government about the faulty installation of a sewer pipeline. Apart from these local actions, Bundy found that simply coping with her daily work life, where she confronted retaliation for her complaints, was so emotionally demanding that she had little energy to spare for any political activities.

Neither Bundy nor Williams included claims of race discrimination in their lawsuits because their harassers were also African American. Among the thirty pivotal cases in sexual harassment law, four involved Black men harassing Black women.[19] These cases reveal the tension between racial and sexual power in the African American community, described by Kimberlé Crenshaw. Because they share a common history of racial exclusion, Black men and women often develop a close bond in the workplace. Yet Black women sometimes find that they confront unwanted intimacy in this context. Crenshaw observes that the women are frequently reluctant to complain about such treatment: "In fact, many Black women fear that their stories might be used to reinforce stereotypes of Black men as sexually threatening. Others who may not share this particular concern may nevertheless remain silent fearing ostracism from those who do" (Crenshaw 1992, 415; see also Marshall 1998).

Sandra Bundy experienced this conflict in the aftermath of her successful appellate case against the District of Columbia Department of Corrections. She claims that other Blacks criticized her for complaining and for bringing a lawsuit:

> See, this is what they're saying: "I mean, we're a minority in this country and here you are a Black woman bringing down a Black brother who is able to—who wants to move up into, you know, and you're holding him back." But that had nothing to do with it . . . because you've got to work too. . . . Sexual harassment has no color. It's not a color thing.

In challenging sexual harassment, Bundy felt forced to choose between her gender and racial identities.

Borrowing Feminist Consciousness

The White women I interviewed, Roxanne Smith and Deborah Katz, were both relatively low on the spectrum of oppositional consciousness. Like Williams and Bundy, neither was an activist affiliated with a women's organization. They also had weaker gender identifications than Williams and Bundy. Yet Smith found it relatively easy to interpret her experiences at work using feminist frames. She realized early in life the importance of economic independence for women, and she blamed outdated male attitudes for her problems at work. Deborah Katz had the least oppositional consciousness of the plaintiffs I interviewed. Yet she too effectively borrowed feminist frames in a manner that helped other women confront sexual harassment.

Roxanne Smith chose to go into engineering because the field offered economic independence. Having a well-paying occupation was important to Smith because of her family background.

> I did not want to end up like my mother, you know, being a divorced woman with no education and not being able to support myself. . . . So, I stuck it out and did it the only way I knew how to do it. You know, I wasn't going to go out and marry a man for his money, or have sex with a man because I could, for money. I wanted to [become an engineer] because I knew I was smart, and I knew I could do it.

Smith's supervisor at Rust Engineering often assigned Smith secretarial duties instead of the engineering work she was hired to do. One of her coworkers, a friend of the supervisor's, made comments to her suggesting that women should not be doing "men's work" and left obscene cartoons posted on her cubicle. After several months, her supervisor asked Smith to do some typing. When she refused, he reprimanded her for being "uncooperative" and put a written memorandum in her personnel file. Smith quit, threatening to sue for discrimination. She thought her treatment was unjust:

> I had just recently graduated and it was a very tough road to hoe for me because, like I said, I had no financial support. A lot of times I had to do without food just to have money to buy books, and at the end of the quarter, I'd have to sell those books when I would like to have kept them. I had to sell them just in order to buy gas enough to get back to my job. . . . And I just felt like after going through all of that to get a degree, to get that sheepskin, and then to finally, finally, land a job during the recession which was something else, to be treated like that.

Roxanne Smith was not a feminist when she brought her claim for sex discrimination against Rust Engineering Company in 1977. She said: "To tell you the truth, at that time, I don't think I even knew what the word meant. I don't think there were feminists at that time." Nor did she think that her acts of filing the lawsuits were inspired by feminism: "It wasn't, I think, a matter of feminist; it was just what I had to do." Now, she is unsure whether or not to accept the label:

If somebody wants to call me that, that's fine. I mean, I'm not going to go to a burn-the-bra rally or anything like that.

There are some aspects of things that they do that I feel are good, but my husband accused me of being a "feminazi." He got that term from Rush Limbaugh. And I said, "That is not true. I am not, just because I won't let some man tell me that I have to be barefoot, pregnant, and in the kitchen . . . no." I mean, I think it's a woman's right [to get an education].

Over the course of Smith's career, she has been disappointed in the slow rate of women's progress in the workplace. She lays the blame on men's attitudes toward women: "I do put the blame mostly on men because it's just the men's attitudes; they're holding these things back. . . . It was like the men who were supervisors or in management were—they were kind of intimidated. . . . That was my impression: 'We can't stand to have a woman know more than I do'—that kind of thing." She cited many instances of sex discrimination that she had suffered and additional experiences with sexual harassment, experiences she considered much more serious than those included in her original complaint. Although she never again filed a formal complaint, she stood up to the harassers in informal ways. In spite of her critique of male attitudes and endorsement of women's rights, Smith is willing to put up with the sexualized atmosphere often associated with male-dominated workplaces:

I've had people, guys tell me jokes and things like that, dirty jokes. Dirty jokes do not bother me, as a matter of fact, a guy using curse words at work doesn't—because I worked with shop guys. Sex harassment to me would be, someone suggesting that you, you know, have sex with them or do something like participate in an orgy with them, or touch you. I do not consider dirty jokes at the coffeepot to be sex harassment.

In addition, Smith thinks that some problems at work arise because of female personalities: "There are some women I feel like that will not stand up for themselves, and I know female engineers that if they ask them to make coffee, they say 'yes, okay.' It's like they're scared of their own shadows. But, maybe they have a different kind of personality than I do." Smith has adopted only some of the elements of feminist oppositional consciousness. While she is aware that the workplace is organized in a way that places women at a systematic disadvantage, she believes that women can challenge those arrangements by standing up to discrimination on their own.

Smith is a member of an organization of women engineers, primarily a networking organization, but does not participate in any political activities beyond voting. Yet at work, she has challenged the negative stereotypes of women that give rise to unequal treatment. Her lawsuit was a small-scale victory. She won only a small settlement of her claim. But the two men who had treated her so badly were fired, perhaps improving the workplace for other women in her situation.

Deborah Katz had a relatively low level of oppositional consciousness, and yet her case, *Katz v. Dole* (1983), set an important precedent expanding the claim of hostile working environment to include cases where there was only verbal harassment. Katz grew up being intrigued by male-oriented occupations. Her grandmother worked for the railroads. When she graduated from high school, she took a clerical position in a small police department where the officers were protective of her and treated her well. She was not intimidated by male-dominated working environments: "I worked with guys all my life. As a matter of fact, I still feel more comfortable talking to guys to this day than women."

Although she was used to working around men, Katz was "surprised" by the working environment in air traffic control. Her supervisors and fellow controllers used vulgar and sexist epithets when addressing her. Some also left notes attached to log books asking her out on dates, and they speculated within her hearing about her love life. Katz tried a variety of tactics to deflect this attention. She avoided eating lunch in the cafeteria, and she dressed conservatively: "Knowing, working with men and how they respond physically, I would dress very conservatively. I always wore some type of cardigan or a blazer, and . . . I would try to downplay my femininity." She also tried to become a member of the team by going bowling and by baking banana cream pies. When these tactics failed, she tried to get tough by introducing vulgar language to her own vocabulary. This strategy had no effect, and she continued to be the object of harassment, which started having adverse effects on her health.

Katz herself was reluctant to deploy feminist oppositional frames to explain her coworkers' behavior. Katz complained about her treatment to the union, the Professional Air Traffic Controllers Organization (PATCO). Supplying the bare bones of an oppositional frame, union officials repeatedly advised her to file a complaint with the equal employment opportunity office of the Federal Aviation Administration, which she finally did. Katz was also initially unwilling to use the antidiscrimination apparatus. She associated discrimination complaints with Black and female employees who were failing but were trying to keep their jobs:

All the EEOC complaints normally that are filed in air traffic they do not take seriously, and rightfully so because this is how people file to keep their jobs. If they're failing . . . in order to grasp to be in air traffic control they file an EEOC complaint, a discrimination complaint, in order to keep their job, even though they should not be there. . . . I can tell you more than a few people who should have been washed out and should have gone someplace else and they filed these grievances and you have problems.

Katz also disapproved of affirmative action programs that lowered required test scores to allow women and minorities to occupy slots: "They lowered the grade to bring in minorities, which I thought was wrong anyhow. Why lower the standards? Why don't you keep your standards high?"

Katz does not describe herself as a feminist. She takes issue with the women's movement position on abortion rights, for example. She told me: "I'm pro-life, and my mother and my grandmother I think were really closet feminists and would have been in the feminist movement if it didn't come to the issue of denigrating women that stayed home and raised their children." While she was an air traffic controller, she declined to join an organization of other female controllers: "I said, 'I worked too hard to integrate.' And I said, 'We already have a union,' and I said, 'That union represents us.' I said, 'I don't need to segregate from them, and also I don't want preferential treatment.'" Katz resented the lack of assistance she received from women's organizations while she was conducting the litigation. She believes that these groups turned her away because her views on abortion made her inappropriate as a feminist symbol: "I did not fit their agenda." After she won her case, she says, some of the same organizations contacted her, asking her to give speeches or to lend support to their activities. She has declined their offers.

Katz does identify with a number of social and political groups, including fundamentalist Christians and conservatives. She gives money to the Christian Coalition and has attended some of their conventions. But her strongest identification is probably with other working people, particularly federal employees. When she was a member of PATCO, she approached conservative senators and representatives to educate them about the issues at stake in the strike. She strongly empathizes with mistreated employees confronting a cumbersome and unresponsive complaint process that has seemingly limitless funds with which to oppose individual employees. She perceives herself as a whistle-blower and would someday like to develop an organization of others like herself who could support employees against the monolithic employer.

Although Katz is certainly at the low end of a conventional spectrum of oppositional consciousness and would never consider herself a feminist activist, her behavior was nevertheless consistent with feminist frames of equality in the workplace. Her career path challenged rigid categories of "men's work," and her personal resistance to sexual harassment challenged the injustice of maintaining a sexually hostile environment.

The four plaintiffs were arrayed along a spectrum of oppositional consciousness. At one end, Sandra Bundy had a well-developed oppositional consciousness from years of union activity and personal resistance to racism. Both she and Diane Williams closely identified with women, particularly Black women, and saw their mistreatment on the job as part of the larger problems women faced in their struggle for economic equality. Deborah Katz came at the other end of the spectrum. In bringing a case for sex discrimination, she feared being lumped with the beneficiaries of affirmative action—women she considered unqualified to hold their jobs. To her, the injustices she suffered were largely particular to her own situation, although she was willing to use the larger category of "sexual harassment" to fight them. Roxanne Smith found herself somewhere in the middle of this spectrum. Although she agreed that women were at a systematic disadvantage in the workplace because of what she considered outdated male attitudes, she nevertheless thought that individual women acting on their own had considerable power to improve their conditions. These four women thus differed in the intensity and maturity of their oppositional consciousness. Yet all four had access to the oppositional frames developed and circulated by the civil rights and feminist movements. By finding lawyers and suing their employers, they used these frames in a public way to assert their rights to equality and justice. Their public claiming of those rights then constituted the basis for a developing oppositional frame surrounding sexual harassment.

Conclusion: Valuing Many Points on the Oppositional Spectrum

The early litigation on sexual harassment reveals a spectrum in forms of oppositional consciousness that range from the committed activist, in the case of some of the lawyers, to the influenced nonactivist, in the case of some of the plaintiffs. Actors at each place in that spectrum play important roles in the entire phenomenon of a social movement. Although a movement cannot exist without activists who in some cases dedicate their lives to the movement, it also depends heavily on nonactivists who are influenced by the movement's ideas.

In the evolution of governmental and social policy on sexual harassment, nonactivists played a crucial role. In judicial policy making, social movement organizations can represent the interests of subordinated groups in class actions and other legal forms that attempt to address wide-scale social problems. But these social problems also create disruptions in individual lives, and with sufficient initiative on the part of the individuals affected, those disruptions can lead to legal disputes. Thus, in spite of its reputation as a nondemocratic route to social change, governed by unelected judges, litigation is in some ways uniquely democratic. A single individual, unsupported by any political party or social movement, can bring about changes in public policy by asking courts to reinterpret existing law to track individuals' changing interpretations of personal experience.

Because we know that many individuals who suffer justiciable injuries do not bring suits for redress, the question arises of why some who suffer an injustice take legal action and others do not. This question, which cannot be satisfactorily answered in this chapter, involves many related factors, including material resources, social networks, and access to legal institutions and actors. In addition to these factors, however, the state of mind of a potential plaintiff undoubtedly affects the likelihood that she will move from anger at injustice to legal action. At this point, adoption of oppositional ideas promulgated by social movements can make the difference between a decision that will, over time, further the movement's goals or a decision that will not further, and may even impede, those goals. All the plaintiffs I interviewed had some exposure to relevant ideas of justice, both through mainstream American culture, which stresses the injustice of discrimination in the workplace, and through oppositional cultures, which stress the larger injustice of current societal structures. From Diane Williams, who works with Federally Employed Women, through Deborah Katz, whose mother and grandmother "would have been in the feminist movement," all had had some relatively close contact with feminist ideas. Williams and Sandra Bundy also had relatively direct access to the civil rights movement, which has functioned as the fountain of inspiration for all the "new" social movements, including feminism. That movement taught those who look back to it that individual responses to injustice, such as refusing to sit in the back of a bus, can have far-reaching collective effects.

The lawyers involved in these cases run the spectrum in oppositional consciousness from almost full immersion in an oppositional community, with the commitment of identity that usually accompanies such immersion, to mere sympathy with oppositional ideals. Again, however, as with the plaintiffs, "mere" sympathy to movement ideals could have a great effect in practice. Being "one of those idealistic liberals," being the kind of person who might browse in the feminist section of a bookstore, or even only having an officemate who was connected with a movement organization could put one in the right place at the right time, and sometimes give one the extra zeal, to push the legal system toward change. In addition, the stories of some of these lawyers show that the very act of representing members of subordinated groups can nurture oppositional consciousness and produce further impetus to engage in acts that confront injustice.

The story of sexual harassment litigation, then, is a story of the impact on public policy of many individuals, with distinctly varying degrees of oppositional consciousness, each of whom played a role in furthering the goals of the social movement. In each case, either their own oppositional consciousness or that of a close acquaintance may well have made the difference between action and inaction. It is not necessary for everyone who acts to further the goals of a social movement to have, among their psychic resources, even a thread of oppositional consciousness. Indeed, the legal system is intended to be structured so that mere individual perception of injustice, unbolstered by larger forces like a social movement, can bring about change. In fact, however, those who do step forward to take action, even in the legal system, are likely to draw as they do so on the cognitive and emotional, as well as the institutional, resources that an oppositional social movement provides. In sexual harassment cases that changed the face of American justice, the interplay between activists and nonactivists demonstrates both the massive and subtle effects of oppositional consciousness.

Appendix: Sexual Harassment Cases Studied

Alexander v. Yale University, * 459 F. Supp. 1 (D. Conn. 1977)
Andrews v. City of Philadelphia, 895 F.2d 1469 (3d Cir. 1990)
Barnes v. Costle, * 561 F.2d 983 (D.C. Cir. 1977)
Barnes v. Train, * 13 FEP Cases 123 (D.D.C. 1974), *rev'd sub nom. Barnes v. Costle,* * 561 F.2d 983 (D.C. Cir. 1977)
Brown v. City of Guthrie, 22 FEP Cases 1627 (W.D. Okla. 1980)
Bundy v. Jackson, * 19 FEP Cases 828 (D.D.C. 1979), *rev'd,* 641 F.2d 934 (D.C. Cir. 1981)
Burlington Industries v. Ellerth, 524 U.S. 742 (1998)
Burns v. McGregor Electronic Industries, 989 F.2d 959 (8th Cir. 1993)

Caldwell v. Hodgeman, 25 FEP Cases 1647 (D. Mass. 1981)

Corne v. Bausch & Lomb, * 390 F. Supp. 161 (D. Ariz. 1975)

Elliott v. Emery Air Freight, No. C-C-75–76 (W.D.N.C. 1977)

Ellison v. Brady, 924 F.2d 872 (9th Cir. 1991)

Faragher v. City of Boca Raton, 524 U.S. 775 (1998)

Garber v. Saxon Business Products, 552 F.2d 1032 (4th Cir. 1977)

Guyette v. Stauffer Chemical Co., 518 F. Supp. 521 (D.N.J. 1981)

Halpert v. Wertheim & Company, 27 FEP Cases 21 (S.D.N.Y. 1980)

Harris v. Forklift Systems, * 510 U.S. 17 (1993)

Heelan v. Johns-Manville, * 451 F. Supp. 1382 (D. Colo. 1978)

Henson v. Dundee Police Dept., 682 F.2d 897 (11th Cir. 1982)

Hill v. BASF Wyandotte Corp., 27 FEP Cases 66 (E.D. Mich. 1981).

Katz v. Dole, * 709 F.2d 251 (4th Cir. 1983)

Kyriazi v. Western Electric Co., 461 F. Supp. 894 (D.N.J. 1978)

Marino v. D. H. Holmes Co., * 21 FEP Cases 452 (E.D. La. 1979)

Meritor Savings Bank v. Vinson, * 477 U.S. 57 (1986)

Miller v. Bank of America, * 418 F. Supp. 233 (N.D. Cal. 1976), *rev'd*, 600 F.2d
211 (9th Cir. 1979)

Munford v. James T. Barnes Co., * 441 F. Supp. 459 (E.D. Mich. 1977)

Neeley v. American Fidelity Assurance, 17 FEP Cases 482 (W.D. Okla. 1978)

Oncale v. Sundowner Offshore Services, 523 U.S. 75 (1998)

Rabidue v. Osceola Refining Co., * 584 F. Supp. 419 (E.D. Mich. 1984), *aff'd*, 805
F.2d 611 (6th Cir. 1986)

Robinson v. Jacksonville Shipyards, 760 F. Supp. 1486 (M.D. Fla. 1991)

Rogers v. Loews L'Enfant Plaza, * 526 F. Supp. 523 (D.D.C. 1981)

Smith v. Rust Engineering, * 20 FEP Cases 1172 (N.D. Ala. 1978)

Tomkins v. PSE&G, * 422 F. Supp. 553 (D.N.J. 1976), *rev'd*, 568 F.2d 1044 (3d
Cir. 1977)

Vinson v. Meritor Savings Bank, * 23 FEP Cases 37 (D.D.C. 1980), *rev'd*, 753
F.2d 141 (D.C. Cir. 1985), *aff'd sub nom. Meritor Savings Bank v. Vinson,* *
477 U.S. 57 (1986)

Walter v. KFGO Radio, 518 F. Supp. 1309 (D.N.D. 1981)

Williams v. Bell, * 487 F. Supp. 1387 (D.D.C. 1980)

Williams v. Saxbe, * 413 F. Supp. 654 (D.D.C. 1976), *rev'd on procedural
grounds*, 587 F.2d 1240 (D.C. Cir. 1978), *on remand sub nom. Williams
v. Bell,* * 487 F. Supp. 1387 (D.D.C. 1980)

Yates v. Avco Corp., 819 F.2d 630 (6th Cir. 1987)

Notes

I am exceedingly grateful to the plaintiffs and lawyers who offered their stories for this paper. For their thoughtful comments on previous drafts, I thank Scott Barclay, Michelle Boyd, Jonathan Casper, Dennis Chong, and Richard McAdams. I would especially like to thank Jenny Mansbridge for the special care and attention that she has given this project over the years.

1. A "case" refers to a single piece of litigation between the plaintiff and an employer, even if it resulted in several published judicial opinions. "Quid pro quo" refers to those cases of sexual harassment in which the employee must submit to sexual advances as a condition of keeping her job or obtaining promotions or benefits.

2. These cases include *Alexander v. Yale University* (1977), the first judicial recognition of a private cause of action for sexual harassment as sex discrimination in education under Title IX of the Civil Rights Act. The other two cases, *Kyriazi v. Western Electric Co.* (1978) and *Rogers v. Loews L'Enfant Plaza* (1981), established tort claims based on facts constituting sexual harassment and were litigated at roughly the same time that the discrimination precedents were being set.

3. Warwick Furr declined to have his interview taped. I took detailed notes during the interview and relied on these notes for this chapter.

4. MacKinnon, however, recognized that racism and sexism were different systems of subordination: "The analogy should not be allowed to obscure the distinctive content and dynamics of sex and race, nor does it imply that sexism and the opposition to it exist only as a derivative form of racism and the movement against it" (MacKinnon 1979, 129).

5. This theory was given its most forceful articulation in Catharine MacKinnon's *Sexual Harassment of Working Women*, published in 1979. Her book, in turn, documents the consensus in the grassroots feminist community about the prevalence of sexual harassment and its economic consequences (MacKinnon 1979, 18–23 and accompanying notes). MacKinnon also quotes Emma Goldman's analysis of the problem in 1917: " 'Nowhere is a woman treated according to the merit of her work, but rather as a sex. It is therefore almost inevitable that she should pay for her right to exist, to keep a position in whatever line, with sex favors' " (MacKinnon 1979, 177, citing Goldman [1917] 1970, 20).

6. Unlike employees working for private employers, federal employees did not begin the litigation process in the EEOC. Rather, they pursued complaint procedures within their respective administrative agencies.

7. Another plaintiff lost her case in federal district court, but since only a per curiam appellate opinion is available, we know less about the district court's reasoning for dismissing her claim (*Garber v. Saxon Business Products* 1977).

8. Also in 1977, a federal district court recognized for the first time that sexual harassment could constitute sex discrimination in education in *Alexander v. Yale University*. The court relied on the appellate opinion in *Barnes* to recognize a private cause of action under Title IX of the Civil Rights Act, prohibiting discrimination in education. The only plaintiff remaining in the lawsuit after the other plaintiffs were dismissed in pretrial motions, Pamela Price, alleged that her professor had given her a bad grade in a class after she refused to sleep with him. Although her claim was allowed to go forward, she lost at trial.

9. See also the cases of *Brown v. City of Guthrie* (1980) and *Henson v. Dundee Police Department* (1982), where the plaintiffs both filed their complaints with the EEOC in 1977.

10. Courts dismissed similar claims against employers in *Marino v. D. H. Holmes Co.* * (1979) and *Neeley v. American Fidelity Assurance* (1978).

11. Bernstein suggests, in the alternative, a standard of "respectful person."

12. Other cases that have adopted the "reasonable woman" standard are *Andrews v. City of Philadelphia* (1990); *Yates v. Avco Corp.* (1987); *Burns v. McGregor Electronic Industries* (1993).

13. Title VII allows awards of attorneys' fees and costs to the prevailing parties in sexual harassment and other discrimination cases.

14. Although Munford won the defendant's motion to dismiss, she lost at trial. After a hearing, the judge found that Munford had been fired for poor productivity rather than her refusal of her supervisor's advances. The appellate court declined to overrule the trial court.

15. He also had a health care practice and lobbied the state legislature on health care issues.

16. The African American women in these cases also come from a variety of socioeconomic backgrounds. They are overrepresented both among the women in managerial and professional positions (39 percent) and in the lower-paid clerical positions (18 percent).

17. Joint Pre-Trial Statement of Facts, *Munford v. James T. Barnes Co.* (1977), quoted in MacKinnon 1979, 259 n. 259.

18. Until the Civil Rights Act of 1994, back pay was the only monetary award available to successful plaintiffs in Title VII lawsuits. They were not able to recover for damages arising from the emotional consequences of discrimination.

19. These cases are *Williams v. Saxbe* (1976), *Barnes v. Costle* (1977), *Bundy v. Jackson* (1981), and *Meritor Savings Bank v. Vinson* (1986).

6   Cristaleño Consciousness: Mexican-American Activism between Crystal City, Texas, and Wisconsin, 1963–80

Marc Simon Rodriguez

Crystal City, Texas, played a pivotal role in the development of the Chicano movement in the United States. Yet research on the movement's origins in Crystal City has failed fully to consider the effect of the Texas-Wisconsin migrant social system, from which Chicanos distilled two separate sources of oppositional consciousness. The residence each year of some migrant farm workers in both Crystal City and Wisconsin facilitated a biregional labor culture based in a dual "home." These workers came to call themselves "Cristaleños," an appellation that would have had little meaning if they had stayed within the boundaries of their family and friendship networks in Crystal City's "Mexican" neighborhoods.[1]

In the 1960s, as the Chicano movement took shape, these community networks drew from the oppositional consciousness of the Texas Mexican farm workers, whose condition of oppression derived, among other things, from the remnants of the Texas-Mexican war and a system of labor that functioned much like a caste system.[2] Its members also drew from the militancy that they found in the Midwest labor movement. That movement had developed a stance of opposition to repressive employment institutions, a repertory of different strategies with which to attack these institutions in court, and experience in creating worker solidarity and displaying that solidarity in public (Salas and Giffey 1998; United Migrant Opportunity Services 1985).

For the Cristaleños of the 1960s labor movement, southwest Texas and Wisconsin constituted nations apart. Former migrants now living in Milwaukee have few regrets about their choosing to leave Texas. They consider Wisconsin, especially Milwaukee, rich in jobs and Crystal City little more than a ghost town.[3] Tomas Rivera, a Crystal City native and former farm worker, has written several books on Crystal City, portraying it as a town of Anglo violence and Texas Mexican poverty. In one dramatic piece a young farm laborer reminds his father that "it is better up north" before he is killed by an Anglo farmer for drinking water while working (Rivera 1971).

In Texas and Wisconsin, both Anglo-dominated worlds, Cristaleños fell at the bottom of the labor hierarchy. Cristaleños preferred the labor conditions and social opportunities available in Milwaukee and elsewhere in Wisconsin to the poor working conditions, social segregation, and labor exploitation in Texas. But Milwaukee was not home, and in any case Wisconsin's agricultural jobs were usually seasonal (Raushenbush 1962, 1966). The constant migration from one venue to another produced a significant impact on identity and on oppositional consciousness. Work in immigration history, ethnic studies, and the developing field of transnational studies has investigated the impacts of migration on identity (Gabbacia 1988; Portez and Stepick 1993; Portez and Grosfoguel 1994; Rouse 1991, 1992; Schiller 1995). Yet except in the case of African American migrations to the urban north, the impacts of migration within the United States have not been studied in depth (Grossman 1989; Phillips 1999). Scholars exploring Chicano communities in the Midwest are attentive to Texas origins, yet have not considered the group part of the world of migrants (Valdes 1991; Vargas 1993). To understand the origins not only of the Cristaleño community but also of the larger Chicano movement in the United States, one must understand the joint Texas-Wisconsin political narrative. To understand the success of the Raza Unida movement, one must understand its synergistic origins in a fusion of Texas and Wisconsin strands of oppositional consciousness.

Oppositional Consciousness in a Texas Enclave

By 1960 Chicanos in the United States Southwest had experienced decades of racial segregation and economic subordination. Jim Crow restrictions on voting rights and public space had minimized Chicano political participation and regulated social contact between Anglos and other races, creating a system of social segregation aptly described as "internal colonialism" (Moore 1970; Acuna 1988; Barrera, Munoz, and Ornelas 1974; De Leon 1980; De Leon 1982; Stewart and De Leon 1993). As one Crystal City activist put it, "The *Mexicano* has been kept in a state of dependency. He's pushed out of the schools . . . the wages, the housing, the health, the government, the distribution of land . . . colonialism is in South Texas" (Parker 1975, 152). Anthropologist Martha Menchaca gives the name "social apartness" to the marginalization and de facto segregation of the Chicano population (Menchaca 1995, 169–75). Yet these segregated conditions also fostered a sense of community pride and self-worth based on shared experiences as laborers, an awareness of personal struggle, and a resentment of Anglos (De Leon 1980; De Leon 1982; Montejano 1989; Zamora 1993).

In Crystal City the evidence of economic disparity was palpable: "The Chicano neighborhood is a collection of wooden shacks on unpaved, muddy streets. On the other side of the tracks, concrete sidewalks and roadways weave past middle class homes and high priced ranch style structures" (Aarons 1970, B5).[4] For Chicanos in Crystal City and Zavala County, plumbing was a luxury and education distinctly substandard (Smith 1978).[5] One report stated that "illiteracy in Crystal City is twenty percent higher than in Mexico" (Thomas 1971, 24; Trujillo 1993).

A strong oppositional culture had developed among the Chicanos in Crystal City, in which anger at the Anglos combined with a deep group identification and, for many, a conviction of the injustice of the Chicano social and political situation. Many had also explicitly recognized the group's common interest in opposing Anglo domination. Yet most individuals in the community still lacked a set of strategies for overcoming that domination and a belief that collective action could be successful.

In 1963, a small group of five impoverished, undereducated yet motivated Cristaleños, later dubbed "Los Cinco," ran for city council. They were elected by a large margin after significant coalition support helped mobilize the Cristaleño migrant vote (Brown 1963; Chandler 1968; Cuellar 1974; Shockley 1974, 40). Chicanos had carried out the unthinkable in Texas politics, where, as one Anglo farmer had put it, "We feel towards the Mexicans just like toward the nigger, but not so much" (Limerick 1988, 247). In an article published in the *Dallas Morning News* on July 28, 1965, reporter Carlos Conde observed that in running for election, Los Cinco "represented the plight of their group. Their average education was about the seventh grade. They dressed in workmen's clothes. They had little knowledge of city economics and government. They deeply resented the Anglos." The success of Los Cinco depended on three groups. On the surface, Los Cinco's challenge to Anglo governmental control depended on the outside resources of the International Brotherhood of Teamsters labor union and the Political Association of Spanish-Speaking Organizations (PASO), who sent organizers from San Antonio (Shockley 1974, 39). These two groups both financed and provided the legal and organizational support for the voter registration drives among Cristaleños that produced Los Cinco's victory (Shockley 1974).[6] They helped with developing strategies and their support made successful action a real possibility. But the door-to-door efforts of a third group—Cristaleño young adults and teens—provided the most politically significant mobilization. Los Cinco youth activist Jose Angel Gutiérrez explained how young Chicanos transformed community traditions by finding ways to pay the poll tax of $1.75 required for each person to vote:

Sell a dozen tamales for $1.75 and you've got your poll tax—now that would make sense [to people who had never voted]—you are getting tamales! It [the food] was all donated through families. Women would make the cakes. Dances? Couples dances for $3.50. The couple would get the two. If they had already had it [poll tax], we would keep it to buy somebody else's. In fact we were buying other people's poll taxes. (Interview, Jose Angel Gutiérrez, April 19, 1995)

Teenage peer groups—including that of Jose Angel Gutiérrez, and future Crystal City city manager Miguel Delgado—formed in the Chicano neighborhoods of Crystal City, at Crystal City High School, and in migrant labor groups (Delgado 1972).[7] Los Cinco candidate Juan Cornejo's brother Robert recruited Crystal City high school students to remind their neighbors to vote and to distribute pamphlets.[8] Future Wisconsin labor activist Jesus Salas, visiting relatives in Crystal City during a break from his college studies in Wisconsin, took part in some of the activities with his friends. Crystal City's "revolt," involving both teenagers and adults, was one of the first actions to bring the Chicano civil rights movement to national attention.[9]

Despite their initial victory, however, Los Cinco fell apart under the weight of Anglo police harassment, economic reprisals, and internal disunion. By 1965, some observers considered the "revolution" in south Texas over. For many Crystal City Anglos, it appeared as if their problems with the Chicanos had passed, as an ethnic coalition of Anglos and acceptable Mexican-Americans replaced Los Cinco at city hall, eliminating all staff appointed under Los Cinco (Shockley 1974, 80–109; Smith 1978, 241–56).

Yet the years between 1965 and the second Crystal City revolt of 1969 were a critical time in the developing consciousness of several youth activists. In this period, some Crystal City activists entered Texas colleges and universities, developed a more mature oppositional consciousness, and began the higher-education wing of the Chicano movement (Gutiérrez 1998, 51; Navarro 1995; Garcia 1989, 15; Rosales 1996, 215–16). The most prominent leader of this wing, Jose Angel Gutiérrez, entered college at Southwest Texas Junior College in nearby Uvalde before the Los Cinco revolt, then transferred to Texas A&M University at Kingsville, where he founded a student PASO organization and graduated in 1966. Gutiérrez went on to write his master's thesis at Saint Mary's University in San Antonio, Texas. His thesis subtitle was "The Empirical Conditions of Revolution in Four South Texas Counties" (Gutiérrez 1968; Gutiérrez 1998, 99–100). Before he finished his thesis in 1968, Gutiérrez founded, with Willie Velasquez and Mario Compean, the Mexican American Youth Organization (MAYO) (Navarro 1995, 80–87; Gutiérrez 1998, 101–3). Following the lead of African American activists, MAYO used race and ethnicity as badges of pride for young Chicano students in direct confrontation with Anglo power. Mario Compean explicitly commented on the formation of MAYO that "[w]hat we needed was an approach similar to what the Black Movement was using" (Navarro 1995, 85).[10] Another MAYO activist remarked, "There was a background: the Selma March in 1965, the Black Power Movement, the Student Non-Violent Coordinating Committee. . . . We were interested in what they were doing" (Navarro 1995, 83). Gutiérrez captured the mood of the MAYO organization when he exclaimed, in an article published by the San Antonio *Express* on April 16, 1969, that "[w]e are fed up . . . and if the gringo doesn't get out of our way, we will stampede over him."

Oppositional Consciousness in Labor-Conscious Wisconsin

As Gutiérrez and Compean were founding MAYO, most Cristaleños' lives still depended upon their yearly migration to the Midwest and Great Plains. Following the 1965 defeat of Los Cinco, most migrants continued to labor throughout the Midwest, some seeking nonmigrant employment in Milwaukee-area industry. Some settled in Wisconsin and continued as activists seeking solutions to the problems faced by farm workers there.

Wisconsin industries required at least a high school education for employment, and the "baby boomers" of the Crystal City migrant community were the first generation in which the majority graduated from high school. High school graduation in Crystal City had improved steadily for Chicano students between 1940 and the late 1950s. Those graduating in the late 1950s and early 1960s were the first generation in which Chicanos represented a majority of high school students in Crystal City. Chicanos as a percentage of graduates went from 10 percent in 1950 to a majority of all graduates by 1960, a fact that led to increased competition for elected school positions (Shockley 1974, 11; Smith 1978, 171–207). By the 1960s, field work had become a summer occupation for some Cristaleño youth, now able to spend the school year as regular students. Some continued to do migrant work during the summers while in college.[11] Geraldo Lazcano, who sold his car after high school graduation to raise funds to settle in Milwaukee, explained the impact of a high school education on out-settlement and migration:

> Life was seasonal. You might begin in June harvesting beets, July clearing the fields, then work canning corn in Wisconsin, tomatoes in Ohio

for Hunt's or Del Monte. You might have five W2's [tax forms]. Everybody did something like this till the 1970s, when with a high school diploma you could apply for other jobs. Then more came to Wisconsin. (Interview, Geraldo Lazcano, August 10, 1992)

Available positions as factory laborers led some of Milwaukee's first Cristaleños to settle in stable year-round occupations that allowed several to purchase affordable homes and duplexes on Milwaukee's South Side (J. Rodríguez 1992).[12] According to a Crystal City Model Cities application relying on the 1960 census, 80 percent of Crystal City's population was engaged in farm work, 85 percent was in need of permanent employment, and 73 percent was trained only in field work (often earning less than the minimum wage of $1.25) (Shockley 1974, 100–101). Migrants from this group who "settled out" in the Midwest thus often sent money back to Crystal City. The Cristaleño network often made the difference between decent survival and pauperism for the families back in Texas.

This labor system provided Midwestern farmers with a dispensable and relatively submissive labor supply and gave workers a sense of potential stability and community within a flux-filled labor world (Provinzano 1971; Wells 1975). Former migrant and Milwaukee resident Jack Orozco remarked on the decision to "settle-out":

Texas was no place to be. No pay. I came [to Wisconsin] in the 1960s. My four sisters came to join me in the 1970s and friends and relatives keep coming. Lots of people are here and the people have been real nice. Other relatives come to Milwaukee and go back to Crystal City. Wisconsin work is better. Texas has only part-time seasonal work. Milwaukee has steady jobs. (Interview, Jack Orozco, August 7, 1992)

Migrants like Orozco maintained friendships and family relations of a circular nature that ebbed and flowed along migrant streams, as family members and friends brought themselves and news of Crystal City to Milwaukee, and in turn carried Wisconsin community news back to Crystal City. These communications expanded the economic potential of the social networks. Many migrants followed similar "chain-migration" patterns of settlement to Milwaukee, but most, like Orozco, also maintained a strong connection to Crystal City. Many Milwaukee residents subscribed, for example, to Crystal City's Anglo-run *Zavala County Sentinel,* and some even wrote letters to the paper from Wisconsin, or sent family news to be published in the "Here and There" section of the paper (Gutiérrez Papers, Raza Unida Inc., Wisconsin).[13] Dale M.

Barker, editor in chief of the *Zavala County Sentinel,* reported that in the decades before the 1990s, Wisconsin was the largest single subscription center outside of Texas, followed by California. Indeed, the majority of the subscribers lived in Milwaukee and were Spanish-surnamed former migrants.[14]

The migrants found progressive Wisconsin surprisingly friendly to their militancy. Labor unions volunteered to help the now-settled migrants, the clergy from many denominations were sympathetic, and when the migrants organized demonstrations progressives of many races came out to help. The progressive publications, university enclaves, churches, and other institutions that served as the activist descendants of the La Follette era, as well as civil rights activists with a national background, provided critical secondary support.[15] For example, many progressive attorneys were attracted to the movement in Wisconsin.[16] David Loeffler, a labor lawyer who had helped teaching assistants form a union at the University of Wisconsin, Madison, and the son of a prominent La Follette Progressive judge in northern Wisconsin, worked for the migrant cause.[17]

These institutions and networks carried strands of a Midwest oppositional culture—and a few individuals within these networks carried a developed oppositional consciousness—that linked back to the German working-class socialist tradition heavily concentrated in the strong craft unions in Milwaukee. These institutions and networks also linked to the more general progressive principles brought to the United States by the German reformers ("the 1848 Club") who immigrated after the failure of the 1848 revolution in Germany (Thelen 1972; Zeidler 1991). They linked as well to a progressive Scandinavian strain in the mix of cultures in the northern Midwest. Milwaukee had a Socialist mayor as late as 1960 (Orum 1995; Zeidler 1991). Wisconsin had also produced, in Senator Robert M. La Follette, a candidate for president in 1924 whose Progressive Party called for recognizing the right of labor to bargain collectively, abolishing child labor, fighting monopolists, and establishing public control over natural resources (Thelen 1985; Commons 1963). (Although La Follette won only Wisconsin's thirteen electoral votes, he polled nearly five million popular votes.) This progressive and socialist tradition, firmly established in parts of Wisconsin's labor movement, was carried on into the 1960s by, among others, individuals who had actually worked with La Follette in 1924. The heritage provided a source of ideology, strategy, and efficacy that meshed well with Cristaleño migrant activism.

Biregional Activism: The Retooling of an Interstate Labor System

Jesus Salas had "settled out" in Wisconsin with his family in 1959, when his father Manuel, after many years as a migrant contract worker in Wisconsin, established a tavern and restaurant close to migrant areas in Waupaca County. Like many Cristaleños, Salas and his family often returned to visit friends and relatives in Crystal City. This contact led to Salas's participation as a student activist and pamphleteer in the Los Cinco struggle of 1963. In 1962, Salas entered what later became the University of Wisconsin, Stevens Point, as an undergraduate and became a student activist. As a student he became aware of the reports on migrant labor that the University of Wisconsin issued periodically, including the important *Migratory Agricultural Workers in Wisconsin: A Problem in Human Rights* released in 1950. In 1964 the Institute for Research on Poverty at the University of Wisconsin began an investigation to update information on the housing and work conditions of farm workers in Wisconsin, under the direction of Elizabeth Brandeis Raushenbush, an economist and the daughter of Supreme Court justice Louis D. Brandeis. The young Salas, who had worked with Wisconsin migrant children in the summer of 1963, was recruited by Raushenbush in 1964 to join the Governor's Committee on Migratory Labor, which she chaired, and to help researchers collect data for the Institute for Research on Poverty.[18] When released in 1966, the report pointed out, among other things, that in 1964 migrant farm workers in Wisconsin's Waushara County failed to earn even the minimum wage, making on average $3.96 a day and only $116.40 for the season, wages that placed them well below the poverty level (Raushenbush 1966, 20). Salas considered this evidence a "call to action" and decided to take his activism off the campus and into the farm fields and canneries of Wisconsin.[19]

The memory and experience of Los Cinco gave Salas the strength and ability to consider becoming active in Wisconsin:

> That political activity had an enduring impact on all of us, especially all of us in Crystal City. We saw the opportunity to struggle for rights in other areas, not just the political arena. Their [Los Cinco's] victory, although it was defeated two years later, really empowered us to improve ourselves not only politically, but economically and educationally. (Interview, Salas, July 27, 1992)

Salas admits that many of Los Cinco and their political faction were "co-opted" by the Anglo power structure after 1965.[20] Some lost their jobs or were forced under threat of legal or economic attack to moderate their views (Gutiérrez 1998, 65–66, 138–39). Yet he still considered the incidents of 1963 pivotal in the formation of what we call oppositional consciousness among young Cristaleños:

> I don't see that you could have the organizing of farm workers or the development of the farm worker's union [in Wisconsin] if that hadn't happened—if Los Cinco hadn't come to the fore in the political arena [in Crystal City, Texas] when they did! In effect, when I speak about organizational activities in the mid-1960s, it is with people that have experienced that situation who become unafraid of the challenge, who start confronting not only the political bosses but the economic ones in central Wisconsin. (Interview, Salas, July 27, 1992)

Political participation and the interconnectedness of migrant life flowed together for many, informing the shape of political activities carried out by young baby-boomer Cristaleños.

One of the central resources for Cristaleño activists—as well as for Chicano rights—developed in reaction to the problems of migrant farm workers in Wisconsin. In 1965, the United Migrant Opportunity Services (UMOS) was founded in Milwaukee, with a Crystal City native as its first staff member. UMOS grew out of the uncoordinated activities of a variety of Wisconsin interfaith church groups, who were then providing "basic necessities," such as clothing and food as well as social and recreational activities, for migrant farm workers. Catholic and Protestant church groups, directed primarily by Wisconsin Anglos, had begun just before 1965 to coordinate their efforts with those of Texas Mexican migrants under the auspices of the federal government's recently created Office of Economic Opportunity (United Migrant Opportunity Services 1985; Parra 1984, 52). UMOS was formed as a facet of the Johnson administration's Great Society, to encourage migrant workers to learn new skills and move out of agricultural work. The organization provided out-settlement assistance, benefits counseling, and housing information (United Migrant Opportunity Services 1985; Task Force on Problems of Spanish Surnamed Americans 1966; Erenburg 1969; Pycior 1993). Crystal City native Genevieve Medina, UMOS's founding staff member, served as an internal liaison between the migrants and the organization.

Cristaleño migrants and activists used UMOS to out-settle themselves and family members, taking advantage of public support for such activities.[21] Cristaleños with high school diplomas and some with a college education also used their liminality and their higher level of training to serve as community bridges between Spanish-speaking farm workers and the opportunities in Milwaukee's labor market.[22] Educated in English yet speaking Spanish in the home, this baby-boom generation was able to use its bilingual background to gain white-collar employment and then help less fortunate migrants find nonagricultural and stable employment, job training, unemployment benefits, and housing (Erenburg 1969).[23] The Cristaleños who provided these services through the publicly funded UMOS also gained political power among the Spanish-speaking population of Milwaukee, as they worked with a number of Anglo liberals. By the late 1960s, the migrant network, with Cristaleños at its core, had been institutionalized at UMOS (United Migrant Opportunity Services 1985).

Cristaleños also provided the backbone of the movement for labor rights in Wisconsin's canneries and more broadly for labor rights for migrants in Milwaukee. In August 1966, Cristaleño organizers led a "March on Madison." The immediate goals of this march were public rest-rooms in the Wautoma migrant area, a state advisory program on workers' rights, enforcement of state housing codes, extending minimum wage legislation to cover migrants, and the placing of more migrant representatives on the Governor's Committee on Migratory Labor (Valdes 1991, 190). Salas also saw the march as a way "to dramatize the plight of migrant workers . . . and to call upon the social conscience of progressive Wisconsin" (Erenburg 1968, 20). The march drew the attention of Texas Mexican cannery workers at the Burns and Sons potato processing plant in Almond, Wisconsin, who contacted Salas for his support. Burns and Sons workers, together with Salas, then founded Obreros Unidos (OU) as an agricultural labor union (Salas and Giffey 1998).

Faced with the immediate desire of workers to organize a union at the Burns operation, Salas reached out for assistance to fellow march organizers Mark Erenburg, then a student of Robert J. Lampman at the University of Wisconsin (Lampman's empirical work on poverty later helped inspire the national War on Poverty); Salvador Sanchez, a Texas Mexican migrant crew leader; and African American student organizer Bill Smith. Salas also lobbied the state AFL-CIO, which replied by sending organizers to Almond to assist in what amounted to a "wildcat" strike on the part of Texas Mexican processing plant workers inspired by Salas's march to Madison. Salas felt he could not leave these workers "out in the cold," and so with no prior organizing experience attempted to organize a union.[24] Through contacts with the University of Wisconsin School for Workers, a Progressive-era creation, Salas learned the mechanics of organizing workers and holding a representative election. The Cristaleño workers at Burns, together with fellow Texas Mexican migrants from nearby towns, helped Obreros Unidos gain the support of the workers, who voted overwhelmingly for union representation. Despite this shop floor victory by Obreros Unidos, the Burns management was unwilling to negotiate.[25] With the legal assistance of the AFL-CIO, Salas and his organizers won significant legal victories against Burns, but the decision came after the migrants had returned to Texas.[26] In this initial effort, Salas had developed a strong organization, which included a newspaper, *La Voz Mexicana*, a lawyers' committee providing free legal advice on the weekends, and a growing cohort of organizers from diverse racial backgrounds (Obreros Unidos 1966; Salas and Giffey 1998).

The Burns strike made Salas aware that he was now considered a leader among all Texas Mexican migrants in Wisconsin. It also clarified for him the existence of multiple strands of migrant consciousness much like those in the Cristaleño migrant world into which he was born. Each set of local experiences in different Texas Mexican migrant communities generated slightly different lessons, but those experiences and lessons converged within the migrant stream each year as workers from towns in and around Crystal City traveled north together. At Burns, workers from south Texas had responded to Salas's coming from within the migrant stream, as they asked him to go beyond marching to engage in union building.

In 1967, Obreros Unidos attempted to unionize Libby's cannery operations in Wisconsin. In January and throughout early 1967, Jesus Salas brought his fellow organizers Erenburg, Sanchez, and Smith to Crystal City and nearby towns to organize Libby workers for the following summer season. In Crystal City, they became involved in the post–Los Cinco attempt to elect a Chicano-chosen slate to office, with Salas giving a speech on behalf of Chicano candidates, including his uncle Julian Salas, a candidate for justice of the peace. Salas also recruited union members in other nearby towns, who eventually joined the La Raza Unida Party.

The efforts in Obreros Unidos brought together strategies from the north and the south. They also fostered among the workers a larger oppositional consciousness, letting them see the connections between organizing migrant labor unions in Wisconsin and Texas and reclaiming control of public office in Crystal City.[27] Thoughout the organizational efforts between 1967 and 1968 Salas relied on Cristaleños, including Francisco Rodríguez, Esequiel Guzman, Rodolfo Palomo, and Arturo Gonzalez, each of whom had participated in the voter registration drives for Los Cinco in Crystal City.[28] Cristaleño roots were key in the development of the Wisconsin-based movement. Salas explained:

They were tied together, so that the leadership was tied together, so that the [youth] leadership of Los Cinco in Crystal City and leadership the farm workers union is the same, it is the same in that it all comes from the same hometown. (Interview, Salas, July 27, 1992)

The Cristaleños, including some MAYO members, together with Anglos and African Americans from Wisconsin, provided Salas with trustworthy organizers.[29] Familiar with farm work and cannery work, these bilingual activists entered a migrant world that welcomed them.[30] The union gained the support of workers, challenged Libby in court for not abiding by labor law, and won the court victories, yet failed to maintain itself as a viable labor organization (Rosenbaum 1991; Wisconsin Employment Relations Board 1967a, 1967b, 1968). In 1968, sensing that organizing Libby field workers would not yield results for Obreros Unidos, the organizers entered the canneries, a move that eventually pitted Obreros Unidos against the AFL-CIO and the Teamsters union, whose labor contracts with the canneries had long excluded Texas Mexican migrant workers. Cristaleño and other Texas Mexican workers, led by Cristaleño organizers, had developed a brand of oppositional consciousness that allowed them to attack labor allies if they too practiced racial discrimination on the shop floor.

In 1969, after Obreros Unidos called attention to the exclusion of migrant workers from cannery labor contracts, the Teamsters in agreement with the AFL-CIO claimed jurisdiction of cannery unionization in Wisconsin, and withdrew their support from the migrant's union (Slesinger and Murragui 1979, 9; Valdes 1991, 192). Eventually the Teamsters extended their contracts to include migrant cannery workers in many canneries originally organized by Obreros Unidos. Salas had hoped that Obreros Unidos could establish a cannery union under the United Farmworker's banner of Cesar Chavez, but Chavez abandoned Obreros Unidos in late 1969.[31] Although their own organization could not reap all the rewards of its work, Obreros Unidos—with its Cristaleño organizers, the support of Progressive Wisconsinites, and Anglo student volunteers—had succeeded with a limited budget in organizing a large number of Texas Mexican migrants and bringing the plight of the migrant worker to the general public (Valdes 1991, 191; Erenburg 1968).

Througout this period, Obreros Unidos placed Cristaleño activists in various sensitive positions, most prominently at Milwaukee's Greenfield Avenue UMOS offices. In 1968, labor leader Caesar Chavez asked Salas to manage the United Farm Workers Organizing Committee's "boycott grapes" effort in Milwaukee (Salas and Giffey 1998, 14–15).[32] With the help of David Loeffler, Salas settled in Milwaukee, left Obreros Unidos to the leadership of his brother Manuel Salas, and headed the UFWOC grape boycott. Other Cristaleño organizers joined UMOS.[33] These radicalized migrants helped promote movements already under way in Milwaukee's Mexican community.[34] Salas explained the influx:

> When we come up from the fields to do the boycotts here we have already been organizing for four or five years in central Wisconsin. We were veterans. As far as the Chicano political movement . . . . we'd come in with our picket signs, 'cause we'd already used that, all ready to go. We brought all the organizers. . . . When we moved down here [to Milwaukee] we knew how to do it. We knew how to organize, we knew how to set up a picket line, we were not afraid to get up there and manifest our rights. (Interview, Salas, July 27, 1992)

By now many of the migrants had not only the minimal components of oppositional consciousness: identification with one's group, identifying and opposing injustices done to the group, and seeing a common interest in combating these injustices. They also had an explicit analysis of their "rights," a repertory of proven strategies, and a conviction of the possibility of success in collective action.

The influx of migrant militants in 1968 led UMOS to participate in Milwaukee's convoy to the 1968 Poor People's March on Washington. Thus the activities of Salas and other Cristaleños in Wisconsin led them from the Chicano movement to participation in the broader civil rights movement in Milwaukee. After 1968, Salas helped Milwaukee's Father James Groppi, an Anglo defender of African American civil rights, in Milwaukee's civil rights activities whenever issues impacting migrants and ethnic Mexicans were addressed (United Migrant Opportunity Services 1985). In this process he became a prominent leader of Wisconsin's larger Milwaukee-based civil rights movement. His oppositional consciousness, and that of other Cristaleño leaders, became more multidimensional (see Stockdill, chap. 8, this volume) as they began to understand and take on the causes of women, African Americans, and poor people in Milwaukee.

In 1969, influenced by the emergence of general activism in the ethnic Mexican community as well as by local and national African American protests, some UMOS employees—led by Cristaleños—called for the ouster of the Anglos who held the main UMOS administrative staff positions. In response, the Anglos resigned their posts when their requests for new contracts were denied (Parra 1984, 55–58). After this call for self-administration and self-help on the part of Cristaleño and other Texas Mexican UMOS staff members, the Office of Economic Opportunity sent an interim management team to aid in the transfer of power. Salas was appointed program coordinator, managing a budget that included federal funds of $900,000 (United Migrant Opportunity Services Inc. 1985, 9). UMOS at this point became fully a center for Cristaleño and pan-migrant activism under Cristaleño and Texas Mexican leadership within Milwaukee's established Mexican neighborhood.

The Cristaleño activists in Milwaukee found themselves only one of many Texas Mexican biregional cultures in the Midwestern states. The Obreros Unidos organizers, who were primarily Cristaleños, joined Chicano activists from other migrant home bases in south Texas, including Carrizo Springs, Corpus Christi, Cotulla, Eagle Pass, and Pearsall, to create a pan-Texas Chicano movement based on a Texas-Wisconsin labor nexus. Cristaleños living in Milwaukee, together with Corpus Christi native Roberto Hernandez and Pearsall native Ernesto Chacon, joined forces to found the Latin American Union for Civil Rights (LAUCR) and *La Guardia,* a monthly bilingual newspaper in Milwaukee (Chicano Studies Program 1985). LAUCR engaged in direct action and community coalition building. In August 1969, *La Guardia* covered the LAUCR role in the establishment of the now-defunct Cooperativa de Credito, a credit union for the Milwaukee ethnic Mexican colony. LAUCR also organized dances and social events and established ethnic Mexican festivals on Milwaukee's South Side, which eventually led to the development of Fiesta Mexicana, an annual summer festival.[35] In this development *La Guardia* became the mouthpiece for several strands of Chicano thought, publishing articles from other national Chicano movement papers as well as the writings of local militants. The paper also opened itself to paid advertising, making available to its readers information on Spanish language radio broadcasts and ethnic Mexican restaurants and taverns.[36] Acknowledging Cristaleño efforts in the larger coalition, Salas remarked, "I think it obvious, the political impact we had."[37] Cristaleños also continued to keep abreast of events back "home." When Crystal City again ignited in protest, the activists in the Midwest answered the call for help.

Biregional Cross-Fertilization: The Rise of Modern Chicano Politics

Jose Angel Gutiérrez returned to Crystal City from his university work in 1969 and formed a Head Start program. This social service agency, with federal funding through Head Start and outside foundation grants, protected Gutiérrez from local Anglo reprisal. Gutiérrez also started a newsletter, which he hired high school students to distribute. According to Gutiérrez:

The important difference was that we had a memory. We knew the mistakes we made in 1963. We knew how we fell apart. . . . We learned how to do it better in '69. The issues . . . were different. You had the political generation that was involved in '63 still involved in '69 all the wiser, and you had the component of young people who were not involved in '63. . . . It was the young people and the women . . . that is part of the metamorphosis of the politics . . . all the disenfranchisement, the poor, the women, the young people took leadership. (Interview, Jose Angel Gutiérrez, April 18, 1995)

The revolt of 1969 grew from a stereotypically American teen culture. In this culture Texas high schools, football teams, and cheerleader squads were institutions of high significance, with Anglo alumni playing an active role in many aspects of everyday school honors and institutions (Smith 1978). Although Chicanos now represented the overwhelming majority of students in Crystal City, they were subject to discriminatory quotas, even for the pompom squad. In the 1962 and 1963 issues of the Crystal City High School yearbook, the *Javelin,* Anglos represented the socially dominant group, despite the fact that Mexican Americans accounted for the largest group of enrolled students. Pompom squad and other student groups were Anglo dominated, with only token Mexican American representation. Jose Angel Gutiérrez was one of the few Mexican Americans to have had prominence in a number of Anglo-dominated student groups, including debate and student government. (By contrast, after the events that follow, the 1970 *Javelin* yearbook adopted many Aztec and Mexican American cultural forms, and Mexican American students dominate the social world of the school—including pompom.)

In Crystal City in 1969, two Anglo cheerleaders had graduated, leaving vacancies on the squad. Diana Palacios tried out, but was rejected because the school already had allocated its quota of one Chicana cheerleader. On November 27, 1969, in the "letters to the editor" section of the *Zavala County Sentinel,* one Chicana asked:

Could it be possible, repulsive as the idea seems to the majority of us, that there are influences within the administration and policy forming groups of the school district that are racist . . . always insisting that the selected cheerleader or twirler groups must not have more than one Spanish-surnamed girl?

After the faculty chose two Anglos to fill the vacancies, Chicano students began to mobilize support for action (Navarro 1974, 187–304).

Because of the efforts of Gutiérrez and the civil rights activities of MAYO, as well as the work of their friends and family members of Obreros

Unidos and UMOS in Milwaukee, the Chicano students in 1969 had a more developed oppositional consciousness than the students in 1963. Among other things they had a good grasp of community action tactics. They put their complaints to the school in April through official channels and were accepted in part. But in June their requests were rejected outright, in what Armando Navarro characterized as a "separate but equal education" decision that refused to challenge the traditional quota system for Chicano student participation (Navarro 1995, 134; Shockley 1974, 120; Gutiérrez 1977). In December 1969, students led by Severita Lara, who had been a distributor of Gutiérrez's newsletter, organized a school boycott and formed the Youth Association, pledged to "total school reform" (Parker 1975, 31). Gutiérrez took a managing role in the Youth Association and began to create the framework for a second and permanent political takeover in the city itself. According to Severita Lara, the boycott was followed by an influx of supportive Cristaleño and other Chicano activists from MAYO and Texas universities (Navarro 1995, 141).[38] Gutiérrez sought to rely as much as possible on outside sources of financing and support, in order to guard against the potential effect of local Anglo economic reprisals. Gutiérrez commented:

> All of this was different in terms of support. We had money from outside. We were independent. . . . not vulnerable. All [of Los Cinco] fell because they couldn't pay their taxes, utility bills [after losing their jobs]. We were all independent. (Interview, Gutiérrez, April 18, 1995)

Remembering the mistakes they had made in 1963, Cristaleño activists moved quickly to counter past weaknesses. First, they worked to deflect the label of "outside agitator" that had damaged the Los Cinco effort in 1963 by bringing in not Anglo Teamsters but activist Cristaleños from the Midwest and other areas.[39]

Ciudadanos Unidos ("United Citizens") formed soon after the Youth Association boycott, organizing activists and parents into a strong community action group. Expressing his larger analysis, Gutiérrez remarked on the structure of Ciudadanos Unidos that "[i]t sought out members who stood for Mexicano social justice. But also it stood for protection of one another against the gringo . . . [to] collectively limit the power of the gringo over La Raza" (Parker 1975, 277)." Julian Salas, later a municipal judge in Crystal City, explained that "[w]hen Ciudadanos Unidos was organized, La Raza Unida was actually born" (Parker 1975, 36). The teenagers and their parents were organized in separate groups, both managed by Gutiérrez. Responding to the Crystal City situation, representatives of the Department of Health, Education, and Welfare (HEW) entered Crystal City, led by Carlos Vela, Texas state coordinator of HEW's civil rights office (Navarro 1995, 143). The boycott ended on January 6, 1970, after Chicano-Anglo negotiations were mediated by the U.S. Department of Justice. The brokered deal meant that protesting Cristaleño students entered class on January 7 without penalties. The activists had achieved many of their goals, including the establishment of bicultural and bilingual education, better testing of Chicano student abilities, and election to student body positions and most titles by majority vote.

Economic reality led teenage migrants such as Geraldo Lazcano and Raul Rodríguez, both participants in the walk-outs and boycott, to settle in Milwaukee after graduation. Lazcano and friends took a bus to Milwaukee, moved in with out-settled family members, and found work in Milwaukee.[40] They carried firsthand news of the changes in Crystal City to Cristaleños in Milwaukee. Rodríguez found employment at UMOS as a migrant job placement recruiter, using friendships formed among migrant workers from Crystal City.[41] By the late 1960s the migrant network had been transformed to serve the needs of a population seeking to settle-out.

The La Raza Unida Party: Biregionalism and the Chicano Political Movement

Following the successful Crystal City school boycott, El Partido de la Raza Unida (RUP) grew from the successful school boycott movement led by Gutiérrez, the student leaders, and the parents. The many layers of the community that had aided in the successful Youth Association movement were retooled to serve the needs of the newly formed RUP. By 1970, RUP had firm community control and the support of a majority of Cristaleños, easily winning three seats on the Crystal City school board; one of the victors was former Obreros Unidos organizer Arturo Gonzalez (Garcia 1989, 57; Navarro 1995, 222). In 1971, candidates for local office in Crystal City were selected from among those who had proven themselves in organizational drives with Obreros Unidos and in other Midwestern Chicano activities. Among them were school board candidate Rodolfo Palomo, who had worked for Obreros Unidos in Wisconsin, and city council candidates Roberto Gamez and Jose Talamantez, both Crystal City High School graduates who had done work with migrants in Wisconsin and the Midwest (Shockley 1974, 189).[42] All RUP candidates won the positions they sought at the city level.

The 1971 victory of RUP in Crystal City not only brought Cristaleños once again from Wisconsin to Crystal City. It also led Jose Angel Gutiérrez to extend the RUP to Milwaukee, with the help of Jesus Salas and

Milwaukee LAUCR activist Ernesto Chacon (United Migrant Opportunity Services 1985, 9). Continued communication across the Wisconsin-Texas nexus brought Francisco Rodriguez, a former UMOS employee and Obreros Unidos organizer, to serve as city manager of Crystal City in 1972 (Gutiérrez 1998, 212).[43] When Rodriguez resigned in 1973, after one year in service, Esequiel Guzman, who had been working for *La Guardia* and UMOS in Milwaukee, replaced him (Navarro 1998, 129).[44]

Continued migration from Crystal City to Milwaukee and back provided a continued transfer of talent across the biregional frontier. In the late 1970s, educated and experienced Cristaleños returned from the Midwest to occupy positions in the RUP government of Crystal City and Zavala County. Jesus Salas, Francisco Rodriguez, Miguel Delgado, and others returned in this period to help RUP efforts.[45] The RUP and Gutiérrez used the network of friends and families that connected the Midwest to Crystal City to recruit qualified Chicanos for governmental posts and candidates for elected office, drawing heavily upon those employed at UMOS and other Milwaukee migrant service agencies. Gutiérrez described Cristaleño informal networks as providing a "job information system, . . . mutual benefit society, . . . insurance company, . . . a communication network—you name it—lots of facets to it, but we added the political dimension to it."[46] Salas described the transfer of Cristaleño activists between the two cities:

> Former organizers for the farm workers union and people who had been involved here in Wisconsin go back and help out the movement in Crystal City. [Francisco] Rodriguez, Esequiel Guzman, Rodolfo Palomo, among others, they all go back to Crystal City and help out with the movement. We never saw it as two different things. For us it was the same. The politics were tied together, and the leadership developed in tandem. I went back in the midseventies after the takeover of [Zavala] county, and I stayed down there helping organize Raza Unida Party. (Interview, Salas, July 27, 1992)

From Local to National: Biregionalism and the National La Raza Unida Party

In 1972, Chicano civil rights leaders from around the nation met to elect a national leadership and to unite the many state Raza Unida Parties that had formed after the victory of RUP in Crystal City. Delegates to the 1972 convention from the Midwestern states of Illinois, Michigan, and Wisconsin were largely former migrant workers from Crystal City or were closely allied with the Cristaleño leadership. Indeed, Gutiérrez used the network among Cristaleños and Texas-based former migrants to take control of

RUP at the national level. Prominent Chicano leaders included Rodolfo "Corky" Gonzales, the founder of the Chicano Crusade for Justice in Colorado; Gutiérrez from Crystal City; and Reies Lopez Tijerina, leader of the New Mexico group Alianza Federal de Pueblos Libres, as well as delegates from most states with significant Chicano populations (Gutiérrez 1954–90, box 24; Acuna 1988, 340–41). At the convention, Gutiérrez met with representatives from Wisconsin and other Midwestern states, many of whom he knew through mutual friendships and organization networks. When it came time to elect a national Raza Unida president, it was Wisconsinite and UMOS employee Dante Navarro, originally from Mexico, together with Ernesto Chacon, a former UMOS employee and founder of LAUCR, who seconded the nomination of Gutiérrez and called for a convention floor vote. With the aid of Cristaleños and their allies, Gutiérrez won the full support of the delegations from the District of Columbia, Oregon, Indiana, Kansas, Maryland, Texas, and Wisconsin, and majorities of the delegates from Arizona, New Mexico, Washington, and Utah (Gutiérrez 1954–90, box 24, "Salazar," p. 2).

Rodolfo "Corky" Gonzales, Gutiérrez's main RUP rival and a longtime out-settled English-speaking Chicano, did not understand this network. He believed that the Midwestern delegates were only Crystal City "plants."[47] Gonzales found it hard to believe, according to Gutiérrez, that Cristaleños had maintained these networks for "twenty years or more." Yet I have found evidence for these connections in Gutiérrez's correspondence with former classmates, including Francisco Rodríguez, who had returned to Wisconsin, and with neighborhood companions living in Milwaukee and elsewhere in the Midwest (United Migrant Opportunity Services 1985, 9; Gutiérrez 1954–90, box 24, Raza Unida Party, Wisconsin folder). Gutiérrez kept in contact with fellow Cristaleños in the Midwest and visited Milwaukee and other areas in Wisconsin several times in 1969–75 to assist Cristaleños and other Texas Mexican organizing efforts (Gutiérrez 1954–90, box 24, Raza Unida Party, Wisconsin folder, correspondence, 1974).

In a letter written on September 27, 1973, to Pedro Ortiz, Gutiérrez stated that "it is always a good feeling to have brothers and sisters or yourselves eager and willing to promote el Chicanismo familiar" (Gutiérrez 1954–90, box 24, Raza Unida Party, Wisconsin folder, correspondence, 1973). For example, Carlos Reyes, Raza Unida Party official and future UMOS board president, wrote to Francisco Rodríguez and often phoned this former city manager.[48] When Gutiérrez sought control of the national party, he tapped these connections (Gutiérrez 1998, 230). Gutiérrez summed up this support system as it functioned in Crystal City:

[Y]ou know if you get beat up you're going to call on your brother and your family for assistance . . . you're not going to call on strangers who don't know or understand you. . . . So, if you're already organized around *La Familia* unit, when you look for help you know where to find it . . . in friends, relatives, or people who are family to you . . . and these people will have another set of people who are family or relatives that are blood to them. And in this way you can organize in a very natural way because you're expanding your relationships from the bottom that are not artificial or contrived, it's a very natural bond. (Parker 1975, 280)

Aware of the political potential of such a network, Gutiérrez used it not only to gain control of the National Raza Unida Party but also to raise funds for La Raza Unida in Crystal City from Cristaleños now settled in the Midwest:

I made it my job to find them [Cristaleños] because that was my fund-raising avenue. I'd go and make them feel guilty, and they'd give me money. I'd say "you *cabrones* left, and I'm holding the bag! If you're not gonna help, you've got to give me money!" And they would. They also became more militant outside of Crystal City. (Interview, Gutiérrez, April 18, 1995)

Among his peers, Gutiérrez was now able to draw on a widespread sense of duty based on a recognition of a group identity of interests and the need for collective action. He knew that their history and family ties would make Cristaleños sensitive to this duty. His fund raising for La Raza Unida reveals the link that he and other activists perceived between Crystal City and the evolution of La Raza Unida Party.

Traditional interpretations of the Los Cinco revolt of 1963 have seen it only as a precursor to the second revolt (Shockley 1974; Garcia 1989; Navarro 1995; Navarro 1998). The Los Cinco revolt now can be seen as providing the initial inspirational and activist training for the leaders of the farm workers' movement in Wisconsin and La Raza Unida Party, neither of which could have been achieved without the migrant experience and the unique cross-fertilization of oppositional consciousness across this biregional migrant frontier.

Conclusion: The Power of Fusion

In this story, the whole is greater than the sum of its parts. The political takeover of Crystal City, Texas, by an ethnic Mexican majority in 1963–65 has long stood out as a critical marker in the development of Chicano politics in the United States. This chapter analyzes the historically significant events following from that takeover, which established the national La Raza Unida Party in the United States, as resulting from a highly fruitful mix of two strands of oppositional consciousness. One strand derived from the traditional anger, folklore, and political wisdom that poor Chicano farm workers had maintained against their Anglo oppressors. The other derived from the progressive labor traditions of La Follette's Midwest.

This attempt to detail the importance of these linkages is a first step toward a more accurate rendering of the larger Chicano movement. The Wisconsin-Texas migrant networks among Cristaleños brought together two strands of ideology and moral conviction in a synergy that had national implications. The Cristaleños adapted institutions created in the nation's capital as a response to the civil rights movement. They activated those institutions by drawing on an oppositional consciousness fused from strands in both segregated south Texas and Milwaukee, Wisconsin. These influences then reshaped kinship and community networks to serve the purpose of labor and ethnic militancy both in Texas and the Midwest. The fusion that made this possible was a fusion of institutions, material support, and human networks. It was also a fusion of ideas, emotions, and commitments. In the historic moment of forging the La Raza Unida Party, two strands of oppositional consciousness had generated an explosion of organizing energy that probably neither strand could have done alone.

Notes

The research for this chapter was supported by a grant from the Franklin D. Scott Fund for Migration Research at Northwestern University. I am particularly grateful to Jane Mansbridge and to my graduate advisor, Josef Barton, for their careful review of earlier drafts of this chapter, and to the many people I interviewed.

1. See Navarro 1998 and Gutiérrez 1998 for the movement's origins in Crystal City; see Shockley 1974, Garcia 1989, and Navarro 1995 for the Texas-Wisconsin migrant social system. Much of the background in this and following paragraphs comes from an initial interview with Jesus Salas (June 27, 1992) and subsequent interviews. Salas, a Cristaleño labor organizer and founder of Obreros Unidos, was a university lecturer and also a labor activist when I interviewed him in Milwaukee and Madison in 1992–2000.

2. Taylor (1932) covers the workings of this segregated landscape. Utilizing some of Taylor's fieldwork, Montejano (1977 and 1989) covers the mechanics of Anglo domination of Chicanos in South Texas. See also Gutiérrez 1968; Quinones 1990, 129; and Valdés 1991.

3. Interview, Geraldo Lazcano, August 10, 1992. Lazcano, who still visits Crystal City annually, called it a ghost town because of its lack of jobs. Lazcano is a factory worker at a major Milwaukee industrial employer. Shannon (1966) found that Texas Mexican settlers in this community near Milwaukee were primarily from south Texas labor-sending areas, including Cotulla, Crystal City, San Antonio, and Laredo. His report also found that steady year-round work was a strong factor in the settlement decision.

4. The poverty and social inequality of late twentieth-century Crystal City is detailed in "Race Antagonism Splits Texas City," *New York Times,* April 14, 1963, 49.

5. Interview, Mark Erenburg, July 22, 1999. Erenburg, A graduate student in Economics working under Elizabeth Brandeis Raushenbush and Robert Lampman, was responsible for much of the data collection on Wisconsin migrant workers and became "Research Director" for Obreros Unidos.

6. Interview, Jose Angel Gutiérrez, April 19, 1995.

7. Interview, Miguel Delgado, February 8, 1997; interview, Francisco Rodriguez, July 25, 1998; interview, Jesus Salas, July 27, 1992. Each of these individuals attended Crystal City public schools in 1960–63; most of them graduated from the high school in that time.

8. Interview, Guadalupe Rodriguez, February 10, 1998.

9. See "Revolt of the Mexicans," *Time,* April 12, 1963, 25; "The Anglo Minority," *Newsweek,* April 29, 1963, 26; and Thomas B. Morgan, "The Texas Giant Awakens," *Look,* October 6, 1963, 71–75. Note that the new energy came from students (in this case high school students rather than college students), a group that Oberschall (1973, 152–53) identifies as a potential source of social movement leadership. Oberschall comments that

> [a]n examination of other revolutionary leaders of the working class or the peasantry would probably reveal much the same pattern of "outside" leadership by the educated sons of the traditional ruling classes or new middle class. . . . If one examines the occupational and social background of protest and opposition leaders in greater detail, it appears that farmers or people with an agricultural background are almost totally absent . . . in the production of leaders. (1973, 152)

In this case we find no outsiders, but rather a pattern of internal upward mobility generating leadership within the group. The father of Jesus Salas was an agricultural labor contractor and the father of Jose Angel Gutiérrez was a barrio physician. Neither leader came from a purely agricultural background.

10. Mario Compean later used the Texas-Wisconsin migrant network to find employment in Madison, Wisconsin, with United Migrant Opportunity Services, Inc. (UMOS).

11. Interview, Victor H. Delgado, July 13, 1992. Delgado's family had migrated most of his life. Yet starting when he was in middle school, the family returned before the end of summer so that the children could attend school. In the 1960s Delgado continued to migrate during the summers while attending college. He later settled in Milwaukee.

12. Interview, David Florez, March 21, 1993; interview, Geraldo Lazcano, August 10, 1992. Florez's father migrated from Crystal City to Milwaukee in the 1950s, has worked as a baker for over thirty years, and owns a home in South Milwaukee, Wisconsin, a working-class suburb. Lazcano owns a home on Milwaukee's South Side.

13. Interview, Oscar Cervera, June 21, 1999. Cervera, who settled in Milwaukee in the mid-1960s, has helped numerous family members move to Milwaukee. He has subscribed to the *Zavala County Sentinel* since his own departure, has sent bits of family news to the "Here and There" section of the newspaper, and passes his newspaper along to other Cristaleños.

14. Interview, Dale M. Barker, February 24, 1997. Barker still manages this small newspaper. With demographic changes in the county, the paper must appeal both to the county's largely Chicano population and the many out-settled residents who subscribe from Wisconsin, California, and other migrant-receiving states.

15. Interview, David Giffey, August 27, 1999. Giffey, a life-long Wisconsin resident, worked with Jesus Salas throughout the Obreros Unidos effort, managing the union's newspaper and press operations. He later moved to Texas to help organize farm workers there under the UFWOC banner.

16. Interview, Fred Kessler, June 4, 1999; interview, E. Michael McCann, June 6, 1999.

Both men joined Obreros Unidos as volunteer attorneys while in their first years of legal practice.

17. Interview, David Loeffler, July 19, 1999. Loeffler was brought in to serve as an Obreros Unidos lawyer by the AFL-CIO in cases before the Wisconsin Employment Relations Board, essentially serving as their labor lawyer in confrontations with growers and canneries.

18. Interview, Mark Erenburg, 1999; interview, Jesus Salas, April 20, 2000.

19. Interview, Jesus Salas, March 22, 1995; interview, F. Rodriguez, July 29, 2000. Salas relied on what McAdam, Tarrow, and Tilly (2001) have termed an "opportunity spiral," originating the day Cristaleños became interstate migrants.

20. Interview, Jesus Salas, July 27, 1992.

21. Interview, Genevieve Medina, June 17, 1992. At the time she was interviewed, Medina ran the outreach section of UMOS's migrant project. Medina was key to the founding of UMOS. She served under the original Anglo managers and aided the transition from Anglo to Chicano migrant control of the organization. She has since died.

22. Interview, F. Rodriguez, July 29, 2000; interview, Manuel Santos, June 17, 1992. Santos, a Cristaleño migrant worker most of his life, found employment first at UMOS and now works at a nearby technical college.

23. Interview, Victoria Silvas, June 17, 1992. Silvas, a Cristaleño migrant worker, joined UMOS after years of activism in Milwaukee.

24. Interview, Jesus Salas, July 27, 2000. Salas used both the labor and progressive movement repertoires (Tilly 1986, 1998) available to him in Wisconsin and tactics that fit the civil rights "master frame" (Snow and Benford 1988).

25. Interview, David Loeffler, July 19, 1999.

26. Wisconsin Employment Relations Board (1966) found among other things that employer harassment and interrogation of employees as to union activity constituted an unlawful interference; interview, David Loeffler, July 19, 1999.

27. Interview, Jesus Salas, July 27, 2000; interview, Bill Smith, April 23, 2000.

28. Interview, Jesus Salas, July 27, 1992; interview, Arturo Gonzalez, February 22, 1997; interview, Esequiel Guzman, February 19, 1997. All three men were in the same Crystal City grade cohort and remained close, despite the fact that Salas graduated from a Wisconsin high school.

29. Interview, David Giffey, August 27, 1999.

30. Interview, Jesus Salas, July 27, 1992.

31. Interview, Mark Erenburg, July 22, 1999; interview, Bill Smith, April 23, 2000.

32. Lucha Oral History Project 1997.

33. Interview, Francisco Rodriguez, July 25, 1998. Rodriguez joined UMOS in 1966 and worked with Obreros Unidos in 1968. He was a close friend of both Jesus Salas and Raza Unida Party leader Jose Angel Gutiérrez.

34. Interview, Esequil Guzman, February 19, 1997.

35. Interview, Ernesto Chacon, October 4, 1996. Chacon, also from south Texas, was key to the establishment of LAUCR with Cristaleños, as well as the early coordination of Fiesta Mexicana.

36. For example see *La Guardia,* August 1969.

37. Interview, Salas, 1992.

38. Interview, Severita Lara, February 15, 1997. Lara saw Gutiérrez as key to the mustering of outside activist and financial support for this student effort. She downplayed the relevance of MAYO membership, and focused instead on the return of Cristaleños from college.

39. Interview, Arturo Gonzalez, February 22, 1997; interview, Esequiel Guzman, February 19, 1997. Both men were solicited by Gutiérrez to return after these events occurred.

40. Interview, Lazcano, August 10, 1992.

41. Interview, Raul Rodriguez, July 16, 1992.

42. Interview, Gonzalez, February 2, 1997.

43. Interview, F. Rodríguez, 1998. Rodríguez, convinced that an activist should not seek to become a permanent fixture in a post, entered intent on resigning within a year to let another person take over the position.

44. Interview, Esequiel Guzman, February 19, 1997. In 1973, Guzman believed that activists should not seek to make careers of government service and thus served a short term as city manager.

45. Interview, Jesus Salas, March 22, 1995; interview, Miguel Delgado, February 8, 1997; interview, Alejandro Nieri, July 14, 1999. Salas and Delgado were Cristaleños. Nieri was originally from Peru, yet had worked among Cristaleños at UMOS for several years and was strongly committed to the Chicano movement. Each of these men, while working for federally supported community-based organizations in Milwaukee, was recruited by Jose Angel Gutiérrez because of his experience with grant writing and management to take over the Zavala County Economic Development Corporation. All earlier incarnations of economic development had failed prior to the grant written by these three Milwaukee-based activists.

46. Interview, Jose Angel Gutiérrez, 1995; Tony Castro, failing to see the migrant dynamic, viewed the Crystal City political scene under the Raza Unida Party as "the old politics of ward campaigning disguised as new Chicano politics" (Castro 1974, 169). The migrant dynamic demonstrates what McAdam, Tarrow, and Tilly (2001) identify as a "scale shift," as the opportunity spirals and brokerage networks that had facilitated the development of the union and migrant movement in Wisconsin became the foundation for the larger national political movement of La Raza.

47. Interview, Jose Angel Gutiérrez, April 19, 1995. See also Rodríguez 2000, where I show how Wisconsin's established Texas-origin activists supported Jose Angel Gutiérrez's rise to leadership of the national party.

48. Interview, Carlos Reyes, July 14, 1999. Eventually Reyes, although not a Cristaleño, went north following the migrant stream to Wisconsin to work for UMOS and the University of Wisconsin.

7   Divided Consciousness: The Impact of Black Elite Consciousness on the 1966 Chicago Freedom Movement

Lori G. Waite

The Civil Rights Movement Comes North

The 1966 Chicago Freedom Movement (CFM) represented a collaborative effort between Martin Luther King Jr., the Southern Christian Leadership Conference (SCLC), and local Chicago activists. It also marked the first time that the SCLC attempted to address racial inequality in the urban North. The decision to shift the locus of protest from the South to Chicago brought to the surface many latent tensions among Black elites. The Chicago Freedom Movement thus helps reveal the divided nature of Black elite consciousness at this moment as well as the cultural and social-psychological factors that affected the outcome of that collaboration. (A more exhaustive history of the CFM can be found in Anderson and Pickering 1986; Garrow 1986, 1989; and Ralph 1993).

The first source of division arose within the SCLC itself over the very idea of a Chicago campaign. Many SCLC activists opposed the notion of going to Chicago because a significant portion of the staff wanted instead to finish what the movement had started in the South. Others objected to Chicago because they knew that its Black population was more diverse and its politics were more complex than in the South. Most importantly, those who opposed a Chicago campaign argued that too many members of the Black elite in Chicago had ties to the political machine. These ties would make them hard to mobilize.

The second source of division arose within the CFM over appropriate strategies and tactics for dealing with the Chicago machine. Most Chicago activists wanted to launch a direct attack against the machine. Most members of the SCLC, however, measured CFM success not in the overthrow of a local political machine but in an increased ability to generate national legislation. These far-ranging disagreements over tactics and goals would limit the movement's power.

A third source of division arose within what should have been the core constituency of SCLC—Chicago's Black ministers. The tensions between the SCLC and prominent Black ministers in Chicago severely weakened the campaign. Much of the tension emanated from the opposition to the Chicago Freedom Movement of the Reverend Joseph H. Jackson, an influential leader of the National Baptist Convention whose church was located in Chicago. Most importantly, however, it was the affiliation of many Black ministers with Chicago's political machine that kept them from supporting a movement that challenged that system. Criticism from Black religious leaders was especially problematic for the SCLC because the Black church had always been the organization's primary base of support in the South. Although the SCLC had encountered opposition from the Black church community during some of its southern campaigns, the clerical opposition it encountered in Chicago was much more intractable.

Finally, during the late sixties tensions were just beginning to surface between "traditional" civil rights activists, such as the SCLC, and a newer cohort of Black elected officials (Reed 1986). Both Black elected officials and the SCLC in Chicago in 1966 claimed "legitimate" leadership in the Black community. The Black elected officials owed their leadership positions to the political machine, whereas the SCLC's leadership status in the Black community derived from its achievements in the South as a protest organization. Black elected officials were threatened by the SCLC's use of noninstitutionalized tactics and perceived the charismatic southern civil rights activists as invading their turf. Chicago's six Black aldermen and many Black ministers opposed the Chicago campaign for similar reasons—they were an entrenched part of the political system. Thus, as the CFM got under way Chicago's Black elected officials *and* prominent Black clergy were caught in the crossfire, forced to choose between the movement and the political system that the movement challenged.

This chapter examines variations in Black elite consciousness within the tensions that surfaced among members of the Black elite during the 1966 Chicago Freedom Movement. Here the term "Black elite" refers to civil rights activists, Black clergy, and Chicago's Black elected officials. The tensions that surfaced during the CFM can be linked to different structural positions occupied in 1966 by members of the Black elite. Not all the Black elite were similarly situated—some were members of the political machine while others were not. The consciousness of different members of the Black elite reflected their structural position. Black oppositional consciousness in Chicago in 1966 did not operate independently of structural location.

The Theoretical Background of Black Elite Consciousness

As one of the first Black intellectuals to analyze the development of Black consciousness, W. E. B. Du Bois, argued in his classic study, *The Souls of Black Folks,* that even within one person the consciousness of

African Americans was not monolithic: "One ever feels his twoness,—an American, a Negro; two souls, two thoughts, two unreconciled strivings; two warring ideals in one dark body, whose dogged strength alone keeps it from being torn asunder" ([1903] 1969, 45). Du Bois's conceptualization of double consciousness has become a standard framework for contemporary scholars interested in the development of Black consciousness. Black feminist scholars (e.g., Davis 1983; King 1988; Collins 1990), however, have argued that the experiences of Black women necessitated, in addition to race consciousness, the development of gender and class consciousness. In effect, Black women have developed a three-pronged consciousness deriving from their experiences with race, class, and gender oppression (Morris 1992, 366). Oppositional consciousness can easily be multiple.[1]

Early sociological studies of the civil rights movement did not include analyses of Black consciousness. The structural models usually overlooked the effects of social-psychological or cultural variables, such as consciousness, on movement origins and outcomes (e.g., Oberschall 1973). Only in the early eighties did movement scholars such as McAdam (1982), Morris (1984), Bloom (1987), and others begin to incorporate social-psychological and cultural variables into structural approaches. In his study of the southern civil rights movement McAdam used the term "cognitive liberation" (1982, 34) to characterize the transformation of consciousness among southern Blacks in the early sixties. Morris (1984) argued that cultural factors such as consciousness raising, music, oratory, and prayer were just as important to the outcome of the modern civil rights movement as the climate of the larger political environment. Bloom's (1987) analysis of the movement called attention to the interaction between consciousness and structure across racial groups. Yet variations in Black consciousness remain relatively unexplored. Black consciousness during the modern civil rights movement was never monolithic. Rather, it varied according to such factors as class position, gender, and geographic region.

By the late 1960s the consciousness of Blacks was perceived as so internally differentiated that Cleveland Sellers, program secretary of the Student Nonviolent Coordinating Committee (SNCC) could ask "What is Black consciousness?" (Sellers 1991, 279). The very question reflected a growing awareness among many Black activists that Black consciousness was not monolithic. In the South before the civil rights movement, Jim Crow laws had placed southern Blacks in similar structural positions, forging, ironically, a relatively unified Black consciousness (Bloom 1987, 145). But in northern settings such as Chicago, where Jim Crow laws and political disfranchisement did not exist, Black consciousness could take many forms. Forms of consciousness that lay latent in the South could be overt and primary in the North. Their structural positions as fuller members of the larger polity allowed many northern Black elites to develop a collective identification with the dominant group based on shared class interests rather than racial solidarity.

After the passage of key civil rights legislation in the mid to late 1960s opened political and economic opportunities for Blacks, class interests became a significant factor in the development of Black elite consciousness. But it would be a mistake to assume that Black elite consciousness is, or was, driven solely by class interests. Other factors also affected its development. For example, although many Black elites in Chicago shared class interests with Whites, the persistence of racism gave them common racial experiences with poorer Blacks. Prominent Black Chicagoans still knew that as long as racism persisted in American society major aspects of their fate were inextricably linked to the fate of poorer Blacks.

Morris's (1992) concept of political consciousness sheds needed light on the complexity of Black elite consciousness. He defines political consciousness as "those cultural beliefs and ideological expressions that are utilized for the realization and maintenance of group interests" (362–63). Both dominant and subordinate groups develop political consciousness—"hegemonic consciousness" among the dominant groups and "oppositional consciousness" among subordinate groups. Here we define oppositional consciousness as "an empowering mental state that prepares members of an oppressed group to act to undermine, reform, or overthrow a system of human domination." That mental state includes identifying with members of a group, recognizing and opposing injustices done to that group, and recognizing a group common interest in ending those injustices. It may include identifying another, dominant, group "as causing and in some way benefiting from those injustices." A mature oppositional consciousness includes other "ideas, beliefs, and feelings that provide coherence, explanation, and moral condemnation" (Mansbridge, chap. 1, this volume; Morris 1990, 1992). Group interests are a necessary but not sufficient factor in the development of oppositional consciousness.

Morris (1992) argues further that political consciousness is rarely monolithic. In some situations Blacks may identify with the class interests and hegemonic consciousness of dominant groups, while in other situations they may identify with the class interests and oppositional consciousness of subordinate groups. Sometimes, as in the Chicago case, Blacks can simultaneously identify with both hegemonic and op-positional consciousness. Many forms of hegemonic and oppositional consciousness appear in social relations, each type resting squarely on the structural relations in which social actors are embedded.

The existing literature on political consciousness tends to overlook the relationship between structural position and political consciousness. Many Black elites in Chicago in 1966 opposed the CFM because of their structural relations with the Democratic machine. The structure of political opportunities in Chicago in 1966 affected their consciousness.

Attention to the effect of structural position on consciousness re-quires some adjustment to the prevailing "polity model" that many sociologists (e.g., Gamson 1975; Tilly 1978; McAdam 1982) use to explain the political situation of dominant and subordinate groups. In the polity model, challengers, such as southern Blacks before 1965, are excluded from the formal political process of a society (Morris 1984, 325). Because challengers are excluded from polity membership they "lack routine, low-cost access to resources controlled by the government" (Morris and Herring 1987, 166; see also Tilly 1978). The chief aim of challengers is polity membership, because until they become polity members gov-ernments will not respond to their interests (Morris 1984, 325; Morris and Herring 1987, 166). Polity members tend to have routine, low-cost access to resources controlled by the government. They thus seek to remain in the polity and "fight tenaciously against loss of power, and especially against expulsion from the polity" (Tilly 1978, 135). In short, the polity model characterizes the relationship between members and challengers as a struggle for power between groups that are inside the polity and those that are outside (McAdam 1982, 38).

The simple member-challenger dichotomy of the polity model cap-tures the political situation of many groups, including southern Blacks, whose interests have been formally excluded from the political process. A problem arises, however, when we apply the model to the political situ-ation of groups such as Black Chicagoans in 1966. Blacks in Chicago had been voting since the turn of the twentieth century (Drake and Cayton 1945; Spear 1967). They could not be classified as challengers because they were not formally excluded from the political process. Moreover, many Black Chicagoans had positions in the polity as elected officials, judges, and so forth, giving them vested interests in the political system. The polity model is thus best used not as a dichotomy but as a continuum. Black Chicagoans were formally but not practically equal members of the polity. During the CFM many Black elites struggled between hegemonic and oppositional consciousness because they were members of *both* the polity and the Black oppositional community. They had, in effect, one foot in the polity and one foot in the challenging group. As a consequence of this dual structural position, during the CFM some Black elites found it hard to choose which consciousness to embrace.

Because the need to reconceptualize the polity model influences how we expect movements to mobilize, this analysis of Black elite consciousness has larger implications for social movement theory. Mobilization, or the "process of increasing the readiness to act collectively by building the loyalty of a constituency to an organization or to a group of leaders" (Gamson 1975, 15), usually takes place over several years, involving many encounters in many places (Gamson, Fireman, and Rytina 1982, 5). But, as Gamson (1975, 15) notes, even when a challenging group has a committed membership that can be quickly mobilized, the group "may lack unity of command. Competing voices, each with its plausible claim to legitimate authority, are often heard—one saying 'March!' another 'Wait!' Who speaks for the group?" In Chicago in the late 1960s, civil rights activists found themselves competing with the machine for the hearts and minds of Black Chicagoans. In situations where hegemonic and oppositional consciousness are not so intertwined, mobilization can be far quicker and more effective. In the South, for example, Black elites saw themselves primarily as members of the Black community and only secondarily as members of the reigning political system. Thus they experienced less ambivalence in political consciousness than northern elites and could be more easily mobilized behind the banner of the movement.

The effects of structural location on political consciousness appear in many social movements. White women, for example, can be torn between a hegemonic patriarchal system rooted in White supremacy and an oppositional gender consciousness. In the nineteenth-century women's suffrage movement, for example, White suffragists used racist arguments to further their gender interests, arguing "that the enfranchisement of white women would further, rather than impede, the power of a white ruling class" (Giddings 1984, 124; see also Davis 1981). Thus despite the fact that the women's suffrage movement had emerged out of the Black movement against slavery, when forced to choose between White supremacy and gender consciousness many White suffragists opportunistically capitulated to the hegemonic consciousness of White supremacy. Like the suffrage movement, the CFM illustrates the problems that arise when members of an elite occupy contradictory structural locations. The primary lesson from the Chicago Freedom Movement is that occupying contradictory locations causes inconsistent responses to social movements.

Data Sources and Methods

Part of a broader study of the 1966 Chicago Freedom Movement, this analysis uses primary data from archives, manuscripts, and interviews in addition to the primary and secondary data produced by recent studies of the Chicago Freedom Movement (Anderson and Pickering 1986; Garrow 1986, 1989; Ralph 1993).

I analyzed documents located at the Chicago Historical Society, the Harold Washington Library, and the Carter G. Woodson Library in Chicago, including newspaper accounts of the CFM and personal papers of various Chicago activists, and political and clerical leaders. In addition, I utilized interview data from the Chicago Freedom Movement Oral History Project[2] and my own interviews. From July 1994 to May 1996 I conducted twenty-four interviews with SCLC activists, Chicago activists, Black elected officials, and Black ministers in the Chicago area and Atlanta, Georgia, who either participated in or knew about the activities surrounding the 1966 CFM. I interviewed respondents in their homes, in churches, in restaurants, and in their places of business. I used a modified snowball sampling technique to obtain their names, compiling an initial list of names from published and archival sources on the Chicago Freedom Movement, then modifying the original list based on the availability of respondents. I also asked each person interviewed which other people they felt I should talk to. All of the interviews were open-ended and semistructured and lasted from one to several hours.

A Brief Overview of the Chicago Freedom Movement

In the late sixties Chicago was the second largest city in America and one of the nation's most segregated. Close to one million Blacks lived in two expanding slum ghettoes, on the south and west sides of the city. Each was hemmed in by barriers in housing and employment (Ralph 1993, 45–46). In the summer of 1965, the deeply segregated schools produced by segregated housing prompted a biracial coalition of Chicago activists, the Coordinating Council of Community Organizations (CCCO), to invite Martin Luther King Jr. and the SCLC to Chicago to lead a fight against de facto segregation in public schools. The hope was that the SCLC would launch a massive campaign against school segregation in the mold of Birmingham and Selma (Young 1996, 381). In response to the uprisings in Watts and New York, the SCLC had recently conducted a tour of northern cities. King wanted to transform the southern movement into a national nonviolent direct action campaign (Garrow 1986, 452). The SCLC thus accepted the CCCO's invitation. After SCLC staff members investigated

Chicago's problems, however, they decided that the movement's objectives should be much larger than an attack on segregated schools.

The SCLC saw Chicago as "the prototype of the northern urban race problem" (Southern Christian Leadership Conference 1991, 292), which required changes on the federal, state, and local levels (299). The SCLC's plan for an open-housing campaign quickly supplanted the CCCO's original plan to oust Chicago's segregationist school superintendent Benjamin C. Willis, because housing had implications beyond the local level. On the local level, the SCLC hoped to raise the consciousness of poorer Black Chicagoans on how to deal with the problems of slum housing. At the state level, the SCLC hoped to secure tax reforms, updated building codes, open occupancy legislation, and enforcement of existing statutes (Southern Christian Leadership Conference 1991, 299). At the federal level, if successful, the Chicago campaign could gain support for the 1966 Civil Rights Bill pending in Congress. This bill was unique because, unlike its 1964 predecessor, it was not directed primarily at the South. The 1966 Civil Rights Bill addressed a national problem—discrimination in the sale and rental of housing (Ralph 1993, 173–74).

From its work in southern cities such as Albany, Georgia, and Birmingham, Alabama, the SCLC had learned two important lessons about conducting a movement. It had learned about the need to crystallize issues so the person on the street could easily understand them and about the need to concentrate the action on specific targets (Southern Christian Leadership Conference 1991, 293–94). In the South the issue had been deliberately reduced to the eradication of legal segregation (Southern Christian Leadership Conference 1991, 293–94). Like the South, Chicago was segregated. But the segregation was not legally sanctioned as it was in the South. Chicago had no segregation laws or discrimination ordinances (Garrow 1986). SCLC leaders defined the issue in Chicago as economic exploitation, seen most clearly in slum housing (Southern Christian Leadership Conference 1991, 294). But Chicago's Black population was so diverse that housing and economic exploitation did not affect all Black Chicagoans deeply the way that Jim Crow segregation had in the South. Andrew Young (1996, 391–92) stated the matter succinctly:

> Chicago lacked the unity of purpose of the South. In Birmingham, whether you were a welfare mother or a millionaire, segregation was a problem. . . . In Chicago, a mother in the slums was concerned about her baby being wrapped in newspaper on the coldest night of the year, while a black millionaire might be more concerned about selling his products in the local supermarket. These were very different issues.

Young's statement speaks to the extent to which Chicago's Black community was stratified along class lines. Chicago's Black poor "had tremendous, immediate material needs" while many middle-class Blacks led relatively comfortable lives (Young 1996, 392). In an effort to unify such a diverse group, the SCLC departed from its usual strategy of concentrating on a single issue at a time and attempted to focus on multiple issues simultaneously in the hope of appealing to a broad constituency (Hine 1991, 289). Specific open-housing demands were drafted to promote three broadly based goals: to bring about equality of opportunity and results; to open up the major areas of metropolitan life of housing, employment, and education; and to provide power for the powerless (Anderson and Pickering 1986, 200). Chicago's large Black middle class seemed to respond more favorably to the open-housing campaign than did members of poor Black communities, who often construed the SCLC's goal as relevant only to middle-class Blacks who could afford to buy a house (Lemann 1991, 239).

The complexity of potential targets in Chicago precluded concentrated action. In cities such as Birmingham, the SCLC had chosen segregated lunch counters because most people could rally around these targets and they would yield some measure of identifiable change. Those targets also encompassed symbolically the whole problem of southern segregation (Southern Christian Leadership Conference 1991, 294). But in Chicago the targets were much more sophisticated, elusive, and difficult to pinpoint (Garrow 1986; Bloom 1987). Because open housing was the movement's central issue, the chief targets in Chicago were not economic elites who owned or operated legally segregated establishments. Instead the movement targeted institutions such as real estate offices, banks, the welfare system, the school system, and the political machine, all of which facilitated de facto segregation and slum housing (Finley 1989, 4). SCLC also targeted White communities where Blacks were barred from living even when they could afford the housing (Finley 1989, 15). Concentrating the action in Chicago proved difficult because racial discrimination was not overt, but embedded in subtle institutional processes.

Chicago is also very large and divided into neighborhoods, making it a logistical nightmare. In 1966 it was ten times the size of Birmingham, Alabama (Reynolds 1975, 47). More Blacks were squeezed into Chicago's public housing projects than lived in most southern cities (Reynolds 1975; Ralph 1993; Biles 1995). The city's size presented major challenges for the SCLC's model of organized disruption, which had proved so successful in southern cities like Birmingham. As Andrew Young pointed out later, because Chicago was so much bigger than southern cities, it was hard to sustain an aggressive movement over a long period of time (*Eyes on the Prize* 1986–87).

SCLC took a series of steps to organize and mobilize Chicago's immense Black population. The staff set up headquarters on the West Side (Ralph 1993, 44, 65) and began organizing tenant unions against slum landlords. Movement strategists devised a "platoon plan" involving preexisting neighborhood organizations in an effort to spread out the task of mobilization (Finley 1989). King and his family later moved into a West Side apartment to dramatize slum conditions (Garrow 1986; Anderson and Pickering 1986; Ralph 1993). On the South Side Jesse Jackson organized Operation Breadbasket, a selective patronage program aimed at increasing Black employment. Breadbasket also facilitated the recruitment of Black ministers into the movement (Massoni [1971] 1989).

From the beginning Mayor Richard J. Daley and his allies denounced the campaign and the SCLC as outsiders. As Daley put it, "We have no apology to any civil rights leaders who come into our city to tell us what to do" (quoted in Biles 1995, 120). Some Black elites echoed the mayor's sentiments. The nationally influential Black minister and one-time King ally, Reverend Joseph H. Jackson, publicly denounced the movement's tactics: "Civil disobedience has never been used to improve a nation, only to destroy a government" (quoted in Griffin and Warden 1977, 263). The most acerbic reactions within the Black community came from Black elected officials. Illinois Congressman William Dawson asked, "What does [King] mean coming in here trying to tell our citizens that we are segregated? Chicagoans know what's best for Chicagoans" (quoted in Reynolds 1975, 46). Ralph Metcalfe, the political boss of Chicago's Third Ward and the highest ranked Black councilman in the Daley camp, told the press, "We have competent leadership in Chicago" (quoted in Ralph 1993, 81; Lemann 1991, 270). Black alderman Claude Holman remarked that "education is needed" before the housing problem could be solved (quoted in Connolly 1989, 84). These remarks made it clear that King and his staff were viewed as outsiders who had no business in Chicago. Most important, Black elites resented what they perceived as an unwanted and unneeded intrusion on their turf.

When Daley refused to provide the SCLC with the sort of confrontation that undermined segregationist forces in the South (Hirsch 1990, 81), the CFM escalated its pace. The SCLC conducted mass marches in White neighborhoods where Blacks were barred from living to highlight Chicago's rigid pattern of neighborhood segregation (Young 1996, 411). The marches were an effort to bring the issue of housing segregation to the public's attention and force the mayor and business elites to the bargaining table (Hine 1991, 289). Prayer vigils, marches, and mass rallies occurred on a daily basis. The march that attracted most national attention occurred on Friday, August 5, 1966. On that day King, accompanied by singer Mahalia Jackson and Chicago activist Al Raby, led a car caravan of from six to eight hundred demonstrators through Marquette Park toward a Gage Park real estate office (Anderson and Pickering 1986, 228; Garrow 1986, 499). As King exited his car, he was struck by a fist-sized rock (Anderson and Pickering 1986, 228; Garrow 1986, 500; Ralph 1993, 123). Twelve hundred Chicago police stood between the marchers and a flurry of missiles, bottles, firecrackers, and bricks (Anderson and Pickering 1986, 228). Andrew Young called Gage Park "the march I would most like to forget" (Young 1996, 413). In the end, thirty people were injured and forty-one arrested (Garrow 1986, 500), prompting a battered King to tell the media, "I have never seen such hostility and hatred anywhere in my life, even in Selma" (quoted in Anderson and Pickering 1986, 228). Andrew Young later commented, "I expected such behavior in the South, but it was a surprise, and an ominous sign, to find such vicious animosity in the North" (Young 1996, 413).

Between August 5 and August 16, multiple neighborhood demonstrations disrupted social order in Chicago (Anderson and Pickering 1986, 233). In response to the growing crisis, the Chicago Conference on Religion and Race, a confederation of lay and religious leaders, called a summit meeting to discuss the Freedom Movement's demands with city leaders (Garrow 1986, 503; Ralph 1993, 72). On August 17 the Freedom Movement began negotiations with some of the city's most powerful people (Finley 1989, 23). Chicago's Black aldermen, however, did not attend these negotiations (Ralph 1993, 152). Rather, those present included leaders of the Chicago Freedom Movement, Daley, the Chicago Real Estate Board, and other civic leaders (Garrow 1986, 503; Ralph 1993, 169). On August 26, 1966, a final agreement was reached. Among other things, the ten-point agreement called for measures by the Chicago Real Estate Board, the Chicago Housing Authority, and the Cook County Department of Public Aid to end racial discrimination (Garrow 1986, 519).

Militant segments of Chicago's activist community called the agreement a sellout (Reynolds 1975; Anderson and Pickering 1986; Ralph 1993). Andrew Young stated that the SCLC felt it had done well considering the tremendous pressure it was under (Young 1996, 415). Although the Summit Agreement, as it was officially called, offered no effective means of implementation (Hirsch 1990, 81), King later wrote that the

Chicago settlement, "if implemented, will be the strongest step toward open housing taken in any city in the nation" (M. L. King 1967).

Black Elite Consciousness and Structure

Understanding the consciousness of Black elites in the course of the Chicago Freedom Movement involves analyzing how the structure of political opportunities in Chicago differed from that in the South. Black Chicagoans had a much more complicated relationship with the political system than their southern counterparts.

The Chicago Machine, Richard J. Daley, and the Black Community

A political machine is an electoral organization held together and sustained through the distribution of tangible and intangible incentives (Walton 1972, 56). In Chicago and other large urban cities, machines were effective in Black communities because they filled a void left by a lack of government services, functioning as social service agencies for both newly arrived European immigrants and southern Blacks who migrated North (Merton 1968, 130). Since the early 1930s the Chicago machine had been synonymous with the Regular Democratic Organization of Cook County, which from 1955 until 1976 was controlled by Richard J. Daley (Guterbock 1980). Daley's regime differed from all others in that he was both mayor and chairman of the Cook County Democratic Central Committee, the organization that charts the party's course. Thus, for twenty-one years Daley ran both the party and city government (Royko 1971; Biles 1995). A long-time machine member had this to say about the extent of Daley's control in Chicago:

> He had amassed and assembled all of the power. And—as opposed to having to go, say, to every county official, every state official, or to the various agencies to seek patronage or seek some sphere of influence— you could go directly to him. . . . [Because] he had amassed all of the power in one office . . . we would often say he had the capabilities of "doing something for you or doing something to you." (Wilson Frost interview, May 9, 1996)

On a national level, Daley's machine was the bedrock of the Democratic Party (Bloom 1987, 210). Locally, as both mayor and party chairman, Daley controlled everything in Chicago from political jobs and slate making to the city budget and the city council. Power was so centralized under Daley that political observers characterized his regime as one-man rule (e.g., Royko 1971). One key reason that the SCLC chose Chicago was that it recognized the extent of Daley's influence both locally and nationally (Finley 1989). But Daley's regime was controversial. He was a complicated man whose mayoralty was extolled by some and damned by others. His detractors in Chicago's Black community accused the machine of "plantation politics" (Travis 1987; Lemann 1991, 302). Black Daley loyalists, on the other hand, lauded his machine's effectiveness and its efficiency in getting out the vote. For the SCLC, Daley was an enigma and far more sophisticated than any southern adversary it had encountered. As Andrew Young put it, "Richard Daley was no Bull Connor, so it was frustrating to me when CCCO leaders tried to tar Daley with that brush" (1996, 406).[3]

The internal structure of the political machine was hierarchical and allowed some of its members to advance from a low-level to a high-level position relatively rapidly. Although the machine provided a means for some within the Black community to move up, it could not do so for all (Katznelson 1973, 104). That many Black elected officials in Chicago were not experienced politicians, however, did not preclude their moving up the hierarchy. Many made it to ward committeeman, a highly sought-after post that controlled patronage.[4] But Daley appointed Black committeemen only if they followed the Democratic organization's agenda. If they did not, they were "vised," or fired. The only Black elites that Daley vised during his tenure were those who displayed "divided loyalty," which meant taking a position in favor of the Black community in opposition to the machine's (Grimshaw 1992, 136).

Although Chicago's Black votes had been largely responsible for putting Daley in office in 1955 and again in 1963, the machine had done virtually nothing to earn Black support (Hirsch 1990; Grimshaw 1992, 113). It provided only minimal services to Black Chicagoans. Overall, Daley's gestures to Chicago's Black community were largely symbolic, designed to appease civil rights advocates (Hirsch 1990, 80). Daley was smart enough not to take Black votes entirely for granted, however. When it was in his interest to do so he spoke at local rallies in support of the SCLC's southern campaign or sponsored local fund raisers for the SCLC (Ralph 1993, 82, 83). Andrew Young (1996, 406) recalled that

> one of the SCLC's most successful fund-raisers had been held in Chicago with the sponsorship of Mayor Daley and Mahalia Jackson: SCLC took home virtually all the money that was contributed. Daley and his operatives actually persuaded vendors not to charge us for expenses. This was not the kind of thing Martin forgot.

But by the late 1960s Daley had all but abandoned Black interests in favor of the White ethnics who were leaving both the city and the

Democratic Party (Hirsch 1990). The machine became a vehicle for the White ethnic middle class, turning its back on the increasingly non-White inner city poor (Hirsch 1990, 81). The official neglect of Black Chicago contributed to racial tensions, culminating in two violent uprisings on the city's predominantly Black West Side in the summers of 1965 and 1966. By 1966, most Black Chicagoans were disillusioned. Many turned against the machine and its operatives, including Black machine aldermen.

The Political Consciousness of Black Elected Officials

The literature on Black political leadership (e.g., Gosnell [1935] 1967, 1937; Wilson 1960; Walton 1972; Bonney 1974; Travis 1987; Grimshaw 1992) characterizes the first wave of Black politicians in Chicago as able, self-made men who learned how to succeed in Chicago's tough political arena. The early leaders were not "militant advocates of civil rights measures" because they believed their numbers were too small to win. But they were nonetheless respected figures in the Black community because people did not perceive them as compliant servants of White bosses (Wilson 1967, vii). In the late sixties, by contrast, a new cohort of Black elected officials had emerged in Chicago who were so silent on race issues that opponents derisively dubbed them the "Silent Six."[5] Chicago's six Black aldermen were also called "frontmen" and "overseers" as well as "Daley loyalists" (Kleppner 1985; Travis 1987; Grimshaw 1992; Biles 1995). Many saw them as no more than the machine's primary operatives in the Black community (Lemann 1991, 273). Although many of their predecessors had been able to build independent power bases in the Black community, Daley saw to it that the six aldermen in 1966 were dependent upon him, forced to deal with him from positions of subservience and weakness (Hirsch 1990, 80; Grimshaw 1992, 110).

When King and the SCLC swept into Chicago in the late 1960s, the six machine aldermen were torn between constituent demands and the needs of the Democratic machine (Ralph 1993, 84). Because in general the machine's interests prevailed, voter turnout in the Black community was at an all-time low (Grimshaw 1992). Thus, when the SCLC stated that its primary role in Chicago was to "raise the issues," smoke out politicians, and force them to respond (Garrow 1986, 449), civil rights advocates had Daley's Black aldermen in mind (Ralph 1993, 85). But the SCLC was faced with a dilemma. It had to figure out a way to "smoke out the politicians" without overtly taking sides. As Andrew Young recalled: "Our problem was how to find a way to force the Daley machine and the Chicago establishment to get moving. But it was tricky: we had to create a momentum without getting tied up in partisan politics" (1996, 406).

Despite King's repeated claims that the system, rather than Daley or any individual, was the enemy (Garrow 1986, 457), Daley and Black elected officials knew that Black dissidents held his administration accountable for the rigid segregation and racial inequality in the city. For example, all of the sites chosen for public housing during Daley's administration reinforced prevailing patterns of segregation (Hirsch 1990, 78). Moreover, Black Chicagoans had not forgotten Daley's refusal to dismiss segregationist school superintendent Benjamin Willis during the school crisis in the early 1960s (Hirsch 1990, 79). From the administration's point of view, if the SCLC's program to create an open city triumphed, this would show that a social movement could accomplish what institutional politics had not—calling into question the legitimacy of the Democratic Party.

When the SCLC arrived in Chicago the tension between King's group and the Daley machine was almost palpable. A Black elected official who was independent of the machine commented:

> When King came here, I mean the Black members of the party they shunned him like a plague. And that's not because, you know, they didn't realize that King was doing a noble work. But they couldn't be seen as, you know, as supporting him because he represented a threat to the entrenchment of the machine in this city. (William Cousins interview, September 20, 1995)

A machine insider, however, accused the media of exacerbating tensions between the SCLC and the Daley administration: "The press was playing the King movement as a movement that would supplant the political establishment. So when people feel like . . . their position of leadership is being jeopardized and imperiled, that's the way they act" (John Stroger interview, January 4, 1996). The media frequently exploited tensions between the two groups. In one article headlined "Civil Rights Critics assailed by Daley" Claude Holman, a Black machine alderman, defensively responded to charges that the Daley administration had taken a backseat to civil rights demonstrators: "The Democratic high command and the Democratic foot soldiers have no apology to make on the question of civil rights. We have nothing to fear. Our record as Democrats is made on the rights question" (Frank J. Maier, "Civil Rights Critics Assailed by Daley," *Chicago Daily News,* April 14, 1966, Municipal Reference Collection Clip File, Harold Washington Library Center, Chicago). Some editorials indicated that Black aldermen were no longer as secure in their positions as they once were. After a group of mostly Black elected officials met with CFM representatives and endorsed most of the movement's demands, one newspaper reported that the group agreed to meet with Freedom Movement members only because "they see their own existence in peril" (Robert Gruenberg, "Daley Machine Seeks Peace on Civil Rights," *Chicago Daily News*, January 1996, Municipal Reference Collection Clip File, Harold Washington Library Center, Chicago). Black aldermen sought a rapprochement with the CFM (Ralph 1993, 143), but only to repair the damage the movement had done to their chances for reelection.

Another, more subtle, factor that created tensions between Black elected officials and the SCLC had to do with competing criteria for legitimate claims to Black political leadership (Reed 1986, x). From the perspective of the Black elected officials, an SCLC-led movement in Chicago would offer Black constituents an alternative leadership model. Black aldermen felt that the more charismatic SCLC leaders were trying to replace them—if not in their offices, then certainly in the hearts and minds of Black Chicagoans. As the duly elected representatives of Black Chicago, Black elected officials felt that only they should serve the interests of Black residents (Ralph 1993, 80–81). Their criteria for leadership were derived from their electoral legitimacy rather than a track record of participating in civil rights protests. A machine insider illustrated why Black elected officials resented the SCLC's presence in Chicago:

> Well, say, suppose I'm in my office and a group decides that they want to meet with me about some issues that they want to consider. Now they might have met in little caucuses and in little groups and they come with some ideas [that] they're the designated spokesmen. Well the first thing that I would take issue with is for them to have met and have made decisions and then say, "Well we're going to picket and here's your sign." Well then I become a follower as opposed to a leader. Now the majority of people elected me so I've been designated as a leader until I'm replaced. (Wilson Frost interview, May 9, 1996)

The Black aldermen considered that they, not the SCLC, were the *elected* representatives of Black Chicago. Despite criticism from opponents that they had not served Black Chicago well, they believed the machine had delivered benefits to the Black community. Moreover, as elected officials they—not the SCLC—were in the position to continue providing benefits. As one machine insider described his position vis-à-vis civil rights activists: "I wasn't one of those soldiers . . . in the street. . . . I was supposed to deliver within the political arena and the governmental arena. And that was my role and that's what I have tried to do" (John Stroger interview, January 4, 1996). Black elected officials guarded their leadership positions closely and resented what they perceived as the SCLC's attempt to usurp their role in "brokering black political interests" (Reed 1986, 2). Asked if it made sense to assume that Black elected officials resented the SCLC's presence in Chicago, a long-time machine member replied:

> I would think that each one of the elected officials would resent someone coming in to take leadership away from them when they have already been designated by their constituents as the leader. . . . But you don't surrender leadership. If you do you are not going to be a leader very long in my opinion. (Wilson Frost interview, May 9, 1996)

Thus the battle lines were drawn. The six Black machine aldermen were not about to surrender their hard-earned leadership to a group of "outside" civil rights activists. They had worked their way up in the system and used the democratic process to get where they were. Frost put it more pointedly: "This is the democratic process. You have been elected; they're self-designated." The crux of the issue "was, or it should have been, on the basis of having elected leaders who were elected to represent the people and carry out the people's agenda . . . as opposed to having someone else bring in an agenda."

Like most Black Chicagoans, the Black aldermen of this era respected King and his accomplishments. Many of them had even participated in the SCLC's southern civil rights campaigns. Nevertheless, they refused to regard King as a leader in Chicago because to do so would have meant relinquishing their own authority. As Wilson Frost put it: "I don't know of any elected official who looked upon King as their Moses."

Thus the source of tension between the two groups was not the goal of open housing. Both sides agreed that adequate housing for Black people was a problem in Chicago. The real issue between the two groups was who would receive credit for implementing an open-housing plan (Wilson Frost interview, May 9, 1996). In an attempt to co-opt the movement and the credit for producing better housing Daley instructed a group of Chicago's Black elites to form their own civil rights organization, the Chicago Committee to Fulfill These Rights. The purpose of this organization was to take the lead in any concerns raised by civil rights protesters (Travis 1987; Ralph 1993, 81). Andrew Young recalled:

> Mayor Daley and his political machine, including his black lieutenants and field soldiers, were then taking the position that they were as interested in abolishing slums and improving conditions for the underprivileged as we were. In fact, they intimated they would take care of everything if we would just get lost. (1996, 405)

Because the SCLC would not "just get lost," pressures mounted. Although all Black machine aldermen felt an intense pressure during the CFM, those with the higher standing in the Black community appeared most vulnerable to CFM pressures (Grimshaw 1992). Former Olympic track star Ralph Metcalfe is a classic example. When Metcalfe heard of the SCLC's Chicago campaign, he publicly stated: "We have competent leadership in Chicago and all things necessary to work out our city's own destiny" (quoted in Ralph 1993, 81). When reporters questioned him about King's decision to make Chicago the SCLC's first northern drive he retorted: "This is no hick town. We have a lot of intellect and can take care of these situations ourselves" (*Chicago Tribune,* Sept. 8, 1965, Municipal Reference Collection Clip File, Harold Washington Library Center, Chicago). But as the CFM intensified, Metcalfe felt pressures from an aroused Black constituency. On one occasion a Chicago activist recalled a conversation with Metcalfe about the CFM and noted that he seemed visibly ambivalent:

> I saw within his eyes that he was with us [but] . . . his lips at the time were sealed in silence and he went along with Daley. . . . [T]here was something about the man that was shackled at the time, and he could not be free to take a stand. (Hatti Williams interview, June 13, 1986)

The traditional view in the literature has been that in this era Black elected officials were machine members first and Blacks second (Wilson 1960). But, as Metcalfe's case shows, the consciousness of Black machine aldermen was not so clear-cut. In the structural framework from which I am writing, the Black elected officials affiliated with the machine could have adopted the positions they took simply because they were following their material interests. But they could also have adopted the same positions because their material interests produced schemas and salient membership groups that led them to interpret reality in ways that disfavored the CFM. The forms of hegemonic consciousness that their structural positions encouraged would then have strongly mediated any oppositional consciousness derived from their structural position as Blacks and, for many, from prior participation in the civil rights movement.

In the first explanation, the material and status interests of Black machine officials would directly have prevented them from working with the CFM. They could, in theory, have maintained a full-fledged oppositional consciousness but concluded that the personal costs of acting on such a consciousness were too great. None of the machine officials that I interviewed, however, suggested that this was their position.

Instead, all of the officials offered some explanation of their behavior that suggested they had, to a greater or lesser degree, adopted
the perspective of the Daley machine on the CFM. Their own positions
of leadership, which they perceived as being threatened by the CFM,
could be described from this hegemonic perspective as both legitimate
and practical. They expressed their concerns for legitimacy with such
phrases as, "Now the majority of people elected me so I've been designated as a leader until I'm replaced." They expressed their practical
concerns in such thoughts as, "I was supposed to deliver within the political arena and the governmental arena. And that was my role and that's
what I've tried to do." To avoid cognitive dissonance (cf. Festinger 1957,
1964), elected democratic representatives will tend to see themselves
as genuinely representing the interests of their constituents. The CFM
threatened that self-image.

Along with trying to reduce cognitive dissonance, the Black machine officials may also have found themselves in social positions that
decreased the amount of positive information they received about the
CFM and increased the amount of negative information. The people with
whom the machine officials worked every day and those with whom they
consulted on matters of strategy would also often be connected with
the machine. The hegemonic consciousness that served their material
interests would be reinforced as legitimate and practical by their significant others. They would see and hear information and interpretations
that reinforced that hegemonic consciousness rather than the competing
oppositional consciousness on which the movement was trying to build.
The similarities among the Black machine officials' reactions reinforce
this interpretation. Compare Frost ("You've been elected; they're self-
designated"), Stroger ("I wasn't one of those soldiers . . . in the street"),
and Metcalfe ("We have competent leadership in Chicago" and "We have
a lot of intellect and can take care of these situations ourselves").

Finally, the Black machine officials might also have developed interpretive schemas that, while making it possible for them to act in accord
with their material interests, promoted a picture of the world as more
complex and more practical than the CFM realized. Their own experience had shown them how they could actually benefit their constituents
in various ways. It was not at all clear to them that the Daley machine was
the root of all evil in Chicago. Even King stated at the time: "The truth is, if
I were the mayor of Chicago, it would take me at least ten years to make
an impact on many of these problems" (Young 1996, 406). Although
most civil rights activists felt that many of Black Chicago's problems
could be laid at the door of the Democratic machine, even they were not

unified in their belief that *all* of Black Chicago's problems could be laid at that door.

Oppositional Consciousness within the Challenging Group

The challenging group during the 1966 CFM was the SCLC-CCCO coalition. The CCCO was unlike any movement coalition that the SCLC had worked with in the South. It consisted of about forty Black and White organizations and included a broad spectrum of indigenous activists whose organizational affiliations ranged across several groups (Garrow 1989, ix–x). Because the coalition was so broad, the SCLC found it difficult, at times, to work with the diverse interests. Andrew Young noted that "[i]n the same movement we had people who wanted major reform of the entire political system in Chicago and others who just wanted the chance to improve their material lives in a very fundamental way—a job, a better school, a home with heat." Southern movements, by contrast, "focused themselves around issues of dignity and citizenship, through which all blacks were affected equally" (Young 1996, 392). Finding an issue that would affect Chicago's diverse Black population equally was far greater a challenge than those in the South. Most CCCO affiliates agreed on the need to overthrow the political machine. Tension arose because the SCLC resisted an outright fight with the Daley machine. While the SCLC did not condone the machine's "parasitic" relationship with Chicago's Black poor (Fairclough 1987, 284), King nevertheless pointed out that attacking the Democratic organization was not the movement's agenda. On more than one occasion he flatly stated that Daley was not the enemy (Garrow 1986, 448): "I'm not leading any campaign against Mayor Daley. I'm leading a campaign against the slums" (quoted in Ralph 1993, 99). It appears that Black aldermen were not entirely alone in thinking that the machine served some of the interests of Black Chicagoans. The SCLC was not entirely sure that this view was incorrect. Andrew Young stated later:

> [The] SCLC could not take on responsibility for running Richard Daley out of Chicago, and we weren't sure we wanted to, even if it were possible. Despite the hostility to Daley in CCCO, there was a lot to admire in Daley's political operation, especially compared to the political dispensation in other big cities. Blacks in Chicago had relatively more access to the political machinery compared to black communities in New York or Los Angles during the sixties. (1996, 406)

From the SCLC's viewpoint, the real enemy in Chicago was much larger than Daley's machine or partisan politics. The SCLC saw the enemy as economic inequality maintained by systematic racial discrimination. But such a broad conceptualization of the problem precipitated disagreements between the SCLC and CCCO over appropriate strategies and tactics. Even people unaffiliated with the movement coalition, such as independent alderman Leon Despres,[6] strongly felt that the SCLC's definition of the situation was too broad for Chicago's context. Despres believed that, rather than attempting to organize a citywide crusading movement, the SCLC should organize the Black community around a specific local election that would undercut the machine's hegemony. He argued:

> [The SCLC] couldn't organize politically [in the South]; here they could. But here there wasn't any activity like that. There wasn't any activity that was keyed to achieving a result that was focused on something. It was all kind of diffuse. They didn't enlist any Black political figures, they didn't enlist any White political figures, they didn't organize by wards. They were just concentrating on this diffuse activity. . . . I think that was the error here. (Leon Despres interview, September 11, 1995)

To critics like Despres, who charged that the movement should concern itself with a local election, James Bevel, the SCLC's chief strategist, responded, "[L]et us be more interested in doing something about the ghetto than in securing candidates" (quoted in Garrow 1986, 448). Bevel nevertheless wanted to wean poor Blacks away from the machine. He saw the first step in this process as raising consciousness, which would be a difficult enough task because Daley, by virtue of his political organization, had significant material advantages at his disposal to maintain Black dependency (Fairclough 1987; Anderson and Pickering 1986, 204). Thus, as Bevel saw it, the most immediate issue for the movement

> was to create a community that was not bought and sold. . . . If you got everybody voting for Daley's hand-picked Black leaders you're wrong. You have to create a movement . . . you got to break out of this hopelessness and this sense of being dictated to unless you will die and starve. We had to break that syndrome. (James Bevel interview, May 30, 1995)

But Bevel's approach was not pragmatic enough for Chicago's activist community. A significant bloc of the CCCO coalition seemed to agree that the movement should concentrate on some form of electoral mobilization. A voter registration drive took place, but in order to protect its tax status the SCLC refrained from engaging in partisan politics (Ralph 1993, 99). Most importantly, the SCLC did not want to wage a war against the machine. According to Bevel, the SCLC did not "think political in the traditional sense. . . . We think constitutional. That which is political is not necessarily in the interest of Black people; that which is constitutional is in the interest of everybody. So we don't tend to be political. We are constitutionalists, which means we operate governmentally rather than politically" (James Bevel interview, May 30, 1995).

Bevel's comments reflect how the SCLC operated as a social movement and as a social movement organization. By 1966 the SCLC considered itself a national movement. King stated as much when he considered the pros and cons of a Chicago campaign. The deciding factor for him was how the SCLC defined itself as a social movement organization: "Well, it seems to me we've got to begin dealing with the North sometime. We can't just concern ourselves with the South if we call ourselves a national movement" (quoted in Young 1996, 385). From the perspective of SCLC, a national movement could not be tied to local interests. The movement's target could not be the Democratic machine in Chicago, but rather systematic racial inequality and racial oppression. Rather than focus on a local election, the SCLC attempted to bring inequality issues in Chicago to the fore as they had done in the South, by appealing to the American creed, which they knew was not realized by Black Americans in either the North or the South. Thus in Chicago, as in the South, the SCLC sought to dramatize how the status of Black Americans was incongruent with the rights and privileges embodied and upheld by the American constitution.

Although most Chicago groups had supported the SCLC's strategy and tactics in the South, by 1966 some groups had become more radical and militant. CORE and the Chicago chapter of the Student Nonviolent Coordinating Committee (SNCC) felt that the SCLC's methods of bringing issues to the fore had become "outdated" (Young 1996, 408). Such critiques became especially popular after the Meredith march in Mississippi ushered in the call for Black power.[7] This radical new call to Black people appealed to militant activists in Chicago and elsewhere more than did attempts at moral suasion. CORE's Linda Bryant Hall recalled that Black power "was the call I needed to adhere to. And so many others of us in CORE, at the same time, felt that way" (Hall 1991, 312).

The appeal of Black power to CORE, SNCC, and other militant groups in the movement coalition revealed the variations in oppositional consciousness among the SCLC and the militant factions of the CCCO. These variations were never more evident than during the march into suburban Cicero in August 1966. Black Chicagoans considered west-suburban Cicero the Mississippi of the North. Black people did not live in Cicero, nor even venture into the area lest they fail to return. Thus the threat of a King-led march into this citadel of White racism was a significant trump card for the movement (Connolly 1989). Radical factions of the movement coalition pressed hard for a march into Cicero. Initially King harbored doubts about a Cicero march, but the radical faction of the movement coalition persuaded him. Linda Bryant Hall recalled:

> Groups like CORE made Dr. King, I think, more militant—kept him more to the left than he probably would have been if we had not been around. Whenever we decided we were going to do something very radical, such as our march into Cicero, that made Dr. King have to say, "Well, maybe it's not such a bad idea." (Hall 1991, 313)

King endorsed the Cicero march, stating, "We're not only going to walk in Cicero, we're going to work and live there" (quoted in Ralph 1993, 166). But to the surprise of everyone, after the mayor's committee signed the open-housing agreement the SCLC canceled the march. Andrew Young later wrote that "SNCC and CORE were vociferous in their opposition" to this decision (1996, 415). Linda Bryant Hall recalled:

> When he called off the march, we were surprised; we were shocked. This is the march we looked forward to. The other marches were nice. But the one in Cicero had special meaning for us. . . . So when Dr. King said he wasn't going to march in that neighborhood, I said . . . well what's it all about? This is *the* neighborhood to march in. (Hall 1991, 313)

Ignoring the SCLC's decision and entreaties from King not to march, CORE's chairman, Bob Lucas, led about two hundred community people into Cicero without the SCLC. According to those who participated, the character of this march differed from the traditional King-led demonstrations because more community people participated who were determined to fight back (Hall 1991). Because the SCLC backed out of the Cicero march, Bob Lucas retrospectively stated that a "lack of courage at critical times" was the SCLC's major weakness during the Chicago campaign (Bob Lucas interview, May 30, 1996).

In short, the SCLC-CCCO coalition was far from unified in its challenges. Variations in oppositional consciousness precipitated disagreements over strategy and tactics. But although some groups in the movement coalition were more radical and militant in their approaches than others, the entire challenging group opposed the status quo and the political machine. Here too, as with the Black elected officials, differences in structural position did not directly affect the participants' actions, but worked through differences in perception and perspective. The members of SCLC had material and status interests in making the organization national and not simply regional. Members of CCCO had material and status interests in defeating Daley. After signing the agreement with

Daley's forces, the SCLC had material and status interests in producing some tangible outcome from their stay in Chicago and maintaining their reputations for keeping their word. Members of CORE had material and status interests in leading the most militant of the protests in Chicago. Yet none of the actors I interviewed posed the issue in material or status terms. Instead, their structural positions influenced who they spoke with about these issues. Those positions also tended to color their perceptions. Leon Despres, whose world was the world of Chicago politics, thought the CFM ought to have enlisted "political figures" and organized "by wards." James Bevel thought the main goal was to "create a community." Bob Lucas thought the movement most needed to display political "courage." Their group memberships, in Chicago politics, SCLC, and CORE, influenced what they saw and heard. Their own past experiences created the interpretive schemas by which they processed and even remembered what they had seen and heard.

The Political Consciousness of Black Ministers in Chicago

As its name, the "Southern Christian Leadership Conference," suggests, the SCLC was a church-based protest organization, led mostly by Black ministers (Morris 1984, 87). The Black church was such an integral part of the SCLC's origin that the Reverend Joseph Lowery, one of the original founders, described the SCLC as "the black church coming alive . . . coming together across denominational and geographical lines" (quoted in Morris 1984, 88). It is no surprise, then, that the Black church community played a crucial role in all of the SCLC's southern campaigns. But when the SCLC attempted to base the Chicago Freedom Movement in Chicago's Black churches, many Chicago natives questioned King's judgment (Hall 1991), arguing that the political machine placed the Black church in Chicago in a relationship with the power structure different from that of churches in the South. Most southern Black churches were relatively independent of White control and could play an active role in the civil rights movement.[8] In most cases, the southern Black church represented the movement's most important source of power. But as CORE's Linda Bryant Hall put it, Black churches in Chicago

> represented something different from what they did in the South. In Chicago, the churches, many of the Black churches—not all of them — many of them had very close connections to the political machine. The political machine supported many of the churches. I mean they did so much as buy pews where the people set. They provided the church with a storefront. They provided the minister, in some cases with a salary. (Hall 1991, 312)

Hall's comments reflect the symbiotic relationship that existed in 1966 between the Daley machine and the Black church in Chicago. Chicago's political machine had not always been the Black church's financial benefactor. Traditionally, Chicago's Black churches had been financially independent, autonomous institutions, largely free from political and economic control by the White community (Drake and Cayton 1945, 427–28; Spear 1967, 91–96). Yet as the number of Black churches in Chicago grew, becoming centers of Black social life, machine politicians recognized how Black ministers could help secure Black votes (Drake and Cayton 1945). Struggling Black ministers were often targeted and persuaded to do business with the political machine in exchange for a new church, a new building, or some other service (Lemann 1991, 256). Once a young pastor had access to the machine's vast resources, success was often practically guaranteed. But doing business with the machine had its costs. Ministers who were openly associated with machine politics were often criticized in the Black community (Drake and Cayton 1945, 428). It is not difficult to understand, then, why in 1966 knowing that a significant portion of Chicago's Black clergy were connected to the Daley machine caused Hall and others to oppose the idea of a church-based movement.

Like that of the Black elected officials, the relationship of Black ministers with the Daley machine was complex. One prominent Black minister confessed that he became "deeply indebted to the Democratic machine" because the machine could supply jobs, day care facilities, and educational centers to Black churches (quoted in Ralph 1993, 84). As Andrew Young (1996, 392) points out, these material incentives made it hard for the SCLC-CCCO coalition to direct people's oppositional consciousness against the machine because the machine itself made it possible for the Black community to get a fairer share of city's resources. Chicago's Black poor were often the beneficiaries of machine or machine-supported church services, such as feeding programs and day care facilities. In many cases, a Black minister who accepted the machine's offer to subsidize day care in his church was responding to the needs of parishioners. As long as the Black poor "had tremendous, immediate material needs" and the machine's services provided for some of these needs, then it was difficult to criticize a minister who accepted those services. Andrew Young put it this way:

> It was not the place of comfortable, middle-class people to condemn a local preacher for abandoning CCCO for day care, commodities for a feeding program, or city grants for a senior's program. . . . I was not

prepared to argue that the Chicago movement was defending a higher principal than day care or food for the hungry. (1996, 392)

Other ministers, such as the Reverend Clay Evans, pastor of Fellowship Baptist Church and one of the few Black ministers in Chicago unaffiliated with the machine, also refused to pass judgment on the otherwise "good men" and "wonderful people" who served their congregations by tapping into Daley's vast supply of resources. As he put it, "Sometime you have to do what you have to do in order to survive." Many of his colleagues, Evans said, avoided taking a stand for the movement because "their job would be threatened [and] their churches also could be condemned" (Clay Evans interview, May 3, 1996). According to Evans and others around at the time, Daley's functionaries also used strong-arm tactics to induce loyalty. City building inspectors, sometimes referred to as the "plainclothes arm of the police department," were known to issue costly citations for fire code violations or faulty plumbing in order to keep Black ministers in line politically (Travis 1987, 354). More often, however, Daley used a more subtle approach such as taking federal money allocated for poverty programs and using it to place Black preachers on the city's payroll (Grimshaw 1992, 227; Lemann 1991, 256).

The use of federal money, possibly more than any other tactic, effectively undermined the autonomy of many Black churches in Chicago. This money placed scores of Black ministers on the city's payroll in various capacities. As Black ministers accepted city jobs in exchange for political support, their independence was completely compromised (Lemann 1991, 256). They became part of Daley's vast patronage army and were expected to deliver for the machine.[9] Daley's practice of doling out city jobs worked extremely well, because, as Evans stated, "most people needed jobs" and "you don't bite the hand that feeds you" (Clay Evans interview, May 3, 1996). The Black ministers who were on the city's payroll had little choice but to treat King "as if he had leprosy because they did not want anything or anyone to disturb their relationship with the Daley machine" (Travis 1987 353).

Despite the number of Black ministers loyal to Daley, the SCLC found a few Black clergy to support the CFM. A small cadre of Black ministers in Chicago had managed to maintain their independence from the machine. Asked how this was possible in the face of temptations, bribery, and coercion, Reverend Evans replied, "Believing in God and my people, that nobody pays me but them" (Clay Evans interview, May 3, 1996). Asked the same question, Reverend Shelvin Hall, another Black Baptist minister unaffiliated with the machine, used an analogy to illustrate his philosophy: "If you don't start eating at the master's table you don't ever miss prime rib, if you understand what I mean. You stay accustomed to neck bones and pig's feet and chitterlings and you can survive on it" (Shelvin Hall interview, April 16, 1996). When Reverend Hall arrived in Chicago in 1955, the year Daley was elected, he was chagrined to find that a great many of his colleagues were eating at the master's table:

> I was amazed at what these guys weren't doing. I was surprised. They weren't doing nothing in Chicago. They couldn't get together because they could be bought off too easily. You can't do nothing when you on the other guy's payroll. How you going to cuss him and kiss him? (Shelvin Hall interview, April 16, 1996)

The SCLC relied upon Operation Breadbasket to recruit Black ministers into the CFM. Headed by Jesse Jackson, then a young divinity student and SCLC staff member, Breadbasket was a selective buying program that used economic boycotts to pressure employers to hire more Black workers (Massoni [1971] 1989, 192). SCLC's introducing Breadbasket into Chicago was a bit of a concession to ministers who agreed with the overall goals of the movement but did not want to involve themselves in mass actions (Massoni [1971] 1989, 194). Evans was one of the first Black ministers whom Jackson recruited through Breadbasket. Evans's support of the movement laid the groundwork for other ministers to participate (Massoni [1971] 1989, 194). As Evans put it, supporting the movement was never a question for him: "It's just always been a part of me to do something like that, because I have experienced racism, bigotry, and so forth. So it didn't take much . . . for me to try to do something about it" (Clay Evans interview, May 3, 1996). But Evans paid a heavy price for his involvement with the CFM. Construction on a new church that was under way was halted for more than seven years (Travis 1987, 354–55; Ralph 1993, 85). In an interview Evans recalled the price he and his congregation had paid for supporting the movement:

> My church was held up for seven or eight years. I was in the process of building a church. I was doing it in stages. And I had been promised funds, money, assistance, and the broker that was handling the deal told me and Jesse [Jackson] about Dr. King that if I supported him that my funds would be cut off. And certainly the person who is the mayor who controls the city can cut your funds off. (Clay Evans interview, May 3, 1996)

While the machine's direct reprisal against Evans is far better documented, he also experienced reprisals from Black colleagues affiliated with the machine. Evans recalled that when he attended a Baptist

Ministers Conference meeting, a colleague physically threatened him as he attempted to discuss Operation Breadbasket's program:

> I attempted to have a discussion or one thing or another as it related to Operation Breadbasket and Jesse and so forth . . . and . . . I was told to not bring it up, and was threatened by a gun and had to leave from that church. . . . I couldn't discuss it or bring it up for it to be voted on. (Clay Evans interview, May 3, 1996)

Joseph H. Jackson, perhaps the most influential Black minister in Chicago in 1966, led Black clerical opposition to the CFM. Since 1941 Jackson had been pastor of Olivet Baptist Church, one of Chicago's oldest and most prestigious Black congregations. Jackson was also president of the National Baptist Convention (NBC) which, with an estimated 6.5 million members, was the largest single organization of Black Americans in the country (Griffin and Warden 1977). Elected to this post in 1953, Jackson oversaw enormous financial investments and wielded substantial influence in Black America (Ralph 1993, 79). Although he was considered one of the most controversial Black leaders in the nation, as president of the NBC Jackson's decisions carried a great deal of weight (C. H. King 1967, 7). If Jackson decided to back King and the CCCO, all of the weight of the National Baptist Convention would follow his endorsement. If he decided not to endorse the Chicago movement, his powerful voice could greatly dampen the momentum that King hoped to develop (C. H. King 1967).

As long as King concentrated his efforts in the South, Jackson supported the movement, although he philosophically disagreed with the use of direct-action tactics. Jackson believed that one could approach civil rights with either of two distinct philosophies, protest or due process of law, and he preferred due process (Ralph 1993, 79). In a controversial speech in June 1961, Jackson lambasted the SCLC's practice of mobilizing the Black church to participate in direct action tactics. "The church," he said, "cannot be used as a rubber stamp for every method employed in the name of democracy and freedom" (quoted in C. H. King 1967, 78).

The new breed of Baptist ministers in the SCLC challenged Jackson's traditional leadership. By 1966 both Jackson and King were influential figures in the national Black community, but King's increasing prominence posed a threat to Jackson's position (C. H. King 1967, 71). Thus when King arrived in Chicago in 1966, his and Jackson's different philosophies regarding social protest, which had already divided the National Baptist Convention,[10] now divided Chicago's Black religious community (C. H. King 1967, 7).

Jackson's camp did not want King and the SCLC in Chicago in 1966. He and his allies felt that the young charismatic SCLC ministers were invading their turf (Ralph 1993, 80). Indeed, "While King was urging Negroes to unite in [Chicago's] Soldier Field, Jackson was urging them to stay at home"; he used radio, press, and television to denounce the freedom movement's campaign (C. H. King 1967, 7). During a press conference Jackson made known the contents of a letter he had written to King in which he criticized Operation Breadbasket and the freedom movement's program to end the slums. Jackson held that the movement accomplished nothing, with "large crowds of people to be used in demonstration and as pressure groups" (Bety Washington, "Dr. King, Rev. Jackson Air Differences," July 7, 1966, *Chicago Daily Defender,* Municipal Reference Collection Clip File, Harold Washington Library Center, Chicago). Jackson also denounced the movement from the pulpit. A former member of Jackson's church recalled that he "was just vehement in his put-down of Dr. King" (Hatti Williams interview, June 13, 1986). Among other things, Jackson accused King and the SCLC of being outsiders and rabble-rousers. When rioting occurred on the west side, Jackson joined Daley to point accusing fingers at CFM organizers, stating, "certain strangers are in Chicago to get youngsters to riot" (quoted in Reynolds 1975, 59).

The cumulative effect of Jackson's opposition is hard to assess. Some scholars conclude that Jackson posed some problems but not enough to handicap the movement (Baldwin 1991, 223). Nevertheless, King and the SCLC had to battle to get a significant amount of the Black church community to side with them. King publicly stated, "I don't believe Dr. Jackson speaks for the Negroes in this country" (Bety Washington, "Dr. King, Rev. Jackson Air Differences," July 7, 1966, *Chicago Daily Defender,* Municipal Reference Collection Clip File, Harold Washington Library Center, Chicago). Asked what the SCLC could have done to neutralize opposition from someone as powerful as Jackson, Clay Evans answered: "Nothing but just keep moving ahead as best as they possibly could with the supporters that he could get. . . . [King] had enough support to do the job, to give him credibility" (Clay Evans interview, May 3, 1996). When asked the same question, SCLC strategist James Bevel shrugged, stating that Jackson's opposition "didn't mean nothing" (James Bevel interview, May 30, 1995). Reverend Shelvin Hall's feelings about Jackson may suggest how other Black ministers who supported the movement felt. Hall refused to allow Jackson to control him, stating, "Jackson couldn't tell me what to do. He was president of the National Baptist Convention but he hadn't paid my mortgage. Since he didn't pay my mortgage, didn't meet my notes, I'm obliged to respect him as my president but I'm not, I don't owe him any loyalty" (Shelvin Hall interview, April 16, 1996).

Although Evans agreed with Hall, he conceded that Jackson's and Daley's opposition locked him out of important political and religious circles. He recalled:

> There was a period of time that I was kind of exiled, and it was very difficult to try to get any favors or . . . elected to anything in the religious body or get any favors from downtown from the political body because J. Daley and I were not good friends, and [Jackson] and I were not good friends.

Evans personally experienced the extent to which the Daley machine had infiltrated Black religious circles in Chicago in 1966. He added:

> [T]he political structure and the religious structure put me in a terrible vise. . . . [P]eople just kind of treat you like you're plague: "Don't associate with Clay Evans because if you do Daley going to get you, or [Jackson's] not going to allow you to have any positions. (Clay Evans interview, May 3, 1996)

Rather than attack the status quo, Jackson and his allies followed the dictates of the Daley machine. As Clay Evans recalled, "Dr. Jackson was right here; he didn't want King to come. Daley was here; he didn't want King to come. So [King] got it from the political and the religious aspect. Neither one of them wanted him in Chicago" (Clay Evans interview, May 3, 1996).

Jackson and other Black ministers who opposed the movement did so in part for reasons of self-interest and self-preservation. Yet an explanation of their behavior that focuses solely on self-interest is not sufficient. As in the other two groups of Black elites heavily involved in the CFM, the differences in the ministers' structural positions did not directly affect their actions. Rather, those differences worked through differences in consciousness, produced in part by the groups to which the different ministers belonged and the interpretive schemas they brought with them to the events.

Joseph Jackson and his allies had obvious material and status interests in supporting the Daley machine. King also had material and status interests in, essentially, overthrowing the conservative leadership of the National Baptist Convention and opening the way for his own followers within that organization. But none of the religious actors in this drama seems to have seen his own material or status interests as particularly relevant to his positions. Jackson's brand of conservative theology drew directly on a well-established tradition. King's understanding of the gospel, on the other hand, drew on an equally strong tradition of social justice within the church. From the Sermon on the Mount through the gospel songs so familiar to the Black community, the theme of God's stand with the weak and against oppression fortified those who believed they should take action in the world to benefit their community. Jackson had many around him to strengthen his position and to tell him only the kinds of information that would make that position seem right and sensible. Similarly, King, in continual strategic discussion with the other leaders in SCLC, would be reinforced in his perceptions of reality. Each set of actors brought to the situation interpretive schemas that selectively reinforced the way they had long come to see the world.

Conclusions: Deconstructing Political Consciousness

Structural position does affect political consciousness. We have long known that positions people are born into, such as race, class, and gender, affect their consciousness. But there is a tendency in the current literature to essentialize these forms of consciousness. That is, we often assume that only women develop gender consciousness, only Blacks develop race consciousness, and only poor (or working-class) people develop class consciousness. Moreover, we assume that all women, Blacks, and poor people develop the same kind of consciousness. Much of the current literature paints a picture of monolithic belief systems attached to undifferentiated groups. But the CFM case presents a more internally differentiated view of political consciousness. It reveals that differences within hegemonic and oppositional consciousness develop in part because subordinate group members—such as Blacks in Chicago in 1966—are not always similarly situated.

Other scholars have discussed the effects on consciousness when members of a subordinate group are not similarly situated. Patricia Hill Collins argues that "[d]epending on the context, an individual may be an oppressor, a member of an oppressed group, or simultaneously oppressor and oppressed" (Collins 1990, 225; see also Stockdill, chap. 8, this volume). Because some Black elites in Chicago in 1966 were members of the political machine and others were not, Blacks as a subordinate group were not equally oppressed. In one context some Black elites were machine members and had developed interests rooted in a form of hegemonic consciousness. But in another context the same elites were also members of the Black community and had developed race-based interests rooted in a form of oppositional consciousness. The CFM presented a situation where Black elites with one foot in the polity and one in the challenging group were forced to choose between the two types of consciousness. The structure of material and status rewards seems to have induced most of them to adopt, with only slight modifications, the hegemonic consciousness that characterized the machine. Others, like Ralph Metcalfe, were ambivalent and conflicted.

When members of a group, such as Chicago's Black community in 1966, are not similarly situated, various factions within the group develop different interests. Members of the machine had vested interests in the maintenance of the status quo while the challenging group wanted the SCLC to overthrow the machine and the status quo. But, as mentioned earlier, the type of consciousness that informed the SCLC's strategy and mobilization work in Chicago in 1966 was not tied to local interests. Rather, King and the SCLC opposed local-interest politics in favor of a more universalistic movement based on the national (and international) struggle against White supremacy. By 1966, the clear targets that symbolized injustice—such as legally segregated facilities—had mostly been eliminated in the South. Rooting out the injustices that remained in Chicago and the nation meant tearing into the very structure of American society (Ralph 1993, 98). Thus a large part of the SCLC's political strategy was oriented toward exposing American injustices in the North and the South (Ralph 1993, 6). In short, the political consciousness of the SCLC encompassed more than ideas about Chicago. As King summarized it, "Chicago represents all the problems that you find in the major urban areas of our country. If we can break the system in Chicago, it can be broken anywhere in the country" (quoted in Garrow 1986, 448).

When subordinate group members are not similarly situated, differences in power and privilege can also affect political consciousness. In the Chicago case, the Black clergy and Black elected officials who were closer to the machine were rewarded if they shared the hegemonic consciousness that characterized machine politics. For example, the disagreement between Joseph H. Jackson and Martin Luther King was largely generational, revolving around different views of religion, but it was also about conflicting political consciousness. Jackson represented a generation of Black ministers who believed in a religion of salvation and redemption, a worldview that was not problematic for the machine. Thus the machine rewarded Jackson for his conservative religious views because they posed no threat to the status quo. In contrast, King and the SCLC represented a generation of Black clergy who refocused the cultural context of the Black church (Morris 1984, 96–97). They held a more militant view of religion, in which the church had an obligation to intervene in unjust human affairs.[11] Jackson's conservative religious views predisposed him to eschew protest politics and civil disobedience in favor of redressing Black grievances through more institutionalized channels. But a core part of the SCLC's approach was disrupting the status quo through protests and demonstrations to create conflict. The SCLC's oppositional consciousness conflicted with the machine's hegemonic consciousness to which Jackson and his allies were closer.

A simple binary-polity model does not capture the complex structural positions that Black Chicagoans occupied as both polity members and challengers. Because members of oppressed groups can occupy positions of power within systems of domination, we need a model that problematizes the notion of a monolithic subordinate group and includes instead a continuum of various positions that subordinate group members may occupy. With a model that effectively captures important structural differences within subordinate groups, we can ask what the effects of those different positions within the polity might be on group consciousness and collective action.

The hierarchical positioning of Black Chicagoans raises the important question of how to mobilize social movements when members of the subordinate group engaged in conflict share certain aspects of oppression but are situated in different structural positions regarding the object of that conflict. Should organizers attempt to target one segment of the subordinate population? If so, how can they know which segment will be the most or least mobilizable? Occupying contradictory structural locations, as we have seen, causes inconsistent responses to movements. How, in this case, can movement organizers predict which way the target population will respond? Social movement scholars have traditionally employed concepts such as collective identity (Melucci 1989) and master frames (Snow and Benford 1988) in order to explain how diverse groups cohere around a particular issue. But as Morris (1992, 369) argues, these concepts "should be solidly rooted within their relevant structural contexts." Otherwise they "assume a reified character appearing to be central causes of collective action." The case of collective action by the CFM in Chicago in 1966 demonstrates how collective identities and forms of consciousness rooted in known structural contexts deeply affect social movement behavior.

Notes

I am grateful to Aldon Morris and Jane Mansbridge for numerous helpful comments. I would like to especially thank the interview respondents for allowing me into their homes and offices and taking the time to share their recollections of the Chicago Freedom Movement with me. I thank also the editor for making insightful suggestions to improve the chapter.

1. I follow King 1988 and Higginbotham 1993 in defining a "multiple" oppositional consciousness as reflecting more than one of an individual's own group identities. A "multi-dimensional" oppositional consciousness (Stockdill, chap. 8, this volume) can include what Kalmuss, Gurin, and Townsend 1981 call "sympathetic consciousness," or identification with the oppression of members of another group.

2. The Chicago Freedom Movement Oral History Project, begun in 1986, is a collection of oral histories of movement participants.

3. Eugene "Bull" Connor was the racist public safety commissioner of Birmingham, Alabama in 1963. Connor's antics included using high-powered water hoses and vicious attack dogs on civil rights protesters.

4. Daley dispensed political patronage (i.e., political jobs) on the basis of a given ward's political performance. The Shakman Decree, which resulted from *Shakman v. Democratic Organization of Cook County et al.* (1972), curtailed the patronage system by prohibiting firing on political grounds. In 1979 the decree was extended to prohibit hiring on political grounds as well. See Grimshaw 1992, 21; Biles 1995, 188.

5. The "Silent Six" label became popular during Daley's second term (Biles 1995, 93). The silent six were Ralph Metcalfe, Claude Holman, William Harvey, Kenneth Campbell, Robert Miller, and George Collins.

6. Despres, a white alderman, was well known for his opposition to the Daley machine and for his support of civil rights issues. At city council meetings Despres spoke up for civil rights to such an extent that he was referred to as the only "Black" member of the city council (Leon Despres interview, September 11, 1995).

7. James Meredith was shot on June 6, 1966, while attempting a "March against Fear" through Mississippi. After the shooting occurred, scores of civil rights groups, including the SCLC, CORE, and SNCC, resumed the march in Meredith's place. One reporter called what began as a lone gesture "the biggest parade since Selma." During the march, on the evening of June 16, 1966, in Greenwood, Mississippi, Stokely Carmichael, the recently elected chairman of SNCC, gave a speech in which he issued the call for Black power (see Hampton and Fayer 1990, 283–95).

8. Both Morris (1984, 5) and Payne (1995, 191–92) make important distinctions between rural and urban Black churches in the South. Payne, however, explicitly argues that in much of the rural South, where Black churches were smaller and not well financed, Black ministers were subject to white reprisals for supporting civil rights activities. Thus in rural areas the church as an institution was slower supporting the civil rights movement than in the cities.

9. Katznelson (1973, 93–100) has noted that under the Republican regime of Chicago mayor William Hale Thompson the Reverend Archibald Carey, a prominent Black minister, dispensed such large amounts of political patronage that his church, in effect, became a political machine.

10. The convention split into two camps—the NBC and the Progressive Baptist Convention—after Jackson defied rules regarding tenure. For a full account see C. H. King 1967.

11. As Morris (1984, 97) reminds us, this "militant" view of religion was not new to the Black church. Rather, this view guided the actions of slave leaders such as Denmark Vesey, Nat Turner, Harriet Tubman, and Frederick Douglass.

8   Forging a Multidimensional Oppositional Consciousness: Lessons from Community-Based AIDS Activism

Brett C. Stockdill

> My role—if nothing else—is to remind people and ourselves that
> AIDS is much more complex than we think. PWAs [People With
> AIDS] can become people with disabilities. That PWAs come in
> all sizes and shapes and colors etc. That sexism has everything
> to do with AIDS. That discrimination has everything to do with
> AIDS. That health is a control issue, and it's a power issue, it's a
> privilege issue.
>
> Jeff, an Asian Pacific Islander gay AIDS activist

Introduction: Social Movements and Multiple Inequalities

Jeff's words reflect a political analysis attentive to multiple inequalities. This analysis appeared frequently in my interviews with AIDS activists of color—in particular, lesbians, gay men, and bisexuals. I will argue that such a multifaceted oppositional political consciousness optimally generates community-based strategies that simultaneously challenge the racism, sexism, classism, and homophobia intertwined in the AIDS crisis.

This chapter, based on fifty interviews with AIDS activists in New York, Los Angeles, and Chicago, analyzes grassroots efforts to increase awareness about HIV/AIDS and facilitate the empowerment of people living with HIV/AIDS.[1] These intracommunity strategies represent the crucial cultural and consciousness-raising work that is at the core of much AIDS activism. Analyzing this work helps us to understand better the interaction between multiple oppressions and collective action—a neglected area in the study of social movements.

Much of contemporary social movement scholarship focuses on forging a conceptual framework that links culture and structure (Mueller 1992; Zald 1992; Morris 1992). Emerging theoretical models emphasize the critical importance of collective consciousness in social movement development. Klandermans (1992) stresses that social movements are socially constructed. Challenging dominant collective beliefs and reframing collective perceptions of social relationships in terms of injustice and inequality is an active process that is central to the development of strategies to undermine oppression.

Much recent research has demonstrated the importance of culture and consciousness in modern social movements, including the Civil

Rights Movement (Morris 1984; McAdam 1988), the Black Power Movement (Allen 1992), the feminist movement (Echols 1989; Taylor 1989; Lengermann and Wallace 1985), the gay and lesbian movement (Cruickshank 1992; Adam 1987; D'Emilio 1983), and the labor movement (Fantasia 1988; Piven and Cloward 1979). The transformation of collective consciousness is a crucial aspect of social movement development. Social movement organizations use cultural symbols to draw people into collective action, attempting to root their messages in the collective beliefs of target groups. Scholars such as Gamson (1992) and Taylor and Whittier (1992) contend that the transformation of collective identities is in and of itself an element of social change. Gamson states that the "construction of a collective identity is one step in challenging cultural domination" (1992, 60), suggesting that changes at the cultural level be given the same status as institutional changes.

However, most sociological research on social movements has focused on consciousness raising and collective action targeting one particular form of social inequality. Little research has been conducted on how people are drawn into collective action within the context of multiple consciousnesses and oppressions. Thus, frame alignment (Snow et al. 1986) and other approaches (McAdam 1982; W. Gamson 1989; Klandermans 1988; Melucci 1989) that attempt to explain how social movement organizations challenge dominant ideology and mobilize new movement participants do not account for the impact of multiple forms of oppression and consciousness. Most work has focused on unidimensional frames—frames that seek to transform consciousness and society on one level. There has been scant attention to collective action that focuses on more than one system of oppression.

While perhaps less visible to many sociologists, some collective action is indeed guided by multidimensional oppositional frames (Collins 1990; Combahee River Collective [1977] 1983). Activists situated at the intersections of multiple oppressions have developed collective action frames that help them strike out against the complex social structures that sustain race, class, gender, and heterosexual oppression. Black feminists (Lorde 1984; Davis 1983, 1990; Smith 1983), other feminists of color (Anzaldúa 1990; Trujillo 1991), progressive Black gay men (Beam 1986; Hemphill 1991; Riggs 1989) and White lesbian feminists (Rich 1986; Pratt, Bulkin, and Smith 1988; Kaye/Kantrowitz 1989) have all advanced such multidimensional frames. Activists have also applied such frames in political struggle. Barbara Smith (1983), for example, notes that Black feminists have been involved in a variety of social change efforts including reproductive rights, health care, child care, the rights of the disabled, violence against women, sexual harassment, welfare rights, lesbian and gay rights, educational reform, housing, women in prison, aging, police brutality, labor organizing, antiimperialist struggles, antiracist organizing, nuclear disarmament, and preserving the environment.

In this chapter, I explore how political consciousnesses attentive to multiple inequalities influence AIDS activism. In the next section, "One-Dimensional Oppositional Consciousness," I examine the ways in which multiple inequalities complicate the fight against AIDS on both the movement and community level. In the third section, "Community AIDS Activism," I analyze grassroots efforts in communities of color to confront multiple oppressions simultaneously, foster multidimensional oppositional consciousness, and galvanize individual and collective action. In the fourth section, "Mobilization and Multiplicity," I discuss the central role played by race in this activism.

One-Dimensional Oppositional Consciousness: Community- and Movement-Level Barriers to Collective Action

Challenging purely biomedical models of disease, Padgug (1989) and others (Brandt [1991]; Patton [1990]; Weeks [1991]; Sontag [1988]) contend that prevailing ideological beliefs and related systemic inequalities shape the definition and spread of AIDS and other diseases as well as the responses of the health care system and other segments of society. Shilts (1987) and other critics (Adam [1987]; Weeks [1991]; Padgug [1989]) show that the perception of AIDS as a "gay disease" in a homophobic society has been central to societal inaction in the face of AIDS. Padgug (1989) observes that gay men were constructed as villains rather than victims, noting that measures proposed to confront AIDS, such as expulsion, quarantine, mandatory testing, and the removal of People With AIDS (PWAs) from schools, jobs, and housing, have been patterned on historical forms of homophobic oppression.

Corea's (1992) research (see also Anastos and Marte 1991; ACT UP/New York 1992) demonstrates how pervasive gender inequality has both obscured and increased the threat of AIDS among women. Corea details the medical community's refusal to study the effect of AIDS on women, the portrayal of women as vectors of transmission (to men and to children) rather than people actually at risk themselves, and the dearth of resources available to women with HIV and AIDS. Other research (Dalton 1991; Drucker 1991; Arno and Feiden 1992; Patton 1990) indicates that the impact of AIDS on poor people, especially people of color, is compounded by the structural assaults of poverty, unemployment, substance abuse, and inadequate housing, health care, and education.

Lusane (1991) notes that the erosion of civil rights legislation, the infusion of crack cocaine, the upsurge of racist violence, and cutbacks in social services during the 1980s and 1990s have intensified these racist assaults, leaving poor communities of color more vulnerable to AIDS. As we begin the twenty-first century, African Americans and Latinos/as continue to be overrepresented among people living with HIV and AIDS.

Social inequalities do not exist in isolation, but have a multiplicative effect (Collins 1990; Combahee River Collective [1977] 1983; Davis 1983). Hammonds (1990) and others (Asetoyer 1992; Cohen 1999; R. Rodriguez 1992; Rumsey 1992) show that race and gender as well as related economic disparities have provided a matrix that makes women of color more vulnerable to HIV infection and simultaneously deflects attention from the problem. Seventy-three percent of women with AIDS in the United States are women of color (Banzhaf 1992). Black and Latino gay and bisexual men also experience disproportionately high rates of HIV infection.

The AIDS crisis has been shaped not only by social inequality emanating from dominant social institutions and culture, but by social inequality on the community and movement level. The existence of multiple interlocking oppressions creates the potential for the oppressed to act as the oppressor (see, e.g., Cohen 1999). Collins (1990, 227–28) writes that domination "operates not only by structuring power from the top down but by simultaneously annexing the power as energy of those on the bottom for its own ends." Multiple forms of hegemonic consciousness extend into the group or community level and coexist with oppositional consciousness. Morris (1992, 364) writes that "individuals and groups oppressed by one system of domination may in fact enjoy a position of privilege and power in the system of domination next door." For example, gay men may contribute to the sexism that oppresses lesbians, and heterosexuals of color may contribute to the homophobia that oppresses lesbians and gay men of color. This dynamic, which I will call "one-dimensional" oppositional consciousness, is expressed in social movements as ideology and strategies that challenge one particular form of inequality but ignore or reinforce other forms.

There has been little social movement research on how one-dimensional oppositional consciousness affects movements. Research outside the field shows that hegemonic consciousness and oppositional consciousness often coexist in social movements and can sow intramovement conflict. Feminists of color (Davis 1983; Collins 1990; Anzaldúa and Moraga 1983; Anzaldúa 1990; Smith 1983) have criticized sexism in antiracist political struggles and racism in the feminist movement.

Other manifestations of the oppressed as oppressor include homophobia and classism in the women's movement (Echols 1989), racism in the gay rights movement (Stockdill 1992; Beam 1986; Hemphill 1991), and homophobia in the Black community (Cohen 1999).

AIDS-related inequality also emanates not only from the federal government, the media, the medical establishment, and other dominant social institutions but from within oppressed communities themselves. Within the context of the AIDS crisis, activists report that racism in the gay community, homophobia in communities of color, sexism in both, and other forms of one-dimensional oppositional consciousness are major obstacles to effective AIDS prevention and intervention. The dynamics of the oppressed as oppressor operate both in impacted communities and in AIDS organizations. Below, I present specific examples of one-dimensional oppositional consciousness drawn from my interviews.

Sexism

As in White communities, battling sexism in communities of color has been central to AIDS organizing according to interview respondents. Marion, an Afro-Caribbean heterosexual woman working with the Caribbean Women's Health Association in Brooklyn, stated that a central aspect of her agency's work involves challenging the "subservient roles" ascribed to women. For example, patriarchal consciousness translates into interactions, such as the refusal of many men of all races to wear condoms, that place women at risk for HIV. Tabitha, an African American lesbian activist, also stated that the refusal of men to wear a condom and the reluctance of women to demand it is a serious problem. She saw the great need for substantial education on "how we [women] view ourselves and our bodies in relation to men and how men view themselves also in terms of health and everything else."

Just as patriarchal consciousness led men to downplay the importance of gender oppression in the Civil Rights Movement and the New Left (McAdam 1988; Echols 1989; Davis 1983), many gay male AIDS activists have failed to pay attention to the impact of AIDS on women (Corea 1992). The White women and women of color interviewed stated that gay men have been resistant to including issues relating to women and AIDS as a priority. Decrying the lack of money for women's programs as "sexist," Yvonne, a Black lesbian minister in Los Angeles, asked, "Why is it that women don't count? And lesbians have been there for our gay brothers the whole time." In some cases, gay men have resented the leadership of lesbians in the AIDS movement, at times leaving organizations that had strong lesbian participation. On a more individual level, women report that men sometimes try to ignore them during meetings or downplay the importance of initiatives targeting women. Ellen, a bisexual White woman, recalled an important meeting during which a male representative from another organization, AIDS Project Los Angeles, "didn't look at us straight in the eye once, didn't acknowledge our existence, only looked at and addressed the men in the room." Maria, a heterosexual Latina activist, noted that when she began working at an HIV clinic in the Bronx there was no information on women and AIDS—"not even a flip chart on anatomy."

Racism

The interviews also suggest that racism within the gay male community is an obstacle to prevention and intervention efforts targeting gay men of color. Prejudice, stereotypes, and exclusion often serve to either render gay men of color invisible or relegate them to marginal positions in relation to the White gay male community. One graphic example illustrating the power dynamics in oppressed communities was described by two gay male activists from the Asian Pacific Islander AIDS Intervention Team (AIT) in Los Angeles. While distributing condoms and safer-sex literature in West Hollywood, they discovered a troubling dynamic in some interracial couples (Asian American men with White men). When outreach workers gave condoms and literature to an Asian American man, he would often immediately give them to his White partner. On one occasion, the White man then returned the condoms to the outreach workers, stating, "He doesn't need these." The interview respondents link such events to the subservient roles some Asian men play in interracial relationships with White men.

Paralleling Black feminist criticisms of the mainstream women's movement (Davis 1983; Lorde 1984), Black gay writer and activist Essex Hemphill (1991) notes that racism in the White gay community has produced a predominantly White AIDS movement that has been slow to deal constructively with the realities of people of color (see also Julien and Mercer 1991; Dalton 1991). Interview respondents presented several interrelated criticisms of predominantly White, mainstream AIDS agencies, centering on a lack of support for services and programs for people of color. One basic criticism addressed the failure to have people of color adequately represented among agency staff.

Interview respondents linked the underrepresentation of people of color to the issue of cultural insensitivity. The most common example they gave was the failure to provide information and services in languages other than English. Other reported forms of cultural insensitivity include not having traditional foods at food banks and organizational events (e.g., distributing Wonder Bread rather than tortillas to Latino/a immigrants). Several respondents pointed out that organizations and events are frequently located in places (such as West Hollywood or SoHo) that are alienating and/or inaccessible to many people of color. One Black gay man commented on the Los Angeles chapter of the AIDS Coalition to Unleash Power (ACT UP/Los Angeles) that:

> there's something about driving into West Hollywood for a meeting. That just turns people of color off because West Hollywood is so insidious in their own racism, in the gay racism. . . . It wasn't really centrally located. A lot of things they did seemed to perpetuate this old boy's club.

These and other problems make it more difficult for people of color to access services. Respondents from other cities related other problems, such as excessive scrutiny of spending by people of color caucuses in ACT UP and doubts about the ability of people of color to articulate group demands adequately at public events.

Respondents of color also criticized many White activists for not seeing how AIDS is linked to racial and class oppression, and to related social issues such as immigration, housing and substance abuse. For example, undocumented immigrants from Latin America are sometimes reluctant to get tested for HIV and seek out other services for fear of deportation. However, mainstream AIDS agencies often do not provide immigrant-specific legal services.

Homophobia

Homophobia has been at the core of the AIDS epidemic. Activists working in communities of color state that constructive community responses have been hindered by apathy, denial and intolerance rooted in homophobic and heterosexist consciousness. Many African-American, Asian American and Latino/a leaders have articulated the same homophobic messages as heterosexual, White male public officials (Cohen 1999). Already lacking accessible healthcare and other resources, gay men of color have sometimes lost the support of their families and communities when they needed it the most (Harris 1986; Dalton 1991; Hemphill 1991). Within the context of the AIDS epidemic, homophobia in communities of color serves to isolate not only gay men but other people with HIV and AIDS.

According to most respondents, cultural taboos on sexuality, particularly homosexuality, have been at the core of resistance to explicit, public messages about AIDS prevention. As do many White churches, many churches in Asian American, African American, and Latino/a communities teach that homosexuality is a sin. Because AIDS is perceived as a gay disease and effective AIDS prevention necessitates talking about homosexuality, these churches resist openly discussing it. As a result, they ignore transmission not only via homosexual sex, but via heterosexual sex and sharing needles. Most of the respondents of color report that homophobia in the Black, Latino/a, and Asian American communities makes coalition building difficult. Churches play a central role in the life of these communities, but, according to respondents, churches in general have frequently resisted doing anything substantial regarding AIDS. As a consequence, challenging homophobia is a prerequisite to AIDS education. Yvonne commented that people often ignore

> the fact that there are gays and lesbians in their church who are African American, who have AIDS or who are HIV positive, who are afraid to come out of the closet because of the church's attitude on homosexuality. So I believe that we need to address homosexuality and religion . . . in order to help people to become more real about addressing AIDS in their own congregation or in their community.

Homophobia is a problem not only in churches, but in a vast array of community institutions. Activists believe that the reluctance of other institutions (including organizations such as the NAACP and the Urban League) to become active in the battle against AIDS has been in large part attributable to homophobia. A Black gay man active in ACT UP/Chicago attempted to get Operation PUSH (a Black community organization founded by Jesse Jackson) to run an advertisement for a conference on AIDS in communities of color cosponsored by ACT UP. PUSH refused to support the conference, stating that such a "pro–sexual liberation" stance was "not appropriate" for the Black community.

Classism

While all the activists interviewed are located within subordinate racial, sexuality, and/or gender groups (there are no heterosexual White men among the interviewees), most were privileged socioeconomically. Most of the activists in this study were middle-class, college-educated professionals. Activists of color were more likely than White activists to talk explicitly about class issues. Several, for example, stated that class divisions often create tensions within communities of color. Being middle class tends to limit their interaction with poor and working-class people, inhibiting the formation of alliances. Activists in the New York–based Black AIDS Mobilization (BAM), where the running joke is that you need a college degree to be in the group, stated that the middle-class professional status of most members of the group makes it difficult for them to gain entree into working-class communities.

Kyle, a Black gay male activist, concluded that "lesbian and gay activism and even AIDS activism to a degree is a privilege in this society, and I think you have to have a certain status in order to do it." He urges people to be mindful of this privilege, particularly when protest involves the possibility of arrest. Aside from the increased likelihood of people of color being beaten, the costs of being arrested include raising bail money and missing work—both of which weigh more heavily on working-class and poor people.

Several activists of color criticized both grassroots organizations in communities of color and ACT UP for lacking a class analysis. An African American HIV-positive gay man in ACT UP/Los Angeles labeled a community-based Black gay AIDS group as "bourgeois," criticizing the organization for not being more confrontational. Although other such comments typically referred to an organization's failure to address class divisions within communities of color, at least two activists also criticized the failure of AIDS activists to recognize the marginalized position of working-class and poor White people within the AIDS crisis. In one instance, Donald, an African American gay man, criticized other members of ACT UP/Chicago for wanting to restrict a conference agenda to people of color and to not include working-class or poor White people. Stephanie, an African American lesbian in ACT UP/Chicago, stated that people are always ready to include Black and Latina women in discussions of women and AIDS, but tend to gloss over the severe impact of AIDS on poor White women.

The most striking class conflict was reported by former members of the Latino Caucus of ACT UP/New York. This conflict, which contributed to the disbanding of the caucus, involved a campaign to challenge the Hispanic AIDS Forum (HAF). Interviewees reported that HAF was located in SoHo—an area worlds away from the majority of the Latino/a population of New York. They also reported that the agency did not have any openly gay or HIV-positive people on its board of directors and thus did not represent the populations most affected by AIDS. Finally, they criticized HAF for not making any substantive attempts to do outreach in the Latino/a community and for failing to set up programs for which it had received grant money. When some members of the caucus proposed a plan to challenge HAF publicly, other members opposed the idea because it involved attacking a Latino organization. The activists interviewed, however, believed that the core issue was class. They stated that opposing members of the caucus (as well as the agency itself) were using race as an excuse to not deal with their own class privilege. According to my interview respondents, the people in HAF who complained that ACT UP used a model alien to the Latino community were reportedly largely conservative and upper middle class. These HAF members reportedly complained that the Latino/a community didn't understand "marching and chanting in the streets." One Latino gay man in the Latino Caucus of ACT UP/New York argued the members' position derived from a "conflict of political ideology," claiming that change in Latino/a communities has indeed come about through street activism, direct action, strikes, sit-ins, and even violence. He felt that the administrators and board at HAF were using this racial argument to protect their lucrative positions in the AIDS bureaucracy.

Simultaneity

Analysis of AIDS activism makes it clear that various forms of social inequality often operate simultaneously, a key element of Black feminist theory (Smith 1983; King 1988; Collins 1990). The interviews reveal many situations in which individual activists and organizations faced the compounded effects of multiple spheres of domination. Middle-class Black lesbians in BAM might be fighting with Black gay men over gender issues and with White ACT UPers over race at the same time that they tried to grapple with their own class privilege. Members of ACT UP/New York's Latino Caucus faced White paternalism in ACT UP, homophobia while organizing in the Latino community, and conflicts over class divisions within the caucus itself. One Asian American activist faced severe difficulties recruiting "buddies" for PWAs in South Central Los Angeles because most Black churches in the community were not interested in getting involved in AIDS work, while most of the current volunteers were White and did not want to travel to South Central.

One interviewee's experience as a poor African American bisexual HIV-positive prisoner vividly illustrates the confluence of different spheres of domination. As a Black prisoner with AIDS, Victor faced the compounded effects of race and class oppression related to incarceration (see Stockdill 1995). He faced prejudice and discrimination from other inmates in prison due to his sexuality and HIV status. While in prison, he wrote various AIDS organizations—including the Kupona Network, a Black AIDS organization in Chicago—but virtually all of these failed to respond to his requests for information and support.

One-dimensional oppositional consciousness, I conclude, can be conceptualized as an ideological bolt that locks together systems of domination. Patterns of oppression within oppressed communities operate to protect hegemonic consciousness and thus reinforce dominant social structures. The concept of one-dimensional oppositional consciousness challenges the rigid dichotomization of cultural/personal and institutional found in much social movement literature and illuminates the links between social structure, collective identity, and individual biographies. More specifically, one-dimensional oppositional consciousness goes beyond Gramsci's ([1929–35] 1987) hegemonic ideology and similar concepts by allowing for multiple, interactive forms of consciousness. An interpretive model incorporating one-dimensional oppositional consciousness creates the opportunity for a richer analysis of collective action.

Community AIDS Activism: Expanding Collective Consciousness

On a practical level, one-dimensional oppositional consciousness presents a complex set of problems for AIDS activists, who have often found that challenging recalcitrant institutions and dominant belief systems is only one aspect of fighting AIDS. There is also a need, they have found, to challenge local movement organizations, educate indigenous communities, and transform collective beliefs. The activists who possess a multidimensional perspective consistently identify battles against multiple inequalities as inseparable from fighting AIDS. These battles often involve challenging one-dimensional oppositional consciousness because they are battles fought within oppressed communities hit hard by AIDS as well as within AIDS organizations themselves.

The organizations analyzed for this section of the paper are primarily community-based organizations within communities of color. In general, they have two primary, immediate goals: (1) to prevent the spread of HIV and (2) to provide treatment, support, and social services to people living with HIV and AIDS. More specifically, organizational efforts focus on the following areas: street level prevention efforts (distribution of condoms, dental dams, and safer-sex information); support services for people living with HIV (treatment issues, emotional support); assistance with related social problems (immigration, housing, health care, substance abuse, food, etc.); promotion of positive images of lesbians and gay men, especially lesbians and gay men of color; and efforts to shape public policy and public opinion around AIDS through education, lobbying, and protest.

Strategies to galvanize multidimensional oppositional consciousness and catalyze both individual and collective action in the face of the

AIDS crisis can be placed into four interrelated categories: constructive dialogue, empowerment initiatives, community embeddedness, and utilization of indigenous cultural traditions.

Constructive Dialogue

Resource mobilization theories stress the centrality of strategies and tactics (Morris and Herring 1987; McAdam, McCarthy, and Zald 1988). Sociological research providing support for resource mobilization theories has focused on collective action utilizing instrumental tactics to effect change on an institutional level. "New" social movement theory and related social psychological approaches assert the importance of "prefigurative politics" or "identity politics," which stress the importance of cultural change (Habermas 1981; Cohen 1985; Taylor and Whittier 1992; Gamson 1992). Joshua Gamson's (1989) research on AIDS activism demonstrates that instrumental and expressive politics are not mutually exclusive but vary according to the target of collective action.

Within this study, respondents reported a range of tactics that varied depending on the target and goals (other factors include the potential for repression; see Stockdill 1996). When activism is directed at communities of color and the gay and lesbian community (as opposed to activism targeting dominant culture and institutions), it is more likely to involve constructive dialogue and less likely to involve confrontation. Strategies to combat one-dimensional oppositional consciousness within oppressed communities and within the AIDS movement itself, by and large, differ from strategies to combat oppression directly emanating from dominant institutions. The activists interviewed stressed the importance of constructive dialogue as a tactic for confronting intracommunity inequality.

For example, when BAM protested the Immigration and Naturalization Service's imprisonment of Haitians with AIDS on Guantanamo Bay, they picketed and engaged in civil disobedience leading to arrests. At the same time, they had internal discussions about sexism in their own community. Within the direct action group ACT UP, women's caucuses and people of color caucuses also have had many in-house "educationals" designed to increase sensitivity to gender and racial inequalities. Steven, an African American gay man in ACT UP/Los Angeles, spoke on how people of color and women in that organization have worked to challenge the perception that only White gay men are affected by AIDS: "It's more than just doing the physical work—it's also the changing of consciousness. . . . You have to tell these White boys over and over, 'No, it's not your fucking disease.' "

Stephanie, an African American lesbian in ACT UP/Chicago—an organization that has engaged in extremely confrontational, militant tactics against pharmaceuticals and the government—advocated a far less confrontational approach for dealing with Black funeral directors who were illegally overcharging the families of people who had died of AIDS. In this case, rather than organizing a demonstration, she and other AIDS activists sat down with the funeral directors and carefully explained that it would be better for all parties involved if the problem was solved through negotiation and without publicity. Although the group conveyed a clear message that "the shit would hit the fan" if the funeral directors did not change their policy, Stephanie stressed that it was crucial to "let them know you're coming at them with respect and brotherhood and sisterhood." Cohen (1999) echoes this strategic thinking: "[I]n contrast to the more aggressive political tactics of civil disobedience used by predominantly white groups such as ACT UP, the political strategies in African-American communities were much less confrontational, with compromise and education being key" (341).

Challenging homophobia in communities of color typically takes place through dialogue on a one-to-one basis or in workshops and pre-sentations. One AIDS organization serving the Caribbean community in Brooklyn set up a home visitor program in which outreach workers went into people's homes to encourage dialogue around the taboo subjects of sex and sexuality. According to one interview respondent, the results were "amazing." A significant change occurred in many families' willing-ness to openly discuss topics related to HIV and AIDS. Similar outreach programs created by other organizations reported success. Activists link this success to the fact that outreach workers are trained in the biology, psychology, and social aspects of AIDS and, most importantly, come from the community themselves.

Activist strategies distinguish between dominant social institutions and marginalized communities. In general, activists appear to work hard to avoid public conflict when responding to hegemonic consciousness and inequality within their own communities. Instead, they try to fa-cilitate dialogue around problematic issues in order to build alliances. Their tactics are shaped by a larger strategy of building coalitions that rest on the existing oppositional culture of oppressed communities, but also seek to expand this culture to include other forms of oppositional consciousness.

Dialogue, however, is only one step toward fostering oppositional consciousness and changing minds. Tabitha, an Afro-Caribbean lesbian, remarked that AIDS education goes deeper than telling people to use a condom: "You have to change people's ideas and the way they look at themselves and they way they perceive their bodies and their place in society; if people don't feel that they're that important to begin with, then, 'Oh what the hell.'" A key element in the transformation of collective consciousness involves empowerment. Particularly for poor people, reframing the situation as a collective injustice, an act of consciousness raising, must be accompanied by a change in the potential participant's sense of agency—on both an individual and collective level.

Empowerment Initiatives

Klandermans (1992) maintains that current theoretical frameworks fail to combine individual and collective analyses. He emphasizes the importance of attention to interconnected levels of micromobilization. Gamson (1992) offers the concept of "microevents"—events that link individual and sociocultural levels and, optimally, facilitate the mobilization of consciousness and action. These interviews suggest that, within the AIDS movement, successful microevents are guided by a model of empowerment that pays attention to the complex social forces affecting people's lives.

Interviewees say they spend a considerable amount of time developing strategies to facilitate individual empowerment. The activists use support groups, educational workshops, and one-on-one interactions to promote the self-worth and dignity of people affected by HIV/AIDS. Community-based service organizations have set up mechanisms to involve clients in decision-making processes and helping other clients. Peer educators are key. In the peer tutor program of Vida SIDA (an alternative AIDS clinic in Chicago), young people from the Latino/a community were trained in the science, psychology, and cultural issues of AIDS and then conducted a door-to-door educational campaign. The peer educators, who were reportedly well received in most homes, loved their jobs so much that they continued to work after funding for the program was cut.

Stephanie noted that a primary aspect of her job at the Chicago Women's AIDS Project was to help develop a sense of "entitlement" among women with HIV and AIDS so that they could demand housing, health care, and other goods. In addition to helping people to see that they are entitled to a certain standard of living, activists emphasize the importance of dealing with the everyday problems in poor people's lives. As Maria, a Latina activist, put it: "If you ask a woman with HIV 'What are your problems?,' she's not gonna tell you 'AIDS.' She's gonna tell you, 'Well, I don't have a house to live in. I don't have food for all my children.'" While doing street outreach, Tabitha encountered a woman who said she didn't want a condom because she had a drug problem and

> when she's high, she doesn't care what she does and her life is so fucked up anyway that she's dying so what the hell does she care if she gets HIV/AIDS? It's no worse than anything else she has to live through. . . . She could just put it together in a way that a lot of policy makers just can't see. That kind of connection is imperative.

Tabitha concluded that in order to mobilize people—whether for individual or collective action—one must use a holistic approach that deals with the various social realities of marginalized communities: "It's got to be linked to providing services that the community needs in some real way." When people see the possibilities of meeting their basic needs, they are more likely to be motivated to take action to change their lives and, in turn, work with others collectively. Several activists in community-based organizations reported that many clients later became activists themselves.

Awareness of the complex layers of adversity that undergird the AIDS epidemic has enabled these activists to develop effective programs. For example, Bienestar, a Latino AIDS program in Los Angeles, offers services that provide for many of the needs of community members. It provides services and information in Spanish. It makes information available at its drop-in center as well as at other sites such as community festivals and day labor camps. Bienestar offers legal services for the immigration issues that complicate HIV/AIDS for immigrants. It offers support groups to address the psychosocial needs of people with HIV/AIDS and their family members. It hires former clients in the Peer to Peer program to do case management.

The need to promote a sense of entitlement among people with HIV and AIDS challenges those resource mobilization theories that treat grievances and discontent as given rather than as shaped by collective and individual meanings, ideas, and values (Mueller 1992). These efforts to facilitate empowerment also indicate that catalyzing oppositional consciousness involves not only sociocultural elements, but the microstructural position of potential movement participants. Frame alignment analyses should therefore incorporate actions aimed at dealing with the concrete socioeconomic conditions resulting from multiple systems of oppression.

Institutional and cultural domination affects people's everyday lives and interactions; they are thus a potential site for oppression and resistance (Collins 1990). As lesbians and gay men of color point out (Smith

1983; Hemphill 1991; Beam 1986; Anzaldúa and Moraga 1983; Trujillo 1991), oppression may exact a severe psychological toll, often resulting in self-hatred and -doubt. Although challenging internalized oppression has been a key element in many movements, including the Garveyite movement, the Black Power Movement (Bennett 1984; Allen 1990), the feminist movement (Echols 1989), and gay and lesbian movements (Adam 1987; D'Emilio 1983; Duberman 1994), social movement researchers have not paid enough attention to this dynamic. Many activists reported how important it is in their work to create ways to challenge internalized oppression and bolster self-images among people of color, gays/lesbians, and women.

We have seen how outreach workers from AIT in Los Angeles identified as a problem the subservient roles some Asian men play in sexual relationships with White men. AIT developed an innovative project to confront this dynamic as well as the general lack of positive sexual imagery of Asians in mainstream culture. According to Rob, the program coordinator for AIT:

> I came up with the idea, this program, "Love Your Asian Body," because I know that self-esteem is running low in the gay and lesbian Asian community. You open up all the papers and magazines and see the ads of what is considered beautiful, what is considered hot, and it's the new clone of the nineties, the West Hollywood gay White male, and so that becomes your standard to work with. That's your standard of excellence.

The campaign's cards and newspaper ads depict two Asians (men with men, women with women, women with men) in a "hot, steamy situation to emphasize loving your body." They give educational information on safer sex and HIV testing, and also advertise events where Asian lesbians and gay men can get more information on HIV and AIDS.

The campaign produced some negative responses from the White gay community and from Asian men with White partners, who complained that the Asian-on-Asian focus discriminated against White men. We may think of these negative responses as "hegemonic Eurocentric consciousness"—which relegates Asians to a subordinate social status in relationships with Whites—reacting to an oppositional antiracist/pro-Asian consciousness. Yet the images seem to have succeeded, at least in part, in their aim. The activists interviewed reported a significant increase in the number of Asians getting tested after the inception of the campaign.

The Love Your Asian Body campaign and others like it illustrate how social movement organizations can work on the micro level to transform identities in order to empower people to take control of their lives. The positive, erotic images of same-sex Asian couples promote both Asian Pacific Islander consciousness and gay/lesbian consciousness. The Love Your Asian Body campaign provides a tangible example of building multidimensional oppositional consciousness.

One of the most powerful, widespread tactics of AIDS activism, which links individual and collective action, is simply being "out"—as openly gay, lesbian, bisexual, or transgendered. Historically, coming out has played a central role in gay and lesbian oppositional culture (D'Emilio 1983; Freedman and D'Emilio 1988; Adam 1987). Given the lack of civil rights protection granted gay men and lesbians and the prevalence of homophobic prejudice, discrimination, and violence, coming out continues to be an act of political and cultural defiance in our society. Several people interviewed stated that being openly gay or lesbian is crucial for facilitating dialogues on AIDS and creating a safe, positive environment for those living with HIV. This means being "out" at all times—at social events, agency meetings, and political rallies and with family and friends.

On a collective level, lesbians and gay men of color have worked to promote visibility in communities of color by taking part in community events such as street festivals, parades, and health fairs. Their participation challenges the construction of homosexuality as a White phenomenon and asserts that they are a part of their respective community of color. In several cases, such high-visibility actions by AIDS activists broke through walls of silence and denial in communities of color and led to more attention to AIDS by community leaders and organizations. For example, after being assigned a space near the end of the Puerto Rican Day parade (a common occurrence for African American and Latino/a lesbians and gays attempting to march in community parades), the Latino caucus of ACT UP/New York broke in closer to the front of the parade. Because they entered the march early, they made it into the media broadcast. The group did a "die-in" in front of Saint Patrick's Cathedral, that, according to one participant, was a "shocking thing to do, especially in the Puerto Rican Day parade, especially in front of Saint Patrick's Cathedral." They had a coffin with a Puerto Rican flag on it and pictures of Puerto Rican politicians with the word "AIDS" printed on top of them. Although their actions shocked many, their signs, props and die-ins received national press coverage, including a half page picture in the *Lucero,* the largest Puerto Rican newspaper in the United States and Puerto Rico. Javier, a Puerto Rican gay man in ACT UP/New York's Latino caucus, stated that "All of a sudden we had blown AIDS out of the closet in the Latino community. . . . It was intense . . . really empowering. . . . It was the big step forward that we needed to start the discourse about AIDS in the Latino community."

Tangled up with homophobia is AIDSphobia—a term coined in recent years to describe prejudice and discrimination against people living with HIV/AIDS. Several AIDS activists interviewed have therefore chosen to be very open about their positive HIV status. Tyrone, an HIV-positive African American gay man, spoke of the "triple whammy," stating that a lot of work is needed to come to terms with being Black, gay, and HIV positive. He articulated the responsibility he and others who are openly Black, gay, and positive have toward those who are not out on these dimensions:

> Those of us who are able to be out about all of those things and have a certain comfortability around it . . . we've got to protect and nurture them [those who aren't] and let them know that there is a place that they can be safe on all, any of those levels, wherever they're at, at that time and making sure they're taken care of in the process.

This attention to nurturing and caring reflects an emotional component of activism. That component lies at the heart of constructing an oppositional consciousness that encompasses compassion and collectivity. Considering the stigmatization (approaching criminalization in some places in calls for mandatory testing, quarantine, and criminal and transmission laws) toward those living with HIV and especially those with full-blown AIDS, being out as HIV positive or as a PWA is inherently political. That is, it raises an issue the public ought to discuss.

Many of the respondents pointed out that creating a safe environment for gays, women, people of color, and people with HIV and AIDS is an essential component of activism. These safe spaces promote collective identities, foster oppositional consciousness, and encourage people to become involved in the steadily evolving networks and organizations of the AIDS movement. The institutional infrastructures and collective identities created resemble the social movement communities that serve as crucibles for innovation and mutual support (Taylor and Whittier 1992). The empowerment initiatives support contentions that cultural change is not merely an antecedent to collective action, but constitutes change in and of itself (see, e.g., Gamson 1992). These cultural initiatives, attuned to microstructural position, make clear the importance of a culture and structure that do not dichotomize.

Community Embeddedness

When activists participate in community events as openly lesbian and gay people of color, one of their goals is to forge and portray a dual collective identity. Their efforts to create multidimensional oppositional consciousness in themselves and others are part and parcel of their efforts to become socially embedded in larger communities. Social movement communities are indeed linked through institutional bases and networks (Taylor and Whittier 1992; Melucci 1989; McAdam 1988).

Interview respondents of color reported varying degrees of affiliation with the White gay community. People of color in ACT UP tended to have more contact with the White gay community, while people of color in small community-based service groups tended to have more contact with communities of color. Even respondents with strong criticisms of the White gay community, who tended to work in autonomous organizations based in racial communities, pointed out, however, that their organizations had links to the larger gay/lesbian community. Primary links take the form of subcontracting, technical assistance, and using meeting space provided by mega-agencies. ACT UP chapters in Los Angeles, New York, and Chicago have provided assistance to various community-based organizations. In New York, ACT UP gave the American Indian House start-up funding for its HIV/AIDS program. These relationships in many cases are based upon the racial community's need for financial and technical resources, which are in greater abundance in predominantly White AIDS organizations.

Overall, a majority of the lesbians and gay men of color interviewed expressed a desire to focus on work within communities of color rather than in the larger gay community, a dynamic discussed later in this essay. They had also developed concrete strategies to become or remain embedded in their Black, Latino/a, Asian Pacific Islander, and Native American communities.

One reason for connecting with organizations in communities of color is increased access to lesbians and gay men in those communities. As in the larger society, homophobia in communities of color causes some lesbians and gay men to hide their sexuality. In addition to the increased visibility of "out" lesbians and gay men that optimally provides a catalyst for others to be out, AIDS organizers also adopt other strategies. Tyrone emphasized simultaneous AIDS work and "general community stuff" because not all Black gays go to gay bars or belong to explicitly gay groups, but are involved in the larger Black community. Sometimes the best way to reach folks, he said, is "under the larger umbrella."

The semantics of advertising have an effect. For example, it is safer, for some, to attend a "Black AIDS" event than a "Black gay" event. Being a part of the larger Black community allows AIDS groups to reach more people. This connection allows organizations to reach those who are often most in need of support and education. Such strategies reflect attention to the social location of potential movement participants as well as a recognition of coexisting hegemonic and oppositional dynamics in the African American community. While heterosexist culture and institutions may force some Black lesbians and gays to remain in the closet, the oppositional infrastructure in the Black community provides channels for activists to reach out to them.

Noel, a Filipino gay man who works at AIT, remarked that he has access to the Filipino community in Los Angeles because he is Filipino, speaks the language, and grew up in the "hood." He knows the gang members, the drag queens, and their families and is considered one of the "homeboys." Marco, a gay Latino activist, recounted that it was easy to start the organization Teatro Viva, a gay and lesbian Latino/a artist organization in Los Angeles, in large part because of his ties to the community:

> because I eat at the same restaurants that my people eat at. Because I go to Burrito King. Because I go to those bars. Not necessarily because I like to sometimes, but I have to be in my community. And those are the people that should be working at these agencies. I don't think it's a secret that we're as successful as we are. We're as successful as we are because we represent our people. That's it.

Most of the activists interviewed emphasized the importance of community immersion and alliances. Strong community ties are extremely important for those actions that may be at odds with community values. In the face of antiaddict sentiment and community concerns with substance abuse/genocide, the people of color caucus in ACT UP/Los Angeles planned a clean needle exchange for several sites in the city. Frank, a White gay male AIDS activist, described how crucial community connections were in setting up the needle exchange in Los Angeles:

> People from ACT UP/LA decided that there needed to be a needle exchange in Los Angeles and so they went ahead and did it. And they did it in a park in the Black community and one in the Latino community. In the Latino community, they had enough connections and talked about this widely enough with people that they could go in and get some community organizations to actually support and kind of cover them to

be able to do this. They didn't establish the same kind of relationship with the Black community. And so the Black community said, "You may not come in here."

Teatro Viva has been successful in gaining the support and active participation of the mothers of gay men. As a way to dramatize civil disobedience, mothers decided to be arrested with their sons during an AIDS demonstration. Drag queens and their mothers have organized rummage sales to raise money for a PWA coalition. The involvement of mothers has been valuable in challenging homophobia and mobilizing support in the Latino/a community.

Interview respondents also described how they tapped into the ever growing Black, Latino/a, and Asian American gay and lesbian communities. Gay/lesbian AIDS organizations of color have often grown out of preexisting organizations and networks. For example, the AIDS Prevention Team in Los Angeles is a project of the National Black Lesbian and Gay Leadership Forum. Different non-AIDS organizations also provide resources and support for AIDS groups. For example, Black and Latino gay bars often provide space for organizational functions related to AIDS. In the fall of 1993, Vida SIDA held a fund raiser at the Baton Lounge, a gay bar in Chicago, in which Black, Latino, and White drag queens performed for free to a packed house. One of the primary methods of mobilization is through informal social networks in gay communities of color. Many interviewees noted that getting people out to different events is often accomplished through word of mouth. As noted by Melucci (1989), reliance on submerged social networks is a key aspect of creating alternative institutions.

Once again, multiple paths shape consciousness raising for gay and lesbian AIDS activists of color. Their "outsider within" status (Collins 1990) in communities of color helps them challenge collective beliefs—in this case homophobic beliefs—and try simultaneously to cement their ties with their respective racial communities. Although challenging and trying to fit in at the same time may seem at odds, communities of color are in fact often contradictory spaces for lesbians and gay men of color. On the one hand, homophobia often leads to ostracism, discrimination, and violence. On the other hand, families and communities of color provide solidarity in a racist society (Julien and Mercer 1991). Roberta, a Black lesbian, points out that lesbians and gay men of color

> need their communities differently than White people need their com-
> munities because all of society is structured to make White people com-
> fortable and people of color generally need their communities more—for

safety, for media access, for financial resources . . . and affirmation. So that homophobia matters in a different way.

All of the people of color interviewed emphasized, as primary aspects of their activism, their racial identities and their loyalty to the larger Black, Latino/a, Asian Pacific Islander, and/or Native American communities. They translate this social identification into conscious attempts to fight AIDS among all people of color, not just gay men and lesbians.

The efforts of these lesbians and gay men of color to achieve community embeddedness shed light on the relationship between fostering multidimensional oppositional consciousness and movement concepts such as multiorganizational fields (Klandermans 1992) and communities of challengers (Lo 1992). A social movement organization's multiorganizational field constitutes the totality of other organizations and institutions with which the organization has relationships. The AIDS groups to which the activists interviewed belonged have tried to maximize the supportive segments of their multiorganizational fields while at the same time realigning other organizations' ideological frames. Other community organizations, including AIDS organizations, may be antagonistic with respect to one or more of the forms of political consciousness the activists are promoting. They may not want to be inclusive with regard to race, class, gender, or sexuality. Within the AIDS movement, the polarization of multiorganizational fields has not occurred to the same extent as in other movements. AIDS activism has encompassed a constant, tense battle to weld together alliances, however shaky, in order to maximize resources—in particular, grants from public and private sources. (One promising area for research is the role that grants have played in the development of the AIDS movement. Virtually all organizations, from small community based groups to mega-agencies to ACT UP, receive some kind of outside funding.)

Lo (1992) maintains that industrial capitalist concepts are not appropriate for groups excluded from the polity, who rely not on industrial market transactions but on community commitment. In these cases, the social relations of a community serve as political resources. Although the organizations in this study always need to acquire outside financial support from the government and foundations, community institutions, networks, and personpower are all crucial weapons in fighting AIDS.

However, Lo presents a limited view of "community" and "challengers" and does not fully explain the importance of the relationships between subordinate groups and the power structure. By limiting his unit of analysis to geographic community, he fails to capture other dimensions of community, such as race, class, sexuality, and gender. In the organizations studied here, communities of color and gay/lesbian communities often transcended geography. These organizations typically targeted a racial community (e.g., the Latino/a community of New York City) or a racial-sexual community (e.g., Asian gay men and lesbians in Los Angeles). Geographic location was not always the central indicator of community. Furthermore, multiple inequalities complicate the field of challengers by creating communities within communities, overlapping communities, and intracommunity challengers. A community may contain intracommunity challengers who seek to challenge and realign sectors of the broader community in order to create a more potent opposition to the overarching power structure characterized by multiple forms of oppression. Thus, in addition to expanding the notion of community, it may be useful to differentiate among different kinds of challengers on the basis of their relationship to particular subordinate communities and dominant society.

Community immersion plays a central role in AIDS activism. Activists attempt to ground constructive dialogue and empowerment initiatives on organizational bonds with communities of color and, to a lesser extent, with the lesbian/gay community. On the fringes of both of these communities, gay and lesbian communities of color have also relied on their own institutional infrastructures and networks to facilitate collective action.

The Use of Cultural Traditions

In addition to community embeddedness, the AIDS activists interviewed also use the language and cultural symbols, images, and traditions of their particular communities in order to promote oppositional consciousness. Frame alignment is most likely to succeed when social movement organizations root their views in the collective experiences and identities of potential participants (Friedman and McAdam 1992; Tarrow 1992). Snow and Benford (1988, 210) link social movement success to narrative fidelity: "the degree to which proffered framings resonate with cultural narrations . . . that are part and parcel of one's cultural heritage and thus function to inform events and experiences in the immediate present."

Language is a core element of culture. Language barriers have created very serious problems within the AIDS crisis. Information on safer sex, testing, treatment, and social services is meaningless if presented in a foreign language. In cities such as Chicago, New York, and Los Angeles, a primary task of AIDS workers is translating all kinds of materials into the language of the target population. This picture is complicated by illiteracy and more subtle sociolinguistic differences. For people with limited reading skills, activists have created comic books with simpler language and pictures. In other cases, outreach workers rely on oral presentations, video, theater, and art. A gay Latino activist noted that gay Latinos tend to be more geographically dispersed than White gays. Many live at home, and many are married to women. Because they do not want to get "caught" in these situations with written information on HIV/AIDS, transmitting information orally becomes crucial. Jeff, an Asian Pacific Islander gay activist, stresses the importance of "cultural competency training" for AIDS workers to make existing services more Asian specific:

> Learning how to say "Ni hau ma?," which is "How are you?" in Mandarin, isn't cultural sensitivity. Sort of acknowledging that you can work with someone who doesn't know the language if you know how to use an interpreter and if you have good people skills—that's culturally sensitive, not necessarily in a patronizing "Oh let me eat your food and learn a little bit of your language."

Leonard, a two-spirited Native American man ("two-spirited" being a term used by Native Americans who feel that the terms "gay" and "lesbian" do not fully capture their cultural-sexual identities), noted that many Indians are more receptive to "AIDS as a story." He describes a few initiatives that Native American activists have developed to teach people about AIDS, beginning with "The Grandmother's Story," an effort by five older Native women:

> They put together a story of AIDS as a creature and talked to our young people about it, and that worked, and that was appropriate culturally. And we had two gay men who put together a dance piece that was very culturally appropriate because the stories were all about Indian people and sort of talking about things that they had experienced and wrapping in the whole issue of AIDS.

Most organizations attempt to connect with the cultural heritage of the target population as a way to promote individual and collective action. Inroads have been made into Black churches in Los Angeles by the AIDS Prevention Team's fan project. For many years, funeral homes and other businesses have distributed fans in Black churches. APT has taken up the tradition. On one side of the APT fan are four images of African masks and the quotation: "He who learns, teaches." The other side lists seven different community organizations that provide testing and/or services to people with HIV. The fans are a culturally familiar device that help to cool off members of the congregation while providing valuable information opening up dialogues around AIDS issues. APT hopes that the fan project will be a step toward productive relationships with Black churches in Los Angeles.

Capitalizing on the success of Spike Lee's movie, one APT poster declares: "Do the Right Thing—We Can't Afford to Do Less!" APT newsletters emphasize both individual and community empowerment, making use of African proverbs and highlighting the positive contributions of African American lesbians and gay men such as Audre Lorde and James Baldwin, both of whom consistently expressed multidimensional oppositional consciousness through their writing and political work. The newsletter includes a question-and-answer column called *The Griot*—a reference to the highly respected storytellers of West Africa.

The Asian Pacific Islander AIDS Intervention Team hands out fortune cookies with safer-sex messages in them. AIT also puts condoms and lubricant in the red lucky envelopes that are traditionally given out during Chinese New Year's celebrations. They use fortune cookies and red envelopes as ice breakers when they talk to people about HIV and AIDS.

Teatro Viva organized a candlelight vigil and rally on Día de los Muertos (Day of the Dead). Día de los Muertos is an important holiday in Latin America and thus holds special significance for Latinos/as. The event also served as a symbolic protest against the silence and inaction surrounding AIDS in Los Angeles. Marco links the success of the event to the use of symbols and collective beliefs in the Latino community:

> The candle idea was a brilliant gesture. . . . That candle meant a lot in terms of Mexico and Salvadoran people's peace protest. It started to take on different meanings, and people were joining those marches that just believed in justice and freedom. . . . It turned into this storytelling thing where mothers were getting up and talking about their sons dying of AIDS. It turned into this really magical, spiritual, very passionate sort of thing. . . . These old ladies would get up and talk about their sons who had died and the secrets the family had about their death. And so it really started to transform how the community started to look at AIDS, but it was rituals, they were just our rituals. . . . Putting AIDS in that context broke down all these barriers that we hadn't been able to break down before.

This action represents not only activists' attention to cultural resonance and the role of rituals (Scott 1985) but collective action itself as a vehicle for increased oppositional consciousness (Klandermans 1992; Fantasia 1988).

APT, Viva, and AIT all promote positive images of being both Black, Latino/a, or Asian, and gay. They hold events at gay bars in their communities. Drag shows—an important cultural tradition in gay male communities—raise both funds and awareness. APT has a weekly aerobics class called "Sweat at the Catch." (The Catch is a gay bar in Los Angeles.) In addition to featuring the APT's trademark images of traditional African masks, the flier advertising this class capitalizes on the gay male community's attraction to things sexy, urging people to "work it till it's Hot & Wet!" The weekly aerobics class includes information sharing and speakers on alternative AIDS treatments, clinical trials, safer sex, insurance planning, and related issues. In the same vein, APT has "hot, horny, and healthy workshops" on safer sex. APT has started to develop educational materials for Black lesbians, using, for example, a glossy photograph of a topless, seductively posed African American woman with information on safer sex for women who have sex with women on the back. Noel stated that outreach materials should be "simple, fun, sexy, attractive, and culturally relevant. Use gay themes." He added that it is good to be controversial: "Let's create controversy because controversy sells. I always figure if it works for Madonna it can work for us colored folks."

In addition to creating "controversy," such sex-positive tactics are used to challenge the antisex, particularly antihomosex, collective beliefs that are part of the antigay/anti-PWA backlash of the AIDS crisis. Portraying homosexuality as positive follows in the tradition of gay and lesbian oppositional consciousness that defies heterosexist gender and sexuality conventions.

The Divas from Viva, three gay Latino men, utilize teatro—short, political skits—which has a history in Latino/a communities in southern California. The skits start off "very Chicano" with "Las Comadres," women gossiping about people in the neighborhood. When the audience is won over, they head into the difficult issues around AIDS including a ranchera (a traditional musical form of northern Mexico) on HIV. The Divas' cultural work taps into both gay and Latino/a consciousness in order to raise people's consciousness about AIDS and to catalyze individual and collective action.

Like the rituals in James Scott's (1985) *Weapons of the Weak,* these cultural tactics often undermine the power of elites. However, there are important differences. While peasant cultures of resistance "require little or no coordination or planning" and "avoid any direct symbolic confrontation with authority or with elite norms" (Scott 1985, 29), these

AIDS activists use their tactics openly as part of a conscious political strategy to challenge dominant norms concerning homosexuality and to promote racial pride among people of color. Scott notes that the character of oppression shapes the form of resistance. Authoritarian rule tends to produce masked defiance. In contemporary America, oppression in the context of the AIDS crisis occurs on the multiple levels of racism, sexism, homophobia, and classism. The multiple levels of need demand intracommunity collective action. The immediate targets of this work are often other members of the community rather than elites. Thus, activists in communities of color often rely on the less confrontational tactics of constructive dialogue and empowerment initiatives. They combine community immersion and existing oppositional cultures to transform consciousness and promote action. What is "new" about these frame alignment processes is that they draw on *multiple* sets of collective beliefs, oppositional cultures, and networks in order to challenge simultaneously multiple forms of hegemonic beliefs, cultures, and inequalities.

Mobilization and Multiplicity: The Centrality of Race

Race and racism have been central forces in the development of the United States. In turn, antiracist struggles have often had a critical impact on other political struggles. The Civil Rights Movement, which grew out of a tradition of protest in Black communities, provided ideological and strategic models for other movements, including the Free Speech Movement, the antiwar movement, the feminist movement, and the gay rights movement (McAdam 1988; Echols 1989; D'Emilio 1983). My interviews suggest that the tradition of antiracist protest worked as a fundamental building block for AIDS activism. Race, moreover, has been a key factor in organizational development and strategy.

As discussed earlier, racism in both the dominant society and within many AIDS organizations has deeply affected the AIDS movement. Most organizations have seen fierce debates over the most effective way of organizing to fight AIDS among people of color. In many cities, people of color caucuses were initiated within ACT UP to combat AIDS within communities of color, although many of these caucuses have ceased to exist as separate entities.

Several interview respondents reported feeling frustrated with these caucuses. The experience of one African American gay man illustrates some of the issues involved. Mike stated that he had worked hard to get people of color, primarily African American and Latino gay men, involved in ACT UP/Los Angeles's people of color caucus. The caucus did door-to-door educational campaigns in the Black community and participated in conferences and ACT UP actions. But the experience was frustrating. Mike felt extremely angry because most Black AIDS activists were reluctant to join the group: "Nobody wants to get involved with ACT UP." (The group was seen as hegemonically White.) On the one hand, Mike was critical of many Black activists, saying that the Black community is "all talk" and that Black activists do not want to march or demonstrate. He described one community-based Black AIDS group as "bourgeois" and felt that they should be doing more direct action. On the other hand, he was also very critical of ACT UP/LA, which he saw as often having the "mentality of a White boy's club." He said, "Why can't I keep these Latino and Black people involved in ACT UP? And it was because ACT UP was very stubborn in its ways and it didn't make Black people feel any more at home than it would have been going to a Republican meeting." In contrast to other committees, he reported that when the ACT UP people of color caucus asked for money they would have to account for "every penny spent. . . . You just get tired of explaining why you spent two dollars to buy a fucking wrist band. . . . Because we didn't really have the support of ACT UP, we never really got off the ground." For Mike, the risk of police brutality helped explain the virtual nonexistence of direct action in the Black community (Stockdill 1996). The people of color caucus eventually fell apart; people just were not interested. Mike concluded by saying:

> Maybe you don't need another ACT UP because ACT UP was specifically a group of White gay men—upper class—who wanted to stop their friends dying. Because of that, ACT UP has always not been all that inclusive of everybody who's been affected of AIDS and that's gonna haunt ACT UP for a long time.

Most respondents of color I interviewed preferred to work with organizations located, geographically and/or culturally, in communities of color (as opposed to within the predominantly White gay/lesbian community). In some cases, this preference followed negative experiences in the White gay/lesbian community. For example, Black AIDS Mobilization split from ACT UP/New York after a period of racial conflict with the larger group. However, members of BAM and other groups had deep organizational roots in their respective racial communities before their involvement in AIDS work. For them, the racial community often served as a prominent reference point both ideologically and strategically. Tyrone, the director of the AIDS Prevention Team, stated that his agency's grants say "African American gay and bisexual men," but "our philosophy is community is first." Here, "community" means the Black community rather than the gay community.

The preference of most activists of color interviewed for working in their racial communities neither precludes working with White individuals and organizations nor signals a prioritization of fighting racism over fighting sexism or homophobia. Rather, the activists tend to echo the analysis of many feminists of color that oppressions are often experienced simultaneously and that it is neither possible nor desirable to give one form of oppression priority over another (see the essays in Smith 1983). The lesbians and gay men interviewed consistently called for a political consciousness and strategy that strike simultaneously at racial, class, gender, and heterosexual oppression. Phil, an African American gay man, said, "We can't compartmentalize all these things. These things are just basically interrelated. You can't look at me and deal with me just in terms of my gayness and not deal with my being an African American."

These activists place such an emphasis on their own racial communities in part because of the lack of resources in these communities as compared to middle-class White gay male communities. They put their energy where they feel it is most needed. The decision to choose race as a primary locus for political activity may also be related to the fact that people usually grow up in communities that are race and/or class based, particularly in racially segregated cities such as Chicago, Los Angeles and New York. Gender and sexuality cut across communities but, in general, race and class do not. Patricia Hill Collins (1990, 226) writes:

> Racial oppression has fostered historically concrete communities among African-Americans and other racial/ethnic groups. . . . Existing community structures provide a primary line of resistance against racial and class oppression. But because gender cross-cuts these structures, it finds fewer comparable institutional bases to foster resistance.

As a result, gender oppression is better able to operate on the personal and family level within Black communities, while racial and class oppressions can be more easily countered by cultures of resistance. Similar arguments have been made for heterosexual oppression by lesbian feminists of color (Smith 1983; Anzaldúa and Moraga 1983; Trujillo 1991).

While there are undeniably lesbian and gay male cultures of resistance (D'Emilio 1983; Kennedy and Davis 1994; Freedman and D'Emilio 1988; Adam 1987; Duberman 1994), they are significantly newer than the cultures of resistance developed by communities of color. Nor are people typically born into and raised in lesbian or gay cultures of resistance. Thus, the cultures of resistance and oppositional consciousness that are more readily available to many lesbians and gay men of color, and within which many continue to live, are racially based. These differences in availability are vividly illustrated by the motto of the National Coalition of Black Lesbians and Gays—"As proud of our gayness as we are of our Blackness." The motto implies that one is likely to already be proud of being Black; the struggle is to construct a collective identity that includes not only racial pride but also lesbian/gay pride. The implied temporal process suggests that racial consciousness can be conceptualized as a building block for lesbian/gay consciousness.

Past research has pointed out that one form of oppositional consciousness can catalyze another form. The antiracist frames acquired by White students working with the Student Nonviolent Coordinating Committee became crucial building blocks for later student, antiwar, and feminist activism (McAdam 1988). Antiracist consciousness and feminist consciousness provided a model for gay liberation frames (D'Emilio 1983). Antiracist and leftist frames gave women in the Civil Rights Movement and the New Left ideological tools with which to construct feminist consciousness (McAdam 1988; Echols 1989). Antiracist consciousness provided a model for disability consciousness (Groch, chap. 4, this volume). However, this research has usually focused on communities, movements, and consciousness as discrete entities rather than as overlapping and intersecting. In these analyses, oppositional consciousness in one form is used by a second group to develop oppositional consciousness in another form. What is unique about the present case is the intracommunity character of consciousness bridging. The activists here use racial oppositional consciousness within communities of color to promote oppositional progay/prolesbian consciousness among gays, lesbians, bisexuals, and straights.

Embedded in communities of color, these activists want to develop a prolesbian/progay collective consciousness both among themselves and among heterosexual community members. They tap into racial oppositional consciousness to challenge homophobia and AIDSphobia. They use constructive dialogue, participation in community events as openly lesbian and gay people of color, embeddedness in community institutions, and the use of racially based cultural traditions and symbols to encourage others in their communities to develop a broader and more overlapping oppositional consciousness. In using racial consciousness this way, they are, in a sense, engaging in a synthesis of frame bridging and frame transformation (Snow et al. 1986) to mobilize consciousness around AIDS and break down the hegemonic barriers around AIDS and sexuality. Their ultimate goal is building a robust multidimensional oppositional consciousness.

Yet while racial consciousness is often utilized, such consciousness is not automatically present among people of color. Several respondents bemoaned the lack of racial consciousness and unity among some people of color. Yvonne expressed resentment of African Americans who can't or won't confront Whites on their racism, remarking: "Some people of color still have a 'slave mentality.'" Noel said that "Asian people are so toothless in terms of affecting social issues," and saw a need for "microinstitutions" in that community to build more political and social power.

Many respondents also stressed the importance of raising consciousness around gender and class, as well as, in the words of one activist, "how to accept differently abled people as part of the whole." Several activists indicated that they saw class as an often overlooked stratifying force that affects consciousness and collective action. Some viewed class as a core element in collective action frames. For example, Javier concluded that: "We have to be able to formulate some type of ideology on class. . . . Until that happens, we won't be able to connect all the isms."

Conclusion

The AIDS activists interviewed for this study have developed a rich repertoire of tactics to defy dominant ideological conceptions of the "other," transform political consciousness and galvanize collective action. These tactics are guided by four broad strategies: constructive dialogue, empowerment initiatives, community embeddedness, and use of indigenous culture. In support of contemporary social psychology approaches to social movements, this study indicates that cultural strategies are part and parcel of collective efforts to undermine domination (in this case, the AIDS epidemic and the inequalities that exacerbate it). The various ways in which cultural elements are incorporated into activism indicate that social movement actors do indeed mediate between individuals and the larger sociopolitical environment. The interview data support the theoretical perspective that grievances are not constant and that social movement actors attempt to reframe perceptions of social relationships in terms of oppression (Snow et al. 1986; Klandermans 1992; Gamson 1992).

Aldon Morris (1992) writes that people are embedded not only within cultural contexts that provide belief systems but also within structural contexts that shape actions and limit options. Because the target populations for AIDS organizations belong to oppressed groups (e.g., poor people of color), potential participants must be convinced that their participation in the movement will meet not only their cultural needs but also their physical needs. The AIDS activists interviewed engaged in different frame alignment processes (Snow et al. 1986), drew upon existing ideational materials and collective identities, and tapped into political cultures in order to create collective action frames (Tarrow 1992), but they also paid attention to the microstructural position of their target populations. Cultural resonance (Snow and Benford 1988) was accompanied by socioeconomic "resonance."

Particularly provocative is the finding that in this case activists developed strategies that simultaneously challenged multiple forms of hegemonic consciousness and oppression in marginalized communities. The activists structured their political work around multiple collective identities, cultural symbols, community institutions and networks, as well as multiple micro-structural positions. The battle over how AIDS is framed within oppressed communities is complicated by the social location of lesbian and gay activists of color. They are often the "other" in multiple communities, the "outsider within" (Collins 1990). They are of color among White lesbians and gay men and lesbian or gay among heterosexual people of color. Conversely, the people they are attempting to "realign" are both supportive and antagonistic, enemies and allies. In this sense, the people they are organizing are simultaneously the oppressor and the oppressed.

The problem of one-dimensional oppositional consciousness necessitates collective action within marginalized communities. For this reason, it also inhibits direct protest against dominant social institutions, such as the federal government, that perpetuate social inequality. Gay and lesbian activists of color must address the expressions of domination within marginalized communities that exacerbate the impact of AIDS. The difficulties of dealing with one-dimensional oppositional consciousness may partially explain the paucity of direct action AIDS activism in gay communities of color. Activists are so busy organizing to challenge intracommunity "isms," provide basic AIDS-related social services, and promote empowerment that they have less time than groups such as ACT UP to protest against dominant institutions.[2]

Challenging collective prejudices with constructive dialogue, facilitating empowerment, establishing concrete ties with impacted communities, and utilizing indigenous culture have three broad outcomes of interest to both AIDS organizers and social movement theorists. The first is individual empowerment. Manifestations of this are people practicing

safer sex and getting tested for HIV and PWAs becoming active participants in their own treatment and case management. The second outcome
is collective consciousness—an increase in the visibility of lesbians and
gay men of color asserting their racial-gay pride (as well as being openly
HIV positive) and challenging oppressive ideology. Finally, such challenges may lead to collective actions, such as taking part in AIDS service
projects, peer education campaigns, and social protest.

This brand of activism provides valuable insight to contemporary
social movement theorists studying identity, political consciousness,
culture, and collective action. Located at the intersections of multiple oppressions, lesbians, bisexuals, and gay men of color active in
AIDS organizing stress in their work the need to challenge all forms
of oppression—on institutional, community, and individual levels. The
community-focused activism does not always directly confront social,
political, or economic elites; however, over time it undermines elite
social power and empowers marginalized communities. Roberta cautions
against minimizing the impact of this intracommunity collective action:

> The actual contours and texture of what would be "activism" would
> be different. I think we want to be careful, 'cause we don't just want
> to say that when activism happens in communities of color, it's more
> moderate, or it's less militant, or it's less confrontational, 'cause that's
> not always true—what's confrontational might be different.

The task of creating a multidimensional oppositional consciousness
is not easy. People who are oppressed on one dimension, such as class,
race, gender, or sexuality, but privileged on other dimensions, often find
it hard to give up the inner conviction of superiority accompanying their
privilege. Yet because the underlying structures of oppression are more
often than not rooted in the same social institutions and systems, members of one oppressed group can come to see the similarities between
their position and the positions of other oppressed groups. Optimally,
that recognition of similarity can be cultivated to forge a more inclusive
vision for social, economic, and political change.

The AIDS activists interviewed for this study had concrete, practical
reasons for trying to expand one-dimensional oppositional consciousness
and create a broader oppositional consciousness among both activists
and communities impacted by AIDS. Only by doing so could they create
sufficient sensitivity and openness to learning and sufficient support for
the movement to make efforts to fight AIDS successful. They developed
several techniques that proved effective in forging multidimensional
oppositional consciousness: engaging in constructive dialogue among

both themselves and community members, finding ways to empower themselves and community members, embedding their efforts in existing community institutions, and drawing on the established cultural traditions in those communities. In the process, the activists welded together different oppositional frames, united cultures of resistance, and carved out protest infrastructures capable of attacking multiple forms of oppression that are at the core of the AIDS crisis and myriad other social problems.

Notes

I would like to thank Aldon Morris, Bernard Beck, Thomas Cook, David Maurrasse, David Naguib Pellow, Lisa Sun-Hee Park, Debbie Gould, and Jane Mansbridge for their excellent suggestions for this chapter. I would also like to thank all the interview respondents for their time and insight as well as their dedication to activism.

1. The findings in this chapter are based on fifty face-to-face interviews with AIDS activists conducted from March 1993 to September 1994. Although these interviews in no way represent a comprehensive treatment of the AIDS movement, they do allow for an in-depth analysis of some of the crucial aspects of the movement. The interviews provide data from both men and women, gay men, lesbians, bisexuals, and heterosexuals, HIV-positive and HIV-negative people, five different racial groups (Native Americans, Asian Americans, Latinos/as, African Americans, and Whites), three major cities, and both service providers and direct action groups. The names used in this account are fictitious.

2. Respondents report two additional factors related to the lack of direct action around AIDS: the fact that AIDS is only one of numerous social problems devastating communities of color and the increased likelihood of police brutality and imprisonment of activists of color (see Stockdill 1996).

9   Complicating Oppositional Consciousness

Jane Mansbridge

The Oppositional "Spectrum": No Single Continuum Will Do

We are tempted to think of oppositional consciousness as simply running along one continuum from less to more. One spectrum might be conceived as follows: (1) recognizing that one group *differs* from another group; (2) recognizing that the groups are not only different but *unequal,* and that one's own group is on the losing side of the inequality; (3) recognizing that those inequalities are *unjust;* (4) recognizing that one's group has a *common interest* in ending those injustices; (5) recognizing that *collective action* can play a key role in reducing or eliminating those injustices; and (6) believing that group action can *succeed* in reducing or eliminating the injustices.[1]

Several necessary but analytically separable dimensions may enter at several points along what might otherwise seem a one-dimensional continuum. Feelings of being a member of, or deeply identified with, a group in a way that is salient to one's *identity,* of *warmth* toward the group and/or its organizations, of *opposition* to another group or groups, and of discontent or *anger* are all analytically distinct and may enter at almost any point along the continuum. The explicit identification of another group (or groups) as the cause and beneficiary of the unjust inequalities can also enter at any point after the recognition of injustice. So can the conclusion that the injustices are systemic. Nor does each point on the continuum require the existence of the prior points. The spectrum, in short, is loosely rather than strictly defined.

Take, as the first point on this loosely defined spectrum, the recognition that two aggregates of people differ on some characteristic. This recognition involves one's consciousness becoming alert to that characteristic, finding it salient. The process is analytically distinguishable from, but in practice often occurs at the same time as, recognizing that one belongs oneself to one of those groups. The separate recognition of identity produces a sense of "us" and "them"; it means I am different from them in a group-related way and need to make sense of that. Because healthy human beings usually like themselves, the analytically distinguishable moment of belonging is often hard to separate from some weak form of positive group identification—warm feelings toward one's

238

own group and others in it. But one may come to have neutral or even strongly antipathetic feelings toward a group of which one is, in others' eyes, a member.[2]

Note that difference need not mean opposition. The members of my family, who live in this house, are different from the members of another family who live in the house next door, but this difference does not necessarily usher in a sense of opposition. I may feel far more warmly toward all members of my family than toward any member of the family next door, but never feel that I (or we) and they are in any sense opposed. The move from "us *and* them" to "us *against* them" is an analytically significant step.[3]

Nor does opposition necessarily require discontent or anger. My son and his best friend used to play tennis against each other all summer, every hour in which they could get down to the courts. Besides their liking each other, one thing that made their interaction so much fun was that they were evenly matched. Although they competed with each other, opposing the other with great energy on the courts, the game would have lost its edge, even for the winner, if one of them had consistently begun to win. A number of traditional rivalries have this quality of opposition without discontent. In Japan high achievers tend to see their competitors as engaging with them in a form of cooperation, each individual or business being raised to greater heights through the opposition of the other. The less equal the opponents and the deeper the opposed interests, the more likely it is that opposition will generate anger and discontent.[4]

Opposition can easily generate inequality if the members of one identifiable group successfully use their oppositional stance toward another group to get greater resources for themselves, either by generating more external resources or by appropriating resources from the group they oppose. Conversely, inequality can also generate opposition. Patterned inequalities easily generate opposition when the disadvantaged see the others' greater resources as diminishing their well-being.

Yet even recognizing inequality, the next stage on the continuum, does not necessarily entail opposition. As John Rawls and many before him have pointed out, some inequalities can benefit the less privileged.[5] Unequal distributions of power, influence, prestige, honor, and material resources can benefit everyone in a society in two ways. They can give everyone an incentive to strive for more of these goods whenever such striving benefits everyone. They can also make the social statement through this unequal distribution that the activities that produce more of these rewards are good. Inequality can thus serve a useful incentive function and a useful normative and attention-directing function. When the inequalities produce largely beneficial outcomes and feelings of envy are weak, inequalities need not produce opposition.

Some circumstances can even produce both inequality and opposition without a conclusion that the inequalities derive from injustice. The "delinquent cultures" of some young peer groups can generate high degrees of opposition to the mainstream without any grounding in a cognitive conclusion that their opposition to the dominant culture is an opposition to injustice.

The key move in the creation of oppositional consciousness is perceiving existing inequalities as unjust. When inequalities derive from a dominant group's exercise of power, in the sense of threat of sanction or use of force, those inequalities are almost always unjust. Because what is just is often highly contested, especially between dominant and subordinate groups, oppositional consciousness requires, at minimum, the conceptual resources that allow members of a subordinate group to draft a definition of just treatment and just distribution that challenges the definitions of the dominant group. It requires, as Morris and Braine point out in this volume (chap. 2), challenging dominant beliefs in the justice of the status quo.[6] Classically it also requires conceiving of an identity of interest among members of the subordinate group in ending these injustices.[7]

As we have conceived it, any minimal definition of oppositional consciousness requires four factors—identifying with an unjustly subordinated group, recognizing the injustice in that group's position, opposing that injustice, and recognizing a group identity of interest in ending that injustice. The definition revolves around injustice. Oppositional consciousness, in our understanding, does not consist simply in identifying with one's own group and opposing another. It requires that one see the group with which one identifies as the recipient of injustice. It requires that one's opposition be opposition to that injustice, and to the group or groups that brought the injustice about. It requires that the perceived identity of interest among the group members be based on bringing this injustice to an end.

Beyond these four key moves, moving to a more than minimal oppositional consciousness requires recognizing some systemic quality to the pattern of injustices, based in the greater power of a dominant group. It requires seeing these injustices as in some degree related, as extending beyond the relations of any two individuals to a larger society-wide system, and as functional for members of the dominant group. It requires, in short, identifying the holders of power as oppressors in a system of domination rather than merely as guardians of the common good.

A key further move is recognizing a need for collective action to redress the perceived injustices or to overthrow the system of domination.[8] As with several other "stages" in the spectrum, this recognition need not follow deductively from the previous stages but may be independently generated. In many cases in human life, each of us can get what we want only if many individuals act collectively. The recognition that a situation requires collective action can be almost purely cognitive, as in figuring out a puzzle, or learned through a fuller mixture of emotion and cognition, the way one learns by growing up in a family. Some people recognize the need to act collectively before others do, usually because their past experience has led them to identify the situational cues more easily. The recognition that a problem requires collective action can appear anywhere along the oppositional continuum.

In addition, when we speak of a "mature" oppositional consciousness, we mean a consciousness that incorporates a well-worked-out, internally coherent set of ideas and beliefs, analyzing the injustices at the core of the system of domination, suggesting how they came into being, and identifying the individuals and interests that benefit from the injustices and/or have intentionally produced them.[9] A mature oppositional consciousness thus incorporates what might be called an "ideology" and a repertory of strategies and potential lines of action.

Finally, a mature oppositional consciousness includes a sense of efficacy, the belief that acting collectively can bring about change. Specific references to comparable moments in history when similar groups succeeded in their goals undergird this sense of efficacy. To be realistic, that sense of efficacy should rise when political opportunity structures open up and decline when repression sets in.[10]

It would be hard to overemphasize the openness, instability, and multifaceted nature of this spectrum. As the history of the Chicago Freedom Movement demonstrates (Waite, chap. 7, this volume), oppositional consciousness can be "internally differentiated" in the sense of taking many different forms among individuals who are differently situated in their material lives and ideological perspectives. Oppositional consciousness can be undercut by "hegemonic consciousness" in ways that are impossible fully to sort out. At the same time, as the AIDS movement in several cities demonstrates (Stockdill, chap. 8, this volume), oppositional consciousness can be "multidimensional," including many or all oppressed groups. It need not remain at the point of focusing only on the injustices against and subordination of one's own group. Indeed, individuals who have developed even a minimal oppositional consciousness regarding one group are often more likely than others to recognize injustice and the workings of power in the subordination of other groups and to feel empathy for their plight.[11]

In several chapters of this book we distinguish oppositional consciousness from oppositional culture. Roughly, we rely on three points of distinction, regarding focus, priority, and locus.

Regarding focus, we make two points. First, oppositional consciousness focuses explicitly on injustice; oppositional cultures often do not. Some oppositional cultures (such as "delinquent peer cultures" or musical countercultures) have little or no reference to injustice. Second, as Morris and Braine (chap. 2, this volume) point out, oppositional cultures are relatively unfocused. They are usually too variegated, too full of unrelated and sometimes contradictory elements, to provide the coherent ideological frame and direction that characterize a mature oppositional consciousness. Oppositional cultures may be almost entirely reactive and resistant, without a picture of a more just world toward which a group should struggle. They can often intertwine and coexist easily with dominant cultures that lead subordinates to accept their destinies as natural.

Regarding temporal priority, oppositional consciousness, with its specific focus on injustice and in its mature forms its developed analysis and strategic repertory, usually evolves from an earlier oppositional culture that has prepared over the years a cauldron of relevant themes, symbols, stories, and pieces of wisdom. Sometimes, however, this prior preparation can be skipped. As Sharon Groch (chap. 4, this volume) points out about mobility-impaired activists, groups without an earlier oppositional culture can borrow major elements of oppositional consciousness from another group that has already developed it.

In addition, individuals who have developed an oppositional consciousness (through either path) can together create a new culture expressing their new consciousness. Groch has coined for such new cultures the term "cultures of oppositional consciousness." Such cultures stress all the attributes of an oppositional consciousness, and are actively created by individuals with such consciousness. Anna-Maria Marshall (chap. 5, this volume), for example, writes of "feminist oppositional culture." In this phrase, the word "feminist" signals a new culture of oppositional consciousness. One job of social movement activists is (in some cases) to create a culture of oppositional consciousness almost from scratch or (in the more usual case) to transform an existing oppositional culture, with its diverse and possibly contradictory strands, into a culture of oppositional consciousness, focused on rectifying injustice.

Regarding locus, we follow ordinary language in, for the most part, locating culture in the group and consciousness in the individual. In general, "culture" refers to the customs, habits, values, and focal concerns of a social group, "consciousness" to the perceptions, thoughts, and feelings of an individual. Occasionally, however, we also follow ordinary language in locating "consciousness" in a group. In this usage, groups can be said to "have" or "gain" oppositional consciousness whenever most individuals in them develop an oppositional consciousness, thus facilitating easier mutual communication and trust.[12]

In our conceptualization, a "mature" or "full-fledged" oppositional consciousness usually describes the mental state of a current or past activist. A minimal oppositional consciousness is more easily accessible to nonactivists. How many strands of a more mature oppositional consciousness are an everyday part of the analytic and emotional world of nonactivists depends on the development of the larger culture of the group.

Motivating Action

Acting for a group requires more than oppositional consciousness. It requires more than recognizing injustice, formulating an understanding of common interests, identifying systemic domination, understanding the need for collective action, devising strategies for action, and feeling sufficiently efficacious to act. Actually acting needs further motivation.

Even Karl Marx was not clear on this point. When Marx wrote that the working class needed to transform itself into a group "for itself" (*für sich*), the short word "for" covered an important ambiguity. Here "for" implies not only "in favor of, on the side of," but also "in support of, in defense of."[13] Defending implies a commitment to act. But being "for" something in the sense of favoring it does not automatically lead one to act to defend it. Moving from recognizing the need for collective action (and thus favoring it) to being willing to act on its behalf requires something else inside the heart and brain.

Like other thinkers of his time, Marx did not work out the logic through which the individuals who constitute a group "for itself" come to *act* for the group. Not until after World War II did game theorists work out the strategic logic that applies to a particular kind of good— one whose structure is such that those who do not contribute to bringing it about nevertheless will benefit from it (i.e., cannot be excluded from it). Until that time almost every social thinker assumed that when an individual was part of an aggregate that would benefit from an action, it would make sense for the individual to contribute to that action.

This is not so. As most social theorists now know, whenever a gain for a group will benefit all the individuals in it whether or not they have contributed to that gain, some motivation for contribution is needed other than wanting one's share of the group benefits. The kinds of goods that social movements try to bring about are almost always these kinds of "nonexcludable" goods (i.e., those goods from whose benefits no one can be excluded). Once some have paid the price to bring legal reforms into being, for example, everyone will benefit, including those who never lifted a finger to bring the reforms about.[14] Forests of paper have been consumed in the last two decades working out the implications of this insight and debating its relevance to collective action.[15] Even those who downplay the force of this insight, however, will agree that, in addition to all the elements of oppositional consciousness we have previously listed—including recognizing systemic injustice and a common interest in removing that injustice, recognizing the need for collective action, and believing that collective action will succeed—motivating the individual to *act* for the collective requires something more.

When we cannot rely on strong inner commitments, getting people to act for a good, a group, or a cause outside their own narrow self-interests involves structuring incentives so that the material, social, and self-enhancing rewards of such action are relatively high and the costs relatively low. Yet activists themselves stress inner drives that relate less immediately to any such external rewards and costs. Activists in social responsibility movements often stress the effort "to realize a moral vision" or "to be a certain kind of [moral] person."[16] Activists in liberation movements, also driven by a moral vision, often have, in addition, a more visceral anger toward the dominant group and empathy with others in the subordinate group. They may feel humiliated when they see another member of their group humiliated, joy when they see a member of their group succeed, and a host of other complicated perceptions and feelings conditioned by a lifetime in a social system that has made them aware of the ways they themselves partake in a collective subordination.[17]

In general, considering oneself a member of a group activates certain social norms appropriate to that group membership. It also activates a set of perceptual biases that filter information relating to oneself and the group. But accepting these norms is not inevitable. Simple acceptance of membership does not entail acting for the group, even when group norms prescribe such action.[18]

As each individual negotiates the contours of his or her self, within a world in which much is given and much suffused with both overt and hidden power, each can be motivated to act for the group by almost as many motives as exist in human experience. Two basic motives, "love" and "duty," not usually separable in practice, are also usually indissolubly mixed with norm-following, self-enhancing, socially oriented, and materially self-interested motives. They can be mixed with hatred, desire for revenge, and a host of other motives that lead people to do something that then benefits their group. Yet "love"—or coming to care so much for the welfare of another, a group, or a cause that you experience its good as your own—and duty are analytically distinguishable. And they both play relatively important roles in the move from simply favoring one's group to acting for it.[19]

Experiencing a group's good as your own can take morally insignificant (but sometimes life-transforming) forms, such as belonging to or even rooting for a sports team.[20] It can take much more significant forms in versions of family loyalty, nationalism, and religious group identification. In any form it provides a motive for acting for the group, and can prompt major material and emotional sacrifices on the group's behalf. Members may try to cultivate in one another feelings of warmth, closeness, sense of likeness, or linked fate with a group, knowing that these feelings and perceptions encourage experiencing the group's good as one's own.[21] But none of these ensures that you do feel pain when the group suffers or joy when it succeeds. Nor do warmth, closeness, likeness, or linked fate lead automatically to the conclusion that you must help the group. Indeed, even experiencing the group's good as your own does not guarantee that you will act on its behalf. You also need some belief that your efforts will in fact help the group. And the costs cannot be too high.

You can also feel a sense of duty—the conviction that you "ought" to act for the good of your group and/or for one or more of the principles motivating a social movement. Like the degree to which one experiences the good of the group as one's own, this principled commitment is analytically separate from any other stage in the "spectrum" of oppositional consciousness. Such a sense of duty could arise at any stage. I could believe it was my duty to act to help anyone in need, whether or not they were members of my group and whether or not my group differed from, was opposed to, was unequal to, or was unjustly dominated by other groups. I could believe it was my duty to act against injustice or for equality whether or not any movement espoused this principle. When a "free-rider" problem arises (whenever the benefits of a collective action are "nonexcludable"), some philosophers (such as John Rawls) hold that one has a "natural duty" to contribute to the collective good. People vary in the degree to which they develop and act upon such convictions of duty.[22] In addition, the experience of duty is heavily influenced by how your community defines your duty, how important that duty is to being a member of that community, who calls upon you to act upon that duty, and how well those who call you to your duty activate the moral strands that have meaning to you as a member of that community. Duty, in short, derives not only from the demands of reason but also from the commitments one has as a member of a community. Some Israelis feel a commitment to help displaced Palestinians precisely because they are Israeli, and thus part of a group that both is committed to fighting oppression and has itself caused this displacement. Many African Americans respond to Jesse Jackson's call to vote on the grounds that their own people gave their lives so that they today might have that right. Moral condemnation and moral praise by respected leaders or peers activate these internal moral commitments.[23]

Activists in many kinds of movements act from a mixture of these kinds of individual motives. But activists in liberation movements, striving to end a system of domination and subordination in which they themselves are members of the subordinate group, have particular reason to experience the good of the subordinate group as their own. The very social cues that mark their subordination, the oppositional culture from which they come, the investments they have made in trying personally to cast off the strands of subordination buried in their psyches, and the recognition of shared struggle with even nonactivist members of the group all reinforce the experience that the good of this group is a good for oneself and a harm to it a harm felt personally.

In practice, the analytically separable motives of love, duty, and hundreds of others intertwine in the lives of most activists. In my own life, the sense of accountability that I feel to the feminist movement comes in part from my having made the good of other women my own, so that I involuntarily cheer inwardly when a woman becomes prime minister or head of a university. It comes in part from a sense of duty to the ideas and individuals involved in the cause, so that I would feel to a degree immoral if I let them down. It comes in part from a principled commitment to a cause that I have reason to think is just, and in part from a simple impulse to rectify injustice, each of which could be separate from any of the other motivations.[24] When I feel anger at seeing a woman treated unjustly because of her sex, I cannot separate out what is empathy, what is rage at similar half-remembered experiences of my own, and what is a response to injustice itself.

My sense of accountability is also deeply intertwined with my relationships with other individuals who have these identifications and commitments. Those individuals inspire me; it is on some of their characters that I have in part modeled my life. They can also implicitly reward and punish me, not only because in some cases I have thrown my social lot in with theirs but also, far more importantly, because the parts of their voices that I take most seriously now play a considerable role among the internal voices that I consider my own. Most importantly, I would not be the person I am if I had not, miraculously, had the time and personal freedom to become active in the women's movement in 1967 and 1968. At that moment the movement itself was in a highly creative stage, I needed its help to figure out tentative answers to important questions about my own life that I had never posed before the movement posed them, and I could take personal, lasting comfort in solidarity with others who both faced the same questions and recognized the need to act together to make the world better for women. The content of the resulting accountability to the movement, and the forms it now takes, derive from a collective past and present, which are as much part of me as any other shaping force.

Experientially, my sense of accountability to the movement comes mostly from having developed an identity in which all these things, mixed together in ways that would be hard to tease apart, simply make up who I am. At this point, parsing out motivations becomes almost impossible. Decisions then seem to flow—not always without consideration or anguish—from the implicit precommitments now embedded in my understanding of myself.[25]

Thus, having laboriously separated out these elements analytically, we find that life complicates matters by mixing them together inseparably. These chapters, grounded in the experience of actual collective action, make clear how closely interwoven is the fabric of motives, self, and others. They make it clear how dependent our selves are on the historical moment and the historically contingent cultural resources available at any given point. When parishioners from different churches in Chicago gathered at a prayer breakfast for Carol Moseley-Braun, what motivated them? A sense of solidarity, of closeness with others in the room (the cluster of affective motivations that lead one to make a group's good one's own)—of course. We human beings need the company of others. But we can get that company in other ways than attending a prayer breakfast in which we will probably be asked to commit our money and our time. Many participants in the collective action described in these chapters seem also to have been inspired by a conviction of duty—to further the good of the group or to fight injustice. Most were motivated by commitment to a cause. Many were brought to take action by the call of a friend or a leader. Particular events had sparked action, and participation in those events had left a memory—of group efficacy or solidarity—that served to prompt actions in the future. Everyone was also drawn there in part by the cultural resonance of that particular event at that moment in history. In short, for most participants in the prayer breakfast, and in all the other activities described in these chapters, many motives had come together to form an identity in which love, duty, and commitment to a cause were taken for granted, parts of the everyday furniture of the soul.

In each of the chapters in this book, however, events take place that ask the participants to move that furniture around a little to accommodate slightly new understandings of self, stretched definitions of solidarity, expanded commitments in duty. Moseley-Braun's campaign encouraged churchgoers to get involved in politics. The disability movement encouraged individuals who were deaf, blind, or mobility impaired to identify with one another. The logical progression of sexual harassment law encouraged lawyers and plaintiffs to adopt a feminist analysis. The progressive organizations of the northern Midwest encouraged Cristaleño migrants to adapt tactics, symbols, and a sense of mission from the labor organizing and civil rights traditions. The Chicago Freedom Movement encouraged African American ministers and elected officials in Chicago to join actions that might endanger their positions of local leadership. AIDS activists in New York, Los Angeles, and Chicago encouraged local groups and their own members to change their practices and ideas regarding race, sex, and sexual orientation.

Work on social movements has documented well how networks of friends and acquaintances get others involved in the movement. The role of crystallizing events is not as well documented. A breakfast, a strike, a march may all suddenly pose the question, "Which side are you on?" and call forth moral, emotional, and cognitive facets of one's identity that were previously relatively dormant. Much of this book shows how oppositional consciousness causes action. But it also shows how action causes oppositional consciousness. When Lynn Feiger took on a set of sex discrimination cases, they turned her into a feminist. When Jesus Salas got involved in union organizing in Wisconsin, he found himself becoming a leader.[26]

One major theme of this book is that the encouragement to expanded consciousness that forms the core of each of these events will be more successful the more it takes as its starting point the existing cultural language and symbolic structure of the participants. Activists and nonactivists then work in symbiosis to craft new symbols and forms that further the expanded project. A female political candidate becomes David against Goliath. A panoply of civil rights and anti–Vietnam War symbols, with a few creative changes, now fits the disability rights movement.

"Discrimination" expands to include sexual harassment. La Raza builds on Black Power. Latino AIDS activists hold a candlelight vigil on the Dìa de los Muertos. But this building process did not work in Chicago. The Chicago Freedom Movement met its cultural and symbolic match in Chicago's black elected officials and church leaders. The CFM did not have access to symbolic resources unavailable to the Chicago elite, and they failed, at least in their immediate goals.

Another theme highlights the ways the non-self-interested motives of duty and love can mingle with "self-enhancing" motives, such as self-esteem, honor, and reputation in the community, and with more narrowly self-interested motives, such as the need and desire for material resources. The analyses of sexual harassment lawyers and plaintiffs, of elected officials and church leaders in Chicago, and of particular organizing strategies among AIDS activists help spell out how movement activism can sometimes succeed by combining material rewards with more altruistic motives in ways that do not drive out the altruism.[27]

These chapters also reveal that the separate characteristics of oppositional consciousness are not indissolubly intertwined. One can have almost any one without the other. "Oppositional consciousness" is thus an additive construct.[28] Some of its features are more common than others. Feelings and analyses differ from individual to individual. More people consider their group's position unjust than see the need for collective action. Some have thought more about causes than about strategies. Some feel more anger than others toward the dominant group. Toward their own group some feel more warmth, some more disdain. Analyses can disagree, as in the Chicago Freedom Movement's confrontation with the black elected officials and established clergy in Chicago. One political meeting, such as the Carol Moseley-Braun breakfast, can gather under its tent an immense range of stances, analyses, commitments, and degrees of oppositional consciousness. One outcome, such as sexual harassment law or the beginning of the La Raza party, can require the participation of a host of different individuals with different degrees and forms of oppositional consciousness.

Finally, these chapters make it clear that action requires more than oppositional consciousness, and more than oppositional consciousness combined with the motivations of duty, love, or commitment to the cause. Even when my principles tell me I ought to act collectively and I identify deeply with a particular group, I am less likely to act if I conclude that my actions are not likely to have a positive effect or that a small positive effect will be offset by major personal costs.[29] Holding oppositional consciousness constant, personal and structural incentives deeply affect any individual's likelihood of acting in any given instance. Some people are more likely to enjoy, or even need, the experience of affecting the world. Some are more vulnerable to shame or blame from others, or more likely to need the affection of others in the group. Opportunity structures at any given moment in history greatly affect whether or not one will act. So does the existing variety of organizations that try to foster collective action on behalf of the group. Levels of repression, friendship networks, communication networks, and group and individual resources of all kinds make individuals with the same level of oppositional consciousness more or less likely to act.

Assorted Difficulties and Problems

Aside from the difficulty of defining precisely a multistranded concept, the problems and difficulties with oppositional consciousness come in two kinds: the difficulties of achieving it and the problems incurred when it is achieved.

The difficulties in achieving oppositional consciousness arise primarily because, as Morris and Braine point out, all cultures among subordinated groups combine not only elements of resistance and opposition but also elements of acceptance, even glorification, of the subordination. In the African American culture of Southern tenant farmers from after the Civil War through the 1930s, for example, one strand of jokes portrayed the "nigger" protagonist as stupid or in other ways innately inferior to the white ruling class. I myself remember as a young woman in high school telling the first man I ever loved, in all seriousness and believing it myself, that the reason he got lower grades than I in our history class was that he was brilliant and creative whereas I was just a memorizer. Until recently and perhaps even now, many a woman, asked what she did for a living, would answer, "Oh, I'm just a housewife," accepting implicitly the common devaluation of work in the home. Simone de Beauvoir steadfastly insisted throughout her life that within their couple it was Sartre who had the more penetrating intellect, not she. Subjects of colonial powers faced the same problem of, to some degree, implicitly accepting the culture of the occupying power as superior.[30]

It is not at all easy in these situations to sort out what in one's own subordinate culture to hang onto and what to drop, what constitutes "aping" the dominant culture and what constitutes a sensible and effective appropriation. Oppositional consciousness helps in taking the first steps in the process, by facilitating one's separation from the dominant group, but it can sometimes go too far in rejecting certain features of the dominant culture that in the long run it would be useful to adopt. The deliberative process—of sorting, sifting, examining, testing against one's experience, learning from the experiences of others—often takes activist leadership, because activists, talking with one another in relatively protected spaces, can more easily come up with new ideas that break through the previous hegemony. But sometimes leaders and activists get in the way. Sometimes they promote a way of being that looks good to them, in the enclaves in which they talk mostly with one another, but that does not work in the lives of others. For others, building a satisfying life may be more important than acting according to the rigid dictates of a particular ideology or set of ideals. In the long run, a combination of activists and nonactivists is probably most likely to sort and sift effectively, creating viable understandings that reject subordination without rejecting some of the most usefully appropriable features of the dominant culture.

In this incremental process, however, some of the more problematic features of oppositional consciousness emerge. A separation from the dominant group, crucial for forging a separate identity, can make it harder to recognize change and subtleties within that dominant group. When African American teenagers start to sit apart from Whites in their school cafeterias, they avoid the major costs of being constantly "on stage" and having to act as tokens when Whites turn to them as exemplars of their group. They help one another by reinforcing their own group ties and rejecting the dominant culture. But they can also harm one another by cultivating an oppositional stance that lumps all Whites into one category and rejects useful features of the dominant culture. In the same way, cohesive oppositional ideologies, useful for stimulating thought, can come to block that thought when situations change. A focus on justice can deteriorate into resentment, blocking vision and corroding the soul. Political unity, a powerful tool for achieving political gains, usually also suppresses meaningful and creative divisions.[31] Much of the opposition to "identity politics," both from outside and inside the subordinate group, focuses on these problematic outcomes of oppositional consciousness.

Nationalism, for example, can overlap with oppositional consciousness. Not all nationalisms are built on a conviction of past or present oppression, but some are. When they are, the extremes to which some of their proponents can go highlight the problems of oppositional consciousness. The experience of daily indignity at the hands of the dominant group cements group identity, fuels anger against the dominant group, prompts attention to a host of injustices, helps locate the source of those injustices in a system of domination, and encourages the thought that all members of the group have an identity of interest in overthrowing that system.[32] The group hatreds to which such a history can give rise are well known. Those hatreds can be countered, in part, by commitments to nonviolence, to loving one's enemy, and—for either practical or idealistic reasons—to remaining in the same polity with one's former oppressors. More often, however, those hatreds give rise to the evils of violence, intolerance, and unthinking separatism.

These problems are real. They deserve considerable thought and investigation. We nevertheless contend that, if oppositional conscious-ness is not a necessity in a subordinate group's acting to overthrow, undermine, or reform a system of human domination, it is at least an extremely useful tool and necessary in many historical circumstances. To condemn oppositional consciousness or try to avoid it would be to divest oneself voluntarily of a highly effective personal and collective means to a desired end. But it would also be foolish to consider all versions of oppositional consciousness an unadulterated good. As with almost any powerful tool, its users should become consciously and then habitually aware of its inbuilt hazards—in this case, primarily an exaggeration of difference from the dominant group, an enforced and biased unity among the subordinate group, and a deafness to new and contradictory infor-mation.[33] Oppositional consciousness does not differ in these respects from the motivating consciousness behind any social movement, but its enmeshment in these traps may be greater, given its roots in central features of the identity of members of a subordinate group.

In addition to understanding the particular dynamics of oppositional consciousness, then, we need also to develop an understanding of the ways, after a system of oppression has been overthrown or has begun to be reformed, that we can begin to repair the damage to self and others caused in the process.

As the bonds of subordination loosen, many strategies become avail-able for loosening those bonds further. To the degree that the social world makes it possible to step out of one's subordinate identity, it can be highly subversive of that identity itself to parody the identity, performing a version that pokes fun at the idea of a stable, "natural" gender, race, or nationality. One need not reject, but can play with the identity that others assign one and that one may at times want to claim oneself. Such playful subversion can support rather than undermine oppositional consciousness, for oppositional consciousness need not be greedy in the sense of eating up all distance from the oppositional identity or refusing all other identities. Play is often highly creative. It also frees one from the quest—which Foucault points out is in any case futile—for one's "authentic" self.[34]

The Problem of Group Essentialism

Group essentialism poses a final thorny problem for the study and practice of oppositional consciousness. Although the rhetoric of some political movements may suggest the contrary, oppositional consciousness does not require that one think of one's group membership as having an essential link with oneself, or of the group itself as being defined by some inner essence. Certain nationalist movements, which resemble oppositional social movements in being based on reactions to continuous reminders of subordination in everyday life,[35] do claim an essential quality of national belonging, often based at least in theory on "blood" or genes. Important strands within the women's movement worldwide, several Black anticolonial movements, and some sections of the African American antiracist movement have also adopted "essentialist" understandings of what it is to be a woman, a Black, or an African American. Yet recognizing and acting against the historical subordination of a group of which one is a member does not require adopting such essentialist understandings. It does require thinking in group terms, both for reasons based on the concept of justice and for reasons based in the existing history of domination and subordination.

The concept of "justice" inherently requires categories. In its thinnest form, justice means treating similar cases similarly. If we define justice as giving each individual his or her due, we mean giving these individuals their due on the basis of some trait or behavior. If a given trait or behavior is held to warrant a certain treatment, and if one individual with that trait or behavior receives the treatment while another with the same trait or behavior does not, we consider the disparity unjust, unless some acceptable reason can be given for the different treatment. Conceptually, such an acceptable reason creates another category of individuals who warrant a different treatment.

This inherent characteristic of the concept of justice means that if any human being anywhere in the world makes a claim of injustice, that person must be thinking of a category of individuals who, for one or another reason, "deserve" a given sort of treatment. Suppose I think that God is unjust in letting my baby die. In making this claim about injustice, I implicitly claim that I am no different and did not act differently in the relevant respects from other human beings whose babies did not die. Any differences between myself and others in the relevant category (perhaps the group of "human beings," perhaps the group of "God-fearing human beings," perhaps some other group) do not justify my being treated differently from them. The claim of injustice requires conceptualizing a relevant category or group.

Oppositional consciousness includes not only the claim that certain treatments are unjust, but also the claim that those treatments derive from a history of unjust domination and subordination. In this history, individuals who have a certain trait or who are capable of certain behaviors have treated those without that trait or who are not capable of those behaviors as inferiors, to be given less favorable treatment. The subordinate group, however, claims that the trait and/or behaviors in question have no relevant relation to the less favorable treatment. There is no relevant functional relation, for example, between having a dark skin and being denied access to a water fountain. There is no relevant functional relation between having female sexual characteristics and being denied the vote.

Just as no claim of injustice can be made without thinking of individuals as members of categories, no claim for rectification based on a history of domination and subordination can be made without thinking of individuals as members of historically meaningful groups. Yet it is perfectly possible to make such claims without restricting the meanings of the lives of the individuals who make those claims to their membership in the relevant group. It is also possible to make claims of injustice or historical domination without freezing or stabilizing the meaning of membership in the group. Indeed, one goal of a group may be to eliminate its own existence as a separate group.[36]

Yet political activity in the name of a group tends to accentuate the significance of the group. The more important a group becomes in the life of its members, the more sacrifices the members are usually willing to make in its name, both from love and from duty. And the more important the group becomes in the life of its members, the more that group can use potential ostracism as a sanction against free-riding.[37] Well-organized and politically powerful groups usually draw on all three sources—love, duty, and fear of sanction—to inspire individual action on behalf of the group. Accordingly, members of a group have an incentive to paint group membership as valuable and important. To some degree they have an incentive to treat group membership as an essential, immutable, and central individual characteristic. Political organizing usually benefits from such essentialism, which makes group membership a matter of personal essence rather than a contingent relationship.

Systems of domination and subordination often reinforce this essentialism. It is often in the interest of a dominant group to portray the group differences that make up the pattern of domination and subordination as natural, God-given, and of the essence of each member, not as merely contingent. But it seems also to be part of a healthy human psyche to like the person one is. When the larger social system makes salient a particular trait that one has, it is often a mark of self-esteem to value that trait positively. Negative external evaluations are often most easily countered by positive internal evaluations, both by the individual and by the group culture. Thus positive psychological mechanisms can sometimes produce essentialist understandings of group membership.

Group incentives to prevent free-riding, the imperatives of political organizing, dominant cultural interests, and the self-protective psychological investments of members of subordinate groups all coincide to build a powerful machine driving toward essentialism. Oppositional consciousness—with its emphasis on group difference, inequality, injustice, the need for and belief in group action, along with feelings of group identity, warmth toward the group, and the stance of opposition to and anger at the dominant group—adds fuel to that machine.

But oppositional consciousness does not inevitably lead to essentialist understandings of the group. Unjust patterns of domination and subordination are produced by power, and they can be undone by power. Those patterns are historical and contingent. Subordinates in a system of domination and subordination can have a strong interest in seeing as mutable and contingent the meanings of group membership that the system has created. Thus, some commitment to ending at least the current version of essentialism is usually built into the goal of ending a system of domination and subordination.

In addition, individuals will always have some interest in seeing themselves not only as embedded in communities that give their lives meaning but also as different in some respects from others in those communities. In every society, each individual has a name that bespeaks individuation. In modern societies where individual freedom has a strong value, individuals often want to see their group identities as relatively voluntary and can make those identities more voluntary by their own efforts. Making a group membership more voluntary need not mean rejecting it. In societies where particular traits and behaviors are highly salient, such rejection may be impossible. But individuals may nevertheless take their own stance toward that membership, perhaps making it central to their lives, perhaps entering fully into it on a temporary basis, perhaps criticizing it, perhaps playing with it or parodying it (or its opposite) from a critical distance.[38]

Currently, U.S. third world feminists are crafting what Chéla San-doval calls a "differential oppositional consciousness," meaning a "form of marginalized subjectivity [that] perceives itself at the center of myriad possibilities all cross working—any of which are fodder for one's loyal-ties."[39] This "tactical subjectivity" can "recenter" itself depending on the kinds of oppression it confronts. Sandoval argues that this kind of oppositional consciousness requires strength, flexibility, and grace:

> enough strength to confidently commit to a well-defined structure of identity for one hour, day, week, month, year; enough flexibility to self-consciously transform that identity according to the requisites of another oppositional ideological tactic if readings of power's formation require it; enough grace to recognize alliance with others committed to egalitarian social relations and race, gender, and class justice, when their readings of power call for alternative oppositional stands.[40]

Activists at the intersection of several group memberships, each with strong claims on their identities and commitments, have often evolved a fluidity of identity that responds to the demands of the moment.[41] They have also developed analyses that respond to overlapping systems of domination and subordination by showing how those systems support one another.[42]

The individuals described in this book—attendees at a political prayer breakfast in a Black church, individuals with disabilities, victims of sexual harassment, migrant workers, participants and nonparticipants in the Chicago Freedom Movement, and AIDS activists—all participated in some negotiation or attempted renegotiation of their identities. The breakfast attendees experienced cultural pulls consciously intended to make them more politically active. The individuals with disabilities unconsciously evolved and then consciously crafted cultures that made claims on their identities. The victims of sexual harassment chose to draw more or less heavily on strands of feminist thought to make sense of their experience. Migrants to Wisconsin and Minnesota from Crystal City, Texas, adopted new identities as activists in a larger progressive community. African Americans in Chicago at the time of the Freedom Movement accepted or rejected the claims that the Reverend Martin Luther King Jr. and his allies made on their membership in the Black community. AIDS activists consciously forged new identities that allowed them to organize across class, gender, and race.

All these negotiations and renegotiations, however, took place upon one bedrock reality—subordinate status in a larger system of domination and subordination. Each individual had to make a decision, indeed many decisions, about how to confront that reality. In most cases, but not all, oppositional consciousness helped the individuals involved to contribute effectively to a social movement designed to end their subordination.

In this book we have striven to highlight the importance of oppositional consciousness to subordinates who in a system of domination and subordination are working for change. We have tried to reveal some complexities within that concept and some subtleties in the way oppositional consciousness is formed. These chapters aim to show variety and change, borrowings and transformations, success and failure. They will have succeeded if they capture a wide spectrum of the ways actual individuals, with their own needs, networks, and symbolic structures, respond to the political and symbolic opportunities presented by their historical moment.

Notes

This chapter has benefited greatly from the suggestions of the reviewers for the University of Chicago Press, Sidney Tarrow, Aldon Morris, and Christopher Jencks. Remaining problems in analysis and interpretation are entirely my responsibility. I began work on these chapters while a Fellow at the Center for Advanced Study in the Behavioral Sciences. I am grateful for financial support provided by the National Science Foundation, Grant #SBR-9601236.

1. As we shall see, the last four stages on this list are crucial for social movements. Similar components, not always conceived as stages, thus appear in others' analyses as well. Piven and Cloward (1977), among the first to produce a list of such components, suggested the following: (1) the system loses legitimacy, (2) people who are ordinarily fatalistic demand change, and (3) the challengers develop a new sense of political efficacy. (McAdam 1982 gave these elements the title "cognitive liberation.") Operationalizing relevant elements for the 1972 American National Election Study, Gurin, Miller, and Gurin (1980) first measured "identification" with one's own class, race, gender, and age group; then "consciousness" of class, race, gender, and age with indexes of (1) power discontent, (2) rejection of legitimacy, and (3) collectivist orientation. (See also Kalmuss, Gurin, and Townsend 1981; Miller et al. 1981; Gurin 1985.) Schlozman and Verba (1979) measured class and race consciousness on the dimensions of (1) concern with fairness, (2) opposing interests, and (3) solidarity. See Klein 1984 on the three stages of political consciousness: (1) recognizing group membership and shared interests, (2) rejecting the traditional definition for the group's status, (3) blaming a system of inequality, not oneself. See Conover 1988 (focusing on the transitions from objective group membership to identification and politicization) on the four elements of group consciousness: (1) group identification ([a] awareness of membership in the group, [b] psychological attachment to the group), (2) well-developed schemas with information on the group's status, (3) attribution of responsibility (for bad group outcomes to others and good outcomes to group members), (4) emotional reaction based on that attribution (see also Conover 1984). See Snow and Benford 1992 on the three "functions" of collective action frames: (1) punctuation [accenting injustice], (2) attribution [of responsibility for committing and redressing injustice], and (3) articulation [creating coherent cognitive packages]. See Klandermans 1997, 38 ff., on the three components of collective action frames: (1) injustice, (2) identity, and (3) agency (on p. 43, he adds [4] attribution). See also Gamson 1992. See Oberschall 1993, 1996, on the four dimensions of social movements: (1) discontents and grievances,

(2) convictions of injustice, (3) the capacity to act collectively, and (4) political opportunity. Note that in many theories these components can apply whether or not the participants are themselves subordinates in a system of domination and subordination (or deeply identified with those subordinates). That is, they extend beyond "oppositional consciousness" per se. The stage of recognizing a common interest derives primarily from Thompson [1963] 1966 and should not be taken literally (see n. 7 below).

2. The National Election Study measures perceptions of likeness by showing the respondent a list of groups and asking, "which of these groups you feel particularly close to—people who are most like you in their ideas and interests and feelings about things." It then asks which single group the respondent feels closest to. The National Black Election Study, based on the NES, also asks how "close" to Black people the respondent feels "in terms of ideas and feelings about things" (Gurin, Hatchett, and Jackson 1989, 76; Tate 1994, 24). The result, which combines feelings of being "close" with a perception of being "like," or having the same "ideas and feelings," is often called "group identification" (see, e.g., Gurin, Miller, and Gurin 1980; Gurin 1985; Conover 1984, 1988; Rinehart 1992). The NES also measures feelings of warmth toward several specified groups through a "feeling thermometer" measuring "cold or unfavorable," neutral, or "warm or favorable" feelings (see Gurin, Miller, and Gurin 1980; Gurin 1985; Conover 1988; and Cook 1989 for a "relative" feeling thermometer).

3. See Ogbu 1990, 150, for the way "immigrant identities" differ from the identities of the dominant group in the receiving society but are not necessarily opposed to those identities.

4. See Fülop 1998 for Japan; note that Thompson [1963] 1966 posits not only an objective identity of interests within the group but also interests objectively in opposition to those of the dominant group. The degree of opposition in interests, perhaps deriving in part from intergroup competition for scarce resources (Miller, Hildreth, and Simmons 1988, 108), derives from an interaction of both "objective" and "subjective" factors. In the tennis example, the common interest in enjoyment presumably outweighs the conflicting interests in competition for scarce resources (the win).

5. Rawls (1971) argues that inequalities are just if they meet certain criteria of liberty and benefit the least advantaged sections of society. Many existing inequalities, of course, are not just, but are held in place by more or less visible systems of power.

6. Gurin, Miller, and Gurin (1980, 31) find this "rejection of legitimacy" the most important predictor of "collectivist orientations." Every social movement theorist who has addressed the issue agrees that oppositional social movements must interpret or reinterpret central problems as unjustly caused. (See, e.g., Turner 1969; Piven and Cloward 1977; Moore 1978; Gurin, Miller, and Gurin 1980; McAdam 1982; Gamson, Fireman, and Rytina 1982; Ferree and Miller 1985; Snow et al. 1986; Snow and Benford 1988, 1992; Klandermans 1989, 1997; Tarrow 1998; Gamson 1992; Johnston 1994; Oberschall 1993; 1996, 94; Conover 1988, 64). McAdam (1982, 50), and later Ferree and Miller (1985, 43–44) and McAdam, McCarthy, and Zald (1988, 713–14; 1996, 9), describe the process as reversing "what Ross (1977) calls the 'fundamental attribution error' "—that is, "the tendency of people to explain their situation as a function of individual deficiencies rather than features of the system" (1996, 9; not the same as Pettigrew's 1979 "ultimate attribution error," in which positive behaviors by in-group members and negative behaviors by out-group members are attributed to internal factors, while negative in-group and positive out-group behaviors are attributed to external factors). See also Major 1994 for the psychological literature. Although a concern for justice is implicit in such conceptions as "exploitation" and "oppression," Marx did not make justice explicitly central in his analyses, preferring a more scientific and less moral language (Buchanan 1982). Writers influenced by Marx, such as E. P. Thompson, followed this lead by not making justice central in their definitions of class consciousness. Building on our own experiences of oppositional consciousness in social movements and on the analyses of previous social movement theorists, however, we have made the perception of injustice central to our

definition. See Kaye and McClelland 1990 for critical perspectives on Thompson, pointing out how he underemphasized the forces of language, culture, increased communication, political opportunity and provocation, and disunity. In spite of Thompson's intended break with some Marxist scholars, he continued to rely unconsciously on economic determinants of consciousness (Sewell 1990, 57). Moore 1978, by contrast, urges us to focus on "the sense of injustice" in understanding working class militance; Steinberg 1995, 1996, cites nineteenth-century workers' speeches that make justice central.

7. Thompson [1963] 1966, for example, writes, "[C]lass happens when some men, as a result of common experiences (inherited or shared), feel and articulate the identity of their interests as between themselves, and as against other men whose interests are different from (and usually opposed to) theirs" (9). Elsewhere he repeats this formulation: "In the years between 1780 and 1832 most English working people came to feel an identity of interests as between themselves, and as against their rulers and employers" (11); "a consciousness of the identity of interests between working men" (807); and "a consciousness of the identity of the interests of the working class, or 'productive classes', *as against* those of other classes" (807, emphasis in original). We do not take the term "identity of interests" literally. In our analysis the phrases "identity of interests" and "a common interest" mean only an assumed common interest among the great majority of the group on the specific point of ending the system of domination. We expect conflicting interests on means, and on many other matters, within the group and even some such conflict as to the goal of ending domination itself. The writings of women of color feminists (e.g., Collins 1990) have taken us some way beyond Thompson's formulation. (See Waite, chap. 7, this volume, for conflicts among means in the Chicago Freedom Movement.) Conceptions of "linked fate" do not make as stringent assumptions as conceptions of "identity of interest." Gurin and Townsend 1986, Gurin, Hatchett, and Jackson 1989, Dawson 1994, and Tate 1994 all analyze versions of a linked-fate question, which on the 1984 and 1988 National Black Election Study is worded, "Do you think that what happens generally to black people in this country will have *something to do* with what happens in your life?" (emphasis mine).

8. Gurin, Miller, and Gurin (1980, 31) call this step "collectivist orientation." Note that in our formulation, recognizing a need for collective action does not include a commitment to acting on behalf of the group, which we argue is importantly a separate move. Our definition of oppositional consciousness differs in this way from the definition of "group consciousness" in Miller, Gurin, and Gurin 1978, cited in Conover 1984, 1988, and Gurin, Hatchett, and Jackson 1989, 81. It also differs in this way from Snow and Benford's "collective action frames," which, among other functions, assign "responsibility for carrying out [the needed collective] action" (1992, 136). Some forms of oppositional consciousness may include such an assignment of responsibility, for example to all members of the subordinate group. But some may not.

9. Snow and Benford (1992) also describe "collective action frames" in much this way. Our understanding of oppositional consciousness includes not only cognitive elements, such as appear in collective action frames and ideologies and are stressed in McAdam's 1982 term "cognitive liberation," but also affective elements such as warmth (e.g., with group identification) and anger (e.g., with the recognition of injustice).

10. See Tilly 1978 and Tarrow 1998, with citations, for "political opportunity structures"; McAdam 1982 on the sense of power and efficacy as a key component of cognitive liberation; and Klandermans 1989, 1997, on the importance of the belief that collective action can be successful. The key component of "agency" in Gamson 1992 and in Klandermans's 1997 summary of conditions for social movements consists of the belief that it is possible to alter conditions.

11. Wilcox (1990) shows that Black consciousness is associated with, and perhaps facilitates, feminist consciousness. Survey data consistently reveal, for example, that African American men are more likely than White men to support the women's movement (Mansbridge 1999). Gay and Tate (1998) indicate that gender identification seems

to enhance the impact of race identification on support for many liberal causes. However, Cohen (1999), along with Stockdill (chap. 9, this volume), shows that oppositional consciousness regarding one's own group in no way guarantees recognizing the injustice done to other groups. As Cohen points out, the very fact of a group's subordination (and therefore its leaders' desire to have the group look respectable both to its own members and to the dominant group) can exacerbate its tendency to oppress a subordinate group in its midst.

12. When we use "oppositional consciousness" in this group way, we produce some conceptual overlap with a culture of oppositional consciousness. The term "culture of oppositional consciousness" is intended to draw attention to symbols, ritual, forms of dress and speech, and other cultural artifacts. The analysis of these distinctions derives from an inductive rather than a deductive strategy. Our coauthors followed their own linguistic intuitions when choosing the words with which to describe the phenomena they portray in this volume. We reasoned that the authors themselves were closer than the two editors to the actions and ideas they were analyzing. After the fact, we consulted and coordinated. Fred Harris (chap. 3, this volume) tacked on the last two paragraphs that appear in his article. Sharon Groch (chap. 4, this volume) changed her wording several times as we worked out the implications of our distinctions. Others changed a word or a sentence here and there. The result is a tentative tripartite distinction among oppositional culture, oppositional consciousness, and cultures of oppositional consciousness. Most cultures of oppositional consciousness are activist cultures (see, e.g., Taylor and Whittier 1992), but the focus on injustice characteristic of oppositional consciousness, and even its more fully developed set of strategies for analyzing structural causation and rectifying injustice, can spread in varying degrees beyond activist enclaves to the larger subordinate group.

13. Marx wrote that the English working class was "already a class as against capital, but not yet for itself" ([1846–47] 1963). The contrast between *an sich* ("in itself") and *für sich* comes from Hegel. Elster (1985, 346, n. 2) comments, "It is widely assumed that Marx himself used these terms [*an sich* and *für sich*] to distinguish between classes that lack and classes that possess class consciousness. As far as I know, he never actually uses the term 'in itself' (*an sich*)." "For itself," the more common term, holds in several languages the double meaning it had for Marx, e.g., for Rabbi Hillel: "If I am not for myself, who will be for me? But if I am only for myself, what am I?" (Avot 1:14).

14. Those not familiar with this problem should note particularly that the resulting "free-rider problem" applies *only* to goods that, once brought into being, can be "consumed" by those who have not contributed to bringing it into being. It is only when noncontributors cannot be excluded from the benefits that it pays each individual (with no motivation other than wanting those benefits) to free-ride, that is, to let others bring the good into being. Then, if the good must also be jointly supplied (supplied by more than one), and if everyone takes the individually rational strategy of letting the others do the work, the good will not be produced. In the less extreme situation, if only a few contribute (or many contribute but give less than is needed), the individual rationality of all the actors results in the good being *under*produced compared to what would have been produced if the noncontributing beneficiaries could have been excluded from the good. Versions of this free-rider problem have been analyzed under many names (the "collective action problem," "common pool problem," "social dilemma problem," and, in the two-person version, "prisoners' dilemma problem"). See, e.g., Olson 1965, Hardin 1982, Mansbridge 1990. Thinking of what would happen if each individual acted only on narrow self-interest serves as a useful heuristic. One should not make the mistake of assuming that such narrow self-interest comprises a major part of human interaction, or the more subtle mistake of modeling behavior as if it were the only human interaction and allowing the other motivations to slip ever lower in one's understanding of human behavior. But with these caveats, parsing out what would strategically follow if each acted only on narrow self-interest illuminates both the probability of certain outcomes if no other motivations are introduced and the resulting

need to explore the full panoply of human motivations. Previous theorists of common interests—such as Plato, Thomas Aquinas, Thomas Hume, Alexis de Tocqueville, and Karl Marx—were hampered in their thinking by not understanding the free-rider logic (see Mansbridge 1990, 1995, 1998). It is therefore also a mistake to see no benefit in the language and thinking of "rational choice theory" (which explores the free-rider logic, among other strategic interactions), although strategic calculations based on narrow self-interest cannot explain the primary motivations of many who contribute their time, money, energy, and sometimes their lives to a social movement.

15. See citations in Ferree 1992.

16. Jasper 1997, 9; Teske 1997, 97. See also Monroe, Barton, and Klineman 1991, 341, and Williams 1985.

17. Jasper 1997 makes the same distinction that we do between liberation movements (which he calls "citizenship" movements") and other movements (which he calls "post-citizenship" and we call "equality-based special issue" and "social responsibility" movements). Thinking of liberation movements as "citizenship" movements, however, obscures their relation to a system of domination that extends far beyond the state, focuses attention primarily on their relation to the state (Jasper 1997, 78), underplays their stress on the need to change social practices and cultural interpretations (Jasper 1997, 324), and neglects the source of these emotions in a shared experience of subordination.

18. I have adapted this brief account of self-categorization theory from Turner 1987 (see also Dawson 1994 and Conover 1984, 1988, who draws on a comparable "self-schema" theory). Yet this theory can take us only so far. We still need to explore, as social movement theorists are doing, the many things that lead some people to characterize themselves as members of groups committed to political action, or "define their situation so that participation is appropriate" (Klandermans 1992, 77). Although membership in some groups is ascriptive, or given, I know of no such groups in which membership in the group so automatically entails action on behalf of the group that in order to act as "themselves" its members have no alternative than to act on its behalf. As soon as two people who do not want to act on the group's behalf find each other, they can create a subgroup of "not very loyal" group members, whose definition does not entail any action for the group. (To avoid this process, participants in many groups try both to make membership in the group valuable—or maintain or increase its value—and to deny that membership to anyone not willing to act for the group. See Friedman and McAdam 1992; Hardin 1995.) Although self-categorization alone thus may explain relatively costless progroup activity, such as the allocation of greater goods to one's in-group in a minimal group experiment, it will not fully explain more costly sacrifices. To explain costly action on behalf of the group, it is therefore not enough to say that people have a "collective identity" in the sense of simply seeing themselves as members of the group. They must also have a motive for action on behalf of the group. If, however, in the process of "enlarging" their personal identities "to include the relevant collective identity as part of their definition of self" (Gamson 1992, 60), individuals come to experience the group's good as their own, this hedonic identification (see n. 20 below) can provide a direct motive for acting on behalf of the group.

19. Several social theorists have independently identified the first two of these motivations, labeling them "affection" and "principle" (Hume [1741–42] 1985), "sympathy" and "commitment" (Sen [1977] 1990), "empathy" and "morality" (Jencks 1990), "we-feeling" and "conscience" (Dawes, van de Kragt, and Orbell 1990), and "love" and "duty" (Elster 1990, Mansbridge 1990). It might clarify the analysis to call the first in this pair "hedonic identification." The second of Knoke's (1988, 315) motivational pair, "affective-bonding" and "normative-conformity," confusingly mixes the motivation of duty with the motivations of avoiding social punishment and acquiring social reward. The motivation of commitment to a cause is captured to some degree by the second of Wilson's (1962) terms "solidary" and "purposive." Turner's (1987) self-categorization theory proposes the motive of acting according to group-appropriate norms. Chong 1991 and Hardin 1995 help

sort out some socially oriented motives (e.g., the desires to gain friendship, maintain social standing and reputation, and avoid ostracism [Chong 1991, 34–35]) and materially self-interested motives relevant to collective action. Teske 1997 explores some of the relevant self-enhancing motives (e.g., efficacy, increased knowledge, a sense of growing as a person). Other self-enhancing motives might include something as simple as a desire for closure, that is, to finish a job once begun. Holmes 1990 investigates some malevolent motives, which can also benefit one's group.

20. Preliminary work indicates, for example, that both testosterone and serotonin (body chemicals associated with hedonic satisfaction) rise when a sports team with which one identifies wins and fall when the team loses (Bernhardt et al. 1998, James 1997). One can presumably identify hedonically not only with a team or group but also with a general collection of political stands ("left" or "right"), or with specific causes (the cause of peace or the cause of the homeless). In some cases, commitment to a group or cause may run no deeper in one's identity than identification with a sports team, or with decisions to grow one's hair long or not wear trousers with pleats. Yet even in a relatively shallow form, the commitment can become such a fully integrated part of one's identity that one will feel violated when asked (or forced) to change. When social theorists talk about "expressive motivations" for collective or altruistic action ("expressive" being a favorite word among economists for motivations that stem from commitment), the phrase nicely captures this kind of relatively shallow expression of self. In social movements, however, most such commitments are also suffused with moral values, which draw from cognitive conclusions about what is right and from moral commitments to do what is right. This moral character, not captured by the word "expressive," usually plays a central role in decisions to give or risk one's life, or make other major sacrifices of narrow self-interest, for a cause.

21. See nn. 2 and 7 above on warmth, closeness/likeness, and linked fate. Survey analysts use these feelings and perceptions as independent variables in a constellation of factors predicted to make action more likely, rather than expecting them automatically to usher in action.

22. On the duty of "fair play" in a free-rider situation, see Rawls 1971. For an application, see Schwartz and Paul 1992, 214–15. On individual variation, see the speculations of Freud ([1930] 1961), who gave the name "superego" to the faculty or collection of faculties that respond to the prompting of duty or "conscience." Psychologists often err in seeing conscience as an internal authority to be placated, as one might placate a parent. This metaphor misses the way the commands of morality and justice not only are located within an individual but have an external authority deriving from the evolution of social learning passed on through the generations, from reason, and from the meaning of membership in a particular community.

The role of individual conscience in human action undoubtedly varies from individual to individual and from culture to culture. Many tight-knit cultures based on close ties and reputational networks may not require a strong internal apparatus of conscience, with its corresponding internal guilt, but can rely more heavily on social shame. Social shaming typically does not distinguish between failures to live up to social norms and failures to live up to what Westerners would consider "moral" norms, which are the typical subjects of conscience.

23. I thank Aldon Morris for the Jackson example; the Israeli example comes from Hochman 2000. This understanding of duty is related less to Kant's conception and more to conceptions in Sandel 1982 and Baier 1987. Analytically we must distinguish between another person activating one's own internal moral commitments and the other doling out social praise or blame (which serve as external sanctions), even though in practice these are almost always mixed. Choosing or accepting membership in a group that will activate one's moral commitments and whose members will praise one for moral activities and blame one for free-riding can act as a form of "precommitment" (Elster 1983). In addition to simple attraction to others with similar moral commitments and admiration for others in the group, an implicit desire for precommitment may help explain why some individuals

find it important to gain friends, maintain standing, and avoid ostracism among other political activists (or morally committed people), who are not usually the most powerful or wealthy people in a community.

24. See Frank 1988 and Jolls, Sunstein, and Thaler 1998 for the impulse to revenge and other impulses to rectify injustices, independent of outcomes to self. It is even conceivable that some part of these impulses is innate.

25. See Batson 1991 for experiments that tease apart the different motivations behind an altruistic act, distinguishing acting to make oneself feel better from acting only to help the other. Understanding the component parts of motivation (such as hedonic identification and duty) can serve a useful analytic purpose, particularly for those who plan to try to operationalize parts of the concept in close-ended survey questions. Such an analysis, however, cannot capture adequately the social or psychological reality of action driven by an at least temporarily relatively coherent sense of self in relation with others (see Teske 1997). Oliner and Oliner (1988) and Monroe (1996), for example, report that rescuers of Jews in Nazi Germany often explained their actions with such comments as "I didn't think about it; I just did it," and expressed the feeling of having "no choice." Cohen (1985), Ferree (1992), Gamson (1992), Monroe (1996), and Teske (1997) rightly point to the demands of "identity," and more broadly "self," that motivate what we problematically call "non-self-interested" acts. Monroe (1996), Teske (1997), and Jasper (1997) further stress the moral dimension of this identity. Teske in particular persuasively attacks my own earlier formulations of these mixtures of motivations. Although Monroe, Teske, and Jasper all studied activists who were not themselves subordinates in the systems of domination and subordination they were trying to end, their conclusions apply to these actors as well.

26. See, e.g., Freeman 1975, McAdam 1988, and Whittier 1995 for the effects of social networks; see Fantasia 1988, Klandermans 1992, 81–82, Teske 1997, 1–3, and Sewell 1996 for the effects of a crystallizing event. See Sapiro 1990 for social movements causing consciousness as well as consciousness causing social movements.

27. Elsewhere (Mansbridge 1990, 1998) I argue that in order not to be extinguished altruistic motivations often require a protective "ecological niche" of material reward, which must be appropriately structured so as not to undermine the altruistic motivation.

28. Gurin, Miller, and Gurin (1980) provide some support for this contention in their statistical analysis. Miller et al. (1981) demonstrate that the components are not only additive but interactive.

29. In some instances such as bearing witness, however, costs may be irrelevant. Jasper (1997, 38) quotes Derrick Bell's (1992, xvi) analysis of his conversation with a Mississippi woman during the civil rights movement: "Her goal was defiance, and its . . . effect was likely more potent precisely because she did what she did without expecting to topple her oppressors. Mrs. MacDonald avoided discouragement and defeat because at the point that she determined to resist her oppression, she was triumphant." Jasper adds, "For many, martyrdom is its own reward."

30. See Levine 1977, 321 ff., for examples of Black jokes; Bair 1990, 269 ff., for Beauvoir; Fanon [1961] 1968 for colonized peoples.

31. See Brown 1988, Chirot 1994, and Scheff 1994 for resentment; Hardin 1982 for the uses and abuses of unity.

32. Johnston's (1994) sensitive discussion of these daily indignities also reveals, in the cases of Catalan, Basque, and Lithuanian nationalist movements, how maintaining opposition to the dominant groups was strongly facilitated by what we would call the "safe spaces" of the church and the extended family.

33. See Mansbridge 1986, particularly chap. 9 for the pressures to deafness and uniformity in a variety of movements that Morris and Braine (chap. 2, this volume) call "equality-based special issue movements" and "social responsibility movements." These pressures can be, and usually are, even greater in liberation movements. Many observers have pointed out that group unity flourishes with the demonization of an "enemy." Turner

1987 points out that the phenomenon of "meta-contrast"—highlighting similarities within the group and differences with outsiders—is inherent in the conceptual framing of a "group." Moreover, the more salient the self-categorization, the greater the "perceptual accentuation of intra-class similarities and inter-class differences" (49). See Taylor and Whittier 1992 and Dawson 1994 for the perceptual minimization of group differences and exaggeration of differences between one's own group and outsiders. Turner and Dawson also explore the positive and negative functions of group-based cognitive biases in absorbing information. See Tajfel 1974 for the first experiments demonstrating an easily triggered and possibly innate human in-group bias. See Brewer and Brown 1998 for a summary of the psychological literature on the behavioral consequences of in-group identity, theories of group identification, whether in-groups require out-groups, and conflict, competition, and comparison. See Taylor and Whittier 1992, Mansbridge 1994, and Groch, chap. 4, this volume, for the potential creativity in movement enclaves where members speak primarily to one another.

34. See Butler 1990 on "drag" as mocking the notion of an authentic gender identity, although she points out that not all parody is subversive; the task is to find or invent strategies that will serve this function. I borrow the concept of a greedy consciousness from Lewis Coser's (1974) "greedy institutions," defined as institutions that require undivided commitment. See Foucault [1976] 1980c for a rejection of the "repressive" hypothesis, which holds that if one were able to remove this or that repressive mechanism, the authentic self would emerge from beneath. (Butler 1990 points to contradictions within Foucault's work on this point.)

35. See Johnston's (1994) closely observed account.

36. Fraser 1997 distinguishes between the political goals of recognition and redistribution. The first involves the continuance of the group in more favorable conditions (as in the gay and lesbian movement). The second may involve the disappearance of a group qua group (as when the working class becomes all middle class, or the proletariat becomes the universal class).

37. See Hardin 1995 on the ways groups benefit from enforced unity.

38. On embeddedness, see Sandel 1982; on being born into embeddedness but taking a voluntary stance toward it, see Hirschmann 1989; on criticism, see Walzer 1988; on parody, see Butler 1990. Because essentialism also marginalizes nondominant or minority referents within a group (see, e.g., Harris 1990; see Cohen 1999 for "secondary marginalization"), fighting this tendency requires recognizing and struggling against processes of marginalization, recognizing the parallels among oppressions, and cultivating mutual understanding on the basis of those parallels (see, e.g., Stockdill, chap. 8, this volume).

39. Sandoval 1993, 49. Sandoval defines U.S. third-world feminism as the political alliance made during the 1960s and 1970s "between a generation of U.S. feminists of color who were separated by culture, race, class, sex or gender identifications but united through their similar responses to the experience of race oppression." The connection, she argues, is a "mobile unity, constantly weaving and re-weaving an interaction of differences into coalition" (Sandoval 1993, 53, n. 2). See also Sandoval 2000.

40. Sandoval 1991, 15. See also Sandoval 1993, 87.

41. Sandoval (1991; 1993, 97; 2000), cites many, particularly within third-world feminism, who have developed similar concepts, e.g., Anzaldúa (1987) on "la consciencia de la mestiza."

42. See, e.g., Combahee River Collective [1977] 1983 and Stockdill, chap. 8, this volume. These analyses are strongest in their understanding of how different systems of oppression support one another. They are weaker on the ways one system of oppression may undermine another, as, for example, when the power system that emerged from capitalism undermined and eventually replaced the power system that emerged from feudalism.

References

Aarons, Leroy F. 1970. "The Chicanos Want In." *Washington Post,* November 11, B1–B5.

ACT UP/NY (Women and AIDS Book Group), ed. 1992. *Women, AIDS, and Activism.* Boston: South End Press.

Acuna, Rodolfo. 1988. *Occupied America: A History of Chicanos.* New York: Harper and Row.

Adam, Barry D. 1987. *The Rise of a Gay and Lesbian Movement.* Boston: Twayne Publishers.

Allen, Pamela. 1970. *Free Space: A Perspective on the Small Group in Women's Liberation.* New York: Times Change Press. Abridged in *Radical Feminism,* ed. Anne Koedt, Ellen Levine, and Anita Rapone. New York: Quadrangle, 1973.

Allen, Robert. 1992. *Black Awakening in Capitalist America.* Trenton: Africa World Press.

Almond, Gabriel A., and Sidney Verba. 1963. *The Civic Culture.* Boston: Little Brown.

American Printing House for the Blind. 1992–93. *Annual Report.* Louisville: American Printing House for the Blind.

Anastos, Kathryn, and Carola Marte. 1991. "Women: The Missing Persons in the AIDS Epidemic." In *The AIDS Reader: Social, Political, Ethical Issues.* Ed. Nancy McKenzie. New York: Penguin.

Anderson, Alan B., and George W. Pickering. 1986. *Confronting the Color Line: The Broken Promise of the Civil Rights Movement in Chicago.* Athens: University of Georgia Press.

Anzaldúa, Gloria. 1987. *Borderlands/La Frontera: The New Mestiza.* San Francisco: Spinsters/Aunt Lute.

———, ed. 1990. *Making Face, Making Soul—Haciendo Cara: Creative and Critical Perspectives by Feminists of Color.* San Francisco: Aunt Lute.

Anzaldúa, Gloria, and Cherríe Moraga, eds. 1983. *This Bridge Called My Back: Writings by Radical Women of Color.* New York: Kitchen Table/Women of Color Press.

Arendt, Hannah. [1963] 1965. *On Revolution.* New York: Viking.

Arno, Peter S., and Karyn L. Feiden, ed. 1992. *Against the Odds: The Story of AIDS Drug Development, Politics, and Profits.* New York: HarperCollins.

Asetoyer, Charon. 1992. "First There Was Smallpox." In *Women, AIDS, and Activism.* Ed. ACT UP/NY (Women and AIDS Book Group). Boston: South End Press.

Bachrach, Peter, and Morton Baratz. 1963. "Decisions and Non-decisions: An Analytical Framework." *American Political Science Review* 57:632–42.

Baier, Annette C. 1987. "Hume: The Woman's Moral Theorist?" In *Women and*

Moral Theory. Ed. Eva Kittay and Diana Meyers. Totowa, N.J.: Rowman and Littlefield.

Bair, Deirdre. 1990. *Simone de Beauvoir: A Biography.* New York: Summit Books.

Baldwin, Lewis V. 1991. *There Is a Balm in Gilead.* Minneapolis: Fortress Press.

Banzhaf, Marion. 1992. "Race, Women, and AIDS." In *Women, AIDS, and Activism.* Ed. ACT-UP/NY Women and AIDS Book Group. Boston: South End Press.

Barker, Lucius J. 1988. *Our Time Has Come: A Delegate's Diary of Jesse Jackson's 1984 Presidential Campaign.* Urbana: University of Illinois Press.

Barnartt, Sharon N. 1994. "Action and Consensus Mobilization in the Deaf President Now Protest and Its Aftermath." In *Research in Social Movements, Conflict and Change,* vol. 17. Ed. L. Kriesberg, M. Dobkowski, and I. Wallimann. Greenwich, Conn.: JAI.

Barrera, Mario, Carlos Munoz, and Charles Ornelas. 1974. "The Barrio as Internal Colony." In *La Causa Politica: A Chicano Politics Reader.* Ed. F. Chris Garcia. Notre Dame: University of Notre Dame Press.

Barringer, Felicity. 1993. "Pride in a Soundless World: Deaf Oppose a Hearing Aid." *New York Times,* 16 May, 1, 14.

Barry, Brian. [1975] 1991. "Power: An Economic Analysis." In *Democracy and Power: Essays in Political Theory I.* Oxford: Oxford University Press.

Batson, Daniel. 1991. *The Altruism Question.* Hillsdale, N.Y.: Lawrence Erlbaum Associates.

Beam, Joseph, ed. 1986. *In the Life: A Black Gay Anthology.* Boston: Alyson Publications.

Bell, Derrick. 1992. *Faces at the Bottom of the Well: The Permanence of Racism.* New York: Basic Books.

Bellarosa, James M. 1989. *A Problem of Plumbing.* Santa Barbara, Calif.: John Daniel and Company.

Bennett, Lerone, Jr. 1984. *Before the Mayflower: A History of Black America.* New York: Penguin.

Berkowitz, Edward. 1980. "Strachan and the Limits of the Federal Government." *International Review of History and Political Science* 17:65–81.

Bernhardt, Paul C., James M. Dabbs Jr., Julie A. Fielden, and Candice Lutter. 1998. "Testosterone Changes during Vicarious Experiences of Winning and Losing among Fans at Sporting Events." *Physiology and Behavior* 65:59–62.

Bernstein, Anita. 1997. "Treating Sexual Harassment with Respect." *Harvard Law Review* 111:445–527.

Best of the Rag. 1985. Louisville: Advocado.

Biles, Roger. 1995. *Richard J. Daley: Politics, Race, and the Governing of Chicago.* De Kalb: Northern Illinois University Press.

Bliss, Susan. 1972. "The Mobilization of DIA." *Performance* 22:3–7.

Bloom, Jack M. 1987. *Class, Race, and the Civil Rights Movement.* Bloomington: Indiana University Press.

Bonney, Norman. 1974. "Race and Politics in Chicago in the Daley Era." *Race* 15:339–350.

Branch, Taylor. 1988. *Parting the Waters: America in the King Years, 1954–1963.* New York: Simon and Schuster.

Brandt, Allan M. 1991. "AIDS in Historical Perspective: Four Lessons from the History of Sexually Transmitted Diseases." In *The AIDS Reader: Social, Political, Ethical Issues.* Ed. Nancy F. McKenzie. New York: Penguin.

Brewer, Marilynn B., and Rupert J. Brown. 1998. "Intergroup Relations." In *Handbook of Social Psychology.* Ed. Daniel Gilbert, Susan Fiske, and Gardner Lindzey. Oxford: Oxford University Press.

Brown, Wendy. 1988. *Manhood and Politics: A Feminist Reading in Political Theory.* Tottawa, N. J.: Rowman and Littlefield.

Brown, William E. 1963–64. "Crystal City: Symbol of Hope." *Labor Today,* December/January, 16–20.

Buchanan, Allen. 1982. *Marx and Justice.* Tottowa, N.J.: Rowman and Littlefield.

Buchanan, Robert. 1993. "The Silent Worker Newspaper and the Building of a Deaf Community: 1890–1929." In *Deaf History Unveiled.* Ed. J. Van Cleve. Washington: Gallaudet University Press.

Burkett, Randall. 1978. *Garveyism as a Religious Movement.* Metuchen, N.J.: Scarecrow Press/American Theological Library Association.

Butler, Judith. 1990. *Gender Trouble: Feminism and the Subversion of Identity.* New York: Routledge.

Callahan, John. 1989. *Don't Worry, He Won't Get Far on Foot.* New York: Vintage.

———. 1991. *Digesting the Child Within.* New York: Quill.

———. 1993. *The Night, They Say, Was Made for Love.* New York: Quill.

Carson, Clayborne, David J. Garrow, Gerald Gill, Vincent Harding, and Darlene Clark Hine, eds. 1991. *The Eyes on the Prize Civil Rights Reader.* New York: Penguin.

Castro, Tony. 1974. *Chicano Power: The Emergence of Mexican America.* New York: Saturday Review Press.

Cerulo, Karen A. 1997. "Identity Construction: New Issues, New Directions." *Annual Review of Sociology.* 23:385–409.

Chamberlin, Judi. 1990. "The Ex-Patients' Movement: Where We've Been and Where We're Going." *Journal of Mind and Behavior* 11:323–36.

Chandler, Charles Ray. 1968. "The Mexican-American Protest Movement in Texas." Ph.D. diss., Tulane University.

Cheadle, Barbara. 1993. *Future Reflections.* Baltimore: National Federation of the Blind.

Chicano Studies Program, University of Wisconsin, Madison. 1989. *The Chicano Civil Rights Struggle in Wisconsin: Interview with Ernesto Chacon, Irma Guerra, and Maria Flores.* Videotape. May.

Chirot, Daniel. 1994. *Modern Tyrants: The Power and Prevalence of Evil in Our Age.* New York: Free Press.

Chong, Dennis. 1991. *Collective Action and the Civil Rights Movement.* Chicago: University of Chicago Press.

Christiansen, John B., and Sharon N. Barnartt. 1995. *Deaf President Now!* Washington: Gallaudet University Press.

Cohen, Cathy J. 1999. *The Boundaries of Blackness: AIDS and the Breakdown of American Politics.* Chicago: University of Chicago Press.

Cohen, Jean. 1985. "Strategy of Identity: New Theoretical Paradigms and Contemporary Social Movements." *Social Research* 52:663–716.

Cohen, Ronald. 1972. "Altruism: Human, Cultural, or What?" *Journal of Social Issues* 28:39–57.

Collins, Patricia Hill. 1990. *Black Feminist Thought: Knowledge, Consciousness, and the Politics of Empowerment*. New York: Routledge.

Combahee River Collective. [1977] 1983. "The Combahee River Collective Statement." In *Home Girls: A Black Feminist Anthology*. Ed. Barbara Smith. New York: Kitchen Table/Women of Color Press.

Commons, John R. 1963. *Myself: The Autobiography of John R. Commons*. Madison: University of Wisconsin Press.

Cone, James H. 1969. *Black Theology and Black Power*. New York: Seabury Press.

————. 1972. *The Spiritual and the Blues*. New York: Seabury Press.

————. [1970] 1986. *A Black Theology of Liberation*. Maryknoll, N.Y.: Orbis.

Connolly, Kathleen. 1989. "The Chicago Open-Housing Conference." In *Chicago 1966*. Ed. David J. Garrow. Brooklyn: Carlson.

Connolly, William E. 1974. "Power and Responsibility." In *The Terms of Political Discourse*. Lexington: D. C. Heath.

Conover, Pamela Johnston. 1984. "The Influence of Group Identification on Political Participation and Evaluation." *Journal of Politics*. 46:760–85.

————. 1988. "The Role of Social Groups in Political Thinking." *British Journal of Political Science* 18:51–76.

Conover, Pamela Johnston, and Virginia Sapiro. 1993. "Gender, Feminist Consciousness, and War." *American Journal of Political Science* 37:1079–99.

Cook, Elizabeth Adel. 1989. "Measuring Feminist Consciousness." *Women and Politics* 9:71–87.

Corea, Gena. 1992. *The Invisible Epidemic: The Story of Women and AIDS*. New York: HarperCollins.

Coser, Lewis A. 1974. *Greedy Institutions: Patterns of Undivided Commitment*. New York: Free Press.

Crenshaw, Kimberlé. 1989. "Demarginalizing the Intersection of Race and Sex: A Black Feminist Critique of Antidiscrimination Doctrine, Feminist Theory, and Antiracist Politics." *University of Chicago Legal Forum* 1989:139–67.

————. 1992. "Whose Story Is It Anyway? Feminist and Antiracist Appropriations of Anita Hill." In *Race-ing Justice, En-gendering Power: Essays on Anita Hill, Clarence Thomas, and the Construction of Social Reality*. Ed. Toni Morrison. New York: Pantheon.

Crescendo, Johnny, and the Piss on Pity Squad. 1993. "Pride." Cassette recording of songs. London: The Entertainers.

Cruickshank, Margaret. 1992. *The Gay and Lesbian Liberation Movement*. New York: Routledge.

Cuellar, Robert. 1969. "A Social and Political History of the Mexican American Population of Texas." Master's thesis, North Texas State University.

Dain, Norman. 1989. "Critics and Dissenters: Reflections on 'Anti-psychiatry' in the United States." *Journal of the History of the Behavioral Sciences* 25:3–25.

Dalton, Harlon L. 1991. "AIDS in Blackface." In *The AIDS Reader*. Ed. Nancy F. McKenzie. New York: Meridian.

Davis, Angela. 1983. *Women, Race, and Class*. New York: Vintage.

————. 1990. *Women, Culture, and Politics*. New York: Vintage.

Dawes, Robyn M., Alphonse J. C. van de Kragt, and John M. Orbell. 1990. "Cooperation for the Benefit of Us: Not Me, or My Conscience." In *Beyond Self-Interest*. Ed. Jane Mansbridge. Chicago: University of Chicago Press.

Dawson, Michael C. 1994. *Behind the Mule: Race and Class in American Politics*. Princeton: Princeton University Press.

De Leon, Arnoldo. 1980. *They Called Them Greasers: Anglo Attitudes toward Mexicans in Texas, 1821–1900*. Austin: University of Texas Press.

———. 1982. *The Tejano Community, 1836–1900*. Albuquerque: University of New Mexico Press.

DeJong, Gerben. 1979. "Independent Living: From Social Movement to Analytic Paradigm." *Archives of Physical Medicine and Rehabilitation* 60:435–46.

Delgado, Miguel A. 1972. "The Fraternization of the Pachuco and the Chicano." Unpublished manuscript.

D'Emilio, John. 1983. *Sexual Politics, Sexual Communities: The Making of a Homosexual Minority in the United States, 1940–1970*. Chicago: University of Chicago Press.

Dolnick, Edward. 1993. "Deafness as Culture." *Atlantic Monthly*. September, 37–53.

Drake, St. Clair, and Horace R. Cayton. 1945. *Black Metropolis: A Study of Negro Life in a Northern City*. Chicago: University of Chicago Press.

Drucker, Ernest. 1991. "Drug AIDS in the City of New York: A Study of Dependent Children, Housing, and Drug Addiction Treatment." In *The AIDS Reader: Social, Political, Ethical Issues*. Ed. Nancy F. McKenzie. New York: Penguin.

Duberman, Martin. 1994. *Stonewall*. New York: Penguin.

DuBois, W. E. B. [1903] 1969. *The Souls of Black Folks*. New York: Penguin.

Dybwad, Gunnar, and Hank Bersani Jr. 1996. *New Voices: Self-Advocacy by People with Disabilities*. Cambridge, Mass.: Brookline Books.

Echols, Alice. 1989. *Daring to Be Bad: Radical Feminism in America, 1967–1975*. Minneapolis: University of Minnesota Press.

Edelman, Murray. 1985. *The Symbolic Uses of Politics*. Urbana: University of Illinois Press.

Edwards, Jean Parker. 1982. *We Are People First*. Portland, Oreg.: EDNICK.

Elster, Jon. 1983. *Ulysses and the Sirens: Studies in Rationality and Irrationality*. New York: Cambridge University Press.

———. 1985. *Making Sense of Marx*. Cambridge: Cambridge University Press.

———. 1990. "Selfishness and Altruism." In *Beyond Self-Interest*. Ed. Jane Mansbridge. Chicago: University of Chicago Press.

Emerick, Robert E. 1989. "Group Demographics in the Mental Patient Movement: Group Location, Age, and Size as Structural Factors." *Community Mental Health Journal* 25:277–300.

———. 1995. "Clients as Claim Makers in the Self-Help Movement: Individual and Social Change Ideologies in Former Mental Patient Self-Help Newsletters." *Psychosocial Rehabilitation Journal* 18:17–35.

Erenburg, Mark. 1968. "Obreros Unidos in Wisconsin." *Monthly Labor Review* 91, no. 6:17–23.

———. 1969. "A Study of the Potential Relocation of Texas-Mexican Migratory Farm Workers to Wisconsin." Ph.D. diss., University of Wisconsin, Madison.

Evans, Sara M. 1980. *Personal Politics: The Roots of Women's Liberation in the Civil Rights Movement and the New Left.* New York: Vintage.

Evans, Sara M., and Harry C. Boyte. 1986. *Free Spaces: The Source of Democratic Change in America.* New York: Harper and Row.

Eyes on the Prize: America's Civil Rights Years, 1954–1985. 1986–87. Television documentary. Alexandria, Va.: PBS Video.

Faderman, Lillian. 1991. *Odd Girls and Twilight Lovers: A History of Lesbian Life in Twentieth-Century America.* London: Penguin.

Fairclough, Adam. 1987. *To Redeem the Soul of America: The Southern Christian Leadership Conference and Martin Luther King, Jr.* Athens: University of Georgia Press.

Fanon, Franz. [1961] 1968. *The Wretched of the Earth.* Trans. Constance Farrington. New York: Grove Press.

Fantasia, Rick. 1988. *Cultures of Solidarity: Consciousness, Action, and Contemporary American Workers.* Berkeley and Los Angeles: University of California Press.

Ferree, Myra Marx. 1992. "The Political Context of Rationality: Rational Choice Theory and Resource Mobilization." In *The Frontiers of Social Movement Theory.* Ed. Aldon Morris and Carol Mueller. New Haven: Yale University Press, 1992.

Ferree, Myra Marx, and Frederick D. Miller. 1985. "Mobilization and Meaning: Toward an Integration of Social Psychological and Resource Perspectives on Social Movements." *Sociological Inquiry* 55:38–61.

Festinger, Leon. 1957. *A Theory of Cognitive Dissonance.* Evanston: Row Peterson.

Festinger, Leon. 1964. *Conflict, Decision, and Dissonance.* Stanford: Stanford University Press.

Finger, Anne. 1994. *Bone Truth.* Saint Paul: Coffee House Press.

Finley, Mary Lou. 1989. "The Open Housing Marches Chicago Summer '66." In *Chicago 1966.* Ed. David J. Garrow. Brooklyn: Carlson.

Follett, Mary Parker. [1935] 1942. "Constructive Conflict." In *Dynamic Administration: The Collected Papers of Mary Parker Follett.* Ed. Henry C. Metcalf. New York: Harper.

Foner, Eric. 1988. *Reconstruction: America's Unfinished Revolution, 1863–1877.* New York: Harper and Row.

Fordham, Signithia, and John Ogbu. 1986. "Black Students' School Success: Coping with the 'Burden of Acting White.'" *Urban Review* 18:176–206.

Foucault, Michel. [1976] 1980a. "Two Lectures." In *Power/Knowledge: Selected Interviews and Other Writings 1972–1977.* Ed. Colin Gordon. New York: Pantheon.

———. [1977] 1980b. "Powers and Strategies." In *Power/Knowledge: Selected Interviews and Other Writings 1972–1977.* Ed. Colin Gordon. New York: Pantheon.

———. [1976] 1980c. *The History of Sexuality, Volume I: An Introduction.* Trans. Robert Hurley. New York: Vintage.

Frampton, Merle E., and Hugh Grant Rowell. 1938. *Education of the Handicapped.* New York: World Book.

Frank, Robert H. 1988. *Passions within Reason: The Strategic Role of the Emotions.* New York: W. W. Norton.

Fraser, Nancy. 1989. "Foucault on Modern Power: Empirical Insights and Normative Confusions." In *Unruly Practices.* Minneapolis: University of Minnesota Press.

———. 1992. "Rethinking the Public Sphere: A Contribution to the Critique of Actually Existing Democracy." In *Habermas and the Public Sphere.* Ed. C. Calhoun. Cambridge: MIT Press.

———. 1997. "From Redistribution to Recognition? Dilemmas of Justice in a 'Postsocialist' Age." In *Justice Interruptus: Critical Reflections on the "Postsocialist" Condition.* New York: Routledge.

Freedman, Estelle B., and John D'Emilio. 1988. *Intimate Matters: A History of Sexuality in America.* New York: Harper and Row.

Freeman, Jo. 1975. *The Politics of Women's Liberation.* New York: David McKay.

———. 1991. "How 'Sex' Got into Title VII: Persistent Opportunism as a Maker of Public Policy." *Law and Inequality* 9:163–84.

Freud, Sigmund. [1930] 1961. *Civilization and Its Discontents.* Trans. and ed. James Strachey. New York: W. W. Norton.

Friedan, Betty. 1983. *Feminine Mystique.* New York: Dell Publishing.

Friedman, Debra, and Doug McAdam. 1992. "Collective Identity and Activism: Networks, Choices, and the Life of a Social Movement." In *Frontiers in Social Movement Theory.* Ed. Aldon Morris and Carol Mueller. New Haven: Yale University Press.

Fülop, Marta, 1998. "Deconstructing the Concept of Competition: The Japanese Version." Paper presented at the Center for Advanced Study, Stanford, Calif.

Gabaccia, Donna Rae. 1988. *Militants and Migrants: Rural Sicilians Become American Workers.* New Brunswick: Rutgers University Press.

Gamson, Joshua. 1989. "Silence, Death, and the Invisible Enemy: AIDS Activism and Social Movement Newness." *Social Problems* 36:351–67.

Gamson, William A. 1975. *The Strategy of Social Protest.* Homewood: Dorsey.

———. 1989. *The Strategy of Social Protest.* 2d ed. Belmont: Wadsworth.

———. 1992. "The Social Psychology of Collective Action." In *Frontiers in Social Movement Theory.* Ed. Aldon Morris and Carol Mueller. New Haven: Yale University Press.

———. 1995. "Constructing Social Protest." In *Social Movements and Culture.* Ed. Hank Johnston and Bert Klandermans. Minneapolis: University of Minnesota Press.

Gamson, William A., Bruce Fireman, and Steven Rytina. 1982. *Encounters with Unjust Authority.* Homewood, Ill.: Dorsey.

Gannon, Jack. 1981. *Deaf Heritage: A Narrative History of Deaf America.* Silver Spring, Md.: National Association of the Deaf.

Gannon, Jack. 1989. *The Week the World Heard Gallaudet.* Washington: Gallaudet University Press.

Garcia, Ignacio M. 1989. *United We Win: The Rise and Fall of La Raza Unida Party.* Tucson: University of Arizona Press.

Garrow, David J. 1986. *Bearing the Cross.* New York: William Morrow.

———, ed. 1989. *Chicago 1966.* Brooklyn: Carlson.

Garwood, S. Gray. 1983. *Educating Young Handicapped Children: A Developmental Approach.* 2d ed. Rockville, Md.: Aspen Systems Corp.

Gay, Claudine, and Katherine Tate. 1998. "Doubly Bound: The Impact of Gender and Race on the Politics of Black Women." *Political Psychology* 19:169–84.

Geertz, Clifford. 1973a. "Ethos, World View, and the Analysis of Sacred Symbols." In *The Interpretation of Cultures.* New York: Basic Books.

———. 1973b. "Religion as a Cultural System." In *The Interpretation of Cultures.* New York: Basic Books.

Genovese, Eugene D. 1974. *Roll, Jordan, Roll.* New York: Vintage.

Giddings, Paula. 1984. *When and Where I Enter: The Impact of Black Women on Race and Sex in America.* New York: William Morrow.

Gilkes, Cheryl Townsend. 1980. "The Black Church as a Therapeutic Community: Suggested Areas for Research Into the Black Religious Experience." *Journal of the Interdenominational Theological Center* 8:29–44.

Goffman, Erving. 1974. *Frame Analysis: An Essay on the Organization of Experience.* Cambridge: Harvard University Press.

Goldman, Emma. [1917] 1970. *The Traffic in Women.* New York: Times Change Press.

Goodwin, Jeff, and James M. Jasper. 1999. "Caught in a Winding, Snarling Vine: The Structural Bias of Political Process Theory." *Sociological Forum* 14:27–54.

Gosnell, Harold F. 1937. *Machine Politics: Chicago Model.* Chicago: University of Chicago Press.

———. [1935] 1967. *Negro Politicians: The Rise of Negro Politics in Chicago.* Chicago: University of Chicago Press.

Gramsci, Antonio. [1929–35] 1971. *Selections from the Prison Notebooks.* Ed. Q. Hoare and G. Smith. New York: International Publishers.

———. [1929–35] 1987. *Prison Notebooks.* New York: International Publishers.

Granovetter, Mark A. 1973. "The Strength of Weak Ties." *American Journal of Sociology* 78:360–80.

Griffin, Dick, and Rob Warden. 1977. *Done in a Day: 100 Years of Great Writing from the Chicago Daily News.* Chicago: Swallow Press.

Grimshaw, William. 1992. *Bitter Fruit: Black Politics and the Chicago Machine 1931–1991.* Chicago: University of Chicago Press.

Groch, Sharon A. 1994. "Oppositional Consciousness: Its Manifestation and Development. The Case of People with Disabilities." *Sociological Inquiry* 64:369–95.

———. 1998. "Pathways to Protest: The Making of Oppositional Consciousness by People with Disabilities." Ph.D. diss., Northwestern University.

Grossman, James. 1989. *Land of Hope: Chicago, Black Southerners, and the Great Migration.* Chicago: University of Chicago Press.

Gurin, Patricia. 1985. "Women's Gender Consciousness." *Public Opinion Quarterly* 49:143–63.

Gurin, Patricia, Shirley Hatchett, and James S. Jackson. 1989. *Hope and Independence: Blacks' Response to Electoral and Party Politics.* New York: Russell Sage.

Gurin, Patricia, Arthur H. Miller, and Gerald Gurin. 1980. "Stratum Identification and Consciousness." *Social Psychology Quarterly* 43:30–47.

Gurin, Patricia, and Aloen Townsend. 1986. "Properties of Gender Identity and Their Implications for Gender Consciousness." *British Journal of Social Psychology* 25:139–48.

Guterbock, Thomas M. 1980. *Machine Politics in Transition*. Chicago: University of Chicago Press.

Gutiérrez, Jose Angel. 1954–90. Papers. Benson Latin American Collection, General Libraries, University of Texas at Austin.

———. 1968. "La Raza and Revolution: The Empirical Conditions of Revolution in Four South Texas Counties." Master's thesis, St. Mary's University.

———. 1977. "Toward a Theory of Community Organization in a Mexican American Community in South Texas." Ph.D. diss., University of Texas at Austin.

———. 1998. *The Making of a Chicano Militant: Lessons from Cristal*. Madison: University of Wisconsin Press.

Habermas, Jürgen. 1981. "New Social Movements." *Telos* 49:33–37.

Hall, Linda Bryant. 1991. "Interview with Linda Bryant Hall." In *The Eyes on the Prize Civil Rights Reader*. Ed. Clayborne Carson, David J. Garrow, Gerald Gill, Vincent Harding, and Darlene Clark Hine. New York: Penguin.

Hamilton, Charles V. 1972. *The Black Preacher in America*. New York: William Morrow.

Hammonds, Evelynn. 1990. "Missing Persons: African American Women, AIDS, and the History of Disease." *Radical America* 24 (2): 7–23.

Hampton, Henry, and Steve Fayer. 1990. *Voices of Freedom: An Oral History of the Civil Rights Movement from the 1950s through the 1980s*. New York: Bantam Books.

Handler, Joel F. 1978. *Social Movements and the Legal System*. New York: Academic Press.

Hannaford, Susan. 1985. *Living Outside Inside: A Disabled Woman's Experience. Towards a Social and Political Perspective*. Berkeley: Canterbury.

Hardin, Russell. 1982. *Collective Action*. Baltimore: Johns Hopkins University Press.

———. 1995. *One for All: The Logic of Group Conflict*. Princeton: Princeton University Press.

Harding, V. 1983. *There Is a River: The Black Struggle for Freedom in America*. New York: Vintage.

Harris, Angela. 1990. "Race and Essentialism in Legal Theory." *Stanford Law Review* 42:581–616.

Harris, Craig G. 1986. "Cut Off from among Their People." In *In the Life*. Ed. Joseph Beam. Boston: Alyson Publications.

Harris, Fredrick C. 1999a. *Something Within: Religion in African-American Political Activism*. New York: Oxford University Press.

———. 1999b. "Will the Circle Be Unbroken? The Erosion and Transformation of African American Civic Life." In *Civil Society, Democracy, and Civic Renewal*. Ed. Robert K. Fullinwider. Landham, Md.: Rowman and Littlefield.

Hartsock, Nancy. 1974. "Political Change: Two Perspectives on Power." *Quest* 1:10–25. Reprinted in *Building Feminist Theory: Essays from Quest*. Ed. Charlotte Bunch. New York: Longman, 1981.

Hemphill, Essex, ed. 1991. *Brother to Brother: New Writings by Black Gay Men.* Boston: Alyson Publications.

Henry, Charles P. 1990. *Culture and African American Politics.* Bloomington: Indiana University Press.

Hering, Kathie. 1996. *ALDA Chicago Style,* January–February, 1–2.

Higginbotham, Evelyn Brooks. 1993. *Righteous Discontent: The Women's Movement in the Black Baptist Church, 1880–1920.* Cambridge: Harvard University Press.

Higgins, Paul C. 1980. *Outsiders in a Hearing World: A Sociology of Deafness.* Beverly Hills: Sage.

Hine, Darlene Clark. 1991. "Two Societies (1965–1968): Introduction." In *The Eyes on the Prize Civil Rights Reader.* Ed. Clayborne Carson, David J. Garrow, Gerald Gill, Vincent Harding, and Darlene Clark Hine. New York: Penguin.

Hirsch, Arnold R. 1990. "The Cook County Democratic Organization and the Dilemma of Race, 1931–1987." In *Snowbelt Cities: Metropolitan Politics in the Northeast and Midwest Since World War II.* Ed. Richard M. Bernard. Bloomington: Indiana University Press.

Hirschmann, Nancy J. 1989. "Freedom, Recognition, and Obligation: A Feminist Approach to Political Theory." *American Political Science Review* 83:1227–44.

Hochman, Dafna Varda. 2000. "Peace with Justice, Peace with Care: Palestinian and Israeli Women Negotiate Peacemaking Models." Senior thesis for the Committee on Degrees in Social Studies, Harvard University (http://www.ksg.harvard.edu/wappp/research/working.html).

Holmes, Stephen. 1990. "The Secret History of Self-Interest." In *Beyond Self-Interest.* Ed. Jane Mansbridge. Chicago: University of Chicago Press.

Horowitz, Donald. 1977. *The Courts and Social Policy.* Washington: Brookings Institution.

Hume, David. [1741–42] 1898. "Of Parties in General." In *Essays Moral, Political, and Literary,* vol. 1. Ed. T. H. Green and T. H. Grose. London: Longmans.

———. [1741–42] 1985. "Of the Parties of Great Britain." In *Essays: Moral, Political and Literary.* Indianapolis: Liberty Classics.

International Center for the Disabled Survey of Americans with Disabilities. 1986. New York: Louis Harris.

Jacob, Herbert. 1994. *Law and Politics in the United States.* 2d ed. New York: HarperCollins College Publishers.

James, Oliver. 1997. *Britain on the Couch.* London: Century.

Jasper, James M. 1997. *The Art of Moral Protest: Culture, Biography, and Creativity in Social Movements.* Chicago: University of Chicago Press.

Jencks, Christopher. 1990. "Varieties of Altruism." In *Beyond Self-Interest.* Ed. Jane Mansbridge. Chicago: University of Chicago Press.

Jepson, Jill. 1993. "Trends in Poetry by Deaf and Hard-of-Hearing Writers." In *The Disability Perspective: Variations on a Theme.* Ed. D. Pfeiffer, S. Hey, and G. Kiger. Salem, Oregon: Society of Disability Studies/Willamette University.

Jernigan, Kenneth. 1976. "Blindness: Of Visions and Vultures." *Vital Speeches of the Day* 43:19–24.

———. 1992–94. *Kernel Books.* Baltimore: National Federation of the Blind.

Johnson, Roberta A. 1983. "Mobilizing the Disabled." In *Social Movements of the Sixties and Seventies*. Ed. J. Freeman. New York: Longman.

Johnston, Hank. 1994. "New Social Movements and Old Regional Nationalisms." In *New Social Movements: From Ideology to Identity*. Ed. Enrique Laraña, Hank Johnston, and Joseph R. Gusfield. Philadelphia: Temple University Press.

Johnston, Hank, and Bert Klandermans. 1995. *Culture and Social Movements*. Minneapolis: University of Minnesota Press.

Johnston, Hank, Enrique Laraña, and Joseph R. Gusfield. 1994. "Identities, Grievances, and New Social Movements." In *New Social Movements: From Ideology to Identity*. Ed. Enrique Laraña, Hank Johnston, and Joseph R. Gusfield. Philadelphia: Temple University Press.

Jolls, Christine, Cass R. Sunstein, and Richard Thaler. 1998. "A Behavioral Approach to Law and Economics." *Stanford Law Review* 50:1471–1550.

Julien, Isaac, and Kobena Mercer. 1991. "True Confessions: A Discourse on Images of Black Male Sexuality." In *Brother to Brother: New Writings by Black Gay Men*. Ed. Essex Hemphill. Boston: Alyson Publications.

Kalmuss, Debra, Patricia Gurin, and Aloen L. Townsend. 1981. "Feminist and Sympathetic Feminist Consciousness." *European Journal of Social Psychology* 11:131–47.

Katznelson, Ira. 1973. *Black Men, White Cities*. New York: Oxford University Press.

Kaye, Harvey J., and Keith McClelland, eds. 1990. *E. P. Thompson: Critical Perspectives*. Philadelphia: Temple University Press.

Kaye/Kantrowitz, Melanie. 1989. "Some Notes on Jewish Lesbian Identity." In *Nice Jewish Girls: A Lesbian Anthology*. Ed. Evelyn Torton Beck. Boston: Beacon Press.

Kelley, Robin D. G. 1990. *Hammer and Hoe: Alabama Communists during the Great Depression*. Chapel Hill: University of North Carolina Press.

Kennedy, Elizabeth Lapovsky, and Madeline D. Davis. 1994. *Boots of Leather, Slippers of Gold: The History of a Lesbian Community*. New York: Penguin.

Kertzer, I. David. 1988. *Ritual, Politics, and Power*. New Haven: Yale University Press.

King, Charles H. 1967. "The Untold Story of the Power Struggle between King and Jackson." *Negro Digest*, May, 6–9, 71–73.

King, Deborah K. 1988. "Multiple Jeopardy, Multiple Consciousness: The Context of a Black Feminist Ideology." *Signs* 14 (1): 42–72.

King, Martin Luther, Jr. 1967. *Where Do We Go from Here: Chaos or Community?* Boston: Beacon Press.

Klandermans, Bert. 1988. "The Formation and Mobilization of Consensus." In *From Structure to Action: Comparing Movement Participation across Cultures*, vol. 1, *International Social Movement Research*. Ed. Bert Klandermans, Hanspeter Kriesi, and Sidney Tarrow. Greenwich, Conn.: JAI.

———. 1989. "Grievance Interpretation and Success Expectations: The Social Construction of Protest." *Social Behaviour* 4:113–25.

———. 1992. "The Social Construction of Protest and Multiorganizational Fields." In *Frontiers in Social Movement Theory*. Ed. Aldon Morris and Carol Mueller. New Haven: Yale University Press.

————. 1997. *The Social Psychology of Protest.* Oxford: Blackwell.

Klein, Ethel. 1984. *Gender Politics: From Consciousness to Mass Politics.* Cambridge: Harvard University Press.

Kleppner, Paul. 1985. *Chicago Divided: The Making of a Black Mayor.* De Kalb: Northern Illinois University Press.

Kluger, Richard. 1975. *Simple Justice.* New York: Vintage.

Knoke, David. 1988. "Incentives in Collective Action Organizations." *American Sociological Review* 53:311–29.

Koestler, Frances A. 1976. *The Unseen Minority: A Social History of Blindness in America.* New York: David McKay Company.

Kymlicka, Will. 1995. *Multicultural Citizenship.* Oxford: Oxford University Press.

Laitin, David D. 1988. "Political Culture and Political Preferences." *American Political Science Review* 82:589–93.

Lane, Harlan. 1984. *When the Mind Hears: A History of the Deaf.* New York: Random House.

————. 1992. *The Mask of Benevolence: Disabling the Deaf Community.* New York: Alfred A. Knopf.

Lawrence, Susan E. 1991a. "Justice, Democracy, Litigation, and Political Participation." *Social Science Quarterly* 72:464–77.

————. 1991b. "Participation through Mobilization of the Law." *Polity* 23:423–44.

Lemann, Nicholas. 1991. *The Promised Land.* New York: Alfred A. Knopf.

Lengermann, Patricia Madoo, and Ruth A. Wallace. 1985. *Gender in America: Social Control and Social Change.* Englewood Cliffs, N.J.: Prentice-Hall.

Lerner, Gerda, ed. 1972. *Black Women in White America: A Documentary History.* New York: Vintage.

————, ed. 1993. *The Creation of Feminist Consciousness: From the Middle Ages to 1870.* New York: Oxford University Press.

Levine, Lawrence W. 1977. *Black Culture and Black Consciousness: Afro-American Folk Thought from Slavery to Freedom.* New York: Oxford University Press.

Levy, Chava Willig. 1988. *A People's History of the Independent Living Movement.* Lawrence, Kans.: Research and Training Center on Independent Living.

Limerick, Patricia Nelson. 1988. *The Legacy of Conquest: The Unbroken Past of the American West.* New York: W. W. Norton.

Lindemann, Barbara, and David D. Kadue. 1992. *Sexual Harassment in Employment Law.* Washington: Bureau of National Affairs.

Lo, Clarence. 1992. "Communities of Challengers in Social Movement Theory." In *Frontiers in Social Movement Theory.* Ed. Aldon Morris and Carol Mueller. New Haven: Yale University Press.

Lorde, Audre. 1982. *Zami: A New Spelling of My Name.* Freedom, Calif.: Crossing Press.

————. 1984. *Sister Outsider: Essays and Speeches.* Freedom, Calif.: Crossing Press.

Lowenfeld, Berthold. 1975. *The Changing Status of the Blind: From Separation to Integration.* Springfield, Ill.: Charles C. Thomas.

Lucha Oral History Project. 1997. Tape-recorded interview of Jesus Salas conducted by Michael Gordon, August 18, 1997, in Milwaukee, Wisconsin.

Lukes, Stephen. 1974. *Power: A Radical View.* London: Macmillan.

Lusane, Clarence. 1991. *Pipe Dream Blues: Racism and the War on Drugs.* Boston: South End Press.

Lynch, Eleanor W., and Rena B. Lewis. 1988. *Exceptional Children and Adults.* Glenview, Ill.: Scott, Foresman.

MacKinnon, Catharine A. 1979. *Sexual Harassment of Working Women.* New Haven: Yale University Press.

———. 1987. *Feminism Unmodified: Discourses on Life and Law.* Cambridge: Harvard University Press.

Maddox, Sam. 1993. *Spinal Network.* Boulder, Colo.: Spinal Network and Sam Maddox.

Madison, James, Alexander Hamilton, and John Jay. [1788] 1987. *The Federalist Papers.* Ed. Isaac Kramnick. New York: Penguin.

Major, Brenda. 1994. "From Social Inequality to Personal Entitlement." *Advances in Experimental Social Psychology* 26:293–355.

Mansbridge, Jane. 1986. *Why We Lost the ERA.* Chicago: University of Chicago Press.

———. 1990. "On the Relation of Altruism and Self-Interest." In *Beyond Self-Interest.* Ed. Jane J. Mansbridge. Chicago: University of Chicago Press.

———. 1994. "Using Power/Fighting Power." *Constellations* 1:53–73.

———. 1995. "Rational Choice Gains by Losing." *Political Psychology* 16:137–55.

———. 1996. "Using Power/Fighting Power: The Polity." In *Democracy and Difference.* Ed. Seyla Benhabib. Princeton: Princeton University Press.

———. 1998. "On the Contested Nature of the Public Good." In *Private Action and the Public Good.* Ed. Walter W. Powell and Elisabeth S. Clemens. New Haven: Yale University Press.

Marshall, Anna-Maria. 1998. "Closing the Gaps: Plaintiffs in Pivotal Sexual Harassment Cases." *Law and Social Inquiry* 23:761–793.

Marx, Karl. [1846–47] 1963. *The Poverty of Philosophy.* New York: International Publishers.

———. [1866–67] 1970. *Capital.* Vol. I. Harmondsworth: Penguin.

Marx, Karl, and Friedrich Engels. [1848] 1954. *Manifesto of the Communist Party.* Chicago: Henry Regnery/Gateway.

———. [1846] 1965. *The German Ideology.* London: Lawerence and Wishart.

Massey, Douglas S., and Nancy A. Denton. 1993. *American Apartheid: Segregation and the Making of the Underclass.* Cambridge: Harvard University Press.

Massoni, Gary. [1971] 1989. "Perspectives on Operation Breadbasket." In *Chicago 1966.* Ed. David J. Garrow. Brooklyn: Carlson.

Mather, Lynn, and Barbara Yngvesson. 1980–81. "Language, Audience, and the Transformation of Disputes." *Law and Society Review* 15:775–822.

Matson, Floyd. 1990. *Walking Alone and Marching: A History of the Organized Blind Movement in the United States, 1940–1990.* Baltimore: National Federation of the Blind.

Maurer, Marc. 1993. "The Continuity of Leadership: Twin Requirements." Reprint of the National Federation of the Blind President's Banquet Address at the annual convention, Dallas, Texas. Baltimore: National Federation of the Blind.

Mauro, Robert. 1991. Letter. *Disability Rag,* September–October, 36.

McAdam, Doug. 1982. *Political Process and the Development of Black Insurgency, 1930–1970.* Chicago: University of Chicago Press.

———. 1988. *Freedom Summer.* New York: Oxford University Press.

———. 1994. "Culture and Social Movements." In *New Social Movements: From Ideology to Identity.* Ed. Enrique Laraña, Hank Johnston, and Joseph R. Gusfield. Philadelphia: Temple University Press.

———. 1999. *Political Process and the Development of Black Insurgency: 1930–1970.* 2d ed. Chicago: University of Chicago Press.

McAdam, Doug, John McCarthy, and Mayer Zald. 1988. "Social Movements." In *Handbook of Sociology.* Ed. Neil Smelser. Newbury Park, Calif.: Sage.

———, eds. 1996. *Comparative Perspectives on Social Movements.* Cambridge: Cambridge University Press.

McAdam, Doug, Sidney Tarrow, and Charles Tilly. 2001. *Dynamics of Contention.* Cambridge: Cambridge University Press.

McCann, Michael. 1994. *Rights at Work: Pay Equity Reform and the Politics of Legal Mobilization.* Chicago: University of Chicago Press.

McCarthy, John D., and Mayer N. Zald. 1973. *The Trends of Social Movements in America: Professionalization and Resource Mobilization.* Morristown, N.J.: General Learning Press.

———. 1977. "Resource Mobilization and Social Movements: A Partial Theory." *American Journal of Sociology* 82:1212–41.

McCarthy, Thomas. 1990. "The Critique of Impure Reason: Foucault and the Frankfurt School." *Political Theory* 18:437–69.

McClory, Robert. 1989. "The Holy Terror of Saint Sabina's: What's a White Boy Like Mick Pfleger Doing in a Parish like This?" *Chicago Reader,* November 17, 1, 24–40.

McKenzie, Nancy F., ed. 1991. *The AIDS Reader: Social, Political, Ethical Issues.* New York: Penguin.

McNeil, John M. 1993. *Americans with Disabilities: 1991–92.* Washington: U.S. Government Printing Office.

McWhinney, Jeff. 1991. "Deaf Consciousness." *Signpost: Newsletter of the International Sign Linguistics Association.* Spring, 13–15.

Melucci, Alberto. 1989. *Nomads of the Present: Social Movements and Individual Needs in Contemporary Society.* Philadelphia: Temple University Press.

Menchaca, Martha. 1995. *The Mexican Outsiders: A Community History of Marginalization and Discrimination in California.* Austin: University of Texas Press.

Merton, Robert K. 1968. *Social Theory and Social Structure.* New York: Free Press.

Milam, Lorenzo. 1993. *Crip Zen.* San Diego: MHO and MHO Works.

Mill, John Stuart. [1859] 1947. *On Liberty.* New York: Appleton-Century-Crofts.

Miller, Arthur, Patricia Gurin, and Gerald Gurin. 1978. "Electoral Implications of Group Identification and Consciousness." Paper presented at the annual meeting of the American Political Science Association, New York.

Miller, Arthur H., Patricia Gurin, Gerald Gurin, and Oksana Malanchuk. 1981. "Group Consciousness and Political Participation." *American Journal of Political Science* 25:494–511.

Miller, Arthur H., Anne Hildreth, and Grace L. Simmons. 1988. "The Mobilization of Gender Group Consciousness." In *The Political Interests of Gender*. Ed. Kathleen B. Jones and Anna G. Jonasdottir. London: Sage.

Milner, Neal. 1986. "The Dilemmas of Legal Mobilization: Ideologies and Strategies of Mental Patient Liberation Groups." *Law and Policy* 8:105–29.

Minow, Martha. 1997. *Not Only for Myself: Identity, Politics, and the Law*. New York: The New Press.

Monroe, Kristen R. 1996. *The Heart of Altruism*. Princeton: Princeton University Press.

Monroe, Kristen R., Michael C. Barton, and Ute Klineman. 1991. "Altruism and the Theory of Rational Action: An Analysis of Rescuers of Jews in Nazi Europe." In *An Economic Approach to Politics: A Critical Reassessment of Rational Action*. Ed. Kristen Monroe. New York: HarperCollins.

Montejano, David. 1977. *Race, Labor Repression, and Capitalist Agriculture: Notes from South Texas, 1920–1930*. Institute for the Study of Social Change, Working Papers Series 102.

———. 1989. *Anglos and Mexicans in the Making of Texas, 1836–1986*. Austin: University of Texas Press.

Moore, Barrington, Jr. 1978. *Injustice: The Social Bases of Obedience and Revolt*. White Plains, N.Y.: Sharpe.

Moore, Joan W. 1970. "Colonialism: The Case of Mexican Americans." *Social Problems* 17, no. 4:463–72.

Morris, Aldon. 1984. *The Origins of the Civil Rights Movement: Black Communities Organizing for Change*. New York: MacMillan/FreePress.

———. 1990. "Consciousness and Collective Action: Towards a Sociology of Consciousness and Domination." Paper presented at the annual meeting of the American Sociological Association, August 9–13, San Francisco.

———. 1992. "Political Consciousness and Collective Action." In *Frontiers in Social Movement Theory*. Ed. Aldon Morris and Carol Mueller. New Haven: Yale University Press.

———. 1993a. "Birmingham Confrontation Reconsidered: An Analysis of the Dynamics and Tactics of Mobilization." *American Sociological Review* 58: 621–35.

———. 1993b. "Centuries of Black Protest: Its Significance for America and the World." In *Race in America*. Ed. Herbert Hill and James E. Jones Jr. Madison: University of Wisconsin Press.

Morris, Aldon, and Cedric Herring. 1987. "Theory and Research in Social Movements: A Critical Review." *Annual Review of Political Science* 2:137–98.

Morris, Aldon, and Carol Mueller, eds. 1992. *Frontiers in Social Movement Theory*. New Haven: Yale University Press.

Mueller, Carol McClurg. 1992. "Building Social Movement Theory." In *Frontiers in Social Movement Theory*. Ed. Aldon Morris and Carol Mueller. New Haven: Yale University Press.

Nagel, Jack H. 1975. *The Descriptive Analysis of Power*. New Haven: Yale University Press.

National Federation of the Blind. 1991. *NFB Song Book*. Baltimore: National Federation of the Blind.

————. 1992. *Architectural Barriers for the Blind: The Myth and the Reality.* Baltimore: National Federation of the Blind.

National Fraternal Society of the Deaf. N.d. *Our History.* Leaflet. Mount Prospect, Ill.: National Fraternal Society of the Deaf.

Navarro, Armando. 1974. "El Partido de La Raza Unida in Crystal City: A Peaceful Revolution." Ph.D. diss., University of California, Riverside.

————. 1995. *Mexican American Youth Organization: The Avant-garde of the Chicano Movement in Texas.* Austin: University of Texas Press.

————. 1998. *The Cristal Experiment: A Chicano Struggle for Community Control.* Madison: University of Wisconsin Press.

Nussbaum, Martha Craven. 1995. "Emotions and Women's Capabilities." In *Women, Culture, and Development.* Ed. Martha Craven Nussbaum and Jonathan Glover. Oxford: Oxford University Press.

Nussbaum, Susan, and Mike Ervin. 1990. *The Plucky and Spunky Show.* A revue performed at the Remains Theater, Chicago, December 2 through 24.

Oberschall, Anthony. 1973. *Social Conflict and Social Movements.* Englewood Cliffs, N.J.: Prentice-Hall.

————. 1993. *Social Movements: Ideologies, Interests, and Identities.* New Brunswick: Transaction.

————. 1996. "Opportunities and Framing in Eastern European Revolts of 1989." In *Comparative Perspectives on Social Movements.* Ed. Doug McAdam, John D. McCarthy, and Mayer Zald. Cambridge: Cambridge University Press.

Obreros Unidos. 1966. "The Migrant Workers Strike in Almond, Wisconsin." Walter P. Reuther Library of Labor and Urban Affairs, Wayne State University, Detroit, William Kircher Papers, box 23, folder 10.

Ogbu, John U. 1990. "Minority Status and Literacy in Comparative Perspective." *Daedalus* 119:141–68.

Oliner, Samuel P., and Pearl M. Oliner. 1988. *The Altruistic Personality.* New York: Free Press.

Olson, Mancur, 1965. *The Logic of Collective Action.* Cambridge: Harvard University Press.

Olson, Susan M. 1984. *Clients and Lawyers: Securing the Rights of Disabled Persons.* Westport, Conn.: Greenwood Press.

Orum, Anthony M. 1995. *City-Building in America.* Boulder, Colo.: Westview Press.

Padden, Carol, and Tom Humphries. 1988. *Deaf in America: Voices from a Culture.* Cambridge: Harvard University Press.

Padgug, Robert A. 1989. "Gay Villain, Gay Hero: Homosexuality and the Social Construction of AIDS." In *Passion and Power: Sexuality in History.* Ed. Kathy Peiss and Christna Simmons with Robert A. Padgug, 293–313. Philadelphia: Temple University Press.

Panzarino, Connie. 1994. *The Me in the Mirror.* Seattle: Seal Press.

Parker, Benny Lee. 1975. "Power-in-Conflict: A Chicano Political Party's Definition of Social Disequilibrium and Anglo-Chicano Power Relationships as Expressed through a Situational Analysis of Public Address in Crystal City, Texas, in 1972." Ph.D. diss., Southern Illinois University, Carbondale.

Parra, Pilar Alicia. 1984. "United Migrant Opportunity Services, Inc.: An Historical and Organizational Analysis of Changing Goals." Master's thesis, University of Wisconsin, Madison.

Patton, Cindy. 1990. *Inventing AIDS*. New York: Routledge.

Payne, Charles. 1995. *I've Got the Light of Freedom*. Berkeley and Los Angeles: University of California Press.

Peck, Gary R. 1982. "Black Radical Consciousness and the Black Christian Experience: Toward a Critical Sociology of Afro-American Religion." *Sociological Analysis* 43:155–67.

Pettigrew, Thomas. 1979. "The Ultimate Attribution Error: Extending Allport's Cognitive Analysis of Prejudice." *Personality and Social Psychology Bulletin* 5:461–76.

Phillips, Kimberly L. 1999. *AlabamaNorth: African-American Migrants, Community, and Working Class Activism in Cleveland, 1915–1945*. Urbana: University of Illinois Press.

Piven, Frances Fox, and Richard A. Cloward. 1977. *Poor People's Movements: Why They Succeed, How They Fail*. New York: Vintage.

Pollack, Wendy. 1990. "Sexual Harassment: Women's Experience vs. Legal Definitions." *Harvard Women's Law Journal* 13:35–85.

Polletta, Francesca. 1999. "Snarls, Quacks, and Quarrels: Culture and Structure in Political Process Theory." *Sociological Forum* 14:63–70.

Portez, Alejandro, and Ramon Grosfoguel. 1994. "Caribbean Diasporas: Migration and Ethnic Communities." *Annals of the American Academy of Political and Social Science* 533:48–69.

Portez, Alejandro, and Alex Stepick. 1993. *City on the Edge: The Transformation of Miami*. Berkeley and Los Angeles: University of California Press.

Pratt, Minnie Bruce, Elly Bulkin, and Barbara Smith. 1988. *Yours in Struggle: Three Feminists' Perspectives on Anti-Semitism and Racism*. Ithaca, N.Y.: Firebrand Books.

Provinzano, James. 1971. "Chicano Migrant Farm Workers in a Rural Wisconsin County." Ph.D. diss., University of Minnesota.

Pycior, Julie Leininger. 1993. "From Hope to Frustration: Mexican Americans and Lyndon Johnson in 1967." *Western Historical Quarterly* 25:468–94.

Quinones, Juan Gomez. 1990. *Chicano Politics: Reality and Promise, 1940–1990*. Albuquerque: University of New Mexico Press.

Raboteau, Albert. 1978. *Slave Religion: The "Invisible Institution" in the Antebellum South*. New York: Oxford University Press.

Raines, Howell. 1977. *My Soul Is Rested*. New York: P. G. Putnam's Sons.

Ralph, James R. 1993. *Northern Protest*. Cambridge: Harvard University Press.

Raushenbush, Elizabeth Brandeis. 1962. "Migrant Labor in Wisconsin." In *Labor, Management, and Social Policy: Essays in the John R. Commons Tradition*. Ed. Gerald George Somers. Madison: University of Wisconsin Press.

———. 1966. *A Study of Migratory Workers in Cucumber Harvesting, Waushara County, Wisconsin*. Madison: University of Wisconsin, Institute for Research on Poverty.

Rawls, John. 1971. *A Theory of Justice*. Cambridge: Harvard University Press.

Reed, Adolph, Jr. 1986. *The Jesse Jackson Phenomenon*. New Haven: Yale University Press.

Reingold, Beth, and Heather Foust. 1998. "Exploring the Determinants of Feminist Consciousness in the United States." *Women and Politics* 19:19–48.

Reynolds, Barbara. 1975. *Jesse Jackson: The Man, The Movement, The Myth.* Chicago: Nelson-Hall.

Rich, Adrienne. 1986. *Blood, Bread, and Poetry: Selected Prose, 1979–1985.* New York: W. W. Norton.

Riggs, Marlon. 1989. *Tongues Untied.* Film.

Rinehart, Sue Tolleson. 1992. *Gender Consciousness and Politics.* New York: Routledge.

Rivera, Tomas. 1971. *And the Earth Did Not Part.* Berkeley: Quinto Sol.

Rodriguez, Joseph A. 1992. "Home Ownership and Ethnic Culture: Mexicans in Milwaukee after World War II." Paper presented at the meeting of the Social Science History Association, Chicago, November 8.

Rodriguez, Marc Simon. 2000. "Obreros Unidos: Migration, Migrant Farm Worker Activism, and the Chicano Movement in Wisconsin and Texas, 1950–1980." Ph.D. diss., Northwestern University.

Rodriguez, Ruth. 1992. "We Have the Expertise, We Need the Resources." In *Women, AIDS, and Activism.* Ed. ACT UP/NY (Women and AIDS Book Group). Boston: South End Press.

Rorty, Amélie Oksenberg. 1985. "Varieties of Rationality, Varieties of Emotion." *Social Science Information* 24:343–53.

Rosales, F. Arturo. 1996. *Chicano!: The History of the Mexican-American Civil Rights Movement.* Houston: Arte Público Press.

Rosenbaum, Rene Perez. 1991. *Success in Organizing, Failure in Collective Bargaining: The Case of Pickle Workers in Wisconsin, 1967–1968.* Julian Samora Research Institute Working Papers Series 11.

Rosenberg, Gerald. 1991. *The Hollow Hope.* Chicago: University of Chicago Press.

Ross, Lee. 1977. "The Intuitive Psychologist and His Shortcomings: Distortions in the Attribution Process." *Advances in Experimental Social Psychology* 10:173–220.

Rouse, Roger. 1991. "Mexican Migration and the Social Space of Postmodernism." *Diaspora* 1:8–23.

———. 1992. "Making Sense of Settlement: Class Transformation, Cultural Struggle, and Transnationalism among Mexican Migrants in the United States." In *Towards a Transnational Perspective on Migration: Race, Class, Ethnicity, and Nationalism Reconsidered.* Ed. Nina Glick Schiler, Linda Basch, and Cristina Blanc-Szanton. New York: Academy of Sciences.

Royko, Mike. 1971. *Boss: Richard J. Daley of Chicago.* New York: Penguin.

Rubin, Gail. 1975. "The Traffic in Women: Notes on the 'Political Economy' of Sex." In *Toward an Anthropology of Women.* Ed. R. Reiter. New York: Monthly Review Press.

———. 1984. "Thinking Sex: Notes for a Radical Theory of the Politics of Sexuality." In *Pleasure and Danger: Exploring Female Sexuality.* Ed. Carole Vance. Boston: Routledge & Kegan Paul.

Rumsey, Sunny. 1992. "AIDS Issues for African-American and African-Caribbean Women." In *Women, AIDS, and Activism.* Ed. ACT UP/NY (Women and AIDS Book Group). Boston: South End Press.

Sacks, Oliver. 1990. *Seeing Voices: A Journey into the World of the Deaf.* New York: HarperPerennial.

Salas, Jesus, and David Giffey. 1998. *Struggle for Justice: The Migrant Farm Worker Labor Movement in Wisconsin.* Madison: Wisconsin Labor History Society.

Sandel, Michael J. 1982. *Liberalism and the Limits of Justice.* Cambridge: Cambridge University Press.

Sandoval, Chéla. 1991. "U.S. Third World Feminism: The Theory and Method of Oppositional Consciousness in the Postmodern World." *Genders* 10:1–24.

———. 1993. "Oppositional Consciousness in the Postmodern World: U.S. Third World Feminism, Semiotics, and the Methodology of the Oppressed." Ph.D. diss., University of California, Santa Cruz.

———. 2000. *Methodology of the Oppressed.* Minneapolis: University of Minnesota Press.

Sapiro, Virginia. 1990. "The Women's Movement and the Creation of Gender Consciousness: Social Movements as Socialization Agents." In *Political Socialization, Citizenship Education, and Democracy.* Ed. Orit Ichilov. New York: Teachers College Press.

Scheff, Thomas J. 1994. "Emotions and Identity: A Theory of Ethnic Nationalism." In *Social Theory and the Politics of Identity.* Ed. Craig Calhoun. Oxford: Blackwell.

Scheingold, Stuart A. 1974. *The Politics of Rights.* New Haven: Yale University Press.

Schiller, Nina Glick. 1995. "From Immigrant to Transmigrant: Theorizing Transnational Migration." *Anthropological Quarterly* 68:48–63.

Schlozman, Kay Lehman, and Sidney Verba. 1979. *Injury to Insult: Unemployment, Class, and Political Response.* Cambridge: Harvard University Press.

Schwartz, Michael, and Sjuva Paul. 1992. "Resource Mobilization versus the Mobilization of People: Why Consensus Movements Cannot Be Instruments of Social Change." In *Frontiers in Social Movement Theory.* Ed. Aldon Morris and Carol Mueller. New Haven: Yale University Press.

Scotch, Richard K. 1984. *From Good Will to Civil Rights: Transforming Federal Disability Policy.* Philadelphia: Temple University Press.

———. 1988. "Disability as the Basis for a Social Movement: Advocacy and the Politics of Definition." *Journal of Social Issues* 44:159–72.

Scott, James C. 1985. *Weapons of the Weak.* New Haven: Yale University Press.

———. 1990. *Domination and the Arts of Resistance.* New Haven: Yale University Press.

Sellers, Cleveland. 1991. Excerpt from *The River of No Return.* In *The Eyes on the Prize Civil Rights Reader.* Ed. Clayborne Carson, David J. Garrow, Gerald Gill, Vincent Harding, and Darlene Clark Hine. New York: Penguin.

Sen, Amartya K. [1977] 1990. "Rational Fools." In *Beyond Self-Interest.* Ed. Jane Mansbridge. Chicago: University of Chicago Press.

Sewell, William H., Jr. 1990. "How Classes Are Made: Critical Reflections on E. P. Thompson's Theory of Working Class Formation." In *E. P. Thompson: Critical Perspectives.* Ed. Harvey J. Kaye and Keith McClelland. Philadelphia: Temple University Press.

————. 1996. "Historical Events as Transformations of Structures: Inventing Revolution at the Bastille." *Theory and Society* 25:841–81.

Shannon, Lyle W. 1966. *The Economic Absorption and Cultural Integration of Immigrant Workers.* Iowa City: University of Iowa, Department of Sociology and Anthropology.

Shapiro, Joseph P. 1993. *No Pity: People with Disabilities Forging a New Civil Rights Movement.* New York: Times Books.

Shilts, Randy. 1987. *And the Band Played On.* New York: St. Martin's.

Shingles, Richard D. 1981. "Black Consciousness and Political Participation." *American Political Science Review* 75:76–91.

Shockley, John S. 1974. *Chicano Revolt in a Texas Town.* Notre Dame: Notre Dame University Press.

Siegelman, Peter, and John J. Donohue III. 1990. "Studying the Iceberg from Its Tip: A Comparison of Published and Unpublished Employment Discrimination Cases." *Law and Society Review* 24:1133–70.

Sigel, Roberta S., and Nancy L. Welchel. 1986. "Minority Consciousness and Sense of Group Power among Women." Paper presented to the annual meeting of the Midwest Political Science Association, Chicago.

Slesinger, Doris P., and Eileen Murragui. 1979. "Migrant Agricultural Labor in Wisconsin: A Short History." Discussion paper no. 565. University of Wisconsin, Madison, Institute for Research on Poverty.

Smith, Barbara, ed. 1983. *Home Girls: A Black Feminist Anthology.* New York: Kitchen Table/Women of Color Press.

Smith, Walter E. 1978. "Mexicano Resistance to Schooled Ethnicity: Ethnic Student Power in South Texas, 1930–1970." Ph.D. diss., University of Texas at Austin.

Snow, David A., and Robert D. Benford. 1988. "Ideology, Frame Resonance, and Participant Mobilization." In *From Structure to Action: Comparing Social Movement Research across Cultures.* Vol. 1, *International Social Movement Research.* Ed. Bert Klandermans, Hanspeter Kriesi, and Sidney Tarrow. Greenwich, Conn.: JAI.

————. 1992. "Master Frames and Cycles of Protest." In *Frontiers in Social Movement Theory.* Ed. Aldon Morris and Carol Mueller. New Haven: Yale University Press.

Snow, David A., E. Burke Rochford Jr., Steven K. Worden, and Robert D. Benford. 1986. "Frame Alignment Processes, Micromobilization, and Movement Participation." *American Sociological Review* 51:464–81.

Solomon, Andrew. 1994. "Defiantly Deaf." *New York Times Magazine,* 28 August, 40–45, 62, 65–68.

Sontag, Susan. 1983. *Illness as Metaphor.* Harmondsworth: Penguin.

Southern Christian Leadership Conference. 1991. "A Proposal by the Southern Christian Leadership Conference for the Development of a Nonviloent Action Movement for the Greater Chicago Area." In *The Eyes on the Prize Civil Rights Reader.* Ed. Clayborne Carson, David J. Garrow, Gerald Gill, Vincent Harding, and Darlene Clark Hine. New York: Penguin.

Spear, Allan. 1967. *Black Chicago: The Making of a Negro Ghetto, 1890–1920.* Chicago: University of Chicago Press.

Starhawk, 1987. *Truth or Dare: Encounters with Power, Authority and Mystery.* San Francisco: Harper and Row.

Steinberg, Marc W. 1995. "The Roar of the Crowd: Repertoires of Discourse and Collective Action among the Spitalfields Silk Weavers in Nineteenth-Century London." In *Repertoires and Cycles of Collective Action.* Ed. Mark Traugott. Durham, N.C.: Duke University Press.

————. 1996. "'The Labour of the Country Is the Wealth of the Country': Class Identity, Consciousness, and the Role of Discourse in the Making of the English Working Class." *International Labor and Working-Class History* 49:1–25.

Stewart, Jean. 1989. *The Body's Memory.* New York: St. Martin's.

Stewart, Kenneth L., and Arnoldo De Leon. 1993. *Not Room Enough: Mexicans, Anglos, and Socioeconomic Change in Texas, 1850–1900.* Albuquerque: University of New Mexico Press.

Stockdill, Brett. 1992. "Building Community: Challenging Racism in the Gay Community." Paper presented at second annual National Lesbian and Gay Graduate Student Conference, University of Illinois, Champaign-Urbana, April 4.

————. "(Mis)treating Prisoners with AIDS: Analyzing Health Care behind Bars." In *The Sociology of Health Care,* vol. 12. Ed. Jennie Jacobs Kronenfeld. Greenwich, Conn.: JAI.

————. 1996. "Multiple Oppressions and Their Influence on Collective Action: The Case of the AIDS Movement." Doctoral diss., Northwestern University.

Swidler, Ann. 1986. "Culture in Action: Symbols and Strategies." *American Sociological Review* 51:273–86.

Tajfel, H. 1974. "Social Identity and Intergroup Behavior." *Social Science Information* 13:65–93.

Tarrow, Sidney. 1992. "Mentalities, Political Cultures, and Collective Action Frames: Constructing Meanings through Action." In *Frontiers in Social Movement Theory.* Ed. Aldon Morris and Carol Mueller. New Haven: Yale University Press.

————. 1998. *Power in Movement: Social Movements and Contentious Politics.* 2d ed. Cambridge: Cambridge University Press.

————. 1999. "Paradigm Warriors: Regress and Progress in the Study of Contentious Politics." *Sociological Forum* 14:71–77.

Task Force on Problems of Spanish Surnamed Americans. 1966. "Report of the Task Force on Problems of Spanish Surnamed Americans." Lyndon Baines Johnson Library and Museum, University of Texas at Austin, Presidential Papers, James C. Gaither Papers, box 327.

Tate, Katherine. 1994. *From Protest to Politics: The New Black Voters in American Elections.* Cambridge: Harvard University Press; New York: Russell Sage.

Taylor, Paul S. 1932. *Mexican Labor in the United States: Dimmit County, Winter Garden District, South Texas.* Berkeley and Los Angeles: University of California Press.

Taylor, Verta. 1989. "The Future of Feminism: A Social Movement Analysis." In *Feminist Frontiers II.* Ed. Laurel Richardson and Verta Taylor. New York: Random House.

————. 1995. "Watching for Vibes: Bringing Emotions into the Study of Feminist Organizations." In *Feminist Organizations: Harvest of the New Women's Movement*. Ed. Myra Marx Ferree and Patricia Yancey Martin. Philadelphia: Temple University Press.

Taylor, Verta, and Nancy E. Whittier. 1992. "Collective Identity in Social Movement Communities: Lesbian Feminist Mobilization." In *Frontiers in Social Movement Theory*. Ed. Aldon Morris and Carol Mueller. New Haven: Yale University Press.

Teske, Nathan. 1997. *Political Activists in America: The Identity Construction Model of Political Participation*. Cambridge: Cambridge University Press.

Thelen, David P. 1972. *The New Citizenship: Origins of Progressivism in Wisconsin 1885–1900*. Columbia: University of Missouri Press.

————. 1985. *Robert M. La Follette and the Insurgent Spirit*. Madison: University of Wisconsin Press.

Thomas, Tony. 1971. "Crystal City, Texas: La Raza Unida Party in Action." *International Socialist Review* 32, no. 4: 22–27.

Thompson, E. P. [1963] 1966. *The Making of the English Working Class*. New York: Vintage.

Thurman, Howard. 1981. *Jesus and the Disinherited*. Richmond, Ind.: Friends United Press.

Tilly, Charles. 1978. *From Mobilization to Revolution*. New York: McGraw-Hill.

————. 1986. *The Contentious French*: Cambridge: Harvard University Press.

————. 1995. *Popular Contention in Great Britain, 1758–1834*. Cambridge: Harvard University Press.

————. 1998. "Contentious Conversation." *Social Research* 65:491–510.

Travis, Dempsey. 1987. *An Autobiography of Black Politics*. Chicago: Urban Research Press.

Treanor, Richard Bryant. 1993. *We Overcame: The Story of Civil Rights for Disabled People*. Falls Church, Va.: Regal Direct Publishing.

Trujillo, Armando. 1993. "Community Empowerment and Bilingual/Bicultural Education: A Study of the Movimiento in a South Texas Community." Ph.D. diss., University of Texas at Austin.

Trujillo, Carla, ed. 1991. *Chicana Lesbians: The Girls Our Mothers Warned Us About*. Berkeley: Third Woman Press.

Turner, John C. 1987. *Rediscovering the Social Group: A Self-Categorization Theory*. Oxford: Blackwell.

Turner, Ralph H. 1969. "The Theme of Contemporary Social Movements." *British Journal of Sociology* 20:390–405.

Tushnet, Mark V. 1987. *The NAACP's Legal Strategy against Segregated Education, 1925–1950*. Chapel Hill: University of North Carolina Press.

United Migrant Opportunity Services. 1985. *Helping People Help Themselves: United Migrant Opportunity Services, Inc. Celebrating 20 Years of Service*. Milwaukee: United Migrant Opportunity Services.

Valdes, Dennis Nodin. 1991. *Al Norte: Agricultural Workers in the Great Lakes Region, 1917–1970*. Austin: University of Texas Press.

Van Cleve, John V., and Barry A. Crouch. 1989. *A Place of Their Own: Creating the Deaf Community in America*. Washington: Gallaudet University Press.

Vance, Carole. 1984. "Pleasure and Danger: Towards a Politics of Sexuality." In *Pleasure and Danger: Exploring Female Sexuality.* Ed. Carole Vance. Boston: Routledge & Kegan Paul.

———. 1989. "Social Construction Theory: Problems in the History of Sexuality." In *Which Homosexuality?* Ed. D. Altman. London: GMP Press.

Vargas, Zaragosa. 1993. *Proletarians of the North: A History of Mexican Industrial Workers in Detroit and the Midwest, 1917–1933.* Berkeley and Los Angeles: University of California Press.

Verba, Sidney, Kay L. Schlozman, and Henry Brady. 1993. *Voice and Equality: Civic Voluntarism in American Politics.* Cambridge: Harvard University Press.

Vose, Clement A. 1955. "NAACP Strategy in the Restrictive Covenant Cases." *Western Reserve Law Review* 6:101–45.

———. 1959. *Caucasians Only: The Supreme Court, the NAACP, and the Restrictive Covenant Cases.* Berkeley and Los Angeles: University of California Press.

Wade, Cheryl Marie. 1989. "Here." Poetry performance video. Berkeley: CM Wade.

Walker, Wyatt T. 1979. *Somebody's Calling My Name.* Valley Forge: Judson Press.

Walton, Hanes, Jr. 1972. *Black Politics: A Theoretical and Structural Analysis.* Philadelphia: J. B. Lippincott.

Walzer, Michael. 1988. *The Company of Critics: Social Criticism and Political Commitment in the Twentieth Century.* New York: Basic Books.

Wartenberg, Thomas E. 1990. *The Forms of Power.* Philadelphia: Temple University Press.

Washington, James M. 1986. "Jesse Jackson and the Symbolic Politics of Black Christendom." *Annals* 480:89–105.

Weber, Max [1922] 1947. *The Theory of Social and Economic Organization.* Trans. A. M. Henderson and Talcott Parsons; ed. Talcott Parsons. New York: Free Press.

Weeks, Elaine Lunsford, Jacqueline M. Boles, Albeno P. Garbin, and John Blount. 1986. "The Transformation of Sexual Harassment from a Private Trouble into a Public Issue." *Sociological Inquiry* 56:432–55.

Weeks, Jeffrey. 1991. *Against Nature: Essays on History, Sexuality, and Identity.* London: River Oram.

Wells, Miriam J. 1975. "From Field to Foundry: Mexican American Adaptive Strategies in a Small Wisconsin Town." Ph.D. diss., University of Wisconsin, Madison.

West, Cornel. 1982. *Prophesy Deliverance! An Afro-American Revolutionary Christianity.* Philadelphia: Westminster Press.

Whittier, Nancy. 1995. *Feminist Generations: The Persistence of the Radical Women's Movement.* Philadelphia: Temple University Press.

Wilcox, Clyde. 1990. "Black Women and Feminism." *Women and Politics* 10:65–84.

Williams, Bernard. 1985. *Ethics and the Limits of Philosophy.* Cambridge: Harvard University Press.

Williams, Paul, and Bonnie Shoultz. 1982. *We Can Speak for Ourselves.* Bloomington: Indiana University Press.

Wills, Garry. 1990. *Under God: Religion and American Politics.* New York: Simon and Schuster.

Wilson, James Q. 1960. *Negro Politics: The Search for Leadership.* New York: Free Press.

———. 1962. *The Amateur Democrat.* Chicago: University of Chicago Press.

———. 1967. Introduction to Harold Gosnell, *Negro Politicians: The Rise of Negro Politics in Chicago* (originally published 1935). Chicago: University of Chicago Press.

Wilson, John. 1973. *Introduction to Social Movements.* New York: Basic Books.

Wisconsin Employment Relations Board. 1966. *James Burns & Sons Farm, Inc.* Decision no. 7842.

———. 1967a. *Memorandum Accompanying Direction of Election.* In *Obreros Unidos-United Workers v. Libby, McNeill and Libby.* Decision no. 8163.

———. 1967b. *Libby, McNeil and Libby.* Decision no. 8163.

———. 1968. *Libby, McNeil and Libby.* Decision no. 8616.

Young, Andrew. 1996. *An Easy Burden: The Civil Rights Movement and the Transformation of America.* New York: HarperCollins.

Young, Henry J., ed. 1988. *The Black Church and the Harold Washington Story.* Bristol, Ind.: Wyndham Hall Press.

Young, Iris M. 1990. *Justice and the Politics of Difference.* Princeton: Princeton University Press.

Young, Robert. [1936] *Analytical Concordance to the Bible.* New York: Funk and Wagnalls.

Zald, Mayer. 1992. "Looking Backward to Look Forward: Reflections on the Past and Future of the Resource Mobilization Program." In *Frontiers in Social Movement Theory.* Ed. Aldon Morris and Carol Mueller. New Haven: Yale University Press.

Zamora, Emilio. 1993. *The World of the Mexican Worker in Texas.* College Station: Texas A&M University Press.

Zeidler, Frank P. 1991. *Ninety Years of Democratic Socialism.* Milwaukee: F. P. Zeidler.

Zemans, Frances K. 1983. "Legal Mobilization: The Neglected Role of the Law in the Political System." *American Political Science Review* 77:690–703.

Zola, Irving K. 1982a. *Ordinary Lives: Voices of Disability and Disease.* Cambridge, Mass.: Applewood Books.

———. 1982b. *Missing Pieces: A Chronicle of Living with a Disability.* Philadelphia: Temple University Press.

———. 1983. "The Evolution of the Boston Self Help Center." In *A Way of Life for the Handicapped: New Developments in Residential and Community Care.* Ed. G. Jones and N. Tutt. London: Residential Care Association.

Index